K

D0594230

THE ROAD TO THE NEVER LAND

AUP Titles of Related Interest:

THE LIFE AND WORK OF SAMUEL RUTHERFORD CROCKETT
Islay Donaldson

POPULAR LITERATURE IN VICTORIAN SCOTLAND
William Donaldson

THE LANGUAGE OF THE PEOPLE
William Donaldson

THE HISTORY OF SCOTTISH LITERATURE
Vol One (origins to 1660) *editor R D S Jack*
Vol Two (1660-1800) *editor Andrew Hook*
Vol Three (the nineteenth century) *editor Douglas Gifford*
Vol Four (the twentieth century) *editor Cairns Craig*

Scottish

THE ROAD TO
THE NEVER LAND

drama

A Reassessment of
J M BARRIE's
Dramatic Art

R D S JACK

ABERDEEN UNIVERSITY PRESS
Member of Maxwell Macmillan Pergamon Publishing Corporation

First published 1991
Aberdeen University Press

© R D S Jack 1991

The publisher acknowledges subsidy from the Scottish Arts Council towards the publication of this volume.

All Rights Reserved. No part of this publication may be reproduced, stored in a retrieval system or transmitted in any form or by any means: electronic, electrostatic, magnetic tape, mechanical, photocopying, recording or otherwise, without permission in writing from the copyright holder.

British Library Cataloguing in Publication Data

Jack, R D S (Ronald Dyce Sadler) *1941-*
   The Road to the Never Land: a reassessment of
   J M Barrie's dramatic art
   1.   Drama in English. Barrie, J M (James Matthew)
   1860-1937
   I.   Title
   822.8
ISBN 0 08 037742 4

Typeset by BEECEE Typesetting Services, Fife
Printed by Athenaeum Press Ltd, Newcastle-upon-Tyne

TO

FIONA CAROLINE JACK

Contents

List of Illustrations   viii

Introduction   1

CHAPTER ONE
Barrie and the Critics   3

CHAPTER TWO
A Victorian Apprenticeship   25

CHAPTER THREE
The Edwardian Journeyman   78

CHAPTER FOUR
The Master and the Myth   155

    (i)   *Peter Pan* and the Pan Myth   155

    (ii) *Peter Pan* and Creation   181

    (iii) *Peter Pan* and Language   212

CHAPTER FIVE
The Road to the Never Land   242

APPENDIX A
Barrie and The Nottingham Journal   262

Notes   265

Index   298

List of Illustrations

1   'queer stove-pipe-hatted heads suddenly bobbing up', Cartoon of the Elders, from souvenir of *The Little Minister* at the Haymarket 1897.   50

2   The homecoming. Scene from *Quality Street*, at the Vaudeville 1902.   83

3   J M Barrie in his Library.   109

4   Cartoon: Pages from my album of bores: The man who *will* tell you the plot of *Little Mary*.   130

5   Hilda Trevelyan as 'Little Mary' wearing the 'Napoleon' hat in *Little Mary* on tour 1889.   142

6   Act 5, Scene 1, *Peter Pan*. Tableau mirroring Napoleon on the *Bellerophon* as painted by Orchardson.   192

7   A sample of the metalanguage invented by Neil, the hero of 'The Blot on Peter Pan'.   237

8   J M Barrie *c*. 1904.   240

Jacket illustrations:

J M Barrie in 1892

Captain Hook: sketch made by the artist who designed the terrifying costume for the first Captain Hook.

All illustrations (except Fig. 7) are reproduced courtesy of the Trustees of the Theatre Museum, Victoria and Albert Museum. Fig. 7 is reproduced courtesy of the National Library of Scotland.

Introduction

Three personal paths set me on the Road to the Never Land. The first was theatrical. It began with my own delight in Barrie's magic and led to puzzlement that his 'fortuna' had been so spectacularly tragic. How could a writer be hailed as a genius by one age and rejected as an oddity by the next? The second was national. As a Scottish critic, who had been involved in the recent revival of interest in that literature, I found it troublesome that the greatest antipathy to the Kirriemuir playwright came from his own countrymen. Did that relate to the definition implicitly or explicitly imposed on a 'Scottish' author? The third was critical, deriving from my earlier study of medieval drama in *Patterns of Divine Comedy*. Increasingly, I had sensed a similarity between Barrie's criticism as professed in *Sentimental Tommy* and the ideas behind medieval literature. Were the methods and aims of the earliest writers of theatrical mythology relevant to the intentions and skills of the man who created Peter Pan?

The areas of research, which these central questions opened up proved so many and so challenging that a detour of one planned year became nine years of study: two contemplated articles became this book. My conclusions are nothing if not radical. I would claim now that the first assessment of genius is correct though itself falsely based. For sentiment I would substitute a great and complex intellect; for the cabbage patch I would substitute the ultimate questions presented perspectivally; for popularity I would substitute a multi-layered text addressing an audience triangle narrowed by intelligence and ending with soliloquy; for the praiser of the past I would substitute intense involvement in the ideas of Nietzsche, Darwin and Roget filtered through the dramatic voices of Shakespeare and Ibsen.

My own mythology fell no less than the myth of Barrie received via the anti-kailyard rhetoric of current literary criticism. To keep some sense of this I have (in Chapter Two) maintained the idea of research in progress rather than writing from an entirely retrospective viewpoint. The final section of that Chapter recounts the first major movement of premise on which the later Chapters are, substantially, built.

My debts are many. They begin with the financial support kindly

1

granted by the British Academy and The Carnegie Trust for the Universities of Scotland. They embrace the patient assistance of staff in many libraries but principally those where the main Barrie holdings are located:— the Beinecke Library, Yale; the Lilly Library, Indiana; the Humanities' Research Center, Austin, Texas; the Berg Public Library, New York; the British Museum and the University of Nottingham Library. I also received a consistently warm welcome and much advice from the librarians of the Theatre Museum in its old and new settings. The list of friends and colleagues, who were drawn into my quest is a very long one. It is easiest to associate names with stages on the Road. Colin Maclean showed interest from the start and more confidence than I, at that time, possessed. Emily Lyle (*The Little Minister*), Pauline Rozendaal (*Quality Street*), Owen Dudley Edwards and Gordon Howie (*Little Mary*), Andrew Birkin and Norman Macleod (*Peter Pan*) are only the names of those who radically changed my thinking at points; the kindness of the many others who helped by reading sections or solving particular problems is greatly appreciated. My typist, Jeanette, once more endured the idosyncrasies of my drafting. As always, my most lasting debt remains with my wife.

                                                                    R D S J

CHAPTER ONE

Barrie and the Critics

'Here was a young Scotchman, able, pure, of noble ambition, and a
first medallist in metaphysics. Genius was written on his brow. He may
have written it himself, but it was there.'

J M Barrie, *Better Dead* (1888)

In his own day, almost all critics accepted that James Barrie was a genius
whose reputation would endure. W A Darlington, drawing on an anecdote
in *Margaret Ogilvy*, one of Barrie's most directly autobiographical works,
poses the question in the words of Cowley before replying in his own:

> What can I do to be for ever known?
> And make the age to come my own?

> Myriads of writers have set out to answer that question as best they could. Not
> many have been able to answer it more honourably than the man who, after a
> long life, could point to *Peter Pan*, *Dear Brutus* and *Margaret Ogilvy*.[1]

In 1938, Darlington was not aware of the irony these words would now
contain. After all, the confident judgement he makes on Barrie's
immortality sounds quite reticent beside the assessments of other respected
writers, anxious to claim the Scottish dramatist and novelist as a genius. His
contemporary, Robert Louis Stevenson, for example, comments in a letter
to the Scottish writer:

> I am a capable artist; but it looks to me as if you are a man of genius.[2]

The dramatic critic, James Agate, is equally sure of his literary stature,
although he anticipates and echoes many other commentators in feeling
emotionally uncertain about aspects of his art:

> Barrie died early this morning. His was an irritating genius, which never left
> one doubt either about the genius or the irritation.[3]

And the first English champion of Ibsen, William Archer, is so convinced of this genius that he uses it as a means of bypassing detailed critical analysis:

> I am content to treat him shortly because he raises no critical question . . . no rational being doubts that Sir James is a humourist of original and delightful genius who happens to have an extraordinary knack of expressing himself in dramatic form.[4]

Barrie, then is a genius, so clearly a genius that his work will live for ever, its value and skill being questioned only by the irrational; so self-evidently brilliant that it transcends the need for lengthy evaluation. Here, indeed, is the material of myth. A Scottish author being raised to giddy levels by his contemporaries! One thinks of the other myths round Burns and Hugh MacDiarmid. But Barrie is being idolised within a British rather than a Scottish context. Arguably, this might be seen as an even greater achievement.

Barrie, like both Burns and MacDiarmid, helped to strengthen these mythologising tendencies by rôle-playing. Variously as the personification of artistic modesty; as the involved man of the theatre; as the idoliser of his leading ladies; as the mysterious friend of children and their mothers or, latterly, as morose hermit, he kept a rapt public wondering and adoring.

Almost every major honour open to a literary man fell to this ninth child of a Kirriemuir weaver and a stonemason's daughter. Granted an Honorary LLD by his old University, Edinburgh, in 1909, he was made a Baronet in 1913, became Rector of St Andrews in 1919 and was awarded the Order of Merit in 1992. (In the field of Letters, only George Meredith, Henry James and Thomas Hardy had gained this last award). He became one of the most popular novelists and the most popular dramatist of his day, so that his election as President of the Society of Authors in succession to Tennyson, Meredith and Hardy must have seemed quite logical. The doors of high society opened to him and when he died, he left £173,467 in his will, almost all of which had been earned by his pen.

All the other authors named above retain their high literary standing. Only Barrie has sunk into obscurity. Interestingly, one of the first powerful voices to be raised against him was that of a Scot. As early as 1903 J H Millar in his influential *Literary History of Scotland* had begun to question Barrie's artistic integrity. Had the genius — and Millar accepts that Barrie has massive talents — prostituted his art for commercial success? Referring to *The Little Minister*, Millar comments:

> By this time Mr Barrie had accurately gauged the taste of his readers, and the cynical disregard of true art — the studied 'playing to the gallery' — which marked that romance and the drama based upon it, has been a prominent feature in all Mr Barrie's subsequent work.[5]

One should point out that a judgement made in 1903 pre-dates *Peter Pan* and all subsequent drama. But Millar's scathing attack, while based primarily on the novels, claimed to be at once all-comprehending and final.

In my experience, most readers today do not see the importance of the date; most are unaware of it. They assume Millar's reaction is to ALL the plays, not to the works of the apprentice and journeyman periods alone. So false myths grow.

Few critics joined Millar in his protest at this time. Some journalists carped a little or found Barrie difficult to assess. But so unusual was developed criticism of the plays, that Max Beerbohm, in 1908, welcomes an attack (which he finds wrongheaded and proceeds to demolish) simply because it is refreshing to find someone not swept away by the Scotsman's reputation:

> I have often scanned the horizon for one who would supply the long-felt want of a furious onslaught on Mr Barrie.[6]

It was not until the First World War that Millar found himself in anything approaching company. As it ushered in an age which increasingly questioned orthodox beliefs and wished life to be shown in darker colours, Barrie, who had been seen as the dramatic mirror of late Victorian optimism, was held by many to be old-fashioned. Even then, he responded with two of his darkest and most successful plays, *Dear Brutus* (1917) and *Mary Rose* (1920). And, despite the comparative failure of his last work for the stage *The Boy David* in 1936, he died knowing that the vast majority of people assumed, with Darlington, that he would for ever be hailed as a major author.

One year before Darlington's comment, however, a particularly striking remark was made about his critical status by Henry Bett. For the first time, someone notes that evaluation of Barrie is in one vital way unusual. 'Probably,' Bett states, 'there is no modern writer with regard to whom there has been so wide a disparity of judgement, as between the critical opinion of the nineties and that of today.' [7] He is not arguing that Barrie has lost his fanatical support among the public but pointing to the emergence among critics of a group, bitterly antagonistic to his work. Barrie evokes extreme emotions. One either hates him or loves him. One either reveres his art or despises it. This implies that if critical orthodoxy become identified with antagonists rather than enthusiasts, Barrie might not merely move down a stage or so in the literary hierarchy but be removed from serious consideration entirely. And that is precisely what has happened. Modern critics who are sympathetic to his writing are few and tend to express their allegiance with a sense of embarrassment.

A further intriguing aspect of this singular state of critical affairs is that the most bitter attacks are delivered by fellow Scots. Usually, of course, a Scottish author — even one of minor ability — could expect a more considered and possibly more favourable assessment in the context of Scottish literature. For a variety of reasons, many of them non-literary, Barrie has lost national support as well. Indeed he may number among his harshest opponents the major Scottish poet of the twentieth century, Hugh MacDiarmid, and one of the finest Scottish critics, Professor David

Daiches. MacDiarmid's opposition is unsurprising. After all he claimed Millar as 'the initiator of many of the leading ideas of the Scottish Renaissance Movement,' [8] which he himself led so brilliantly. As a proud Anglophobe and a Communist, MacDiarmid could scarcely be expected to have much in common with a writer who made his name in England while worshipping Eton and the box-office in equal measure. Nor does he, being at once brief and dismissive:

> There is perhaps little that can be said to the credit of the late J M Barrie except his love of hard work.[9]

He is grateful that Barrie signed an important petition supporting him at a time when he felt particularly oppressed but this gratitude cannot cloud a negative literary judgement unsupported by textual analysis:

> I had little enough in common with Sir J M Barrie, little liking for his work, and never met him in the flesh.[10]

The intensity of Professor Daiches' opposition is more puzzling. His brief article in *The Listener* does raise some quite sophisticated critical problems, which will be discussed later. But behind the title 'The Sexless Sentimentalist' lurk the views of Millar. In many ways the usually generous Daiches even outdoes the earlier literary historian, replacing 'falsity' with 'perversity', 'playing to the gallery' with 'a streak of real cruelty'. Again, this time because of the brevity of the piece, there is little detailed literary discussion. We are deprived yet again of seeing the precise literary grounds on which his argument is based. Ironically its conclusion echoes (from a diametrically opposed viewpoint) Archer's judgement that such evaluation is in Barrie's case unnecessary:

> Clearly, something within him helped to twist his view of human relations into the pattern I have been describing. For those who want to explain rather than evaluate his work there is much more to say.[11]

Indeed there is much more to say. But surely it cannot be a solely psychological account? Surely in deference to the tastes of so many people over so long a period of time, the works which pleased, even enthralled them will repay scrutiny? Surely this is especially so when the author in question appears to have fallen from a position above criticism to one below it?

I have attempted just such a detailed reassessment. If much of it reads like a case for the defence that is in part because the critical climate is nowadays so negative and in part because I was one of the 'embarrassed few' mentioned above. My research has moved me from the modest hope of restoring his literary respectability to the much more ambitious hope that I may, through showing how much his art has been misunderstood, encourage a complete revaluation of his dramatic aims and status. Inevitably, the hostile critics often have some right on their side. Yet many of them have accepted rather than examined the perjorative generalisations about him. Others use such emotionally charged language that it is difficult to avoid the suspicion that they are in part arguing away a troubled reaction to Barrie the man as well as the writer. What, then, are the major lines of attack?

The first is overtly or covertly psychological. There has always been a tendency in both Scottish and English literary studies to devalue a writer by attacking his or her personality. Barrie has suffered from this diversion of attention more than most. As has been seen, within his own lifetime he managed to create the positive image of a modest, eccentric individual whose final years were spent in melancholic brooding.[12] He might have been pitied but clearly he was also loved and admired. His critical fall from grace has gone hand in hand with a much harsher viewing of his nature.

In most periods, the question of whether character assassination had any part to play in evaluating a drama or novel would at least have been seriously addressed. Barrie, however, began to lose his reputation in the period roughly between 1918 and 1940. During that time very powerful critical influences urged that although psychology and literature were separate disciplines, the key to the latter might be found in the former. The First World War led to a period of troubled self-examination in which the works of Freud were in a sense rediscovered and applied to a variety of areas of experience, including literature. The valuable counter-balancing ideas of the New Criticism with their emphasis on impersonal concern for the literary work as independent object and consequent opposition to extrinsic concerns such as authorial intention post-dated this period of Barrie's downfall. Even then, one would have thought that the 'psychological' writers might have been more conscious of difficulties than they showed themselves to be. Had Barrie, after all, not presented a curiously complex view of art in *Sentimental Tommy*, which suggested that the artist was a purveyor of deceit, both in the sense of deceiving himself and his audience? The latter was a major aim and, to be satisfying, had to be complex, challenging:

> To trick people so simply, however, is not agreeable to an artist.[13]

Yet, if anything, the evidence on which the psychological attack is mounted is too obvious. What triumph is there in reading complex Oedipal interpretations of other works when the author in *Margaret Ogilvy*[14] seems to be trumpeting 'mother fixation' in our ears? And what, ultimately, is the value of producing long books on the nature of the man if the grounds for his fame, his books, have been thoroughly discredited? The answers to these problems I have presented in Chapters Three and Four.

Of course, as has been implied, Barrie's novels are often strongly autobiographical. From them we can learn of a childhood dominated by the powerful influence of his mother; of the trauma he experienced at the death of his elder brother David and of his frustrated realisation that he could never replace that shade in her affections. The narrator in the novels is usually a thinly disguised Barrie, recounting with, at times an embarrassing honesty the emergence of an emotionally maimed adult personality. His failure to maintain sexual relationships in marriage is relentlessly analysed as are his compensatory love for children and particular attraction to situations in which that love can initiate a friendly rivalry with their mother while threatening to supplant the father.

Few outstanding men of the Victorian or Edwardian eras have so artfully and, apparently, artlessly defined their own Oedipus complex. Evidence which, in an earlier, optimistic age, had been generously interpreted as eccentricity now raised questions of homosexuality or paedophilia.[15]

There being at this time no detailed research available to counter charges which had not been admitted by his earlier idolaters, the darkest interpretations of his nature gained enough credence to make the man more interesting than his work. These charges still direct much modern criticism.

I am not challenging all the assumptions which psychologically orientated critics have made about Barrie.[16] He is in many ways a disturbing psychological study, whose obsessions undoubtedly had an effect on his art. But at least Andrew Birkin's fully researched, sensitive study *J M Barrie and the Lost Boys* has attempted the sanely balanced view of the man which the writer awaits.[17] Birkin does not seek to present Barrie as other than a troubled individual. Indeed his researches bring alive more poignantly than before the picture of a childhood dominated by rejection, inferiority and guilt. Using the evidence of the Barrie Notebooks much more fully than earlier writers he confirms the adult's sexual immaturity and probable impotence; his search for substitute fulfilment through flirtation and the almost parasitical relationship with the boys of the Llewelyn Davies family.[18] Yet the Barrie who emerges from all this, while not the wholly sympathetic figure presented by a Darlington or a MacKail,[19] is even further from the dark, threatening image of perversion created by his earlier detractors. This is partly because Birkin writes in a more liberal age than that of the 1940s and 1950s. Homosexuality is not now a matter of great moral concern. Paedophilia, however, is still repugnant to us and here Birkin brings the strongest possible evidence in Barrie's defence — from the Llewelyn Davies boys themselves:

> I had written to Nico [Llewelyn Davies] asking him whether he felt that Barrie had been platonically in love with George and Michael. In a later letter he wrote. 'I'm 200% certain there was never a desire to kiss (other than the cheek!), though things went through his mind — often producing magic — which never go through ordinary minds of such as myself . . . All I can say for certain is that I . . . never had one word or saw one glimmer of anything approaching homosexuality or paedophilia: had he had either of these leanings in however slight a symptom I would have been aware. He was an innocent — which is why he could write *Peter Pan*.[20]

This conclusion is probably rather simplistic. Barrie may have had some paedophiliac tendencies — he did, for example, take photographs of the boys undressed or undressing with suspicious frequency. The idea of *Peter Pan* as an 'innocent' play is also not one which withstands close critical scrutiny. But, by using all available sources, Birkin reclaims for Barrie the status of a vulnerable, generous human being largely unaware of a sexually darker side to his emotional make-up. For myself, I must admit that such concerns still seem at best peripheral to the problem of literary evaluation. The fact remains that many writers on Barrie use the idea of perversion to call into question the validity of his art or to explain its limitations.

Ironically, the only full-length Freudian study of Barrie did not appear until 1971, providing a late formulation of ideas, much earlier current. Harry M Geduld's *James Barrie* opens by discussing at length the events centring round the death of Barrie's elder brother David, fatally injured by a fall on the ice in 1867. The author, then a very young boy, had tramautic feelings of guilt, strengthened by his mother's illness and her clear indication that James could never adequately fill the emotional gap left by a favourite son. All this is first outlined by Geduld and then confirmed through lengthy quotations from Barrie's novel about his mother, *Margaret Ogilvy*. This, Geduld tells us, 'provides the prototypic story discernible through numerous variations in all of his novels and plays.' [21]

What follows is a dogged attempt to reduce all Barrie's extremely varied output to the unity of this pre-ordained premise. Inevitably the evidence is strongest in *Margaret Ogilvy*, where the prototype is consciously spelt out by Barrie himself, and in the other 'autobiographical' novels. But even here, there is the uncomfortable sense that only the discovery of the prototype is important. Anything which, to an open mind, suggests concerns beyond the purely personal, such as the description of the Chartist riots in *The Little Minister*, is played down or ignored. The continuing, subtle theorisings about the relationships between art and childbirth are not considered. Barrie's constant formal experimentations, the theatrical dimensions to his dramas and indeed anything which suggests literary variety is not addressed with any seriousness. Yet, undeniably most of the novels do contain a strongly self-analytical element. It is only when Geduld turns to the plays that a note of real desperation sounds.

The essential barrenness of the prototypic quest in this area reveals itself in various ways. Most obviously, there are situations where the material is so unhelpful to Geduld's cause that the discovery of the protoype involves him in ingenuities of an extreme kind. In the discussion of *Quality Street*, for example, we are invited to accept that 'Valentine Brown's preference for Phoebe corresponds to Barrie's infatuation with Margaret Ogilvy' on the grounds that 'the narrator of *The Little White Bird* . . . expressed the same taste for older women.' [22] (On such general grounds practically every major world dramatist could at some point be proved to have a mother complex). The Barrie figure, we are told, is divided in the play, being represented in actuality by the uncharitable brother James and in fantasy by the lover Valentine. The awkward fact that James — so central to the prototypic interpretation — never appears at all in the drama is ingeniously converted into 'appropriateness' through the idea of 'absenteeism'. Valentine's loss of a hand in the Napoleonic wars becomes a symbolic castration. Phoebe and Livvy, we are told without explanation, 'are fused into their prototype — the invalid Margaret Ogilvy who is to be cured by the one who deserted her.' Having suitably manipulated his material, Geduld then moves on to the conclusion he had by definition to reach, that Valentine accepts Phoebe (Margaret) and sends her (now non-existent) rival off in a carriage to brother James. There may be some dim and distant subconscious coding of this sort in the play but one is left with the strong sense that only a critic who had decided a priori to unify his study through consistent discovery of the same prototype would have had the determination to unearth it and the presumption to imply that this is the most valuable comment that can be made about Barrie's first major dramatic success.

Never does Geduld admit failure. *The Admirable Crichton* is praised for its satiric subtlety and for 'allowing the fantasy to work itself out without expressing or justifying the author in a prototypic situation'. That does not mean that the prototype cannot be rescued, as it were against the author's will.

> But the prototypes are not absent from the play. Crichton, Tweeny, and Lady Mary are recognizably personae of Barrie, Margaret Ogilvy, and Mary Ansell; and the incompetent Lord Loam . . . is a characterization of the 'negligent' parent, David Barrie Senior.[23]

Why is it that a complex argument has to be mounted for *Quality Street* but mere statement suffices for *Crichton* when, on Geduld's own evidence, the latter is the less personal and more obliquely prototypical of the two?

If, on the one hand, Geduld lays himself open to suspicion of having decided his conclusion in advance, the few sections of his analysis which move beyond the overtly psychological are disappointing. Barrie's most famous drama, *Peter Pan*, for example can be dismissed in three pages. Apart from the prototypic argument (drawn mainly from the later Dedication rather than the play) there is a brief recapitulation of its stage history, a short statement of major sources and a listing of other works which might rival it as 'the world's most popular children's play'.[24] As to why on literary grounds it might deserve that title, there is nothing.

In a sense Geduld's book was inevitable. Since 1921 various influential writers had been proclaiming the value of a Freudian work on Barrie. There was, however, a central paradox. As his reputation sank further and further, due largely to psychological criticisms, so the value of demonstrating at book length the limitations of so minor an author became increasingly questionable. He fell to the supposed implications of a Freudian analysis before that analysis was fully formulated. It is no coincidence that Geduld is an American. Barrie's higher reputation across the Atlantic at least made a full-length study seem worthwhile. In Britain at the time when he was writing, a book on Barrie was unlikely to attract either academics or publishers.

I do not deny that Geduld makes some interesting points nor that his central thesis has value. But I do believe that a study of this sort should show more willingness to conceive of exceptions; of plays and novels which do not fit into the overall scheme. It should be balanced by awareness of variety at other levels, paying some attention to 'varius sis' as well as 'tamen idem'. It should convince us that the author has done research in these other areas as well as dutifully following his chosen leitmotiv. Geduld does not so convince. His final condemnation of Barrie as a narrow and limited author whose work seldom rises above his own personal concerns thus seems to me largely the outcome of an approach which is itself narrow and limited, finding personality dominating because only personal issues have really been addressed.

Of course Geduld's strong reservations merely confirmed what most people now believed. Yet his Freudian criticisms bypassed close study of the texts, this time on the grounds that the man was more interesting than his work and the work only interesting in giving an insight into the man.

Geduld's book runs to 187 pages. By contrast, David Daiches' article in *The Listener* is only two and a half pages long. It has, however, damaged Barrie's reputation just as much if not more. Daiches is, after all, an outstanding scholar and sensitive critic with a deserved reputation in both English and Scottish literature. Yet 'The Sexless Sentimentalist' is also largely concerned with personality. Daiches rightly sees that Barrie's plays are essentially mythic, dealing 'in the elemental things of life.' [25] But he proceeds to invalidate their universal application on two grounds. First, Barrie's mother-complex and emotional immaturity resulted in a distorted view of the human situation.[26] Secondly, he did this wilfully to take his "revenge . . . on life for daring to pose adult problems involving real human relationships.' [27]

Barrie's work, then, is too idiosyncratic to be truly universal but it is also an act of wilful cunning. It is false both through nature and intention. Now, the problem of intention is a notoriously elusive one. Moreover, all the evidence clearly suggests that Barrie not only was painfully aware of his sexual inadequacies and his inability to cope with some aspects of adulthood, he was unambiguous about these subjects in his writings. Would a 'shamelessly cunning' author, intent on passing off his vision as normal, admit his mother-complex so openly as Barrie does in *Margaret Ogilvy* or analyse his marital feelings so relentlessly as Barrie does in *Tommy and Grizel*? Would he admit in a letter, "What is chiefly the matter with my own work I think is that life has always seemed so drab a thing to me that I keep at arm's length of it'? [28] Surely this argues for openness rather than deviousness? He did also attempt in *The Wedding Guest* to mirror directly the mutual sexual passions that were outwith his own experience but it was, on that level, a failure. Barrie, whose Notebooks, novels and plays constantly examine the interrelationship between life and art, is concerned about another type of honesty — being true to one's own vision. Admittedly, the comparative failure both commercially and critically of *The Wedding Guest* concentrated his mind wonderfully. But the attempt had been made. It may be true that from then on he avoided direct presentation of adult love in his plays wherever possible but he was already (even in *The Wedding Guest* itself) moving further and further away from naturalistic drama. The idea of love could be presented through structures associated with myth and fairytale, modes which naturally attracted a poetic mind. Overall, the evidence suggests to me an author admitting his limitations and seeking out forms which minimised them rather than practising any sort of literary Macchiavellianism.

Professor Daiches' other assertion that a writer dealing 'in the elemental things of life' must present 'normal expectations' and avoid a 'distorted rendering of the human situation' also begs some questions. Even if we accept the premise, however, surely Barrie is intent on minimising such a danger? His return to myth and fairy-tale is also a return to areas of experience where the 'normal' is not highly valued. As Lévi-Strauss and others have pointed out, these myths are not ludicrously erroneous history but a sophisticated coding or ordering of reality. Almost all fairy-tales, measured against the criterion of normality, would seem distorted. Daiches does not, unusually for him, make clear what precise genre expectations he is measuring Barrie against and although his stress on the 'elemental' suggests some awareness of artificiality, the drawing in of 'the savage naturalism' of *The House with the Green Shutters* for favourable comparative comment betrays an underlying belief that naturalistic criteria may be used to assess Barrie's work.[29]

That is to approach the problem from the authorial viewpoint. If instead we concentrate on the audience, it becomes immediately apparent that Daiches must assume that millions of people over more than a century have had so little insight into their own experiences as to call 'charming' what was in fact insidious; to rejoice in a comic skill without suspecting that, ultimately, it was turned against them. Indeed, if Barrie has mastered an art which is at once populist and misanthropic he must surely be one of the most subtle and daring writers of all time. Using in sentimental comedy the most commercial of forms, within the genre with the closest audience involvement, he would have to walk a constant referential tightrope and forever risk the appearance of clearsighted critics ready to expose his trickery. He would be the ultimate master of ambiguity. Though this claim may seem astounding, I believe that Professor Daiches is here very close to the truth. There is a sense in which Barrie *is* a deceptive artist, rejoicing in his skill to deceive but the precise definition of that deception and the literary theory which supports it is one of the most complex areas which I shall address.

Many writers who preferred to deal with the elemental and to present it through creatures and situations bearing only a symbolic relation to ordinary life were themselves nothing if not idiosyncratic. Was Swift normal? Was he so idiosyncratic that the general validity of *Gulliver's Travels* must be denied? Surely the case is, rather, that minds who view the world from an unusual angle often highlight those truths they see in a more powerful manner than 'normal' minds, which probably do not feel the need to write in the first place?[30] For instance, Barrie feared physical love, but because of that he saw with rare intensity the joys of a parenthood to which he could never aspire. That led in turn to a novel view of art, based on this counterpointing of literary and natural creativity. It also permitted him to dramatise with peculiar poignancy in *Dear Brutus* the all-consuming love of father for daughter and the horror of even considering disruption of that bond:

> MARGARET [shuddering]: I didn't like her saying that about your losing me.
> DEARTH: [the one thing of which he is sure]: I shan't lose you.
> MARGARET [hugging his arm]: It would be worse for you. I don't know how I
>   know that, but I do know it. What could you do without me?   (p. 1039)[31]

The realisation that he was unusual in having in some ways stopped before adulthood also led to an interest in different timescales and so to a unique approach to questions of youth and maturity, mutability and death. These issues ultimately lie behind dramas as different as *Quality Street, Rosalind, Peter Pan* and *Mary Rose*. The capacity to transcend time is, as Wordsworth clearly saw, a feature of fantasy literature and a reason for not condescending to its practitioners:

> Forgers of lawless tales! we bless you then,
> Impostors, drivellers, dotards, as the ape
> Philosophy will call you: then we feel
> With what, and how great might ye are in league,
> Who make our wish our power, our thought a deed;
> An empire a possession: Ye whom Time
> And Seasons serve, th' elements are potter's clay
> Space like a Heaven fill'd up with Northern lights;
> Here, nowhere, there, and everywhere at once.

What comes through most forcefully in Professor Daiches' article is the itensity of his reaction to Barrie. Almost every condemnation is strengthened by an adjective or adverb — 'real cruelty', 'positively masochistic pleasure', 'fierce resistance', 'disturbing cunning'. It is a reaction whose extremity he recognises at the end in the form of a partial recantation. 'Perhaps I have over-stressed the calculating side of Barrie.' As the genuine response of a brilliant critical mind it is something which cannot be discounted in a study such as this. It also confirms Bett's discovery that Barrie attracts ardent disciples or ardent detractors. Yet, in the last analysis, 'The Sexless Sentimentalist' is another example of condemnation of the artist sustained primarily through negative hypotheses about the man and his intentions.

The studies by both Geduld and Daiches embrace Barrie's novels and dramas without asking whether the criteria involved in judging the former can be applied to the latter. Has he fared any better amongst those modern critics whose major interest lies in the theatre? Certainly, there are fewer sustained diatribes but, while his great dramatic rival Shaw continues to be adulated in a series of book-length studies, only too often Barrie's fate is dismissal in a brief paragraph contrasting his superficiality and sentimentality unfavourably with Shavian depth and wit.

In John Allen's *A History of the Theatre in Europe* a lengthy and deeply considered evaluation of Shaw exists beside a brief description of Barrie, granting him inclusion solely on commercial, populist grounds.[33] The *Revels History of Drama in English* repeats the proportional value judgement. Shaw is lengthily reassessed in a manner which profits from ongoing critical debate while adding creatively to that debate. For Barrie the usual formulae are trotted out; in two pages he is credited with 'whimsical humour', 'whimsical fantasy' and 'Scots whimsy', whatever any of these may, precisely, be. A reference to his 'insubstantial fantasies', unaccompanied by any attempt to define either word, leads to an equally imprecise conclusion, that he satisfied the audience's need for 'some sort of escape' from realism.[34] Not only is Barrie rejected; it seems that all involvement with his work has ceased. Any of the questions he raises can safely be bypassed for they cannot have any substance. If Archer felt justified in treating Barrie briefly because he assumed general agreement on genius, most Histories of the Theatre reflect an antithetical position. They practise economy convinced that their readers will consider more space or exactitude a waste of critical energy.[35]

One of the problems underlying such a black and white opposition relates to the audience. Of all the major genres drama relies most heavily and intimately on audience reaction. It is rather more difficult to generalise about what an audience's reactions should or should not be, when those tastes are starkly defined by box-office receipts. And, however much the critic in his study may prefer Shaw, the fact remains that of the eleven plays written before *Man and Superman*, only *Arms and the Man* was produced in the West End. After that Shaw favoured the small Court Theatre, which specialised in short runs of radical plays. Barrie, by way of contrast, regularly filled the largest West End theatres with long-running plays in the face of massive competition from other would-be popular playwrights.

Nor is Barrie's drawing power confined to his own period. The bitter truth for those who want to dismiss him is that even today he remains dramatically much more successful than his critical position would suggest. In 1988 in London there were two Barrie revivals, the more recent being a production of *The Admirable Crichton* at *The Haymarket*. Starring Edward Fox and Rex Harrison, it has received generally enthusiastic reviews. In the same year in Edinburgh *Mary Rose* was imaginatively produced at *The Lyceum*, once more to journalistic acclaim. The fact that the dramatic publishers French still find it worthwhile to keep acting copies of these plays in print as well as *Peter Pan, Dear Brutus* and *What Every Woman Knows* bears witness to the frequency with which amateur groups return to the work of the Kirriemuir dramatist.

Yet even this success is turned against him. He is condemned as a populist without sufficient attention being paid to why he is the most successful populist and whether populism is not the first requirement of any practising dramatist. The tastes of the Victorian, Edwardian and modern theatregoer in favouring him are then condemned as superficial. This permits the contrast with Shaw to be re-established in all its apparent simplicity:

> While Shaw whetted the intellectual appetite of his audience, Barrie played on the sentiments of his and gave little more than a hint of social criticism . . . Barrie in general sought neither to criticise nor to penetrate below the surface of life.[36]

One might note in passing the sophistic device of assuming that if Shaw wrote successful, socially relevant drama, Barrie must be trying to do the same. Barrie didn't fail to penetrate beneath the shadow of life; he wasn't interested in Shadows (in the Platonic sense) but in Forms. Only once different literary methods and different conceptions of reality are allowed for, will comparisons of this sort be truly valuable. Yet the simple contrast between depth and shallowness, head and heart remains the major leitmotiv when Shaw is set against Barrie.

No-one who has read Barrie closely, and particularly no-one who has studied the many drafts from manuscript to stage presentation, should be satisfied with such an oversimplification. True, Barrie is a pragmatist in assessing what the audience wanted and presenting his message in a form which he knew would prove acceptable. Like Shakespeare he was a working dramatist for whom empty houses meant economic suicide. True, he favoured clear structures and happy endings. I hope to be able to prove, however, that in his best plays he handles myth in such a way as to open up questions of some complexity not solved on all levels by the solution chosen for any particular dramatic performance. In terms of Chehov's distinction Barrie at his best poses questions in a new way, while Shaw both poses and answers them. We are concerned then with different types of intellectual endeavour. Barrie hopes that the audience will continue the process of creation while Shaw presents a brilliant but closed intellectual argument. Arguably, the former approach makes better use of the unique characteristics of theatre while the latter is an extended branch of oratory.

The ability to present a simple story line which does not exhaust the potentialities of the topic it embodies but is part of a wider questioning opened up by quite subtle linguistic techniques is one of Barrie's greatest skills. It lies behind the frequently expressed confession of theatregoers that the ending of ostensibly happy plays leaves them unaccountably sad. In 1902, referring to *Quality Street, The Times* critic proved himself aware of these symptoms:

> For the charm of a genuine Barrie, while it is undeniable, is at the same time not very easily explicable. In the ultimate analysis we believe that the pleasure of a genuine Barrie will be found not so much in what the work — whether novel or play — says as in what it implies.[37]

Given the frequency with which commentators admit their difficulty in pinpointing Barrie's strengths, it is something of a relief to find at least one working towards a solution rather than escaping from the situation through unconvincing references to his 'whimsicality'.

I strongly believe that we would do better to concentrate less on Barrie's subconscious and more on the ways in which he disturbs our own. Nor is it only through careful working and reworking of mythic ideas that he achieves this end. Perhaps the most striking omission of all in critical approaches to his drama is the failure to welcome its poetic power. Barrie has the mind of a poet, though his infrequent metrical experimentations are disastrous. In prose the case is different, his constant revisions revealing the particular care lavished on key images and metaphors. Once again, the effect is to stimulate the audience's own imagination by encouraging a variety of possible associations. The early symbolic leitmotiv of the cuckoo in *Walker, London* provides an example where the associations are, comparatively, restricted. How often, though, in less controlled contexts does Barrie's dialogue reveal a poetic mind?

> MRS PAGE: And so, dear Charles, we have succeeded in keeping middle-age for women off the stage. Why, even Father Time doesn't let on about us. He waits at the wings with a dark cloth for us, just as our dresses wait with dust-sheets to fling over our expensive frocks; but we have a way with us which makes even Father Time reluctant to cast his cloak.
>
> (*Rosalind*, p 798)

Or his extended stage directions?

> She is already wearing her evening gown because she knows her children like to see her in it. It is a delicious confection made by herself out of nothing and other people's mistakes. She does not often go out to dinner, preferring when the children are in bed to sit beside them tidying up their minds just as if they were drawers.   (*Peter Pan*, p 505)

It should be made quite clear at this point, that I do not believe Barrie to be necessarily a better dramatist than Shaw. My contention is that they have different strengths. Shaw's have been enthusiastically identified by a line of critics beginning, characteristically, with Shaw himself; Barrie's have not. In this connection I would further argue that, not only his poetic abilities, but also his love of the theatre must be taken into acccount. Here, there is one very real contrast with Shaw, for if serious radical thinkers in the Victorian era welcomed the Irish dramatist, theatre managers much preferred the Scot. Cyril Maude, recounting his life at *The Haymarket*, pays tribute to Barrie's ability to become part of a theatrical team without diminishing his authorial status. He identifies *The Little Minister* as the play which initiated the success of his theatre, emphasising the harmony that existed in production among playwright, scenic artists, musical composer (Sir Alexander Mackenzie) and cast. Of Shaw at rehearsals for *You Never Can Tell*, he remarked by way of acid contrast:

> From the first the author showed the perversity of his disposition and his want of practical knowledge of the stage.[38]

Ideas being so important in Shavian drama, it is not surprising that he also proved much less malleable than Barrie over textual alterations. 'On the question of cutting, Mr Shaw's attitude was nothing less than Satanic.' [39] Barrie on the other hand combined a passion for rehearsal involvement (he attended rehearsals for *The Little Minister* from 10 a.m. until 6 p.m. for two months) with a belief in multiple texts and multiple interpretations. His view of art made him ready to accept the definition of theatre as the pooling of different talents. Both ideas also appealed to and strengthened his belief in an unending revision process. When Thomas Hardy, attending rehearsals for *Mary Rose*, spoke wistfully of Barrie possessing that 'sixth sense', the sense of the stage, which he did not himself have, he probably did not realise how much that original gift had been enhanced by months of hard work in study and stalls. [40]

Dramatic critics, then, may not be quite so antagonistic as Geduld or Daiches. But the prevalent mood of approach via Shaw, and the presentation of their relationship in terms of a contrast which implicitly blames Barrie for not being Shaw, while failing to acknowledge his own very different dramatic strengths is, in its own way, just as much an escape from thoughtful literary evaluation as the evasions of unreserved adulation, unreserved contempt or psychological detraction.

If we move from theatre critics viewing Barrie within a British context to those who are concerned primarily with Scottish drama, we find the same low evaluation and agreement with the generalisations outlined above. There are, however, some additional arguments and emphases. On the positive side, Scottish critics are readier to accept Barrie's continuing popularity with a certain group of people. He is, for example, more frequently presented by amateur dramatic companies in Scotland than elsewhere and he is still more effective in drawing people to the professional theatre than many excellent modern writers. Usually these facts are discounted with the one word 'bourgeois' which is in Scotland even more of a derogatory expression than in England. But in both countries it is part of the strange paradox that the dramatic establishment spends a good part of its time despising the group which form the vast majority of its clientèle.

On the negative side there is an essentially nationalistic argument. This has three major strands. First, it is argued that he is a literary traitor through having made his name in London. Secondly, his dramas are found to be lacking in specifically Scottish themes. Thirdly, there is the often stated but all too seldom examined contention that he mocked his own people in order to please Southern audiences.

Whether a Scottish author makes his name in Scotland or elsewhere is ultimately a matter of complete irrelevance to the question of his literary abilities. Behind the objection lies the age-old anger against a geographically close, numerically superior race and the fears that it may swallow up a smaller, distinctive culture. That is why a Scotsman becoming the talk of Rome or Paris is triumphant proof of internationalism but a Scotsman finding popularity in London finds his patriotism called into question.

Barrie has suffered more than most from such feelings, acknowledged or unacknowledged. But on what grounds? He is blamed for making his name in the London theatre. What other theatre could he have used as a vehicle for his talents? He was a self-made man, living by his pen, and there was no active repertory theatre in Scotland, when he set out to make his name. When he had money and a name he was one of those most involved in creating that repertory movement both north and south of the Tweed. The slow development of the *Scottish Playgoers Company* in Glasgow from 1909 onwards has been traced by George Rowell and Anthony Jackson.[41] It lacked audiences and folded again at the outbreak of war in 1914. With the exception of *The Boy David*, all of Barrie's full length plays had been performed before that date and it, anyway, opened in Edinburgh. Bridie did write plays with stronger Scottish themes for predominantly Scottish audiences. But playwriting was only a minor part of his income and in his day there was a settled repertory company, anxious for such material. With great regularity, Scottish critics find him a better or more interesting playwright than Barrie. In no other country, so far as I know, is this generally held.[42] I suspect that behind the preferences lies the 'patriotic' argument, in this case applied even where no practical alternative existed.

The tendency to look for Scottish themes and characters in works by Scottish authors is in itself a quite understandable and valid activity so long as description is not confused with evaluation. It would be one thing to study Shakespeare, looking for Scottish concerns, quite another to argue on those grounds that *Othello* must be inferior to *Macbeth*. Yet some Scottish critics do openly claim that, to be within the Scottish tradition, authors must 'articulate their Scottishness' in just this way. Clearly, once a native literature has been so narrowly defined, Barrie will only be one among many, who is condemned as peripheral. In a sense I am less concened with extreme opinions such as this; more so by the larger number of critics who support such a bias without fully admitting it either to their audience or, one suspects, to themselves. In Volume Four of *The History of Scottish Literature*, there is a chapter on early twentieth century drama by David Hutchison. In it one can detect not only the desire to find Scottish themes but a consistent preference for those dramatists who employ them most frequently. Two pages only are devoted to Barrie, a decision which in itself amounts to a negative judgement on the first major Scottish dramatist since David Lindsay in the sixteenth century and the most popular Scottish dramatist of all time. Although there are brief accounts of *The Admirable Crichton, Peter Pan* and *Mary Rose*, the section opens with the question of Scottish themes and ends with a relieved transition to Bridie, whose 'case is more interesting'.[43] Presumably this can only be due to his providing a wider range of Scottish topics. The tendency to judge Barrie on what he says rather than how he says it, is yet another evasion of detailed literary consideration of the texts. It is particularly marked among those approaching him within the context of Scottish Literature.

The third major 'nationalist' criticism is also the most bitterly advanced. Barrie is accused of holding his fellow Scots up to ridicule for the benefit of the English. Although the other prose works are included in this, there can be no doubt that the major thrust refers to the drama. It is the idea of large theatre audiences doubling up in laughter at witty depictions of Scottish stereotypes, which alienates many people from Barrie. Even if he were guilty of the charge, it would still remain a non-literary judgement, based on the false equation of message with medium. In suggesting that laughter is being raised for the wrong people at the expense of the wrong people, a critic is moving into the realms of sociology and politics.

Genre considerations are also relevant. Barrie is writing comedies. Surely it is not surprising that he finds the people he knows best a natural source of humour. Are Scots never funny? Are Molière and Goldoni to be ostracised for mocking their fellow Frenchmen and Italians? Are Congreve and Sheridan to be rejected by right-thinking Englishmen? Although basic questions such as these are seldom addressed, it soon becomes clear that this is not the central issue. The bone of contention is not funny Scots but funny Scots as the butt of English laughter.

I emphasise this because only if laughter at Scots *per se* was the source of anger could the favourite method of proving Barrie's guilt be adequate. Listing dramatic situations where Scots are successfully parodied is pointless. Here the context is all. One of the few critics to appreciate this is Ian Campbell, who notes for *Mary Rose* that while Cameron the ghillie is 'thoroughly laughed at for his provincial mannerisms' the major butt proves to be the very English Simon. The latter lacks both Cameron's knowledge and quiet dignity.[44]

> SIMON [with a groan]: Phew, this is serious. What was that book you were reading, Cameron, while I was fishing?
> CAMERON: It iss a small Euripides I carry in the pocket, Mr Blake.
> SIMON: Latin Mary Rose!
> CAMERON: It may be Latin, but in these parts we know no better than to call it Greek.   (*Mary Rose*, p 1116)

> CAMERON: . . . there iss much in Mr Blake which I am trying to copy.
> SIMON: Something in me worth copying!
> CAMERON: It iss not Mr Blake's learning; he has not much learning, but I haf always understood that the English manage without it.
>   (*Mary Rose*, p. 1117)

Similarly, if MacPhail in *Walker, London* is a stereotype of the over-serious Scot, he is matched by Nanny O'Brien an exaggerated portrait of Irish verbosity and Kit Upjohn, a parody of the Englishman whose only outstanding quality is his ability to play cricket.

Strangely, the very critics who blame Barrie for presenting an idyllic picture of Scottish peasant life usually centre their concern about his comedy round the treatment of these innocents. Are the elders in *The Little Minister* not mocked for their presbyterian rigidity? Are the Wylie family in *What Every Woman Knows* not at their most amusing when their unworldliness comes face to face with sophisticated London living? The answer is yes, although one might reasonably ask how Barrie can be blamed at one and the same time for being sentimentally idyllic and cruelly satirical. But Barrie knew how to draw laughter from every aspect of a situation. The elders provide amusement but retain all the dignity that is associated with honest naivety. And they are not the focus of the major comic reversal. That position is reserved for Rintoul, a latter day version of the hated Johnny Cope. In the same way the unworldliness of the Wylies is thoroughly exploited in terms of comic potential but balanced by a sympathetic awareness of their quiet inner strength. It is one of their number, Maggie, who is the architect of the plot and the English arch-sophisticate, Lady Sybil, who is outwitted by it. Context is all and context regularly reveals a controlled, for the most part gentle, treatment of national traits in Barrie's dramas.

Finally, there are those Scottish literary critics who deal with the novels as well as the dramas. Among their number there is little difficulty in deciding who has been the most influential. George Blake's *Barrie and the Kailyard School* appeared in 1951 and remains the one book whose arguments are known by all those interested in the period.[45] Blake at his most charitable damns Barrie with faint praise. Like so many others he does so through unsubstantiated generalisations. The chapter devoted to the Kirriemuir playwright is twenty one pages long but contains only one extended quotation from his works. The passage in question is taken from an episode in *Auld Licht Idylls* where preparation on the sabbath of a child for baptism poses comically grave theological problems. Stylistically, that passage is a masterpiece. Simply reported dialogue is contrasted with the heavier rhetoric of the minister's speaking voice. The sad conclusion is carefully understated and the whole passage united by a tone mingling wit with sympathy. Blake comments:

> This sort of guff might appeal to a cockney commercial traveller as a true picture of the sort of thing that could happen in Scotland, where they all wear the kilt and eat haggis.[46]

Unfortunately this is not untypical of the mode of argument practised by Blake. Here he avoids the single opportunity he has granted himself of assessing narrative art. Instead of looking rationally at how Barrie writes, he mocks what is being said after carefully parodying it.

Ultimately, however, Blake is not so much offended by what Barrie says as by what he doesn't say. Blake was himself a novelist. His best books — for example, *The Shipbuilders* — are realistic studies of social conditions during the industrial development of Scotland. What then is his major dissatisfaction with the works of Barrie?

> The fact is that the Industrial Revolution knocked the old Scotland sideways . . . And what had the Scottish novelists to say about it? The answer is nothing, or as nearly nothing as makes no matter.[47]

Now, most of Barrie's novels are set in an age prior to the Industrial

Revolution. To criticise these for lacking industrial comment is as sensible as blaming Scott for not addressing the problems of eighteenth century Scotland in *Ivanhoe*. Others, such as *The Little White Bird*, are creation myths while yet others, like *When A Man's Single*, focus on art in relation to another type of creativity, childbearing. Variety and artifice characterise Barrie's non-dramatic works, so it is hardly enlightening to treat them all as failed attempts at anticipating *The Shipbuilders*.

Interestingly, Max Beerbohm was faced with an earlier example of this type of non-argument directed at *What Every Woman Knows*. He defended Barrie as follows:

> Mr Massingham . . . has made excellent use of the best recipe of all, which is to blame your man for not having set out to do something quite alien from his actual purpose . . . If the play pretended to be the key of sober, realistic comedy, I, too, should be awfully angry about it. Realistic comedy is the form to which most of the playwrights of the time devote themselves. To the majority of plays that I criticise the test of actual life is the test that I apply, therefore; and it is because so few of them do not crumble under this test that I am so seldom able to praise. But in *What Every Woman Knows* the key of fantasy is struck from the outset, and to that key I attune my ears.[48]

It is a pity that Blake is in this sense tone deaf. Barrie set so many of his novels and dramas back in time precisely so that they might transcend the sort of particular references in which social realists delight.

Occasionally Barrie does try to re-create actual living conditions. He hopes, for example, that playgoers will accept the values and the atmosphere of *Quality Street* before the central fantasy is enacted. But Blake is ready even for this. Realism is not village life — realism is railways and the growth of the city. This is confidently asserted despite his own admission that the basic culture of Scotland is 'still parochial' and the fact that Leclaire's study of British fiction in the 1880-1900 period shows a predominance of regional and rural themes.[49] Subtle studies of sheltered lives lived in a state of quiet endurance but finally being rewarded (as in *Quality Street*) are also judged to be untrue to life because Blake is committed to the twentieth century's tendency to equate realism with pessimism. This permits him to evade the mimetic conclusion that happy endings are realistic mirrors of a confident society. It also permits him to find naturalism in George Douglas Brown's artificially constructed *The House with the Green Shutters* where the conclusion involves a single family in three suicides and one murder. It is clearly difficult for Barrie to impress a critic who judges him against false criteria and, whenever he does by chance threaten to meet those criteria, narrows their scope to exclude him. Yet so many subsequent writers have echoed Blake's conclusions that they now represent critical orthodoxy in Scotland.

Blake is also responsible for strengthening Millar's link between Barrie and the so-called Kailyard school of authors. In this context he is first damned by frequent association with inferior authors, held to be members of the same group. In fairness to Blake, he does from time to time clearly assert that Barrie writes better than the others:

> When all that is said and done, in James Matthew Barrie we are dealing with a
> writer who could have written ten Crocketts and twenty Ian Maclarens into a
> cocked hat at any moment.[50]

The fact remains that he *is* placed in the same school and is sometimes
viewed as the 'guiltiest', having squandered the greatest potential. There is a
grey area here which Blake does not seek to enlighten. Equally, when he
presents his hierarchy of authors, Barrie's position is left unclear:

> Once we have dealt, however, with a group of Scottish writers on three grades
> of excellence — Scott on the topmost tier, Stevenson on a lower level, Neil
> Munro and John Buchan derivatively with them but below decks in the larger
> assessment of these matters — we are left with a collection of small fry: the
> men of what has been called the Kailyard School. James Matthew Barrie
> excepted, none of these was anything but a reasonably competent commercial
> novelist.[51]

A variety of interpretations are here possible. Barrie belongs to one of the
higher grades, although this grade is not specified; Barrie belongs to a
higher rank among the Kailyard but still is one of the small fry; Barrie is
only a competent commercial novelist, any additional literary quality being
provided by his plays or Barrie is a better commercial novelist than the
others. Experience shows that most readers accept the second and fourth of
these propositions as the most likely. Barrie, therefore, becomes one of the
small fry and after a while even the distinctions of quality carefully drawn
by both Millar and Blake come to be of little importance. Soon it is not
unusual to find him last in the list rather than first. Hugh MacDiarmid, for
example, refers to 'the writers of the popular Kailyard school — Ian
Maclaren, S R Crockett, J M Barrie and others.[52]

If there is a tendency to group the Kailyard authors more closely together
than the variety of their work warrants, so there is a tendency to
oversimplify the nature of Kailyard writing. One of the most sentimental
tale collections, Ian Maclaren's *Beside the Bonnie Brier Bush*, is taken not
only as the worst extreme of the Kailyard but as a shorthand method of
referring to ALL Kailyard composition:

> The Scots storyteller either followed Scott and Stevenson through the heather
> with a claymore at his belt or he lingered round the bonnie brier bush, telling
> sweet, amusing little stories of bucolic intrigue as seen through the windows of
> the Presbyterian manse.[53]

It is easy to ridicule if you use one of the most overtly sentimental, poorly
written books as your 'type'. Of Barrie's prose works only the early
'Thrums' stories are anything like *The Bonnie Brier Bush* and they are
rescued from excesses of sentimentality by his wry and, at times, chilling
wit. The major novels, ranging as they do from the overt fantasy of *The
Little White Bird* to the pessimistic view of life and art presented in
Sentimental Tommy deserve, like the plays, to be examined without
reference to the blanket term of Kailyardism.

At last a more enlightened study of the Kailyard phenomenon has appeared. Thomas Knowles in *Art and Commerce: Aspects of Literary Sociology in the Late Victorian Scottish Kailyard* has moved behind the journalistic generalisations, seriously to consider the aims of these writers within their own social context. Knowles points to a number of instances where Barrie does in fact deal with social problems but accepts that these are of minor importance to his art. He also challenges the idea that realism must be equated with bleakness, arguing that it should involve 'descriptive balance' rather than 'the total illumination of the unseemly'.[54] If critics wish to appeal to twentieth century attitudes they are free to do so but they must make clear that they are superimposed from the limited view of one age on another, not regarded as absolutes. Quality Street and Thrums are, like all Barrie's literary worlds, stylised and artificial creations but they are not nearly so far from truth within their period and setting as the voice of cynicism would like to suppose. Why, otherwise, would Thomas Hardy of all people call *A Window in Thrums* a 'faithful representation of reality?'[55]

Knowles relates the art of the Kailyard specifically to the ideology and prevalent tastes of the period. On the one hand, influenced by Robertson Nicoll and the *British Weekly*, Barrie did see his art as having an essentially moral purpose, aimed at highlighting the values of human kindness and generosity. On the other hand, and Nicoll again was an influence, he saw the artist as having a duty to identify and enlist public taste on his side. Preferred topics; preferred literary modes were accepted and adapted rather than openly flouted.

A moral art is not necessarily unrealistic; a commercially aware art is not necessarily hypocritical. It depends on the use made of the accepted forms. Barrie, I hope to prove, used these forms creatively and subtly in a manner consistent with his advanced view of art as ever-changing and self-creating. Knowles' research provides the most reliable sociological base for such an approach.

The critical climate may now be a little more sympathetic to a thorough reassessment of Barrie's literary standing. Birkin has provided an excellent study of the man; Knowles has looked intelligently at the social background. Most important of all, three literary critics have recently produced balanced reactions to his work drawn from close attention to the texts. Leonee Ormond covers both plays and dramas in a regrettably brief book, drawing on a detailed knowledge of some of the early manuscripts.[56] She is quick to point to his shortcomings but considers him an author worthy of serious attention. Jacqueline Rose is a structuralist, applying the insights of that critical method to *Peter Pan*. The story 'without an author' and with no fixed text lends itself admirably to such an analysis. Rose finds it a work of challenging complexity, defying easy critical generalisations:

> The story of Peter Pan cannot be fitted into a framework which sees the child as a historical entity which literature reflects. It shows history as a divided entity which is given a false unity in the image of the child.[57]

To these book-length studies may be added a rare, sympathetic evaluation in a modern History of English Literature. Alastair Fowler refuses to link Barrie's dramas with the Kailyard or view them as the end of a second-rate popular traition. Instead his section on Modernist Drama opens with Barrie in the company of Wilde, Pinero and Shaw. For once the Scottish dramatist is accepted as providing 'a strong challenge to naturalistic realism'; is connected with expressionism and seen to be employing sentimental material for quite 'unsentimental aims'.[58]

Fowler concludes, 'Barrie's tragedy was that he easily got away with anything audiences could treat as whimsy; so that critics have not troubled to probe more deeply'.[59] In a sense this Chapter has been an extended variation on that theme. A further tragedy is that those who wished to probe did so as biographers, psychologists, sociologists and nationalists rather than literary critics. When attempts were made to find a place for him in literary or dramatic history, too often he was drawn in as a shadowy contrast for greater writers (Shaw) or as part of a loosely defined school (Kailyard). In these cases he was judged according to false criteria despite having made his own literary aims much clearer than most.

CHAPTER TWO

A Victorian Apprenticeship

The Early Plays:
Walker, London: The Professor's Love Story: The Little Minister: The Wedding Guest

'He accepted the theatre just as he found it, and sat down inside and for ten years you would hardly have known it was his deep design to join in the game of keeping it open.'   Howe

With the ideas noted in Chapter One at the forefront of my mind, I decided to focus on the full-length plays, beginning with those cited above. Barrie's careful composition methods were my starting point. I traced each play from its origins in his Notebooks[1] through MSS and production drafts to the latest extant text. This exercise in generative criticism was, I felt, true to the author's own spirit and would provide a full base from which to define areas where further enquiry was necessary. I also looked at those writers who were his early rivals in the London theatre, to provide a wider context of reference. I did not, at this stage, anticipate that the evidence provided would be so surprising but the Chapter seeks to trace both the procedure and the emerging consciousness of a need to re-define, radically, initial questions and my research priorities.

The four plays considered are not Barrie's first offerings to the London Theatre. 1891 had witnessed both a full-length tragedy and a one-act parody.[2] For the first of these, Richard Savage, he had joined his name to that of his collaborator, Marriott Watson: but he presented the one-act satire, Ibsen's Ghost, anonymously. Ironically, critics found the serious work unintentionally amusing but took the lighthearted attack on Ibsen seriously. The Times reviewer, for example, witnessed Savage's suicide 'not only without a pang, but even with some sense of relief'.[3] But his only concern over the short drama was whether the Norwegian playwright's reputation would last. He concluded. 'Probably the clever little parody . . . comes just soon enough to be not too late'.[4]

25

The Times also, in its Review of Drama for 1891, found Barrie the most likely candidate for the title 'new Molière' although the writer conceded that *Ibsen's Ghost* was 'too slight' to allow such prophecies to be made with confidence.[5] Barrie — an avid reader of *The Times* — must, nonetheless, have been encouraged by this judgement. His Notebooks reveal that he had planned a fullscale assault on the theatre, building on his already secure reputation as a prose writer. *Richard Savage* and *Ibsen's Ghost* were the first salvos. If he needed official sanction for this break with his past writing practice, he had now received it.

The major plays which followed share a number of features. Most significantly, Barrie consistently views them as products of his theatrical apprenticeship. Despite the commercial success of *Walker, London* and *The Little Minister* in particular, he did not allow any of them to be included in the *Collected Plays* of 1928.[6] This decision is seen as a reflection of his modesty by those who accept that persona at face value. As will be seen, however, in a theatrical context this diffidence was a clever invention of the theatre-manager J L Toole. Barrie adopted it with a melodramatic enthusiasm, inconsistent in my opinion with a truly retiring disposition. He was insecure rather than modest and especially insecure when entering that mysterious, stage world about which he had fantasised as a child in Kirriemuir and as a schoolboy in Dumfries.[7] That is why all four plays begin carefully from his own experience, real and literary. They are all 'Scottish' plays in the sense of deriving much of their comedy from the confrontation between Scottish and English values.[8] Only *Walker, London* does not have a Scottish setting and it is played out on a Thames houseboat similar to that which Barrie had shared in 1887 with his friend Thomas Gilmour.

This gives each a secure base, strengthened, critics argue, for all but *The Wedding Guest* by the fact that their plots rely to a considerable degree on the novels and prose works for which Barrie was already famous. At the same time, he saw more clearly than others that his appeal to his reputation as a prose writer posed other problems. It is no coincidence that 1891 was the year in which Guy de Maupassant wrote 'I believe the work of dramatising the novel is a dead art'.[9] In England many writers had assumed that these genres could be translated without any clear assessment of the unique features differentiating the two. Barrie may not have been immediately successful in dramatising his prose but he did accept from the outset that the study was not the stalls and all his subsequent painstaking revisions are made in the awareness that this distinction is an important and complex one.

I believe that there is in fact quite a close relationship between *The Wedding Guest* and one major Barrie novel, *Sentimental Tommy*, but even if this were not accepted, it is certainly based on another literary mode which he believed he had conquered. It was, as Geduld argues, an attempt at 'the Ibsenite problem play',[10] whose major traits he had already captured so skilfully for the purposes of satire. Even this literary transition from one literary mode to another would involve a real challenge. It is one thing to please comfortable audiences with a brief parody of a rather unpopular dramatist: quite another to imitate his bleak vision, even in a form which also draws from Pinero and Wilde.

Already, the similarities which draw these four plays together into a natural group can be seen to co-exist with and even to imply variations. If they derive from prose works, they do so in markedly different fashions and for contrasting dramatic ends. *The Wedding Guest* is a problem play; *Walker, London* is a farce; *The Professor's Love Story* a comedy and *The Little Minister* a mythic romance. Despite his conservatism in founding them on known literary and experiential worlds, Barrie experiments in different and often quite daring ways. Both similarities and variations are my concern, as is the crucial relationship between these early experiments and his mature drama. But one final, simple fact separates these plays from the others. Ten days after *The Wedding Guest* had ended its run, Queen Victoria died. These plays belong to the era of certainty and optimism which she embodied. They are an Edwardian playwright's Victorian apprenticeship.

WALKER, LONDON

Walker, London opened in Toole's Theatre on 25 February, 1892. The actor-manager J L Toole himself took the leading comic rôle of Jasper Phipps; his leading lady Irene Vanbrugh played the bluestocking, Bell Golightly, and a young actress, Mary Ansell, impressed the first night audience as the exuberant Irish girl, Nanny O'Brien. The plot is slight and centres on three love affairs, carefully differentiated and each bound on a troubled course towards marriage. Of these the relationship between the talented cricketer Kit Upjohn and Bell, the Girton graduate, is developed so as to satirise excessive reliance on brawn or brains. Kit gets off more lightly than Bell, who embodies all the fads and eccentricities of the determined Victorian feminist. Contrasting with this extremely volatile match is the quieter union between Andrew MacPhail and Nanny. On one level this is the stock opposition between serious Scotsman and funloving Irish girl, but the main focus is on MacPhail's morbid fears that he will fail his final medical examinations.

It is the third partnership which acts as the catalyst for all the misunderstandings and regroupings which constitute the storyline. The comic barber, Jasper Phipps, jilts his faithful fiancée Sarah in order to have one last fling among the upper classes. Passing himself off as one of his own clients, to whom he bears a striking resemblance, he becomes 'Colonel Neil', famed African explorer, falsely gains credit for rescuing Bell from drowning and so becomes one of the houseboat guests. He flirts determinedly with all the women aboard, even briefly becoming engaged to Bell, but is caught finally by the persevering Sarah, to whom, 'in his own way', he has remained faithful.

Certain themes do emerge from this lighthearted tale. The capacity of lovers to delude themselves; the folly of judging life on intellectual grounds alone; the barriers that need to be broken before different social classes can mix — all of these are considered. But Barrie is more concerned to amuse than instruct. It is, in short, 'a trivial story', 'a box of frivolous theatrical tricks as ephemeral as yesterday's newspaper.' [11] Yet it ran for no fewer than 511 performances and no other Barrie play survived so many consecutive presentations. Why should this be so? It cannot simply be referred to the trivial tastes of Edwardian audiences, for there were many frivolous plays in London at this time, none enjoying the continued success of Barrie's farce.

Nor did the critics of his own time drown the work with superlatives. True, Clement Scott in *The Daily Telegraph* saw its author as a worthy successor to Thomas Robertson. Such a comparison, however, is merely a polite way of suggesting that it is skilfully superficial.

> He is a Robertson of today, a Robertson up-to-date — not so sentimental, but quite as human, as observant, as pungent, as laconic, and a Robertson who has that same dramatic mastery over the simplest and apparently the most trivial details of life.[12]

J F Nisbet in *The Times* is even more insistent. He likes the play but fears that its humour may prove too subtle for London.

> Whether the general public will care for Mr Barrie's thin extract of humour, which they may find more piquant than satisfying, is a question.[13]

Why, then, was that question answered so positively?

For the first answer, it is helpful to return to Barrie's Notebooks. How did he first come to see the houseboat tale as suitable for the theatre? Interestingly, the earliest relevant jotting in Notebook 6 concerns neither a character nor a theme but a visual effect:

> 71)   Flirtation scene through blinds in houseboat
> (Shadow pantomime).

Later, in Notebook 7, he is still toiling with this one powerful moment:

> 21)   *Houseboat.* Scene 1 Day Scene 2 Night Girl flirting in 2.
> Shadows seen through blind.[14]

This incident will, in fact, be postponed in the play until the climactic movement when Jasper is trying to escape with Sarah. Another ambitious visual effect is introduced at this juncture when the crane which has been set up for cricket practice is used to move the sleeping Sarah in her chair from the upper deck down to a punt. The tension involved in this unusual method of escape is cleverly counterpointed against the happy sounds and cosy shadows of the minuet being danced in the warmth behind the blinds.

The triviality and ephemeral social concerns of *Walker, London* make it unlikely that we will ever see it performed again. Yet it *has* to be seen (even if only with the mind's eye) to be fully appreciated. It was not the houseboat which was original. Other plays had been set on houseboats. It was the young Barrie's ability to visualise the potential of that setting with its various levels and enclosed acting areas which provided its dramatic power. Look at the careful stage directing implicit in the first words of the text.

> Scene A house-boat on the Thames. The blinds are down. Time: morning. A canoe and punt on bank at the bow are tied to house-boat. Someone in distance is playing a penny whistle. W G is lying on plank lazily writing a letter. Presently he sleeps. Nanny is on deck fishing. Mrs Golightly is seen pulling up blind in saloon. The table is set for breakfast on deck. The opposite blind is also going up, giving a view of river and towpath. Mrs Golightly sits at window and knits. Andrew is seen in the saloon with no coat, waistcoat or collar. Bell is in the cabin. Nanny raises the line. She has her hair only partially done.
>
> (p 3)

Every character is precisely pictured and given a distinct area of the stage. The penny whistle adds atmospheric sound. The drawing of the blinds reveals in turn the breakfast table and then the further bank.

George Shelton, who later became famous for his performance as Smee in *Peter Pan*, played the part of Jasper's old ally Ben in *Walker, London*. He admits that the complex set filled the actors with dismay at first but confirms that 'as the dialogue proceeded, Barrie indicated where the speaker should be upon the stage, whether upon the upper deck or in the saloon, or in the punt alongside; and all went well'.[15] The young playwright clearly had thought out the presentation with the eye of a Stage Director.

Although *Walker, London* is not an ambitious work when viewed as a narrative, it was in many ways a very ambitious piece of theatre. Not only the actors but even the scenic designers are agreed on that. As Barrie had visualised everything with such care, Joseph Harker found it easy to understand what type of backdrop was required. Later he would identify that backdrop as the most satisfying of his whole career. So striking was it, that Clement Scott reserved a significant part of his notice to praise Harker's work:

> As if by magic — and in this case Mr Joseph Harker, the scene-painter, is a magician — we are carried right away from dull, unromantic London to the lovely reach of pure Thames scenery under the Cleveden Woods at Maidenhead. Just opposite the picnic cottage and within earshot of the Cookham lasher, among the reeds and the water-rushes and the long purples that grow about Formosa, a houseboat has been moored.[16]

Barrie's visual imagination, which later produced in Tinker Bell the most famous wordless character in British theatre, is powerfully at work even in his first major play.

As these examples prove, it was part of a wider interest in stage effects of all kinds. The young Barrie accepted that writing for the theatre involved teamwork and the cultivation of techniques markedly different from those of the novel. In this there was a hangover from those first childhood fantasies played out in the wash-house at Kirriemuir. *Walker, London* was written for the idol of his schoolboy days, J L Toole. While at Dumfries Academy, Barrie had attended a performance given by Toole on one of his provincial tours. Shortly afterwards the Dumfries Academy Dramatic Society put on a triple bill. Two of the plays were works in which Toole had starred and the third was Barrie's own juvenile drama *Bandalero the Bandit*. The show produced some self-righteous outrage in the town but also a generous letter from the great man himself in which he jokingly suggested that one of the boys might later write a play for him. Doubtless to his extreme surprise this 'prophecy' was realised.

Indeed, if Barrie shared the credit for *Walker, London* with the production team, in a sense he passed the major credit to Toole. So dominant was this actor-manager that the programme has his name emblazoned across it three times to Barrie's one; the performance is billed as celebrating not Barrie's first solo full-length play but Toole's return to the stage from illness. (Toole specialised in 'returns' either from illness or the provinces.) Toole it is who makes the final curtain speech, and most reviewers emphasise Toole's triumph, rather than the dramatist's contribution.

A major implication of this experience was Barrie's early realisation that a working dramatist never completes a script. He brings a version to the theatre which is at once adapted to meet acting strengths and practical limitations. Many of the long soliloquys intended for Toole in the earlier drafts are cut down because Toole's reputation had largely been founded on the expressiveness of his face. Often, he preferred to mime. So, ironically, in giving him more dialogue, Barrie had underestimated this actor's part. But while these speeches disappear after rehearsal, so the phrase 'Sarah, I'm slipping!' and variations on it increase at the same stage. This is because the posters advertising the play showed Toole in costume uttering these words.[17]

From the outset Barrie realised that revision was an endless theatrical process. He was still inserting new material for the three hundredth performance[18] and was always open to the lessons taught by those who had spent their lives in the theatre. This openness did not imply any loss of confidence in his own rôle. Barrie may have been an apprentice playwright but he was also a celebrated writer, whose works often explored the theme of art's power. The evidence provided by all those associated with *Walker, London* confirms that he haunted the theatre as a welcome figure, ready to learn but gently firm on all matters of importance. In casting, for example, he had decided that Mary Ansell should play Nanny. Irene Vanbrugh records her experience when she went to ask for that part:

> I approached the shy little author, confident at seventeen that my position as Toole's leading lady would intimidate him into giving me a choice of either part. How young but how foolish I was and how quiet but how firm he was![19]

Changes of dialogue were only allowed on his authorisation. Inevitably, a cast whose senior members specialised in farce introduced new witticisms from their own store. George Shelton records one rehearsal at which Barrie called them to account:

> As the gags came along Barrie, in his quiet way, said 'Out,' and so it went on until every gag was banished.[20]

This touch of authority gained Barrie lasting respect in the theatre, as did his willingness to subject himself to the corrections and antagonisms of constant rehearsing. On these grounds he became a favourite of the acting profession and theatre critics alike. But it was on the first night of *Walker, London* that Toole chose to make that modesty part of the night's dramatic impact. Five nights before, Oscar Wilde's first play, *Lady Windermere's Fan*, had opened at the *St. James's*. On the curtain call, 'Wilde, a fat man in evening-dress, wearing a fur-lined overcoat, had strolled into view smoking a cigarette and, the applause subsiding, had continued to smoke while he assured the audience that he was so glad the acting had not quite spoilt his little play'.[21] Outrage at this condescension gripped the acting profession. So, when Toole took his own curtain call at the end of *Walker, London*, he used the opportunity to boost his own dramatist and reply for his fellows. Barrie, he pointed out, was so nervous that he had left the theatre. Nor did he smoke![22]

Wilde's self-conceit was one of the reasons for his play being so severely treated by the critics. *The Times* denounced the author as one of those 'literary and artistic triflers' whose reputation depends on their remaining unintelligible. Over and over again it was argued that he had condescended to the theatre, providing a plot riddled with inconsistencies and successful only as a vehicle for his own epigrammatic wit.[23] Later, in the same year, Shaw's first play, *Widowers' Houses*, was similarly attacked for embodying a haughty superiority to the theatre and a failure to understand the unique demands of drama. The reviewer in *Lloyds*, for example, regrets that it is 'In no sense a drama, but a succession of dialogues in which the author sets forth his views concerning Socialist questions'.[24] The other side of the coin is that trivial, unambitious *Walker, London* meets with an enthusiasm which we now (distanced from those inner strifes of the London stage) find astounding:

> We do not need to go to Norway or Belgium, or Spain for the new dramatist when we can get so good a one from bonny Scotland.[25]

Barrie had established himself as a dedicated man of the theatre with a keen eye for the new opportunities it offered.

I have no doubt that he deserved this reputation. He saw himself as a working dramatist and as such must be evaluated. In addition, the idea of a medium which was constantly in flux and in one sense knew no ending appealed to Barrie the critic, already formulating a theory which saw literary and sexual creativity as different fatherings of developing children. It was, further, a challenge to Barrie the workaholic perfectionist. In the last analysis, *Walker, London* may have appealed to London audiences because it was an undemanding escapist drama but it appealed for so long and to so many because a man of great literary ability and instinctive dramatic skill had laboured on its slight plot with a carefulness that was to become his byword.

This care can be illustrated in four different ways. First, I shall examine the Definitive text itself and then look in order at the relationship between that text and the Notebooks, the prose sources and the earlier dramatic versions. Barrie was determined that his first major theatrical venture, even if it were only a farce, should not be attacked for slipshod craftsmanship.

That said, it would be idle to pretend that the Definitive text does not in some ways betray the inexperienced hand of the apprentice. Most notably, there is an unhealthy reliance on letters read aloud at key moments in order to introduce characters or explain the plot. None of these characters, with the exception of Jasper (and perhaps Sarah) are more than stereotypes of the kind then popular on stage — Scottish doctor, English cricketer, Bluestocking. Moreover, the tone of gentle farce is, on occasions, disrupted by lurchings into near melodrama.

> SARAH: You don't happen to have a villain on board?   (p 12)

> SARAH: [*starts to her feet*] Jasper's voice — he's on board this boat.
> [*Has almost gone off.*] He is found! Found, found! [*Assumes fighting position and cries*] Jasper Phipps, hi! . . . . His wedding clothes! . . . He is gone!

> (p 36)

It as if Barrie, like *The Times* reviewer, feared lest his humour might not satisfy Toole's robust audiences. If this be the case, his insecurity is reflected in some rather abrupt tonal variations, moving unhappily in and out of melodrama.

One major character also fails to convince. It is not surprising that Irene Vanbrugh wanted to move from the rôle of Bell to the comparatively minor one of Nanny. Barrie is caught between his genuine admiration for the 'new' woman and his belief that love must bring her back to the rôle of man's servant-ally. In the comic context of *Walker, London* this confusion is exaggerated rather than concealed. Bell descends from determined logical ideas to exchanging baby-talk with a lover, whose brains are in his cricket bat:

KIT: [*taking her head in his hands and speaking with great solemnity*]. Does 'oo love me, 'ittle pet?

BELL: [*with great solemnity*]. 'Es, me loves 'oo. Does 'oo love me? [*Nestles closer to him*].

(p 45)

From this Barrie would learn never to expect a leading lady to play a part in which she could not shine!

These weaknesses are counterbalanced by obvious strengths. Great thought has gone into producing a clear form, working from morning (Act 1) through noon (Act 2) until evening (Act 3). Each Act concludes on an intensely dramatic note, focusing on Jasper and Sarah. First, Jasper is surprised by his fiancée at a moment of hubris; secondly he escapes from her frantic searching and finally they sail off on the punt together, Jasper for the first time shouting out the play's title. This introduces a neat pattern of repetition and variation, escape leading to reconciliation. The love affairs, too, are neatly differentiated and the various 'humours' viewed through the contrasting eyes of youth (W G) and age (Mrs Golightly).

At the centre of this clear, dramatic presentation of plot there stands one major original idea and one major original character. The idea is that of having one's honeymoon prior to the wedding and on one's own. The character is Jasper, as close to Toole's acting strengths as Bell was distant from Irene Vanbrugh's. Essentially he too is a stereotype, defined by obsessional characteristics. Visually, there is his dizziness; verbally there is his repeated use of 'sister'; psychologically there is his compulsive flirtation.[26] But such is his energy as he strives to maintain the triple deception of being Colonel Neil, a brave rescuer and a Casanova that he ceases only to be defined by these characteristics. The major comic moments centre on the conflicting worlds of lower class reality and upper class illusion which he desperately strives to keep separate.

Linguistically too they are always on the point of collision. Colonel Neil would have realised the proper African contexts of 'caravan' and 'Alhambra' but to a barber they have much more down-to-earth references:

MRS GOLIGHTLY: What is a caravan like exactly?

JASPER: Hum-ah-well, a covered - in - van, you know, with brooms and baskets all over it and with two horses.   (p 21)

MRS GOLIGHTLY: The Alhambra is in Spain, you know.

JASPER: Oh, I thought you meant . . . oh!   (p 24)

And already Barrie, through Jasper, is developing his skill in irony. Jasper the lover is accepted in marriage the only time he checks to make sure such an outcome is impossible; Jasper the duper of women fails to realise that they are anxious to dupe themselves; Jasper the free spirit turns in terror to his fiancée and the barber's shop at the very moment he has won the most superior of the upper-class heroines.

In these areas lie the 'originality' and the 'inventiveness' attributed to the play by J F Nesbit and Granville Barker respectively.[27] As dramatic apprentice Barrie's conscientiousness is matched only by his energy and this idea points to a different sort of preparation and to the Notebooks.[28] Barrie used these famous jotters for the noting down of concepts, situations or dialogue if and when they occurred to him. They were initially the product of his busy days as a journalist and to the end he retained the journalist's economical desire to use as many of them as possible.[29] But he did make a clear distinction between ephemeral newspaper articles and those works on which he hoped to found his literary reputation. For these, the ideas were usually given a longer period of incubation and he wrote, revised and re-revised with enthusiasm.

The Notebooks reveal that his first thoughts on *Walker, London* originated about four years earlier. In Notebook 6 (1885-8) he has already devised the obsessional plea of 'Be a sister' and the idea of using both houseboat and plank as part of the stage setting. Notebook 7 (1887-8) introduces the character of the flirtatious barber. Initially, though, he intended the Bluestocking to have the leading part. Only in 1888 does he decide to have the 'Barber (as) leading character'.

Ironically, the Notebooks devote more space to the topic of a title than to anything else. Those suggested vary from *Woman's Wit* to *Tub-on-Thames*, from *Baby Bluestocking* to *The Floating Lady*.[30] From these Toole and Barrie settled finally on *The Houseboat* but this was subsequently refused on the grounds that a play so named already existed. It was out of desperation, then, that the ingenious title of *Walker, London* was adopted. 'Walker', being a slang interjection expressing the fear of being hoaxed, cleverly combines both a clue to Jasper's deceptive rôle and the trickster's last cry of relieved triumph.

His earlier prose works play a much greater part in determining the final form of *Walker, London*. Although he was aware of the generic leap he was about to make and its attendant problems. Barrie did not scruple to use again material from three of his most popular works. *When A Man's Single, Lady Nicotine* and *An Edinburgh Eleven*. The idyllic atmosphere of the houseboat setting had already been evoked in *When A Man's Single*:

> Rob stood on the deck of the house-boat Tawny Owl, looking down at Nell, who sat in the stern, her mother beside her, amid a blaze of Chinese Lanterns. Dick lay near them, prone, as he had fallen from a hammock whose one flaw was that it gave way when any one got into it . . . Mary, in a little blue nautical jacket with a cap to match, lay back in a camp-chair on deck with a silent banjo in her hands. Rob was brazening it out in flannels, and had been at such pains to select colours to suit him that the effect was atrocious.[31]

When A Man's Single also provides the original of W G (Will) and the flirtatious barber passing himself off as a gentleman.

But the specific rôle chosen by Jasper to carry off his deception — that of African explorer — is most fully treated in the essay collection *An*

Edinburgh Eleven. There, 'Africanus Neil's' prototype is discovered in Joseph Thomson, the explorer whose identity could 'always be proved by simply mentioning Africa in his presence'.[32] From this source too comes Andrew McPhail's farcical fear of failing his medical examinations and his attempt to conceal it beneath a façade of worldly nonchalance. *An Edinburgh Eleven* mainly consists of portraits of those among the Edinburgh University staff who had impressed Barrie when he was a student there. In the Chapter devoted to Professor Chrystal of the Medical Faculty, Barrie tells the story of an anonymous student very much like Andrew who with lordly air had persuaded his friends that he would prefer to fail. On learning that he has passed, he shrieks:

> 'I'm through: I'm through!' . . . His cigar was dashed aside and he sped like an arrow from the bow to the nearest telegraph office, shouting 'I'm through!' as he ran.[33]

If one adds to these examples, the discussions on smoking drawn from *My Lady Nicotine*, it becomes clear that much of *Walker, London* is derivative. Why, then, do the critics seldom mention this aspect and why can W A Darlington confidently assert that 'to the casual eye' the play bore 'almost no relation at all to the novel (*sic*) from which it came?' [34] There are three major reasons for this. The powerful ideas of the original honeymoon and the barber-gentleman were new; Barrie borrowed lightly from different prose works rather than concentrating on one and, in later drafts, cut down on borrowed dialogue. As a result he was congratulated on dramatic originality rather than condemned for excessive reliance on his own earlier prose.

Walker, London also allows us for the first time to follow Barrie through his labours as a practising dramatist. A comparison of the Definitive text with the MS in the Lilly Library of the University of Indiana and with the typed version presented to the Lord Chamberlain reveals, from another viewpoint, the painstaking care lavished on this light farce.

Many of the changes introduced from MS to Lord Chamberlain's text are simply those we would expect in a transition from draft to full text. In the Indiana MS Barrie occasionally leaves gaps. In Act 1 of the Lord Chamberlain's version, the letter sent by Jasper to Sarah explaining his reasons for deserting her is read out in full by Mrs Golightly. In the Indiana MS there is a space in midpage with only two words 'The Letter', indicating that Barrie has delayed composition. Similarly the word 'Soliloquy' in the draft prepares us for Bell's lengthy weighing up of the rival claims of her two suitors near the start of Act 2. In each case it seems likely that Barrie wished to develop the personalities of his major characters before returning to speeches in which they give detailed accounts of their respective philosophies.

In this category too we may place those occasions when Barrie simply changes his mind during composition. The clearest evidence for this centres on names. In the Indiana MS Jasper begins his adventures as Colonel Kay but becomes Colonel Neil. More subtly, although Nanny O'Brien and Bell Golightly are throughout the Indiana MS called Baby O'Brien and Nanny Golightly, there are internal signs that Barrie is already having doubts, as when W G remarks that they call Miss O'Brien 'Baby', adding 'though it is a rotter of a name.' Certainly it becomes less and less appropriate as Nanny's mature, worldly-wise character unfolds.

This evidence is especially important because Barrie was an author who laid great stress on getting exactly the right name for his creations. Only when that name harmonised with the character's personality did he feel that the latter came firmly into focus. As Colonel Kay, Baby and Nanny develop from vague ideas into individual dramatic rôles Barrie becomes dissatisfied with the names he had initially chosen and alters them either within the draft or in revision.

If the Notebooks show care being taken over the broad conception of plot, so a comparison between the Indiana MS and the Lord Chamberlain's text reveals those changes in detail made by an artist who is wholly absorbed in the development of his fictive world. Always he is working towards greater character consistency, clearer plot formulation and more powerful dramatic effects. And he is so completely involved in this process that he can follow through the implications that each variation has for the rest of the plot.

For the best example of this one may return to the much-altered title. The Indiana MS is still headed *The Houseboat*. What critics have not realised is that the witty use of 'Walker' is first to be found in the dialogue of the original manuscript. When describing her fiancé to Mrs Golightly, Sarah had called him 'a barber by trade, hookey walker by nature.' Once the new title was decided upon, Barrie substituted 'deceiver' for 'hookey walker,' thus reserving the first use of the crucial word for the dénouement, when the disappearing Jasper shouts it across the water to Mrs Golightly. Careful revision preserves the unexpectedness of the climax.

The Lord Chamberlain's text was only finalised in time to receive its licence one day before the first performance. Most of the changes between it and the MS, therefore, are the result of those celebrated rehearsals attended by Barrie but masterminded by Toole. What the young playwright appears to have learned above all is that the leisurely anecdotal style of the Indiana draft still betrayed his earlier training as a novelist. Sharpening of dialogue, highlighting of dramatic climaxes and simplification of form were all necessary to convert the material conceived in the study into powerful drama. This implied a good deal of cutting. Revisions aimed at achieving these goals continued long after he had received the Lord Chamberlain's licence. In terms of the play's evolution, therefore, this text represents an intermediary, if important, form. But one further type of alteration made at this stage should be analysed before drawing in the 'Definitive' [35] text.

It reflects on the problem of changing mode. The 'Definitive' text does contain one or two passages discreetly borrowed from the prose works. Many more are to be found in the Indiana MS but the majority are deleted in the Lord Chamberlain's text and are not resuscitated. It is, therefore, at this intermediary stage that Barrie most resolutely breaks the direct links between prose narrative and play. Usually the deletion simply speeds up the dialogue. In the Indiana draft, for example, W G's initial bantering with Baby (Nanny) included the following exchange:

BABY: The time will come when you'll give anything for a kiss.

W G: Look here, Baby, you have no right to bring such a charge against a fellow. And him as big as you. Little boy! Why you should just have seen me at breakfast with our tutor, old Jerry, that's all. The other fellows were frightened to open their mouths, but what do you think I did?

BABY: Something silly, Will.

W G: I asked old Jerry as cool as you like to pass the butter! And I won't be called Will. My name is W G.

(p 3)

In the Lord Chamberlain's text and the finalised version the joke about Jerry and the butter, which has been borrowed almost verbatim from Chapter 4 of *When A Man's Single*, is omitted, so that the script reads:

NANNY: Pooh! the time will come when you will be willing to give anything for a kiss.

W G: Rot! You have no right to bring such charges against a fellow.

NANNY: A fellow! You horrid little boy.

W G: Little boy! I'm as tall as you.   (ADD 53493F)

Here the effect is simply to speed up the action by deleting a quietly amusing joke, more likely to please a leisurely reader than a theatre audience. In Act 2 another borrowed passage disappears but this time the decision is related to a more complex dramatic situation. In all versions the subject of smoking — one of Barrie's lasting obsessions — is used to clever comic effect. The character who farcically tries and fails to give up cigarettes is Kit. But in the Indiana MS it is Jasper who first expatiates on the problem at length in answer to an abrupt question from Baby (Nanny). This has not been dramatically anticipated and serves only as a mildly amusing digression:

BABY: Why do men smoke?

JASPER: Some so as not to get sick in the company of smokers, and some because they begin it at school and are afraid to leave off. A lot smoke for economy, because it makes them work harder, and then at picnics it drives away the midges from the ladies, and it keeps you cool in summer and warm in winter.

BABY: Does nobody smoke because he likes it?

JASPER: None.[36]

All Jasper's ideas had been anticipated in a longer list provided by Dick Abinger in Chapter 12 of *When A Man's Single*. The clumsiness of this interpolation must have been obvious at rehearsal but the deletion also confines the problem of smoking to Kit alone, economically contrasting his problems with love and the weed against Jasper's flirtations and contented pipe-smoking.

At this stage too the extra soliloquys disappear, allowing the 'agonised groans and facial contortions' [37] of Toole their full expressive power. Indeed, in all ways, the acting edition received by the Chamberlain, was a much more consciously theatrical text than the Indiana draft. It was also much shorter. But there were further revisions as a comparison between the Chamberlain's text and the finalised version reveals. The emphasis in this reworking is on strengthening the theatrical effects at moments of crisis and on developing (perhaps in imitation of Ibsen) an, until then quite minimal, symbolic level of application.

The major addition at this stage, however, belongs to neither of these classes. It is the comic exchange between Nanny and Andrew in Act 1, where they discuss national stereotypes:

> ANDREW: You're a bonny wee lassie.
>
> NANNY: No compliments, but I can see you're a Scotchman now, and I used to doubt it.
>
> ANDREW: Why?
>
> NANNY: Because you never say 'Bang went saxpence whatever', and then you don't wear the national costume.
>
> ANDREW: What national costume? [*Nanny points to her skirts and to his legs.*] Oh, it's only the English tourists that wear that; besides you're not national either, for though you're an Irish girl, you don't flirt!
>
> NANNY: No, never. Oh! there's a fly in my eye!
>
> ANDREW: Fly in your eye! Oh I must operate at once.
>
> (p 7)

The introduction of this episode does suggest that London audiences enjoyed 'national' comedy. But it does not lend any weight to the 'Barrie as mocker of his homeland' contention. In fact, the comedy derives from Andrew's passionate rejection of that stereotype as part of a typically English vision. Further humour derives not from Andrew's use of the word 'lassie' but from his failure to see that Nanny *IS* flirting and so fulfilling her national stereotype, while he so energetically denies his. Neither Nanny nor Andrew returns to the subject of national identity nor do they load their conversation with the 'hoots mons' and 'begorrahs' of contemporary music hall convention.[38] In Andrew's seriousness and lack of romantic fervour Barrie draws on another myth about Scotsmen, one which he will use again. But in *Walker, London* he creates a situation which involves mockery of all three nations, making as slight and as reserved a bow to the comic potential of stage Scotsmen as he can.

The strengthening of theatrical effects at crucial dramatic moments involves further directions for the shadow dancing scene, which first had appeared all those years ago in Notebook 6. Now, limelights are introduced to heighten the contrast between Jasper's isolation and the joy of those dancing inside. An even more radical change is reserved for the end of Act 3. The original plan had been for the sleeping Sarah to be spirited to safety on W G's crane. In practice, this must have involved a good deal of movement and noise, likely to awaken more lethargic mortals than Sarah. There was the danger that if (against all the evidence) she remained absolutely asleep, tension might inappropriately lapse into farce. By having her wakened by a cuckoo cry in the final version, Barrie achieved a more convincing finale without sacrificing any of the drama.

The last moment of all is also revised. The words 'Walker, London' end the play in both Lord Chamberlain's and Definitive text. But in the former, as the 'invaders' sail away, Mrs Golightly reveals that yesterday the 'Colonel' had given her his telegraphic address. After searching in her purse, she finds a scrap of paper and reads out the key words. In the Definitive text this becomes part of a shouted exchange between houseboat and punt:

> MRS GOLIGHTLY: Your address?
> JASPER [off]:   Walker, London.
> ALL: Walker, London.   (p 52)

This minor alteration brings together many of the improvements detected in Barrie's revisions. It is more dramatic, being part of a dialogue with chorus: it is shouted out rather than read quietly: it gives the last effective word to the comic lead and it is more realistic — why should Jasper have written down a demonstrably false address? Why had Mrs Golightly not read and questioned it earlier? Above all, it reveals a playwright whose second thoughts are usually an improvement on his first; whose concern is with such details that he controls even the most minute of theatrical effects.

The most important additions, however, pertain to the cuckoo and the symbolism surrounding it. There is no cuckoo in the Indiana MS. In the Lord Chamberlain's text its call is heard only after Jasper has been cross-examined on his African experiences in Act 2. On hearing it, he becomes dizzy and when it calls out three times, Nanny is startled:

> NANNY: Listen to that cuckoo.
>
> MRS GOLIGHTLY: Yes, we never heard it till you came to us Colonel and now we hear it a dozen times a day.[39]

It sounds once more immediately afterwards and Jasper vows to shoot it. But, despite this melodramatic intention, there is no further reference to it. In the Definitive version, however, the cuckoo is so firmly related to the action that Walbrook entitles his Chapter on *Walker, London*. 'J L Toole and the Cuckoo.' This is because, in the version he saw, the cuckoo's call occurs at almost every crucial moment in Jasper's career. The symbolism is not subtle but it does at once emphasise the barber as a free spirit while underlining the more serious aspects of his swashbuckling.

The houseboat on this level of application becomes the nest into which Jasper has infiltrated himself. He successfully passes himself off to the mother (Mrs Golightly) and her fledglings as one of the family. Finally, the nest becomes overcrowded, nature reasserts itself and he returns to his own kind (Sarah). The leitmotiv is clearly established and its implications *explicitly defined* for an audience who would not expect to be intellectually challenged. In the final version, for example, the bird's first call is accompanied by an explanation, provided by old Ben:

> I tell you what I believe — you're the cuckoo in the hen's nest and that's your
> mate a-calling to you.   (p 17)

The mate is Sarah and the call is usually heard when she is nearby. At the end of Act 1 the cry annoys Jasper and shortly afterwards he sees Sarah searching for him. As it represents the call of nature, urging him to return to his own kind, inevitably it helps Sarah, the girl from his own class. At the end of Act 2 his shout of 'Damn that cuckoo' alerts her to his whereabouts and he only narrowly escapes discovery, while in Act 3 it is the bird's call which awakens her and finally brings them face to face. In various ways Barrie's dialogue has suggested that the medieval law of 'kynde' still works strongly in Victorian England. The symbolic use of the cuckoo underlines this.

Those critics who detect a sadder, more wistful message underlying the dominant farcical tone of the play are in part reacting to the associations of the symbolism. Jasper is an intruder, his adventure is doomed to failure and its continuation can only result in destruction of the idyllic family group. The story line, however, does not obey the fuller logic of the symbolism and the end is conceived through a retreat from illusion and a happy resolution involving three marriages. A distinction is made between those who hear and understand the cuckoo's warning (Sarah and Jasper) and those who hear but ignore it (the women on the houseboat). They are puzzled by the call but question no further because they are anxious to accept Jasper as the romantic adventurer of their imaginings. The tension between happy, particular, narrative conclusion and a more complex, universal, melancholy logic of metaphor or symbol will be used more subtly and consistently by Barrie in later dramas. Already, however, he is experimenting with a technique which will allow him to escape from the confines of light comedy and farce while obeying their central conventions.

Walker, London, then, for all its trivial story and fleeting social appeal, has great importance for anyone interested in Barrie's development as a playwright. It guides the student away from the study into the theatre, reminding him that judgement should only be made after the fullest possible realisation of that context. It highlights a tireless craftsman, creating, revising, recreating in accordance with his own perfectionism and with the successive demands of the stage. Barrie seems to see *himself* as an apprentice discovering the unique features of his chosen genre and explaining how far these may be stretched. The introduction of the cuckoo (at however late a stage) indicates an interest in universalising poetic techniques and the possibility of counterpointing explicit and associative levels of meaning. The apprentice, even at this earliest stage, reveals his ambitiousness.

THE PROFESSOR'S LOVE STORY

Arguably, Barrie's next offering, *The Professor's Love Story*, did not advance his reputation, although once more it provides interesting evidence of quite radical experimentation concealed by a conventionally romantic story-line. Strictly, he claimed to be moving from farce to comedy. But *Walker, London* had been very gentle farce and the plot of *The Professor's Love Story* does, intentionally or unintentionally, have farcical undertones. It centres on an absent-minded workaholic professor who claims to be suffering from a mysterious illness which prevents him from studying. In fact (unknown to him!) he is in love with his secretary, Lucy White. A more convincing version of the 'liberated' woman than Bell Golightly BA, Lucy handles Professor Goodwillie's illusions cleverly. She also fights off a rival, the delightfully useless Lady Gilding. As the latter cannot conceive of someone as low-born as Lucy being romantically interested in the professor, she reveals to her a plan for rousing the interest of Goodwillie by fainting in his presence. Lucy uses the plan, wins her unworldly suitor but then comes under dual pressure from her own exaggerated sense of guilt and the stern disapproval of his sister. That lady's views on love are of the school of Dickens' Miss Havisham but a long-lost love letter restores Miss Goodwillie's faith in men. She then reconciles her brother and Lucy who seem, at the curtain, set to live happily ever after in a romantic academe.

In many ways, *The Professor's Love Story* builds on the perceived strengths of *Walker, London*. Great care has again gone into creating a romantic visual setting, a point seized upon by Hammerton:

> The cleverly conceived setting of the play, in an atmosphere of sunshine and haycocks, came with a freshness similar to that produced the moment the curtain went up on *Walker, London*.[40]

Patrick Chalmers underlines the idyllic atmopshere created, referring to 'harvest fields, far-blue hills and bowers of honeysuckle'.[41] And throughout there is the same attention to visual effects. In Act 1 alone there are Lucy's hypocritical use of her handkerchief; Dr Cosens' by-play with the thermometer and Sir George Gilding's destruction of his wife's hat. In addition there are a series of mimed confusions as the professor fails to distinguish the separate purposes of glass, pillbox and ink-bottle; or coat and dressing-gown. The most noteworthy device of all, according to *The Times*, occurs at the denouement. There the playwright introduces the 'somewhat novel effect of a love story, told by dint of shadows on the window-blind.' [42] It is not, of course, a novel effect but a variation of the device used for the saloon dance in *Walker, London*.

Barrie further consolidates on his first major success by increasing the comedy dependent on national characteristics. *The Professor's Love Story* is set in Thrums and deals more thoroughly with Scottish country life than any of his other plays. The 'Scotch comedy' is centred on a sub-plot, which focuses on the cautious and circumspect rivalry between two farm labourers for the hand of the professor's housekeeper. The idea of the man, so slow in courting that he loses his girl had appeared in Scottish literature as early as 'Robene and Makyne', usually attributed to Henryson. Barrie adds a rival, just that bit more passionate, who talks his friend out of marriage and then demands material rewards for achieving an end he had, himself, coveted:

> HENDERS: That butter dish o' yours is a bonny thing — I'll take the butter
> dish. Also your picture o' Bobby Burns sitting on a tree playing
> the concertina, also six knives and forks, also a spade, also three
> sackfuls o' potatoes.   (p 123)

Almost all the humour is directed at the Scottish male's reputation for canniness and lack of romance. Characteristically (for Barrie) the 'pursued' woman is much more intelligent and passionate than either. Despite that, hers is a philosophy of quiet stoicism. She prefers Henders but is willing to take either. Occupying so low a place in a male-dominated, hierarchical society, she sees love as a probably unattainable luxury. As she admits to Lucy:

> I'm doubtin' it's not for common folk like me, Miss. We have our wistfu'
> hopes, but in the end we maun just tak' what we can get.
>
> (p 114)

The ridiculous Professor Goodwillie is also a Scottish stereotype. Barrie probably intended us to admire him as a man of the people, who has gained status through continued work but the dramatic context emphasises the ridiculous lover rather than the determined academic. There is also something about a lover, so lukewarm that he cannot define the source of his own feelings, which makes us wonder (even in a farce) whether this is not too ridiculous; or — if it is not — why Lucy should want such a confused individual in the first place.[43]

Parallels with *Walker, London*, then, merge into issues central to Barrie's standing today. Arguably, *The Professor's Love Story* not only provides ammunition for those who see him as a mocker of his fellow-countrymen, it is also dominated at points by extreme sentimentality. William Archer, in particular, shared this belief, relating an attack on its extravagant sentiment to a largely justified criticism of Barrie's reliance on 'irrelevant anecdote'.[44] I also think that I could find more reasons for supporting David Daiches' belief in idiosyncrasy invalidating universal relevance[45] in this play than in the others considered. Barrie's own ambivalent sexuality may have encouraged him to believe that others could accept such a man. But even the usually supportive *Times* finds such 'postulates strange and debateable.' [46]

Let us accept, then, that *The Professor's Love Story* is unashamedly sentimental and idiosyncratic. Let us accept that it involves situations which rely for their success on a predominantly English audience finding Scots amusing. Each of these admissions, however, needs to be viewed in context. The sentimentality of *The Professor's Love Story* is not primarily romantic sentimentality; the practicality of Lucy and Goodwillie's passionate myopia together guarantee that. Barrie is at his most self-indulgent when the professor recalls his life as schoolboy and student. Many of the incidents he revives are romanticised memories from the playwright's own past which, whatever their value for Barrie, are embarrassingly personal for the audience. They are also the source of the anecdotal looseness earlier noted in an otherwise tightly controlled plot. These weaknesses are the very ones Barrie himself referred to when lamenting that, initially, he had not treated the theatre with proper respect.[47] Not until *Quality Street* would he find a form which permitted him to integrate fantasy and realism in a way which avoided these tendencies, and allowed the vocabulary of sentimentality to serve an unsentimental purpose.

It is because the Victorian plays of Barrie invite us to use real life (however idyllically conceived) as a measure of their credibility that David Daiches' reservations are more relevant to them than to the mature drama. The reinforcing sub-plot in *The Professor's Love Story* (like the cuckoo in *Walker, London*) is an attempt at universalising the play's message but the base is still naturalistic rather than mythic. Max Beerbohm, reviewing the 1916 revival, incisively defines the major difference between the old and the new Barrie as imitators of Nature. The plot is incredible but so would many of Barrie's later plots seem if presented in précis form.

> The intention of the play (*PLS*) was to reproduce real life. Nowadays Mr Barrie treats life in a frankly fantastic manner. But he sees what he twists. The reality is there, right enough, despite the mode of its presentment. Life is shown as it isn't, and yet — life is the formula for Mr Barrie's recent work. And here we have an exhilarating development from his early work, whose formula is 'Nothing that exists purporting to be life'.[48]

Professor Daiches accepts the universality of application of the later works but implies that they still seek to be realistic in the manner of *The Professor's Love Story*. They are not; and the consciously artificial modes Barrie will choose are such that he is able to isolate those aspects of human experience, which his particular vision can illuminate, while avoiding those which may reveal his limitations. He would not always define this range correctly but his later creation of imaginatively consistent yet inherently fantastic dramatic worlds are at once a signal of recognised weakness and an attempt legitimately to bypass them. This does not negate the critical pertinence of asking whether a given personality can present a universal view but it forces a precise framing of that question. For the later Barrie one must enquire whether an author working within an artificial literary construct designed to minimise naturalistic realism and provide the higher Platonic Realism of form or myth can never have valuable views even in a world so re-defined.

When *The Professor's Love Story* was revived only *Dear Brutus* and *Mary Rose* of Barrie's unchallenged dramatic successes had not yet captivated the London stage. Beerbohm 'sympathises with Mr Barrie on the sudden and sorry resurrection of his old self. It must be very tragic for a man of mature genius . . . to be brought face to face with his old self's image'.[49] This underlining of an obvious fact has special relevance to the last of the issues raised. The comedy of the Scottish stereotype, however assessed, while a genuine concern in this group of apprentice dramas, can only relevantly be raised for two of the other full-length works — *What Every Woman Knows* and *Mary Rose*. Though the occasional Scottish character may appear in others, there is no sustained attempt to make it a source of comedy.[50]

The tendency noted in Chapter One to define Scottish Literature in terms of specifically Scottish content will always result in a narrowing of the canon consulted for authors who do not share that definition of their literary rôle. For Barrie the dramatist, however, the part of the canon preserved on these criteria is largely that which he himself dismissed. Even in these plays the charge of 'treacherous mockery' seems to me persuasive only when the incidents supporting it are de-contextualised. But the grounds for argument are there. The trouble about canonical dilution of this sort is that it refuses to consider Barrie's decision drastically to reduce such material in his mature works because that decision also removes those works from the defined area of critical concern. It is surely a bizarre situation in which the only grounds for making Barrie a Scottish author are the grounds on which that Scottishness is denied? Certainly, it is a biassed critical situation, where thematic concerns confine attention to the weakest works, permitting generalisations on sentimentality, incredibility and superficiality which, at the very least, are much more difficult to sustain for the Barrie of *Quality Street, Peter Pan* or *Dear Brutus*.[51]

It is, of course, the inadequacy of *The Professor's Love Story*, which makes it a natural focus for discussing negative criticism. Certainly, it encourages parallels with *Walker, London* which, usually, redound to the favour of the earlier work. Both, for example, evolve slowly in the Notebooks but *The Professor's Love Story* does so as two separate ideas. The first of these, 'The Bookworm', consumes rather than complements the second, 'The Self-Made Woman'[52] Moreover, if both plays have a successful and an unsuccessful leading rôle, undeniably Professor Goodwillie is much more of a dramatic disaster than Bell Golightly had been. If she is unconvincing, he is simply unbelievable and one can only sympathise with *The Scotsman* reviewer when he laments that the dramatist had 'allowed his [Goodwillie's] peculiarities so to overcome him that he appeared to be on the verge of insanity.' [53]

The next major question which arises is whether Barrie had in this instance set himself simply to write a popular play without continuing the radical experimentations covertly begun in *Walker, London*. There is after all no use of Ibsenite symbolism here and the ending is unequivocally sentimental rather than tonally ambivalent.

It was a major box office success both in the United States, where it opened at the *Star Theatre*, New York in December 1893 and in London. There it began its run at *The Comedy* on 25 June 1894, later transferring to *The Garrick*.[54] Although its 144 performances fell well short of *Walker, London*'s marathon run, they compared very well with contemporary offerings and have to be seen in the context of a much weaker cast than that amassed by Toole. Indeed the actor-manager E S Willard, who bought the rights for the play in America and England, was considered by many to have given a tired performance as Goodwillie. Walbrook shares this view, linking it with a belief that Willard was by now disillusioned with the stage.[55] To this was added criticism of the 'Scotch accents' adopted by Royce Carleton and F H Taylor and lukewarm appreciation for Bessie Hatton's Lucy. Against this background, Willard's contention that the work was a 'safe' one having 'all the right ingredients for popular success — romance, sentiment, a little sly satire, a happy ending' [56] appears to confirm the image of a Barrie working to popular order. Had he indeed given up his attempts at innovation in an attempt to woo and win the box-office?

This attack on Barrie the populist can, even in the vulnerable case of *The Professor's Love Story*, be countered in two different ways. The first involves discussing those experimental techniques employed in the play itself. The second involves the larger question of the degree to which any dramatist can afford to be anti-populist; to ignore the tastes of the audience who are his only direct consumer.

As novel-plays *Walker, London* and *The Professor's Love Story* could not be more different. The houseboat drama used a variety of prose works as sources for its interrelated plots but never drew heavily from any one. In the double plot of *The Professor's Love Story* Barrie chooses instead to use, very thoroughly and for the sub-plot alone, a single Chapter of *Auld Licht Idylls*.[57] He has consciously set himself new tests in structure and genre translation, the latter contrasting in every way with that he addressed for Toole.

He is just as successful in his realisation of the new demands. Essentially this time he is converting a short story into part of a double dramatic plot. Carefully he extends the rôles of his three Scottish peasants, allowing them to move at times into the main plot.[58] He excises minor characters, shortens the time-scale, coalesces two chases into one, polarises the characters of the male suitors and develops brief interchanges into full-scale farcical situations. He also avoids what must have been a great temptation — to lift rather than re-write most of the dialogue, for Chapter 8 of *Auld Licht Idylls* is so dominated by direct speech that it already reads like a chattily annotated playscript. The lessons here will serve him well in the even more ambitious task posed by dramatisation of *The Little Minister*.

If the sub-plot is an adaptation of one of his own stories, the structure of the play as a whole imitates one of his dramatic idols, Shakespeare. Barrie was to write versions of *The Taming of the Shrew* and *Macbeth*; to use Shakespearean character names and a performance of *As You Like It* in *Rosalind*; to make his own contribution to the Bacon debate[59] and, of course, to employ echoes of Shakespearean drama in many of his major plays, most notably *Dear Brutus*. In *The Professor's Love Story* he uses the Renaissance device of universalising his message through a counterpointing sub-plot. The upper class comedy of an unworldly man, relentlessly courted by two women is set beside that of a down-to-earth woman (Eiffie) somewhat less wholeheartedly pursued by two men (Pete and Henders). While the pursuit in the main plot involves a primarily intellectual competition, on the lower level this is translated into a physical race. While both Lucy and Lady Gilding view the situation in romantic terms, Effie is more concerned with economics. While Professor Goodwillie passionately does not know with whom he is meant to be in love, Pete and Henders unpassionately know only too well. This aspect of the play has been thoroughly worked out with Barrie's usual ironic skill. Unfortunately the final irony was one he had not anticipated. So successful was his translation of the earthy ménage à trois from the *Idylls* that, dramatically, they overshadowed rather than complemented the romantic posturings of the Professor and Lady Gilding. As a result the sub-plot fails to produce the universalising result, contributing rather to that uneven 'patchwork' effect identified by Archer.[60]

If Barrie can be defended (if not excused) on grounds of experimentation, the charge of rampant commercialism can also be countered in an even more down to earth manner. A working dramatist cannot be aggressively unpopular and survive. Over and over again Barrie makes this point himself both with regard to drama and, of course, humour. He makes it in the Notebooks, he makes it in his Letters and (inevitably) his Prose heroes make it on his behalf:

> When I say a humorous thing mysel I'm dependent on other fowk to tak note o' the humour o't, bein mysel ta'en up wi' the makkin o't.
>
> (*A Window in Thrums*, p. 41)

If Tammas had been trying to win over a paying London audience, his problem would have been intensified. Had he then compared the practice of his, supposedly radical, rivals, he might have been surprised. In fact these writers are all acutely aware that, in the theatre especially, innovation has to be disguised in reasonably conservative clothes. Wilde seems to escape criticism because of his unique vein of wit but his plays closely follow theatrical conventions even if they seek to subvert them. More serious dramatists such as Jones and Shaw, while embarking on quite radical reforms, knew that any revolution must emerge from prevailing tastes.

Jones in *The Liars* addressed an unusually serious problem, that of deceit, but he set it within the melodramatic and comic conventions to which the play-going public were accustomed. The bland ending of that play, at odds with its moral logic, shows the degree to which he was willing to compromise his art in order to placate his audience.[61]

Shaw was not one to compromise his ideas, and his bitterness against the English theatre grew throughout the 1890s. At the same time, he realised that the criticism of *Widowers' Houses* for being too homiletic was not entirely undeserved. As a result the attack on popular theatre contained in the Preface to *Three Plays for Puritans* confesses the necessity of combining radical thought and traditional presentation. Of *The Devil's Disciple*, which opened in New York three years after *The Professor's Love Story*, he confesses:

> It does not contain a single even passably novel incident. Every old patron of the Adelphi pit would, were he not beglamoured in a way presently to be explained, recognise the reading of the Will, the oppressed orphan finding a protector, the arrest, the heroic sacrifice, the court martial, the scaffold, the reprieve at the last moment, as he recognizes beefsteak pudding on the bill of fare at his restaurant.[62]

I am not suggesting that Barrie at this stage launched such an overtly radical assault on the values of the London stage as Shaw did. But I do think that the degree of his non-conformity has been grossly underestimated because his innovations are more subtle, relating to the medium primarily and to the surface message only insofar as it is defined by that medium. Even *The Professor's Love Story*, one of his most blatantly commercial works, takes some risks in the name of experiment and art.[63]

THE LITTLE MINISTER

If, in all these ways, it is easy to understand Barrie's own low opinion of *The Professor's Love Story*, the situation with regard to *The Little Minister* is much more puzzling. The simplest level of the problem is succinctly defined by Cynthia Asquith:

> He spoke disparagingly of the play, *The Little Minister*, which he said he didn't intend to include in any future edition of his works. Ungrateful of him, for it earned him eighty thousand pounds in its first ten years![64]

Indeed, all the evidence indicates a stronger revulsion against this play than any of his other early dramatic works. When it became a film in 1935 (starring Katherine Hepburn) Barrie refused even to walk the ten minutes from his door to *The Tivoli* in order to see it.[65]

Nor is Cynthia Asquith exaggerating the commercial success of the play. After a quiet opening in Washington, it ran at *The Empire*, New York with

Maude Adams in the leading rôle for 300 consecutive performances, netting American record receipts of $300,000.[66] On 6 November 1897, the British production, starring Cyril Maude and Winifred Emery, opened at *The Haymarket* to conflicting reviews but complete audience satisfaction. Two weeks after that opening, the *Pall Mall Gazette* records, the playgoers of London and New York were together paying £4,000 a week to see it.[67]

The American production went on tour, taking advantage of 'the golden age' of the theatre in that country before the advent of cinema and radio. In England Cyril Maude identified the play as 'the most important and not the least successful' of a fortunate series at *The Haymarket*.[68] This he attributed in large part to the brilliance of the piece itself and, while Barrie became increasingly hostile to it, successful revivals were staged at *The Duke of York's* in 1914 and *The Queen's* in 1923. Indeed, for a brief period in January 1923, five Barrie plays — *Peter Pan, The Little Minister, What Every Woman Knows, The Will* and *Alice Sit-By-The-Fire* — figured on the London stage simultaneously. Of these only *The Little Minister* was excluded from the *Collected Plays* as chosen by the playwright.

This again proves that Barrie was not simply a dramatic materialist. But it reveals more. He was capable of self-criticism in the face of essentially favourable reviews and despite the awareness that everyone had praised his courage in adapting a long, sprawling novel for the stage. This was a much more ambitious exercise in imitation than that undertaken in either *Walker, London* or *The Professor's Love Story*. Even *The Scotsman* critic, who had grave reservations about the play as a play, admitted that 'great skill' had been shown in moving from one genre to another.[69] Of contemporary writers, Darlington praised him for 'boldly simplify[ing] the story' and Howe correctly noted that, unlike so many other novelists, he refused to see the stage as posing 'a shorter but not different task, a kind of subdivision of his accustomed labour'.[70] Walbrook takes the matter further. For him, *The Little Minister* is not only a milestone in the commercial history of the drama, it is also the play which proved that novels could become successful theatre. Until Barrie, and in spite of minor successes like *The Prisoner of Zenda* (1896) and *Under the Red Robe* (1896), the dramatisation of prose works seemed, in the main, a recipe for failure. Walbrook has no doubt what the triumph of *The Little Minister* means:

> Had he [Barrie] failed he would, as they say, have put the hours of the English dramatic clock a long way back. Luckily for the British drama he succeeded. From that memorable night [the *Haymarket* opening] dates the brilliant chapter of stage history in which the names of Clemence Dane, John Galsworthy, Arnold Bennett, W Somerset Maugham, Morley Roberts, Thomas Cobb, and other men of letters, so happily shine.[71]

This, no doubt, overstates the case but Barrie's achievement is a real one. Walbrook was writing in 1922 and it is against this eulogistic background that Barrie maintained his own disfavour.

One of the grounds for his reaction can be traced back to the most bitter review he had yet received. While major English journalists were either thrilled or lulled by *The Little Minister*, the voice of Edinburgh, *The Scotsman*, chose the opening of that play to voice acute disappointment. Barrie, it argued, had now had long enough to prove himself as a playwright. 'Pretty, rather over-sentimental successes' (*The Professor's Love Story*) and embarrassing failures (*Richard Savage*) could not conceal his potential but was it ever to be realised? If *The Little Minister* were the answer to this question, then 'Hope is now replaced by disappointment in the hearts of those who think seriously about our national drama,' for here is more triviality.[72]

Perhaps the writer was in too much of a hurry to urge Barrie out of apprenticeship into accountability. But he had accurately defined his fellow countryman's serious approach. Barrie had, once more, attended rehearsals with almost masochistic dutifulness for six weeks prior to the opening. He had sat with Maude from morning until late evening on a little platform specially rigged up in front of the stage. Moreover, even if he were still trying to find a unique voice rather than courting final judgement, the evidence suggests that this play was by far his most adventurous technical experiment so far. As will be seen, this radically new approach went hand in hand with failure of nerve and while Barrie, almost certainly, would not have defined that failure so simplistically, his later reactions suggest that he shared the sense of disappointment just as acutely.

Ironically, one of the major dissatisfactions expressed by *The Scotsman* critic arose from what was undoubtedly one of Barrie's prime dramatic strengths, his awareness of visual impact. Howe, referring primarily to *The Little Minister*, stresses this in the context of his praise for the novelist turned playwright:

> There is no part of the theatre's art which is more frequently foregone by the novelist in the theatre than what we may speak of as its visual possibilities . . . and there is no part of the theatre's art which, by Barrie, is more surely seized.[73]

Walbrook notes the care with which scenic detail and contrasted costumes assault the eye. Winifred Emery as Babbie wanders

> barefooted and barelegged among the reddened leaves of Caddan [*sic*] Woods, in her dress of leaf-green serge, loose bodice, leather belt, scarlet berries in her flying brown hair

and compares this with Gavin's 'trim, black-coated' shyness.[74] But he also calls attention to the conclusion when the two lovers kiss in fairy-tale union. This, he claims, is 'one of the most vivid memories of those who saw the play' not because of the sentimental love but because of 'four queer stove-pipe-hatted heads suddenly bobbing up from the other side' providing an unexpected but from all accounts theatrically effective farcical denouement.[75]

The hats belong to the Scottish elders of Thrums and it is on this moment

1. 'queer stove-pipe-hatted heads suddenly bobbing up' (*The Little Minister*)

above all others that the attack on Barrie as an encourager of English ridicule at the expense of Scots simplicity hinges. *The Scotsman* columnist, addressing himself to the major hope of '*our national* drama,' finds this moment 'decidedly unpleasant' and quite correctly links it to the tonal insecurity which bedevils the whole play:

> The piece begins and is carried on for an act and a half as light comedy, then it takes a more sentimental turn and concludes as what may be almost called 'screaming farce'.[76]

While I believe the general case against Barrie's supposed 'humorous treachery' to be markedly overstated and while *The Times* critic (presumably an Englishman) reacted to the Thrums characters in the sympathetic way the playwright almost certainly intended,[77] I am willing to concede that this criticism does have social validity.

There is some evidence that Barrie shared this feeling. If one compares the earliest texts[78] with the Definitive Edition, you discover that lines asserting Scottish superiority to Englishmen have regularly been introduced into the latter. In Act 2 Scene 2 both the comment on Babbie's English ignorance (p 162) and the triumphant Jacobite song (p 163) are additions. To these situational superiorities may be added the linguistic superiority produced by the insertion of Nanny's dense dialect (p 148). Barrie apparently saw that the balance between presenting the Thrums elders as serious, moral men and farcical bigots had moved too strongly towards the latter. He had falsely judged the, always precarious, tonal balance and sought now to redress it in favour of Scottish values.

These adjustments were too little and too late. The damage was done despite a marked playing down of this type of humour in *The Wedding Guest*, silence in the next five major plays and an attempt to address the same mixture of dignity and simplicity more patriotically in *What Every Woman Knows*. No form of repentance, however extreme, could counterbalance the image of those hats. Soon, English critics were going to accept the bitterness felt north of the border without examining its justification. When assessing the 1914 revival of *The Little Minister*, *The Times* echoes accepted Scottish opinion. Barrie's comedy holds up 'an imaginary Scotland for English consumption'.[79] Only a few thoughtful voices paused to consider the grounds for such attacks. Beerbohm again comes to Barrie's defence. Contrasting the stage version of *The Little Minister* and *Beside the Bonnie Brier Bush*, he comments:

> It is true, doubtless, as most Scotsmen assert, that Mr Barrie's characters were not true to Scottish nature. But, at least, they were not stagey. They were inventions from within Mr Barrie's own brain; and very delightful inventions they were too — presented with a salt humour that saved us being cloyed by the inherent sentimentality.[80]

Rightly he again reminds us of the artifice; the fallacy of presuming that all drama and Barrie's in particular, must work according to naturalistic criteria.

Is his justification a fair one? One line of exploration clearly suggests that it is. Through symbolism in *Walker, London* and the double plot in *The Professor's Love Story* Barrie had falteringly moved towards universal concerns, while retaining an essentially naturalistic story line. In *The Little Minister* he began to move towards fantasy and myth. In the Notebooks he had carefully observed,

     171)   The Weaver Revolution was 1839.
     172)   Gavin 1838.[81]

By 1897 he had moved the time back twenty one or twenty two years before these riots. Why?

Concerns of this sort relate directly to the transition from novel to drama, where everyone is agreed on Barrie's success in adapting narrative to meet the requirements of an art form in which everything depends on dialogue and situation. Stressing the sentimental plot line of love overcoming all forces, they conclude that the play is 'more conventional than the novel' and, having established this, feel justified in criticising it for defying naturalistic expectations. In particular they cannot understand why a high-class lady such as Babbie must masquerade as a gypsy nor why the relationship between the romantic plot and its historical background is kept so vague.[82] It is a pity that no one notes the paradox involved here. It is accepted that Barrie has been careful in his revision. Yet the very sources of discontent have been created by the changes. In the novel, Gavin's story was carefully linked to historical events such as the Chartist risings. In the drama, the links are so slight that one sympathises with *The Times* reviewer's plaintive plea for someone to explain to him why Thrums was under attack at all! If Barrie had left well alone the perceived critical problems would not have existed.

The answer seems to be that Barrie, while not abandoning the conventional sentimental plot, wanted also to introduce the modes and methods of fairytale and myth. The idea of a highborn lady going in disguise among the lower classes itself belongs to this realm. Close analysis of the revision process reveals that his alterations often go beyond what was simply demanded by the stage and result in the closest possible conformity with the rules governing folk – and fairytale narrative as defined by Olrik.[83]

For example, *The Little Minister* as novel had a many-stranded narrative. It tells of the old dominie/narrator's love for the minister's mother and how he has been fated to move out of her life; it tells of the minister's struggle to be accepted by his 'Auld Licht' congregation particularly highlighting his conversion of the alcoholic, Rob Dow, and the latter's final Christlike sacrifice; it tells of the minister's love for the mischievous Babbie and it links all these to historic and legendary material such as the Chartist risings and the Legend of Caddam Wood. Of these strands, the third provides the major focus of the drama. The dominie and the mother disappear entirely. Gavin's relations with the congregation are introduced only in the context of his passion while historical and legendary details are drastically cut. The movement from many-stranded novel to single-stranded play is a logical way of making the transition to the stage. But notably this is the first time Barrie has adopted so simple a dramatic form. *Walker, London* had three interrelated love plots. *The Professor's Love Story* had used a main plot counterpointed against a sub-plot. And one of Olrik's major rules is that the fairytale must be 'einsträngig' (single-stranded).

The cast list is also rigorously shortened. Not only the dominie and his mother disappear but the large body of Scottish presbyterians is cut to four. Amusing but inessential figures such as Wearyworld the policeman also go, any necessary functions they may have performed in the novel being taken over by one or other of the smaller group. This again is what we would expect, if only because a play must be shorter and more dramatic. But Barrie goes beyond these naturalistic expectations and again his changes bring *The Little Minister* closer to the mode and methods of the fairytale. Olrik noted that the major focus in such works was limited to two characters although others may be onlookers. In moving from novel to play Barrie had already ensured that Gavin and Babbie would hold the major spotlight throughout with the Scots presbyterians performing the choric function. But subsequent *dramatic* revisions carry this process even further. A comparison between the MS submitted to the Lord Chamberlain and the final version reveals further cuts in almost all the minor parts. The comic interchanges between Halliwell and Rintoul in the final act, for example, are shortened. But most obviously Barrie further diminishes the rôle of Dow. Already deprived of his heroic sacrifice in the transition from novel to drama, he loses in the revision of the Lord Chamberlain's MS the few dramatically important moments which still remain for him.

In that MS Dow was given the last word in Act 1. After Gavin had challenged Whamond's authority and picked up the rose given to him by Babbie, it was Dow who shook his fist and darkly prophesised that he would murder the minister's new-found love:

> DOW: You flisk-mahoy, if I catch you near the minister again, I'll wring your neck like a hen's. (ADD 55635A)

This raises a series of questions centred on Dow's intentions, making them the major source of interest rather than Gavin's romantic act. In the final version Dow is present but does not speak a word. Instead Whamond challenges Gavin to lift the flower. Gavin does so and the interest is transferred to his new courage in love as he struts defiantly offstage.

At the opening of Act 4 in the Lord Chamberlain's MS, Dow is again the centre of attention. Still intent on murdering Babbie he has abducted her but she has escaped. This has happened offstage but now he is quizzed by the elders and desperately tries to justify himself by lying and blustering. In the final version he is not allowed either to relive his adventures or make any real emotional impact on the audience. Even his later pathetically ridiculous attempt to claim the glory for himself when things seem to be working well is excised:

> DOW: [*triumphantly*] I call everybody to witness it was me that brought this about — firstly by running awa wi' her and secondly by letting her escape.   (ADD 55635A)

By now every major dramatic moment associated with him has either disappeared or been played down. He becomes, in fact, one of the chorus of villagers, distinguished only through being Gavin's most unexpected conversion and, in a blinkered, foolish way, his most loyal ally. From being a serious rival for dramatic attention he is reduced to exemplifying one of Gavin's ministerial rôles.

Olrik further stresses that the two central characters are always polarised.[84] Once more Barrie's revisions bring Gavin and Babbie into conformity. In the drama they are consciously conceived as opposites, illustrating in extreme form the romantic belief that love draws contrasting personalities together. This was the opposition whose visual underlining Walbrook had noted so enthusiastically. Tonally, there is also a marked difference between novel and drama. The latter has its darker moments but essentially works through comic methods towards a suitably happy ending. The frame of the novel, on the other hand, had been the wistful yearning of the dominie-narrator for reunion with Gavin's mother and his attempts to live vicariously first through Gavin and then through his granddaughter, for whom ostensibly the story is being written. At the end, especially, Barrie strikes that note of wistfulness which his reading public so adored:

> When I found Gavin in the rain . . . I cried to God, making promises to Him if he would spare the lad for Margaret's sake, and He spared him; but these promises I have not kept.   (p 340)

A similar ending would, of course, have been quite out of place in dramatic comedy and so Babbie runs joyously into the arms of Gavin, having outwitted her father and proved that love conquers all. But in the final dramatic version only, that love is symbolised through the planting of a rose tree, confirming that they lived happily ever after and were fruitful. This is once more the land of myth and faery. Even the particular idea of roses defeating death is singled out as a common topos in this type of storytelling:

> Hundreds of folk songs end, not with the death of the lovers, but with the interweaving of the branches of the two roses which grow up out of their graves.[85]

Barrie was to use fairytale themes and fairytale form in later works. In these cases it is clear that this was his intention from the outset. Not so in *The Little Minister*. It remains quite possible that the needs of the drama, the folk-tale basis of his material and his own psychology with its openness to myth and fairytale guided his hand unconsciously. Yet, the variety of fairytale devices introduced into the drama and in particular the revisions of the play itself (always pushing further in this direction) suggest that what may have started out as a largely instinctive reaction to external demands became a conscious experiment in mythic drama. Certainly the play in finalised form obeys every one of Olrik's laws and the novel (despite its extensive use of folk material) very few.

In both, the associations between Babbie and the fairy world had been stressed. Notably she most often meets Gavin in woods or by a well, both traditional bridges to the other world. These, however, assume greater importance within the compact dramatic structure as does the emphasis on the number three (e.g. the triple blowing of the horn). What is more significant is the reliance placed on what Olrik calls 'fairy logic' in the drama. It is the introduction of this logic within a work which elsewhere seems to conform to the laws of psychological consistency which, with some justification, puzzles the critics and lessens the power of Beerbohm's defence. By removing the reasons for Babbie's longing to be a gypsy, Barrie made her character less understandable on a naturalistic level but strengthened her possible associations with witchcraft and the supernatural.[86] Her easy assumption of the rôle becomes an essential part of her mystery, encouraging us to think in terms of magic rather than genealogy.

Babbie's language with its effortless movement from English to Scots also loses its rational explanation. In the novel her ease in both registers is rationally explained through details of her upbringing. Lord Rintoul had farmed her out to his gardener's family and there she learned the dialect. In the play, however, she is presented as living entirely in Rintoul Castle with the English laird. Her fluent use of Scots thus becomes another mystery related to the everchanging nature of her personality, the conflict within her of opposing forces and worlds rather than an apparent riddle solved by the melodramatic discovery that she is a foundling.

Clothes too play an important part in both novel and drama. Interestingly, Barrie does not follow other Victorian writers in emphasising their moral connotations. Rather they are related to disguise and the fairytale idea of transformation. But once more the drama endows them with greater mystery. In the novel, after Babbie's first entry into Thrums to warn the villagers, her cloak is found by Gavin who buries it in his garden. It is dug up by a dog, found in a quarry and proved to belong to the English soldier Captain Halliwell. This brings it down to earth in more ways than one. It becomes part of the 'discovery' plot and loses its earlier associations with magic ('it is the cloak that has bewitched me'). The importance of the cloak burial is to prove that the minister, despite himself, is loyal to Babbie. In the drama Barrie makes the same point but centres Gavin's loyalty round the rose she gave him. In refusing to part with the rose, Gavin proves his love by protecting a symbol of love which then becomes a leitmotiv. But Barrie leaves the cloak as a device unrelated to the realistic core of the plot. It remains associated with Babbie's supernatural powers, worn or cast off as she moves from one world to another.

All of these changes strengthen the fairytale logic at the expense of realism, making Babbie more and more of a mystery or of the essence of woman as defined by mystery. The play therefore moves much more daringly in the direction of myth than does the novel. And it is this mythical emphasis which determines Barrie's treatment of the historical context for, as Roland Barthes has argued, all mythologising involves dehistoricising:

> In passing from history to nature, myth acts economically; it abolishes the complexity of human acts, it gives them the simplicity of essences, it does away with dialectics, with any going back beyond what is immediately visible.[87]

Barrie in his novel gave full accounts of the Chartist risings and established clear if more distant links between enacted events and Jacobite loyalties. In the play these links do not disappear but they are minimised. The reasons for the weavers' revolution are not clearly explained because this is more than a particular revolution, it is any uprising against authority. The Jacobite songs and the secret passages in Rintoul Castle are not, as in the novel, linked directly to the dramas being enacted. They merely strengthen by association the idea of freedom overcoming authority. Likewise the detailed accounts of contemporary attitudes to gypsies, which played a large part in the novel, are cut out. Those that remained in the Lord Chamberlain's MS, such as the following speech from Whamond in Act 1, were deleted in the next dramatic revision:

> WHAMOND: He has only treated them as the scum they are. The mark their gipsy fire burns in the ground is not so black as the mark they leave on every soul that hearkens to their ribald tongues. They are thieves and triflers, and they were beginning to settle down in Thrums and turning it into the mouth of Hell. The next thing we should have heard was that our young men were running after their shameless lassies, and may be wanting to marry them.

> (ADD 53635A)

Why, if these changes are so obvious, do almost all critics continue to judge the play against naturalistic criteria? In part, this is probably due to their conventional expectations. *The Scotsman* critic certainly finds it disturbing that a comedy should break the laws of probability as if it were a 'comic opera or wild farce'.[88] But even those like MacKail who see the fairytale element, clearly do not accept that this frees the author from the laws of likelihood.[89] Nor can I blame them. Barrie has not yet found a form which could adequately signal his desire to use types of fantasy as a means of exploring life. In his most enduringly successful plays the movement from domestic scenes to fantasy is clearly marked out. In *The Little Minister* Babbie and Gavin as real lovers in a particular situation, Babbie and Gavin as fairytale types, Babbie and Gavin as exemplars of mythic themes, Babbie and Gavin as supernatural and mortal co-exist within an ultimately sentimental, conventional plot.

It is impossible to be sure whether this confusion reflects Barrie's unconsciousness of what was implied by his recasting of the novel. After all, some simplifying method was necessary if only to reduce length. Already he had shown an interest in drama as a means of exploring universal ideas. My belief is that these two motivations pushed him in the direction chosen but that, only after *The Little Minister* had been exposed in all its potential strengths and acutal weaknesses, did he fully realise the literary problems besetting a popular dramatist, wishing to be thought-provoking in this particular way.

My supposition that Barrie's own intentions for *The Little Minister* were confused is based on his dissatisfaction with the play and his subsequent, more carefully structured, experiments in mythic and/or fairytale drama. The evidence which suggests that these intentions, however defined, were subject to damaging outside influences is so strong that one moves from supposition to fact. Never before and never again was Barrie, the modest yet principled man of the theatre, to allow friends so far to detract him from his original design.

The exact details of this story are complex. The young playwright had not wished to dramatise his lengthy novel in the first place. The initial drafts were done by his agent Arthur Bright. When Barrie took over, he was pressurised variously by Elizabeth Marbury, a vivacious New York play-broker; by his own admiration of Maude Adams' virtuosity[90] and by the energetic theatre manager Charles Frohman. They all praised his ability and were keener on the project than he was. To what degree they interfered with his usual process of writing and revision is unclear, but interfere they certainly did with the aim of giving Babbie's rôle greater dramatic dominance. Marcosson claims that Frohman

> began to adapt several important scenes which might have been dominated by Gavin Dishart, the little minister, into strong scenes for his new luminary.[91]

Although be believes such scenes were made with Barrie's consent, the implication is that the superior writer had allowed at least two businessmen to interfere in his composition for commercial reasons. MacKail sums up the situation:

> Bright had begun it, Frohman had knocked it about; the early view of the Auld Licht legends had gone further and further out of sight. It was a manufactured article and much of it painfully manufactured at that.[92]

Never again would Barrie allow his literary children to have surrogate parents of this sort.[93]

To sum up, Barrie must have been aware that this his first major experiment in the drama of myth and fairytale had adopted two logics without finding a form to reconcile them. If this betrayed a populist's reluctance to break radically with convention, the renouncing of sole authorial responsibility for at least one major character was a different type of literary abdication than that he was to support in *Peter Pan*. It was also a major breach of the serious artistic creed which justified the experimentation in the first place.

It is notable that many critics, while praising the virtuoso nature of Babbie's part, remark that it lacks a consistent centre.[94] It is not surprising that this should be the case as she is a multi-author creation. Her relationship with Gavin also introduces the mythic oppositions I have referred to. Only some of these confirm the essentially positive picture highlighted in the sentimental conclusion. True, on the optimistic side Babbie and Gavin enact a tale of transformation common to fairytale. Here the rôle of the gypsy and the emphasis on clothes are all-important. Barrie tries to reinterpret the Cinderella myth. Instead of a man raising woman, through love, to a higher class, he presents a variation. In temporal terms it is the woman (Babbie) who descends in class but spiritually she is raised through Gavin's religion, finding in the manse her proper home. Later in *A Kiss for Cinderella* he will formulate the idea more fully and make it the controlling idea for a whole play.

Complementing this and aided by the polarisation of characters earlier noted is the Androgyne myth — love as a reconciling of opposites. Gavin and Babbie, as their costumes proclaim, are not only from different social worlds, their natures are entirely different. The little minister represents orthodox religion, obedience to authority/convention, reason, seriousness and responsibility while she is a pantheistic, pagan creature, anarchic, instinctive, humorous and irresponsible. The controlling image here is that of Babbie as gypsy in George Borrow's sense.[95] In *The Romany Rye* (1851) he had stressed the freedom of the gypsy as a roguish influence harmless in itself but causing others to reassess the narrowness of their own codes. So Babbie gives Gavin the power to love freely and learn the lessons of instinct while he controls her excesses of irresponsibility. At their best the two extremes may complement and educate one another.

Yet there is a darker side to this. It also involves an element of sacrifice. And while most of the concessions initially are Gavin's — he risks reputation, job, even his life — the conclusion is on his terms and the major compromise Babbie's. Her gypsy life will be reduced to a sort of therapeutic charade within the framework of accepting her fate as a minister's wife. Occasionally, we are told, 'when the blinds are down and the shutters are on' she will dress in gypsy clothes again for Gavin's benefit:

> GAVIN: [*gloriously*]: Yes. He will pretend not to notice. And presently there will come popping into the drawing room a barefooted girl in a gypsy frock, with rowan berries in her hair, and he will pretend to be shocked, and he will exclaim — Babbie [*coming quickly forward with left hand raised and still carried away*] 'Woman stand forward'   (p 184)

The ideal of synthesis in real terms involves the destruction of all Babbie's anarchic freedoms.

When the supernatural rôle of Babbie is highlighted, the logic of the myth becomes even darker. She does not only inhabit a different social or personal world from Gavin. As has been suggested, she participates in the world of faery as well. Their meetings by wood or well confirm this but again it is her gypsy nature which is crucial, especially as it is now a mysterious rather than an explicable rôle. Gypsies have, from time immemorial, been associated with supernatural powers either for good or evil. At times Babbie is seen as a good power, likely to provide Gavin with a valuable, if different, type of spiritual understanding. This understanding is associated with joy and music:

> GAVIN: What have I to forgive you — for bringing me the great glory of my life? Your song! Babbie, your song has come to me for evermore. (p 181)

But at best, as supernatural force, she has an ambivalent definition. She ostentatiously wears red rowanberries in her hair. This could mean either that she is herself a witch or that she is protecting her life against witchcraft.[96] In the play she is much more often connected with darkness and the devil than with the powers of light. It is the dark-clothed Gavin whose symbol is the light of the study. These associations admittedly are often introduced by the 'Auld Licht' chorus whose proneness to superstition makes them unreliable witnesses. But any dramatic power relies on the audience sharing this fear. Gavin admits that spiritually she seems a temptress, 'Everything a woman ought not to be.' The witching songs and the legendary material introduced by Barrie reinforce the Scottish proverbial saying that 'witches, warlocks and gypsies soon ken ae the ither' and make sure that Babbie is more often feared as witch than welcomed as spiritual guide.

Ronald Bryden perceptively notes that 'there is a recurrence in Barrie's writing of half-dreamed figures who try to share if not to take possession of the lives of living people.[97] He also rightly sees Babbie as an early version of the succubus in 'Farewell Miss Julie Logan'. In that story, however, the supernatural dominates throughout and what remain for Babbie dark possibilities are fully realised. The heroine of *The Little Minister* remains primarily a lovable and real character but the confusion surrounding her is increased by the introduction of another possible level of interpretation (the supernatural) and another elemental vision (woman as tempter).

The mode chosen to simplify a novel, whose own structure was far from perfect,[98] had opened up far greater complexities than the dramatic form could resolve. This horrifying expansiveness comprehending naturalistic, fairytale, mythic and allegoric logics can best be demonstrated by re-examining the ramifications of one parallel: Babbie as gypsy. The optimistic logic of romantic tale, of fairy story and of allegory suggests a conclusion along the sentimental lines favoured by the popular conventions of the Victorian stage. This, of course, is what the Collected and Definitive texts give us with the rose tree and the kiss. Babbie here is the gypsy of romance (married), of freedom (modified). There is, however, another use of gypsy presenting a different view of Babbie and women. This is the gypsy of constant change and ultimate mystery, the view taken by Thomas Dekker when he calls them 'Moonmen — mad, changing always.' [99] Barrie links Babbie with the moon imagistically and has moonlight settings. He also encourages us to see her as a creature who is always changing her form (cloak), her speech (Scots/English) and her attitudes:

> BABBIE: Will I — or won't I? This line — but that line — no. I don't believe I will . . . Haven't you seen that I do everything for fun? It tosses me in the air; I am just a bubble.   (p 167)

Later he will devote a whole play to exploring this idea. But in *Seven Women* it is analytically developed without recourse to supernatural possibilities. In *The Little Minister* it adds yet another mythic idea but one which is not strongly enough stressed or carefully enough integrated to provide a satisfying resolution of the various conflicting strands of thought within the play. As Babbie moves from flesh into mystery and the supernatural of folk legend or religious allegory so a stricter and more savage view of life and love emerges.

Before I began my researches on the earlier texts of this play I was committed to the viewpoint that Barrie had created a text which needed multiple endings to resolve its disparate levels of logic. The bleaker, elemental view of love seemed to me to be embodied in the references to passion as a battle demanding dominance and subservience. In the Notebooks I found the first supportive evidence. There are few references in Barrie's Notebooks to a romantic dramatisation of *The Little Minister*. First, he wanted to use gypsies as a means of exploring 'yearnings to go back to savagery'. Then, when he comes to make entries specifically about the play, images of dominance and slavery intrigue him most:

> Girl crouching before man because clothes + stockings off. Taken against her will. Yet they captivate her, as she wishes a man to subdue her.

> First her independence, 2nd hates herself at feeling it go, 3rd proud to be his slave — Their talk of this — her pride in making him say she is his slave and he her master — Her wistful humbleness about future. [100]

In the earlier dramatic drafts, including that for the Lord Chamberlain, both of these lines remain very strong indeed. Explicit discussion of the gypsies' evil powers both as tempters and savages are introduced in sermons by Gavin and comments from the elders:

> WHAMOND: . . . to make him an outcast on the face of the earth, like the abominable gypsies.
> GAVIN: Egyptian vagrant, idle teller of fortunes to the foolish and the vagrant.   (ADD 53635A)

By sacrifising such passages Barrie lost the clear line of religious allegory where Babbie's submission in love is the fitting victory of virtue over pagan caprice. He also destroyed the major moral rôle of the elders as voices of warning. As Babbie became less threatening so the Scots characters moved from choric prophecy to near farce.

If this suggests artistic dishonesty reaping its own unanticipated punishment, the second area of revision reveals Barrie sacrificing the major radical idea of the Notebooks. Though some references to domination/ servility remain in the Definitive text, they seem at best incongruous, at worst asides in doubtful taste.[102] In the first drafts this savage vision of love's power was set against romance and sentimentality. Most important of all, the 'alternative' ending was in fact the original one. Barrie had not wished to end with rosebuds and farce but with submission as a sign of love's animal powers and, allegorically, as the yielding of dark instincts to Christian morality.

That this was a very serious intention is shown by the different versions he had planned for the American and English openings. In Washington and New York the play would have concluded with the father's romantic vision of love as 'Cupid birds', leading into the following dialogue:

> RINTOUL: Don't be alarmed Mr Dishart. It is only her way of trying to get round the pair of us. [*Lifting cane*] If you would just let me bring this about her shoulders for once, I think I might forgive her in time.
> GAVIN: [*pleasantly*] Ah, Lord Rintoul, no one has the right to punish her now except her husband.
> BABBIE: [*Startled*] Oh! [*He's unaware he has said anything disgusting. Gavin opens the door for Lord Rintoul who goes into manse, leaving door open.*]
> GAVIN: [*Returning to Babbie gloriously*] Babbie — my wife!
> BABBIE: Yes, but what was that you said just now to father?
> GAVIN: [*Seriously*] I have forgotten — what was it about?
> BABBIE: [*rather breathless*] If you have forgotten — it doesn't matter. [*She looks around and a fit of shivering seizes her — this should go on till every bit of her is shivering*]
> GAVIN: [*putting arms round her*] Beloved, you are shivering — why?
> BABBIE: I don't know why — you lovely, fussing husband! [*sweetly*] Gavin you will always be kind to Babbie won't you in case she doesn't last!
> GAVIN: [*He is lovingly drawing her to Left away from the house as if to sit at wall — she is warmer now*]. No, dear, let's go in by the door.
> [*They enter manse hand in hand — The head of Nanny alone rises over dyke watching them with beaming face*][103]

A slightly toned-down version was planned for London, given to the Lord Chamberlain and passed by him:

> GAVIN: Ah, Lord Rintoul, I am her husband, you see no one must cane her now except myself.
> BABBIE: Oh! [*she stands looking in horror at audience while GAVIN unaware that he has said anything startling opens door to let LORD RINTOUL exit into manse*]
> GAVIN: [*coming joyously to Babbie*] Babbie — my wife! [*He is surprised to see her looking agitated*]
> BABBIE: Yes, but — what was that you said just now to father?

GAVIN: [*innocently*] What did I say?
BABBIE: Well?
GAVIN: I only said I am your husband [*with rapture*] your husband!
BABBIE: But after that?
GAVIN: And that no one must cane you now — except myself.
BABBIE: Did you mean it? That you — that you would —
GAVIN: Only if you deserve it.
BABBIE: [*after making a face*] Gavin, I — I feel sure that you are the right man for me.[104]

CURTAIN

None of these denouements survived rehearsal. Instead farce and the elders' astounded faces were introduced.

With this background it becomes much easier to understand why Barrie disliked one of his most profitable plays so much, for here commercial success *had* been bought at the price of artistic integrity. The same work had witnessed the most radical step forward in his dramatic thinking[105] and the most disastrous betrayal of that creativity whose mystery he idolised. Variously and literally he had compromised on his first ideas; his right to sole authorship; the implications of his chosen mode and the problems of matching psychological complexity to a single, acted conclusion. Later he would confront every one of these issues with extreme seriousness. At this time, however, criticisms such as those raised in *The Scotsman* must have wounded him not only because of what he had let *The Little Minister* become but because of what he knew it might have been. Particularly he must have been aware that the desire to give his leading actress a virtuoso part had led to an irresponsible and overambitious attempt to make Babbie at once the centre of a romantic comedy, a fairytale, a myth and an allegory. Most poignantly of all he must have regretted that his decision to opt for a sentimental, farcical ending rather than one which emphasised the more serious lines of allegory and savagery led to the alienation of many Scottish critics. Those hats were, after all, a sign of his own lost integrity.

THE WEDDING GUEST

The fourth and last play of this Victorian apprenticeship has always been regarded as an aberration — a single, catastrophic attempt at more serious drama in the Ibsenite mould. Even the lone voice of unstinted support, William Archer's, evaluates it in this context of enthusiasm for the Norwegian dramatist:

> Hitherto, Mr Barrie has only trifled with the stage, but now we can offer a very sincere welcome to our new dramatist.[106]

Geduld sums up the more prevalent view:

The Ibsenite problem play reduced to melodrama.[107]

To assess the rights and wrongs of this situation in relation to Barrie's early dramatic experimentation, I shall first recount the plot. On the very day of his wedding to a young innocent (Margaret Fairbairn) Paul Digby is faced by his former mistress complete with their illegitimate child. During the ceremony the mistress (Mrs Ommaney) faints. Although this awakens Paul to the situation, his bride remains unaware and the marriage is completed. Later and gradually the young wife learns the truth. At first she reacts with strident moral revulsion. Later she decides that he must adopt the baby but Mrs Ommaney refuses to accept this. The impasse is finally broken by the intervention of Margaret's aunt, a spinster who had, many years ago, also refused to marry the man she loved on moral grounds. She claims that she had erred in this and now suffers more than anyone. This leads to a reconciliation between Margaret and Paul and a wholly unlikely sympathetic alliance between the sister and Mrs Ommaney.

It is easy to see how such a play has been branded atypical and indeed in some obvious ways it is. People had come to expect from Barrie a surface plot which was light and sentimental. Despite the contrived happy ending *The Wedding Guest* offered instead a serious psychological drama. Walbrook records the audience's puzzlement:

> For here was their gentle ironist; their optimist their sentimentalist ladling out scenes as harrowing and remorseless as those of Ibsen himself.[108]

As psychological drama it forced Barrie to attempt what, arguably, he found most difficult — direct depiction of passionate adult relationships.[109] He tried very hard to succeed in this area, revising with his usual meticulousness but as he only had stage passion to imitate the result is often unsatisfactory. Frequently he lapses into melodrama as in the dialogue which opens Act 3:

> MRS OMMANEY: Is that you Jenny? Have I been asleep? [*Sitting up and yawning*] Are you there? How dark — [*Rising bewildered*] Why — what [— *Disturbed*] Something has happened! [*A match is heard being struck; she goes toward entrance*] Jenny!
> [*Enter Paul carrying lamp*] You!
> [*Paul looks anxiously at her.*] Why do you look at me so?
> PAUL: Thank God!
> [*Puts down lamp and sinks into chair.*]
> MRS OMMANEY: When did you come here? Let me think.
> [*Presses her hands to her temples.*] Ah! [*Flings open bedroom door.*] Come out! [*Seizes lamp and enters bedroom, returns.*] Where is she? Your wife!   (p 248)

Barrie also escapes by way of childish dialogue (a device he had used in *Walker, London*) or via madness. His attempts at the latter must have tested the acting skills even of Violet Vanbrugh:

MRS OMMANEY: What fun, what fun! Run away from me. No, no! [*Waves hand as if beckoning Paul forwards.*] Looking for your wife are you? Ha, ha! In here, Mr Digby — [*Pointing to the bedroom door*] — with your child. Where else should she be? Wife and child, wife and child.

(p 240)

Not only the critics but the audience sensed his awkwardness. *The Wedding Guest*, therefore, also stands apart in being the least successful commercially, of all his full-length plays with the exception of *The Boy David*. It had a single, troubled run at *The Garrick* with the leading actor, H B Irving, transferring midway to another production at the *St James's*. His rôle was taken by Martin Harvey who, though by all accounts equally proficient, was less of a box-office attraction. Though Barrie had learned from his experiences with *The Little Minister* not to rely too heavily on other members of the theatrical team, he was faced on this occasion by an aggressive stage-director in Dion Boucicault the younger, antagonistic to many of his intentions and clear where authorial authority ended. This led Barrie to complain during rehearsals about his 'bleeding and broken play.' [110]

While it is certain that this time he held true to the intentions expressed in his Notebooks, it is also evident that *The Wedding Guest* merits fewer entries than any of the works so far considered. The idea of a 'Play. Scotch Wedding — The other woman steals in while it is in progress' had occurred as early as 1895. Four entries further on he records 'Ibsen drama = drama with a past.' [111] Most of the entries round the crucial period refer rather to the novel *Sentimental Tommy*, also the gravest of his prose contributions so far. Perhaps *The Wedding Guest*, therefore, had not been so fully thought out? Perhaps it was an attempt to please those critics, outraged so far by his apparent triviality rather than a composition to which he was emotionally committed?

Finally, it seems to be generally agreed that he was not so well served as usual by a cast which, with the exception of Irving, Vanbrugh and Brandon Thomas (who played Margaret's optimistic garrulous father) was full of unknowns. Walbrook's comments on this are of particular interest because, if he is right, the performance accentuated rather than underplayed the drama's melodramatic tendencies:

> *The Wedding Guest* suffered from an excess of the sort of acting which so blackens every shade and whitens every light that the whole of the dramatist's appeal to the imagination of his audience evaporates in a sort of orgie of histrionic obviousness. [112]

This is so obviously the opposite of Barrie's usual advice, which consistently asks for underplaying and concealing of the obvious that one assumes this approach, being the remit of the director, was one of the major points of contention between him and Boucicault.

If the drama gives way to melodrama; if the dialogue is often un-convicing; if the director was at odds with the author and the cast unhappy, it has to be added that even the comic content lacks Barrie's usual flair.

While Mr Fairbairn's humour of optimism provides the odd moment of hilarity, his rôle is also a pathetic one, tied in to the moral concerns of the drama. Most of the moments of fun centre, for the last time until *What Every Woman Knows*, on the opposition between English and Scottish stereotypes. In this area, having just received his strongest 'nationalist' rebukes, he is at once conservative in technique and over-careful that Scots should be seen to advantage. The Scottish butler Meikle, who anticipates Crichton's mixture of superiority and servility, is a major spokesman for his nation:

> PAUL: We English give Meikle a good deal of amusement, Miss Ripley.
> MEIKLE: Beg pardon, sir, I do my best to keep it in. [*Tries not to laugh at the quaint ways of the English*].   (p 216)

The child-nurse-mother, Jenny Geddes (first in a series of dramatic characterisations of this sort) and the 'grande dame' Lady Janet continue this effort to redress any 'English' balance detectable in *The Little Minister*:

> PAUL: She is said to be very formidable. A grande dame.
> ARMITAGE: I thought there were no Scottish grandes dames.
> PAUL: My young friend, there are only Scotch ones.   (p 220)

Apart from this change of emphasis the comedy is all very foreseeable, an exercise in apology showing little if any sign of developing literary skill.

For all these reasons *The Wedding Guest* remains a flawed work. Again Barrie's own reaction was negative. Not only did he exclude it from the *Collected Plays*, he refused permission for it to be revived and, of course, only returned to this type of theatrical melodrama to parody it in *Alice Sit-By-The-Fire*. My purpose in what follows is not, primarily, to rescue it in evaluatory terms but to re-define it in relation to Ibsenism, to its literary sources and to Barrie's other early plays.

The first obvious critical tendency is to dismiss it as a serious rival to Ibsen's practice. The plot of *The Wedding Guest* fails to catch his carefully modulated sombre voice of social protest and moral perplexity. It is, therefore, relegated to the level of the more limited English dramatic tradition related to *Lady Audeley's Secret*. Leonee Ormond at once gives it this particular, theatrical context:

> His choice of subject reflects a contemporary vogue for plays about women with a past. Oscar Wilde's *Lady Windermere's Fan* and Arthur Pinero's *The Second Mrs Tanqueray* both date from 1892-93.[113]

In itself this is not at all misleading. Barrie had a great enthusiasm for Pinero and for that heroine in particular. In 1913 he wrote enthusiastically to his rival, 'the woman is a masterly study bound to hold her place in the annals of dramatic writing.' [114] *Lady Windermere's Fan* had been the immediate theatrical rival to *Walker, London*. When Mr Fairbairn proposes, as a solution to his daughter's problems, the convenient geographic removal of Mrs Ommaney to Australia, Barrie may well be satirising the ending of that play in particular.[115] In terms of plot, however, it seems clear to me that the closest English parallel is Pinero's *The Profligate*, a case earlier advanced by Howe.[116] There, the importance of the wedding rice is also anticipated while 'profligate' is the young nurse-mother's preferred name for Mrs Ommaney.

This theatrical framework is encouraged by emphasis on the story line of *The Wedding Guest* and supported by the vocabulary of the Notebooks. 'Grande dame' and 'the woman' apply more easily to this English tradition than to Ibsen. But had Barrie sacrificed the multi-level approach begun in *The Little Minister* for a straight story line? Was he primarily interested in Ibsen as social dramatist? These are the terms in which he is seen to fail but I do not think they accord with the evidence.

My first reason for suggesting a radical reassessment derives from the current definition of Ibsenism in the English theatre of his day. Shaw in his 1890 lecture to the Fabian society, entitled 'The Quintessence of Ibsenism', had made sure that this quintessence accorded with Shavianism. He did this by emphasising the surface themes while obscuring the deeper levels of symbolic and mythic application. As Einar Haugen puts it, Shaw wished to 'annex' Ibsen as a socialist. So successful had he been in narrowing the definition of Ibsenism, he was accepted by most as the major British disciple of the Norwegian playwright although his dramas remained 'in most respects unlike Ibsen's both in style and theme.' [117]

Secondly, most modern critics of Ibsen now accept that the Norwegian's early plays, like Barrie's, constitute a continual 'experiment in combining myth and realism.' [118] His more mature plays (also like Barrie's) seek a satisfactory comprehending form involving melodramatic surface plot and mythic subplots. Only once this has been understood does Walbrook's parallel between *The Wedding Guest* and *The Master Builder* become understandable. In Ibsen's play the story involves a middle-aged man who loses his head over a young girl. She drives him to take a desperate action, leading to his death. On the mythic level, dominated by the symbol of the tower, the master builder becomes Sacrificial King and Promethean rebel. He even becomes a type of the creator, the artist (builder) who vies with God in trying to create happiness but finds youth and new creativity supplanting him.

Barrie's early use of the cuckoo as an open-ended symbol is reminiscent of Ibsen's use of the duck in *The Wild Duck*. *The Little Minister*'s mythic opposition between convention and traditional morality; Christianity and paganism as well as Babbie's mixture of benevolence and witchcraft may have more than an incidental relationship with Rebecca and *Rosmersholm*. Barrie's play, for all its imperfections, does try to emulate Ibsen in working simultaneously on a variety of levels — narrative, fairytale, myth and allegory. This fact is only obscured because of British critics' overconcern with surface meaning. Barrie's dramas are sentimental; Ibsen's are sombre. Ergo they are poles apart. In *The Wedding Guest* for the first time the Scottish playwright adopted a serious narrative line. Now he was claimed as a poor disciple of Ibsen by those who misunderstood the art of both. Like *The Master Builder* the surface plot of *The Wedding Guest* tends towards melodrama and is set in two different mythic patterns, the one moral, the other essentially concerned with literature and art. Neither of these patterns was highlighted in the précis I offered because I based it closely on Geduld, whose psychological interpretation of the drama is sustained by his electic view of the plot in terms of surface structure alone.[119]

How, then, does the multi-level approach work? Morally, it is structured round oppositions between childishness and adulthood; irresponsibility and responsibility; false love and true charity. Margaret is the only one who, as she reacts to the successive revelations concerning her husband's guilt, passes from negative to positive poles in each. Innocent, irresponsible, hating she becomes experienced, responsible and loving. Her father by way of contrast remains for ever stuck in an irresponsible immaturity of spirit which makes all his love ultimately selfish and which prevents him from sharing in the generosity of soul which finally draws together all the other main characters.[120] These themes will surface later in *Peter Pan*; earlier, the same oppositions had underpinned *Little Eyolf*.

The other mythic pattern is the fullest dramatic expression to date of Barrie's view of art as the shadow of childbirth. In this hierarchy, Mrs Ommaney (having the baby) stands at the top. Beneath her are, on the female side, Margaret (being married) and, then, Lady Janet (the spinster). Paul is an artist and therefore essentially selfish and sentimental. He stands above his father-in-law, however, because his versions of painted reality are creative and give pleasure while the old man's fictive optimism is merely a selfish verbal twisting of nature. Characteristically, in this hierarchy it is the 'free' Lady Ommaney, who inspires Paul the artist while the conventional Margaret does not even understand that aspect of his make-up. In these ways one set of values is counterpointed against another. This particular view of creation had been central to Barrie's thought for some time; Ibsen had a version of it in *Hedda Gabler*, where Thea is symbolically fecund with Eilert's book but physically barren; Hedda is unable to bear the kind of symbolic 'child' she does want and is physically pregnant with the child she does not.[121]

The Wedding Guest, then, is not the only one of Barrie's Victorian plays to lack mythic undertones. Instead it surpasses *The Little Minister* in the carefulness of its mythic planning. However troublesome both 'melodramatic realism' and childish talking may be on a psychological level, both are justified by the logic of myth as Ibsen's similar experiments indicate. Indeed the force of the play's symbolism (symbolism which otherwise might merely have been held to be decorative) will only be realised when the extent of Barrie's debt to Ibsen is accepted.

First, there is the rice, symbol of fertility. At the end of Act 1 it is conventionally thrown at the married couple as a sign of future childbirth. Later when Margaret lets the rice run through her fingers it is a sign of despair in the face of Mrs Ommaney's proven fertility; when finally Mrs Ommaney throws rice at the departing couple, she indicates that she is giving up that major advantage. The hierarchy of womanhood is also symbolically underlined. — Mrs Ommaney having the child Margaret the ring and Lady Janet the letter. Many of the most embarrassing moments in the drama, such as Margaret's strange order to the baby to kiss the ring are only justifiable in symbolic terms — making the proof of love subjugate itself to the sign of love. Likewise strange stage directions are explained — 'Mrs Ommaney looks bitterly at her left hand on which there is no ring.' This signifies Mrs Ommaney's awareness of her major vulnerability, lacking the sign of divine blessing. Baby and ring must join. She strives to achieve this by using the child as a weapon and, in her madness, calling herself Margaret. The closest she gets to triumph is when Margaret throws away her ring but secretly retrieves it. Through charity, Margaret justifies her divine gift, conquers and converts Mrs Ommaney. She offers Paul the eternal sign (ring) along with the hope of future physical fruition (baby) but only after she too has tried an immoral shortcut, demanding that Mrs Ommaney should hand the child over to her (baby and ring).

There are many other intriguing symbolic patterns — not least effective the ring given in love (Act 1), used as weapon (Act 2), thrown away (Act 3) and regained (Act 4). But another symbol relates more specifically to Paul's rôle as artist. This is the locket bearing his picture, fittingly worn in Act 1 by his lover-inspirer Mrs Ommaney. In Act 2 it is opened by Lady Jane revealing the source of this stranger's power. In Act 3 it is offered, empty, to Margaret who, as yet, does not understand that her husband is Mrs Ommaney's lover. In making Mrs Ommaney do this, while suggesting that Margaret fill it with Paul's picture, Barrie economically conveys through symbolism an apparent act of generosity, which really is a trick and a challenge. 'Create your own picture of Paul', Mrs Ommaney is covertly saying. 'It will be the same as, yet inferior to the one I possessed when he was the great artist I made him.' In another sense, Mrs Ommaney's profession, offer and retention of the locket signifies her lack of power. Her child is the unanswerable proof of physical union but the locket remains an inferior sign of union in religious terms. By offering it — the 'shadow' of human creativity — she hopes to win through a devilish moral test the sign of divine charity, the eternal ring; to gain the man by proferring his image.

This is Barrie's most successful use of complex symbolism so far. It is at this level that *The Wedding Guest* shows the greatest literary skill, just as the triple level of application proves Barrie a more thorough (and arguably more perceptive) disciple of Ibsen than Shaw. He has gained credit for neither because critics did not perceive the deeper structure and so made their judgements on, at best, a third of the play's complex pattern.

The other major experimental development in *The Wedding Guest* can equally be linked to Ibsen. Barrie's interest in visual effects, from broad scene-setting to specific lighting effects, though derived from his own theatrical enthusiasms, was shared by the Norwegian writer, himself a painter.[122] *The Wild Duck*, for example, had different lighting corresponding to the mood of each of its five Acts. Outdoor scenes, mimed activities and leitmotiv actions (for example the crocheting of the shawl in

Rosmersholm) attracted Ibsen as much as Barrie. It is mime whose theatrical effectiveness is most ingeniously developed in *The Wedding Guest*. Many of the major highlights — such as the interrupted wedding and the progressive stages of Mrs Ommaney's fit in Act 2 — are played out without dialogue. The conclusions of each Act (the focus, as always, of Barrie's most fastidious revisions) are also in this case mimed. The throwing of rice by all but Mrs Ommaney in Act 1 leads to the throwing of the rice by Mrs Ommaney alone in Act 4. The central Acts conclude with Paul covering his sleeping mistress and dropping the ring when his wife returns it. So, mimes in which Margaret's victories of marriage and future fertility are symbolically linked, frame pictures of her rival's power to enchant and undermine. Such a carefully contrived relationship between visualisation and theme would surely have pleased the Ibsen who stated that composition involved the capacity 'to see in such a way that whatever is seen is perceived by his audience just as the poet saw it.' [123]

What this approach finally uncovers is the fourth type of experiment involving dramatic translation of the prose works. Far from being linked to his major novel of this period only through a few stray parallels between Mrs Ommaney and the Painted Lady. *The Wedding Guest* echoes the major themes of *Sentimental Tommy* very closely. Barrie does not this time either borrow dialogue or transfer characters. Instead he faithfully re-enacts in a markedly different story the same conflicts between fertility and barrenness; adulthood and childishness; marriage and free love; the creativity of woman and of male artist, which are part of the experience of Tommy, Grizel and Elspeth; Mrs Sandys, the Painted Lady and 'magerful' men.[124] Tonally in each he made the decision to present a bleaker surface plot instead of relying on the subtler, poetic levels of application to counterbalance overt sentimentality.[125] In this, the novel proves a more successful experiment than the drama but they stand together not only through shared themes but also in the sustaining of a vision, darker than any for which Barrie enthusiasts had earlier been prepared.

I had begun my researches by focusing only on the full-length plays, justifying the narrowness of approach through the thoroughness of the generative critical method. Every stage of textual evolution had been observed from Notes to 'definitive' form. The only wider context initially intended had been theatrical. I had studied the successes and failures (both domestic and foreign) on the London stage at that time. But detailed consideration of these four dramas soon forced a further perspective upon me. It became clear that Barrie was obsessively interested in unique features distinguishing one genre from another. One could not study the apprentice plays without realising how, clinically, he had decided to explore drama's variety and the various ways of crossing genre boundaries. In turn he had attempted farce, comedy, romance and social drama. Each sub-genre had also illustrated a fresh method of theatrically translating his prose works. It was, therefore, impossible to study the plays adequately with only a passing knowledge of the 'novels' on which they were to some degree based. If Barrie the actor-manqué was finding out how well fitted his genius was to the new demands of the theatre, Barrie the word-wielder was continuing to explore the wider limits of his craft.[126]

In fact, even at this stage I realised that he was at once more subtle and more ambitious than I had supposed. To do justice to his mind, I would have to match its tenacity and range. If already I had been led into one further branch of study, it seemed more than likely other unexpected areas would open up. The principle of interconnections almost certainly implied that the generative approach would have to be applied to the shorter plays as well. And if the evidence also pointed towards Ibsen and ultimate issues in literary criticism before Barrie had even dropped the style of 'apprentice', a choice had to be made at once.

What had seemed to me a possible academic 'sabbatical' from my beloved Middle Ages, could cease now with one or two articles. These would suggest new approaches while admitting their limitation of focus. The alternative was to turn two years of study into a much longer period. I wrote the articles, hoping that this would decide me in favour of the former alternative.[127] Unsurprisingly, they drew me towards the latter. I was, like so many before me, under the spell of the Barrie enigma. I returned, therefore, to the findings of this Chapter. Three major conclusions emerged among many suspicions, hopes and anticipations.

I The Apprentice   The word 'apprentice' had been Barrie's; my research had already shown the propriety of that term as an assessment of literary method, stage of development and dedication to all aspects of wordcraft. Implicit in my findings was another justification. An apprentice has to subsume pride; he has to learn. That was not easy for Barrie the self-made man and established prosewriter. But he schooled himself, not only through reverence to other members of the creative team (Toole; Harker; Boucicault etc) but through attention to audience reaction. I confine myself to two crucial examples of this learning process.

The major practical drawback to *Walker, London* had been the failure to provide an adequate female lead. Never again would Barrie make that mistake. Indeed, with Babbie in *The Little Minister* he would be guilty of providing a plot which suffered from being a vehicle for the virtuosity of Maude Adams or Winifred Emery. But *The Professor's Love Story* intervened and, although there is a tendency to discount it entirely as an embarrassing failure, the part of Lucy is clearly a successful reworking of the 'new woman', a type inadequately represented by Bell Golightly in *Walker, London*. His assessment of the distinctive features of drama led Barrie to see the importance of the female lead. A key member of the creative team, she was also the romantic focus anticipated by the audience. The importance of that audience lay, for Barrie, in the unique intimacy of communication afforded by the theatre, though inadequately encouraged by the convention of the 'proscenium arch'.[128] To give Maude Adams and the others a challenging rôle thus served a double purpose. And if critics tend to pass Lucy over, actresses do not. Fay Compton, whose repertoire is extremely wide, comments:

> As I look back I believe it [Lucy] to be the most difficult part I ever played.[129]

The apprentice not only learned the lesson of the female lead; he learned it *at once.*

A second clear example of this learning process relates to the spirit of self-contradiction, which he identifies as a characteristic of his writing from the early, journalistic days in Nottingham. An Imp, he tells us, then urged him to compose 'articles which meant the reverse of what they seemed to say.' [130] In *Walker, London*, he had introduced the open-ended symbol of the cuckoo to achieve this.[131] In *The Professor's Love Story*, he sought to achieve counterpoint through levels of plot. Audience reaction taught him that he was more effective in imitating Ibsen than Shakespeare, so (in *The Little Minister*) he attempted a more ambitious use of poetic openness. On this occasion, the audience still seemed content. He was, himself, conscious of the confusions resulting from that experiment. As a result (in *The Wedding Guest*) he moved to the opposite extreme, planting carefully contrived symbols with carefully limited associations at every stage of the action. This was as much a failure of the playwright-dictator as *The Little Minister* had been of the playwright-midwife. But the reasons for imperfection could not be deduced simply; the associative experiments were too closely inter-related with other variants of plot and structure. What Barrie the apprentice *had* learned, was that no play so far had succeeded in this crucial area of communication. In Augustinian terms he was wiser only in false ways. He, therefore, excluded all four from the *Collected Plays*.

Barrie had proved himself a much more disciplined apprentice than I had first supposed.

II Ibsen My second lesson involved facing the limitations of my own expectations from another angle. I had not expected Barrie to be so deeply influenced by Ibsen. One reason for this lay in the Shavian appropriation of the Norwegian author's reputation within the domain of his own social drama. Another lay in my acceptance of Barrie as a Christian author associated with Christian journals. In his prose works, he often reflects not only the religious faith of his characters but attributes that belief to his Barrie-narrator. A third originated from my acceptance that *Ibsen's Ghost*, as a parody of the 'master', placed him at once on the side of the conservatives, gaining easy laughter from the outraged Victorian response to a resolutely pessimistic world-view.

As the latter dilemma produced the simpler answer, I shall discuss its implications first. It confirmed my initial suspicion that the generative approach would have to be extended to the one act plays. When I returned to the Beinecke Library I read the first version of the parody. Two holograph notes immediately caught my attention. The second disavowed responsibility for the ghastly singsong ending and the sub-title of *Toole up to Date*. Barrie, writing retrospectively (and ironically) on the copy he had first sent to Toole, now blames the actor-manager for these features:

> I added a sub-title, 'Toole up to Date', because he said it would make him feel more at home. I let him turn suddenly into Ibsen because Thea turns suddenly into Hedda. I even let him wind up with a song and dance. He never insisted on these novelties, he just looked wistful.[132]

The first note is even more interesting. It is an apology without repentance.

> I have sometimes wondered what treatment I meted out to the characters and how I could have made play, even for twenty minutes with the dramatist I have always known to be the greatest of his age.   (IB 6.2 p 1)

I think this is the benevolent comment of the older man on the confidence of youth. It does not deny the worth of the play nor the method used. Indeed, parody is the most obvious way of presenting a counter message along the lines suggested by Barrie's Imp. It is no coincidence, therefore, that he often returns to this mode for shorter pieces. But, evaluatively, there is no doubt — for Barrie, Ibsen is the supreme dramatist.

Ibsen's Ghost invites another type of dual reception. It is on one level a quite hilarious treatment of Ibsen's characteristic methods carried to excess. The heroine's melodramatic rejection of conventional morality and the dramatist's reliance on symbols produce excellent moments of comedy:

> THEA: I let him [Judge Brack] do it, I wanted him to do it; and even that is not all, for Parson Greig kissed me on Tuesday, and Henrik Barsam on Wednesday and Baron Kleig on Thursday, and I am going mad, mad, mad.
> PETER: Ghosts. So the bolt falls. Thea, men don't do these things.
> THEA: They do, they do, and oh Grandpapa, I like it.
> PETER: She likes it. Ghosts.   (Ib 6.2 p 7)

But Barrie, by entwining a plot drawn mainly from *Hedda Gabler* and *A Doll's House*; symbolism mainly from *Ghosts* and *The Wild Duck*, with side-references to practically every other Ibsen play then known, also reveals how thoroughly he understands the model he mocks. The fact that he will use in his own dramas the very techniques he parodies turns *Ibsen's Ghost* into a work of creative literary criticism incorporating humour and reverence.[133]

As a work of literary criticism, it confirmed one of my darkest suspicions. Barrie is not only interested in the message and the medium as sustainer of that message; he is interested in the medium from a theoretical point of view as code or, relativistically, as perverter of message. *Peter Pan* and the Pan myth will represent the most thorough exploration of this line in his thought but it existed prior to any dramatic practice. In *Ibsen's*

Ghost, the most obvious symptom of this concern is the use of different translations by different members of the cast. The comic potential of this idea co-exists with some rather uncomfortable implications. Are we understanding Ibsen fully when two scholars can produce such different versions of his text?

> THEA: 'So well,' that is your cue.
> PETER: No, 'other women' is my cue. I am using Gosse's version, you know.
> THEA: I am using Archer's   (Ib. 6.2 p 8)

The power of the artist as creator links with this fear as characters check on alternative versions before bowing to their dramatic fate:

> THEA: [*whsipers*] Archer's version says that you have taken the pistol.
> PETER: [*sadly*] So does Gosse's. [*Takes pistol*].[134]   (ADD MS 53475L)

Other possible means of communication and non-communication add to the hilarity while broadening the linguistic complexity. In answer to a simple question, the Grandfather mimes 'elaborately' and at length:

> THEA: That means yes! How much easier it is than talking.
>   (ADD MS 53475L, p 9)

Ridiculous in context but used by a dramatist who will make the most radical miming experiments yet known on the English stage. Where too is my seemingly safe assumption that overuse of letters in *Walker, London* was an example of the prosewriter slowly coming to terms with a different genre? A year earlier, it would seem, Barrie had parodied Ibsen's overuse of precisely that device and so was only too aware of the inherent dramatic dangers. His excision of letters in his farce must indicate awareness that the device was too sophisticated for his audience rather than failure to adapt to a new genre.

If acceptance of this suspicion gave warning that a simple 'Kailyarder' might challenge his critics to read both contemporary and modern accounts of language as the conveyer/perverter of meaning, it also announced in subtler tones that they must understand what is ultimately implied by the claim of the artist to be creator. That, in its turn, leads to the literary/fantastic issues confronted by Wordsworth or Tolkien. It also points to the theological/philosophical issues involved when we confront language as the most developed means devised by man in his, ultimately doomed, attempt to imitate through sounds the infinite variety of Nature. The critic, then, has to discover what visions of Nature dominated when Barrie wrote and what Barrie's own view of Nature might be.

III   Darwin   Already the last of these problems had revealed itself in a manner which demanded attention. Was the simple, accepted view of Barrie as the champion of Victorian optimism and as upholder of the harmonious Christian world-view sill tenable? When, in *Ibsen's Ghost*, George asks if there is a 'k' in Christianity, Thea retorts, 'There is nothing in Christianity.' The audience laughs; Barrie reassures; Margaret Ogilvy smiles. But if the text is teaching how disparately meaning is conveyed and if every literary technique has been parodied only to be later adopted, can we securely assume that Barrie's irony implies complete rejection of Thea's viewpoint?

An apparently endless quest in all directions of human knowledge seemed to be opening up! But at least the new questions being posed were transforming apparent critical paradoxes into consistent convictions of a complex mind. Barrie had, after all, warned over and over again that he was not one person but several. This is a feature of almost all his prose personae. It is a belief clearly stated as early as 1888:

> Most men are hero and villain several times in a day, but Rob went through the whole gamut of sensations in half an hour.
>
> (*When A Man's Single*, p 169)

The inability to hold to one idea or perspective, he tells us, was a major reason for his move to the more controlled dramatic form. But surely kindly, sentimental Barrie did not harbour non-Christian views of the Universe?

If one unsought-for conclusion of the early research had been Barrie's Ibsenite tendencies, the other had been what Geduld defined as 'personal sadism'. This perception was the psychologically-oriented critic's logical reaction to seeing Babbie and Gavin engaged in battles for domination. My own puzzlement at discovering that the dramatic version of *The Little Minister* had originally ended on a similar note added to the evidence on which Geduld's thesis was based. But nothing suggested that Barrie was a sadist while everything suggested that he was concerned with accurate imitation of Nature as refracted by the changing vision of a multiply-defined personality. What, then, was the most powerful alternative view of Nature? Without doubt Darwinism.

It would have required a considerably less curious mind than Barrie's to have been ignorant of those claims which had rocked society. Someone as interested in the history of Edinburgh University as the author of *An Edinburgh Eleven*[135] could scarcely have failed to note that the originator of *The Origin of Species* had also been an Edinburgh student. The distinctively Scottish philosophical background which shaped both Barrie and Darwin has been expertly analysed by George Shepperson in 'The Intellectual Background of Charles Darwin's Student Years'.[136] Having traced the influence on Darwin of John Miller, Lord Monboddo and others, Shepperson concludes:

> Darwin's ideas clearly belonged to the same environment as the Scottish philosophy — which is scarcely surprising if one remembers the important fact about the Scottish philosophers that is generally ignored is that they were the dominant philosophical school.[137]

This being the case, it is hardly surprising that the reception of Darwin's theories in Scotland was at once pronounced and capable of being differentiated (especially in academic circles) from the reaction in England.[138]

Where, however, is there any clear indication that Barrie went beyond acquaintances with these ideas to even limited acceptance of them? Such was my own unconscious conditioning by another Scottish tradition (the 'literary' denigration of Barrie by Blake) that I thought there would be none until I read his leaders in *The Nottingham Journal* (see Appendix A) and re-read *Auld Licht Idylls* (1888). What view of Nature opens that book? A starving sparrow and a frozen bantam-cock serve as prologue to the vision of a weasel which 'had gripped a water-hen' as a type of the 'fierce struggle among the hungry birds for existence.' [139] From the battle of the birds and animals one moves to the bitter conflict fought by the weavers against the background of Waterloo. Where, the schoolmaster laments, is there anything but barbarity to be found in a society typified by the 'Roup?' And what proves to be the 'standard pastime' of the Scottish ploughman? Reading. And what does he read in his bothy? Blake would have anticipated one side. He subscribes to the *Saturday Review* and *The People's Journal*. But also, open, lie other books, 'including one of Darwin's'.[140]

Darwin's theory of evolution in its broader applications will be discussed in relation to the more overtly philosophical plays. His theories of language will be drawn in when the question of communication attains primacy. His impact on creation theory will have relevance to Barrie's views on art and fantasy. In the Scot's early writings, however, the conflict implied by the evolutionary drive of natural selection remains relentlessly sexual. The open book was, therefore, as likely to be *The Descent of Man* (1871) as *The Origin of Species* (1859). How often is the primitive battle of man to merit woman re-enacted in Barrie's Victorian work? Darwin comments:

> It has ever been the custom among those people for the men to wrestle for any woman to whom they are attached; and, of course, the strongest party always carried off the prize.[141]

What else is the conflict between Pete and Henders in *The Professor's Love Story*? What other principle lies behind the plot of *Walker, London*? In *The Little Minister*, the apparently sadistic exchanges between Gavin and Babbie are, almost certainly, intended to be the latter's method of rousing the masterful, the 'magerful' [142] in a man, over-refined by conventions of society and the ideals of theology:

> Man is more powerful in body and mind than woman, and in the savage state he keeps her in a far more abject state of bondage than does the male of any other animal; therefore it is not surprising that he should have gained the power of selection.[143]

Barrie did not accept every word. He believed woman's mind to be superior to man's. But he saw the power of love as an appeal to primitive powers. After Babbie had proved Gavin's ability to be 'magerful', it probably would be best for him to return to some of his civilised ways. After all, the 'magerful' men in *Sentimental Tommy* triumph to destroy. But their attraction in part derives from this darkness:

> We danced together and fought thegither a' through the ball, and my will was no match for his, and the worst o't was I had a kind o' secret pleasure in being mastered.[144]

And the greatest tragedy of all, in the eyes of Barrie's women, is to be without the capacity to be drawn backwards into barbarity. Aaron Latta, lacking any shred of virility, loses Jean Sandys in a revival of the primitive sexual challenges described by Darwin:

> If Aaron had fought and been beaten, even if he had just lain there and let the man strike away, if he had done any thing except what he was bidden, he would have won, for it would have broken your father's power ower me. But to write the word![145]   (*ST*, p 112)

Barrie's originality lies in rejecting the view of man's mental superiority (based mainly on comparative brain size).[146] He replaces a simple paternalistic vision of nature with a 'battle of the sexes', redolent with irony and paradox. Instead of man triumphing over woman in both society and primitive nature, a woman tempts man backwards into the folk-memory, there to establish his superiority in strength. Having done this, she then returns him to the present, there to re-prove himself in a battle of wits where the odds are in her favour. Darwin's thesis holds that only the more adaptable (favoured) creatures in any species are the guarantee of that species' survival. The battle will be the most intense at the highest levels of development.

> Consequently, each new variety or species, during the progress of its formation, will generally press hardest on its nearest kindred, and tend to exterminate them.[147]

Barrie agrees. He also accepts that the logic of such a view is the cherishing of the genius, the super-person. But within civilised society (the arena of the mind rather than the body) Darwin's 'battle' does not cross sexual boundaries. Man, being superior in both aspects, competes with man for a mate and if the parallel process of natural selection 'depends on the success of both sexes', it is only as synthesis; all conflict is 'between the individuals of the same sex' within a hierarchy which places man constantly above woman.[148] Like Shaw, Barrie thought the evolutionary evidence less clear. Indeed, over and over again he suggested that mental and spiritual development favoured the female. *Sentimental Tommy's* surprisingly consistent belief in this had been a major factor in Grizel's attraction to him. Pan, of course, tells Wendy that 'one girl is worth more than twenty boys' but the most powerful evidence lies in the clear maturity of heroines such as Lucy, Maggie Wylie or Kate (in *The Twelve-Pound Look*) when set against the puerility of their male counterparts.

In the immediate context of drama and *The Little Minister*, these views provide a rationale for the different types of 'mastery' debate, which looked so odd initially. They also explain the polarisation (and the ironic tone underlying that polarisation) of body and mind, natural and civilised, wild and conventional. More generally, however, one is reminded of James Ramsay's comment in Woolf's *To the Lighthouse*. 'Nothing is simply one thing . . . the lighthouse will be either a misty, hazy edifice or a stark, barred tower. It all depends on one's perspective. And yet — the lighthouse, being neither is equally both.' Barrie complicates not by allowing one view to dominate — the Christian or the evolutionary; the man or the woman; the advantages of primitivism or civilisation — instead he counterpoints the one against the other in order to satisfy the Imp which rejoices in self-contradiction. This is, as yet, an aim which has not been adequately embodied in art. But the complex questions are to some degree clarified and it is not in Barrie's nature to compromise or to shield himself from judgement. His days of apprenticeship over, the journeyman prepares a major theatrical assault.

CHAPTER THREE

The Edwardian Journeyman

Plays of 1902/1903:
Quality Street; The Admirable Crichton; Little Mary

'How wretched the lot of those whose life is cast among fools not
capable of understanding him! What was that saying about entertaining
angels unawares?'   (*Sentimental Tommy*)

'It's easy to you that has just one mind,' he retorted with spirit, 'but if
you had as many minds as I have!'   (*Sentimental Tommy*)

Barrie had made it clear that his Victorian plays were the work of an
apprentice to a complex art form. In 1902 he brought two plays to major
London theatres without any such apology. *Quality Street* and *The
Admirable Crichton* were intended to mark his arrival as a serious and
revolutionary playwright. Few critics opposed the claim of maturity then; in
our own day, Leonee Ormond confirms Barrie's judgement:

> *The Wedding Guest* marks the end of Barrie's apprenticeship in the theatre;
> 1902, the year of *Quality Street* and *The Admirable Crichton*, witnesses his
> advent as a mature dramatist.[1]

And Bernard Shaw, writing in 1904 after the addition of *Little Mary* to the
repertory, places the Scottish dramatist in distinguished company:

> Who are the first rate authors? Pinero, Jones and Barrie. I omit for the
> moment Shakespeare, who is played out, and Shaw, who is not yet played in.[2]

But do these plays, the focus of this Chapter, establish Barrie as a radical
new voice? Can the populist invite revolution?

QUALITY STREET

When *Quality Street* opened in Ohio, New York and London's Vaudeville, critics found in its story of sheltered lives little more than developed craft. Here again was a play adapted from one of Barrie's novels — drawn this time from a sub-plot in *Sentimental Tommy*; here again was fantasy, fairytale and sentiment. *The Times* reviewer, for example, considered the plot 'thin', verging at times on 'the namby-pamby, so that we almost sigh for a wolf in the little sheep-fold.' He avoids the word 'sentimental' but instead notes that we have been 'laid up in lavender,' a covert reference to Pinero's reworking of the Cinderella story, *Sweet Lavender*.[3] Modern commentators have also longed for the wolf while accusing Barrie of continued populism:

> [With *Quality Street*] he was back in the realms of romance and sentiment, where the public preferred him to be.[4]

> His instinct for dramatic effect combined with his impish sentimentality was everything that the more comfortable theatre-goers wanted at the turn of the century; it re-assured them at a time when the society they most valued was being eroded or re-examined by the new writers and dramatists.[5]

If Barrie believed he was altering theatrical tastes, it seems that his audience then and now didn't realise this was happening. How, if at all, can this paradox be resolved?

A précis of the plot of *Quality Street* seems to add ammunition to the viewpoints just cited. Here is a quiet society of maiden ladies reading romances in a blue and white room in a genteel street in a small town. Far away the Napoleonic wars may thunder, but they only directly impinge on the lives of Miss Susan and Miss Phoebe Throssel when they take away the latter's admirer, Valentine Brown. True, there is a moment of black irony when Phoebe mistakes this piece of news for the proposal she has long expected, but courageously she recovers, quenching personal sorrow with patriotism. Act 2 takes place ten years later. The blue and white room has been converted into a school room where the sisters cope, at times hilariously at times pathetically, with the brutality of youth and the opaque mysteries of algebra. The return of an ex-pupil and of Phoebe's admirer from the war serves to emphasise how much the sisters have aged. In a last, desperate throw Phoebe dresses herself up in the clothes of her youth and gets invited to a ball by Brown, who believes she is her own niece. This new rôle permits her to don a witty, biting personality and generally to enjoy the life of the frivolous romantic heroine. It also allows her to chide her suitor for his earlier insensitivity, a triumph which is cleverly undercut by his confession that he loves not the niece but the absent aunt. The last Act returns us to the blue and white room and a farcical situation with the sisters unable to rid themselves of the non-existent niece, whose entrance into the house has been noted by their eagle-eyed neighbours. Determinedly they await the drama of her exit while the desperate sisters fear they are doomed eternally to share living space with an illusion. A maid tells Brown of their situation; he enters their dream world by taking away a bundle which appears to be the niece, before returning to marry her 'aunt'.

This was the first play which satisfied Barrie enough to be included in the *Collected Edition*. I shall discuss it in relationship to the Notebooks, to *Sentimental Tommy* and the early dramatic drafts; I shall also consider how far it bears out the views on art expressed in his prose works. Surprisingly, there has never been a consistent attempt to connect the highly complex literary theory of these 'novels' to Barrie's later drama. Yet the two, as Lynette Hunter noticed, are inextricably combined:

> The struggle to control and change his style in the novels became a search for greater artistic responsibility in expression which he finally achieved in the written form of his plays.[6]

In *The Wedding Guest* in particular he had explored theatrically the problems of composition, just as so many of his prose works had reflected on his own artistry. This bias would continue. Yet with the exception of Beerbohm, his contemporaries remained stolidly blind to this crucial dimension of his dramatic message.

Even the simple story line of *Quality Street* involves an incisive satirical attack on the controversial romantic heroine as expected by Victorian audiences and defined by the male imagination. Shaw had earlier made a similar protest but, until 1904 and the Vedrenne-Barker management at the Court Theatre, the only one of his plays to be produced in the West End was *Arms and the Man*.[7] Barrie tried to introduce a new type of heroine, modest intelligent and virtuous, to the very people who had created the opposed convention. In *Sentimental Tommy*, Miss Ailie, the spinster who wins the lone suitor, is explicitly described in terms which contrast with the flighty attractiveness of romantic youth:

> somewhat beyond middle-age, and stoutly, even squarely, built, which gave her a masculine appearance.[8]

And the love affair, though comically viewed, is opposed in placid uneventfulness to the melodramatic, whirlwind passions favoured in the commercial theatre at the turn of the century and in the pages of romantic novels:

> You must listen now (will you?) to so mild a thing as the long thin romance of two maiden ladies and a stout bachelor, all beginning to be old the day the three of them first drank tea together and that was ten years ago . . . That was how it began, and it progressed for nearly a year at a rate that will take away your breath.   (*Sentimental Tommy*, pp 278,282)

It is this staid love which triumphs, while elsewhere the novel depicts the tragic fate of those like the Painted Lady and Tommy's mother, who put their trust in passion and fantasy.

In transferring this message on to the stage, Barrie did make a few concessions. Miss Phoebe, though not beautiful, is certainly not 'masculine'. She is witty and possesses more charm than the other Quality Street spinsters. She is also the youngest. Further than this he was not prepared to go. In particular he emphasises in the opening stage directions that the actresses must not flaunt themselves as romantic heroines might. Rather their rôles should be underplayed:

> None of them should have any oddities of appearance or gesture . . . There must be no exaggeration or attempt to make broad effects . . . They should always behave as refined ladies and never as comic figures.[9]

The idea of the non-romantic heroine in a non-romantic love affair, is therefore, boldly presented. In her youthful rôle as Miss Livvy, Phoebe specifically blames the superficial nature of men for the valuation of beauty above brains — 'As soon as you see a lady with a pretty nose you cannot help saying that you adore her.' She also defines the callous flirt, whose part she rather enjoys playing, as a 'horrid, forward, flirting, heartless little toad.'

Why, then, did Barrie not gain credit for this brave attempt to question the tastes of his paying public? The answer appears to lie largely in the presentation. Ellaline Terriss was well known to be a headstrong actress. Clearly she found herself ill at ease in a part which did not immediately attract the audience adulation to which she was accustomed. *The Scotsman* reviewer wryly rounds off a lukewarm analysis by condemning 'her trick of ignoring all but the audience.'[10] Beerbohm concurs:

> Miss Terriss . . . walks and talks very prettily, and is very pretty altogether But never for one moment does she forget herself, still less merge herself for us in the part she is playing.[11]

A pretty romantic figure, therefore, overplayed a part intended to represent an ageing, quiet spinster. One does wonder why Barrie permitted this, allowing the vanity of his actresses to blur an attack on that very weakness. As Beerbohm notes, though there is much talk of aging, the actresses simply refused to age. As a result the intended dowdiness was replaced by charm and Miss Terriss merely changed from appearing young to appearing even younger.

An interesting contrast is revealed when Fay Compton's performance, as Phoebe in the 1921 revival, is set against the 1902 interpretation. She conveyed the wittiness of the non-romantic heroine by following Barrie's instructions — 'all through the play Miss Compton acted very quietly.' [12] Interestingly, too, the darker spirit of these days led to a more serious reception of the play as a study of different types of warfare:

> Seen in the light of the actual experience of war, *Quality Street* impressed the Londoner of 1921-2 as a far more realistic thing than it had seemed on that night of laughter and cheers in the little Vaudeville theatre twenty years before.[13]

Barrie's intention to replace romance with reality, fancy with worth had appeared in his Notebooks as early as 1892, when he jotted down, 'Girl's greatest glory in love is being loved for what she really is.'[14] The critics remained blind to these aims. They were absolutely sure that he had rejected the latest of his Victorian experiments, *The Wedding Guest*, to return to safer comic ground and the more conducive appeal of fantasy. A few, like *The Scotsman* reviewer, lamented this as a retreat from serious drama; most welcomed it as a return to the writer's natural strengths; all accepted it as fact. It is easy to see how such an over-simplification occurred. First, in broad terms, Barrie *had* moved back to comedy and myth, much as in *The Little Minister*. Secondly, nobody had fully understood the artistry of *The Wedding Guest* with its use of text and sub-text anyway. In *Quality Street* Barrie matched the multi-textuality of the one to a refinement of the reality/fantasy combination employed in the other. A full appreciation of the complex form and literary techniques adopted in *Quality Street* demanded an awareness of both types of imitation.

The Wedding Guest, it will be remembered, used symbolism as a means of controlling form and underlining meaning. It also relied very heavily on poetic methods and on visual effects in the manner practised by Ibsen. All of these devices are carried into *Quality Street*. Originally, it was called *Phoebe's Garden,* a title preserved in the earliest known draft now in Austin, Texas.[15] At all stages of the play's development the metaphor of the garden is used to trace, yet poetically to widen, the implications of Phoebe's progress. This is not a work which involved Barrie in as many revisions as usual but the importance of this leitmotiv is reflected in the high proportion of changes centring on it. A comparison between the Lord Chamberlain's text and the Definitive text reveals a growing concern to erase other images so that the 'garden' may alone symbolise the heroine, her state and her qualities.[16] The crucial dialogue in Act 3, for example, when Phoebe uses the metaphor to explain her guilt begins thus in the earlier version:

VALENTINE: Never!
PHOEBE: That casket which contains all the admirable qualities that go to the making of a perfect female.
VALENTINE: It is what she is.
PHOEBE: That garden —
[LCP1902/27N]

In the Definitive Text, the intruding casket image has been removed:

VALENTINE: Never.
PHOEBE: That garden —
VALENTINE: Miss Livvy, for shame.
PHOEBE: Your garden has been destroyed, sir; the weeds have entered it, and all the flowers are choked.   (p 323)

When Barrie revises, the passages chosen for special attention nearly always reflect his major dramatic interests. The idea of Phoebe as garden permits

2   The homecoming. Scene from *Quality Street*, at the Vaudeville in 1902.

Valentine in Act 1 to associate her with innocence, constancy and modesty via daisy, hyacinth and violet, yet leave the rose (flower of love) unglossed, unfulfilled. In Act 4 his garden-poem provides the heroine with proof of love through the flower-emblem of that passion. Yet, just as the cuckoo in *Walker, London* had joyous and serious associations, so the garden has graver connotations. Most obviously it is the sign of nature's inevitable subjugation to time. A brief spring moves into age and decay. It also reminds us of mutability. In a play where Miss Phoebe may seize her moment and outwit time, the other spinsters must sit quietly awaiting death in loneliness. The idea of the sheltered garden, admired but unvisited, also accurately symbolises the sheltered gentility of Quality Street ladies, praised for their refinement, but ignored sexually. Or there is Miss Phoebe aptly topping Valentine's romantic use of the metaphor in order to underline his brutal assumption that women stand still in time awaiting the return of man:

> You, who think you can bring back the bloom to that faded garden and all the pretty airs and graces that fluttered round it once like little birds before the mast is torn down — bring them back to her if you can, sir; it was you who took them away.   (p 321)

In *The Wedding Guest*, visible symbols — rice, ring, baby — had played an important part in delineating meaning. In *Quality Street* the visual sign of youth is ringlets and that of age, the cap. At the start of Act 1, Miss Susan and Miss Willoughby wear caps already; Miss Fanny, Miss Henrietta and Miss Phoebe do not. This division is too broad, however, as Miss Susan is quick to point out. Phoebe's ringlets alone do not need the aid of papers. As in *The Wedding Guest*, therefore, visual signs establish a hierarchy, in this case one of youth and marriage-potential. Miss Phoebe's second Act appearance in a Quaker cap, only to let her ringlets down later, economically underlines the fact that age is to some degree an attitude of mind; that individual determination can open up opportunities within the passive social code. Yet the presence on stage of only one spinster without a cap silently demonstrates how difficult it is for timid ladies, held in the grip of gentility, to catch that one moment when marriage may offer itself. The play may conclude with Valentine putting Phoebe's cap in his pocket (so implicitly equating marriage with eternal youth) but Miss Susan is still there wearing hers.

This use of metaphor and the visual power of the stage to relate the sentimental optimism of the surface plot to a wider, more pessimistic vision is very effective. Time and again those who have simply given themselves up to the play's dramatic power ask why an ostensibly happy story leaves them darkly disturbed. *The Times* reviewer, it will be remembered, used *Quality Street* as further proof 'that the pleasure of a genuine Barrie will be found not so much in what the work — whether novel or play — says as in what it implies.' [17] In this he was undeniably right. Barrie had decided that his dramas should work on many levels rather than one, that they should be poetically open-ended rather than homiletically sealed and that they should range over many issues from the personal to the metaphysical.

In these ways, *Quality Street* resembles rather than departs from *The Wedding Guest*. Formally, however, it is *The Little Minister* to which it returns, as well as to that play's mythic content. Barrie had justly been criticised for failing to separate the worlds of realism and fairy tale when dramatising the story of Babbie. Learning from this error he adopted for *Quality Street* the circular form of the Shakespearean Romance. By opening with a domestic scene, moving into the fantasy of disguise at the ball and then returning to domesticity, he formally distinguished the different worlds and logics he was invoking. The fact that all his other enduringly popular plays — *The Admirable Crichton, Peter Pan, Dear Brutus* and *Mary Rose* adopt this structure or a variation on it indicates how well it was adapted to Barrie's particular skills.

My own earlier article on the relationship between the episode of the Hanky School in *Sentimental Tommy* and the plot of *Quality Street* highlighted Barrie's determination to retain the basic formal pattern of the novel — misunderstanding leading to partial resolution, then to a deception which first complicates then totally resolves the situation.[18] But he also strove for greater simplicity in the theatrical version. That process continued through successive drafts, the tendency always being to discard inessentials. Phoebe's part alone develops (much as Babbie's had done); the rôles of the other spinsters and servants are cut, occasionally quite ruthlessly.[19] All this contributed to greater clarity which pleased the critics and an unchallenged heroine, which doubtless pleased Miss Terriss.

Some critics related the central fantasy to the tale of Cinderella:

> The ball scenes are essentially a variation on the Cinderella story — in which the prying spinsters take the place of the ugly sisters and the possibility of Livvy's being unmasked replaces the twelve o'clock deadline.[20]

The trouble with this is that these general parallels relate to inessential elements within the original fairy tale. None of the crucial features of ill-treated heroine, unnatural father, heroine's flight and King Lear judgement listed by Bettelheim, nor the source of psychic utility (the child's feeling about its parents) are retained.[21] Given Barrie's policy of deleting inessentials, it seems that the fairy tale is not the true key to the ball scene.

What Barrie has seen — anticipating the Dutch writer, Jolles — is that a simple form can in itself become a type of structuring principle, taking shape in language. Jolles argued that the universal forms in which the world may linguistically be organised are few in number. He lists the following and I have set beside each class the Barrie play or plays, which most obviously anticipate these structures:

The Legend	The Soldier of Christ	(*The Boy David*)
The Saga	The Tie of Blood	(*Alice Sit-By-The-Fire*)
The Myth	A revelation of the cosmos seen as unchanging	(*Peter Pan*)

The Riddle	'To answer riddles is to gain admission to a circle of initiates'	(*Little Mary*)
The Proverb	Compresses meaning into a memorable formula	
The Case	See below	(*Quality Street; The Admirable Crichton*)
The Memoir	'The unique features of a typical event'	
The Tale	'Takes place in a world which is deliberately set against our own world as other, different, better'	(*A Kiss for Cinderella; Mary Rose*)
The Joke	'Attacks inadequacies in language, in logic, in ethics'	(*Little Mary*)

The definition of the 'case' provided by Robert Scholes, following Jolles, is 'a hypothetical narrative that relates some possible human situation to some set of norms and values . . . not to illustrate a particular value but to test the norms themselves.' [22] This is a more fruitful approach to the moral and social implications of *Quality Street* than regarding it as 'a little fairy story with characters not pretending to be more than shadows.' [23]

In another major fashion, *Quality Street* controls where *The Little Minister* did not. This advance is more subtle and the clue lies in a distinction between the former and ALL of Barrie's other 'mythic' dramas. The titles on the preceding list refer (like *The Little Minister*) directly or obliquely to character. *Quality Street* highlights a setting and a social context. Of course, *Phoebe's Garden* had earlier contextualised in a primarily romantic manner but with the character still named. Barrie's revision of the title suggests a playing down of the specific in favour of the 'case' and a movement of emphasis from love to manners. These tentative conclusions are given support by the superficially puzzling introduction to Phoebe:

> There seems no sufficient reason why we should choose Miss Phoebe as our heroine rather than any one of the others.   (p 275)

This does not mean that, having chosen her, Barrie will refuse to differentiate Phoebe from the others. But it defines her status as a 'case' in Jolles' sense. She is one plain, intelligent product of Christian gentility among others. Any differentiation has been ordained by the artist in relation to his elected dramatic purpose.

If *The Little Minister*'s structural ambitiousness lay in the mixing of realism and fantasy, its mimetic ambitiousness lay in confronting opposed philosophies. In *Quality Street*, Barrie sought to replace diffuseness with control for both. Structurally, he uses the Act division to mark off

Naturalism[24] from Fantasy. Dramatically he uses his set clearly to divide the blue room from the world outside. In each case he has simplified through 'boxing off'. In so doing, he has proclaimed his artifice more directly. The opening Stage Directions for *Quality Street* not only emphasise the distance of one world from another (through the bowed window . . . we glimpse . . . the street . . . and through the street, the shop . . . and through the shop, the world); they also let us see those representatives of the world who have strayed into the street (recruiting sergeants; soldiers; clergy etc.[25]) We are, therefore, in a literary act of imitation observing an emblem of the imitative process containing both viewer and viewed. Neither vision is without its limitations — Barrie is cut off from Nature by the failure of words to embody; the spinsters observe not the Napoleonic wars but those who have strayed from the wars into the limbo of the street.

One further simplification and the energetically dissipated effect of *The Little Minister* becomes the controlled analysis of *Quality Street*. This concerns the philosophies presented. Babbie and Gavin had set paganism against Christianity; witchcraft against religion; barbarism against refinement — the list of oppositions suggested were vague and almost endless. *Quality Street* covers many of the same issues but has a much clearer focus. Christian gentility looks out at a great distance on the battling world described by Darwin. And although, as usual, Barrie does not find for one rather than the other, this particular pattern of his dramatic kaleidoscope presents a much more precise and negative view of Christianity than, earlier, he had dared.

Following in part St Paul and in part the code of the socially genteel, the spinsters of *Quality Street* have chosen geographically to distance themselves from Nature and physical love. If 'Gentlemen in the street are an event', a man in the Blue and White Room is a near miracle. And if one enters, he has to be sanitised in order to face their purity.

The Recruiting Sergeant has to stand on a piece of newspaper; Valentine Brown has to be a suitor moving, *with no trace of sensuality*[26] towards Christian marriage. The ladies, in short, will not compete in either of the major battles defined in *On The Origin of Species*:

> I should promise that I use the term Struggle for Existence in a large and metaphorical sense, including dependence of one being on another, and including (which is more important) not only the life of the individual, but success in leaving progeny.[27]

The problem is, that while Darwinian ideas account for the framework of this 'case', they do not account for the tone. There is a bitter criticism implied, which the biologist's maintained religious beliefs excluded.

Indeed, I find *Quality Street* in some ways frighteningly direct. While they are not condemned as black against Darwinian white (Phoebe's near tragic heroism is based on Christian striving and Christian suffering), Christianity's values are searchingly examined via a controlled, analytically conceived dramatic structure. When all the representatives of Christianity in the play appear not just to be protecting themselves from the evidence of Nature but wilfully blinding themselves to it; when their opening remarks present such a false, even smug,[28] view of the Napoleonic Wars; when an entire set emblematising Art as a translation of Nature is devoted to showing how *far* the character-types are from the proper object of their contemplation, then surely Barrie must wish to question the validity of the creed.

Ironically, this has not been seen. Almost all critics are as protected from the literary truths of *Quality Street* as the sisters from Nature in Art. The fact that most of the writer's audience shared the faith represented is, ultimately, irrelevant. It is everyone's unquestioning faith in Barrie's traditionalism, which prevents valid conclusions by shutting off the proper range of questions. Such critics only see the Romance plot or if they accept the wider challenge so strongly implied by title, structure, setting, symbolism and imagery, they do so within a specifically social framework.

> Although the play ends sentimentally and conventionally with the marriage of two people whose love triumphs over both internal and external obstacles, the play also raises an interesting question: how is a 'woman of sense' to deal with the restrictiveness and emptiness of the social conventions which seem to prevent her finding a 'man of sense'.[29]

True. But the social question derives from theological belief; the theology dictates morals which are socially reinterpreted; and that vision looks out at history from a blue and white room whose colours inadequately translate those of Nature's sky.

Quality Street: Nietzsche's World-View[30]

While this draws Barrie closer to Ibsen's message as well as his methods, I am certain that another major thinker lies behind the Scot in this area. The writer is Nietzsche. I shall be arguing that his philosophy may well provide the foundation for Barrie's radical approach to morals and theology. As I intend also to suggest that the German proved a catalyst for Sir James's perspectivist view of life and utilitarian approach to art, the grounds for my own belief must be carefully prepared.

The most obvious starting point is chronology. When did Nietzsche's ideas reach Britain? The first extended treatment in English of Nietzschean philosophy is Max Nordeau's essay in Book III of *Degeneration*. That is dated 1895. A year later, Tille published the first two Volumes of his English translation of the *Collected Works*, and in 1898 there appeared Havelock Ellis's three influential Nietzschean Essays in *The Savoy*. Given the undoubted impact of these texts, it seems highly likely that Barrie would have been acquainted, at least with the major Nietzschean ideas prior to *Sentimental Tommy*. After all, here was a philosopher who, uncompromisingly, went further than Darwin in demolishing the benevolent Christian world-picture. But he also encompassed theories of literature and language in a jargon-free text, often using maxims or even fictions to present his views.

He was, therefore, more popular with literary and political figures than professional philosophers. Shaw and the Fabians in particular welcomed his freethinking:

> Nietzsche is undoubtedly the deepest, though most biassed, psychologist of human institutions that our century has seen. His analysis of the Christian . . . ideal . . . is . . . the most telling and brilliant psychological analysis ever made.[31]

If anything was guaranteed to make Barrie consider a writer it would be Shaw's appropriation of him. The relationship between these two great dramatists was one of intense respect in the context of differently defined artistic goals. The frequent dramatic contests, later to be revealed, and the consistently perceptive critical comments on the rival's work result from this. In their letters, each records what an honour it is to know the other and the evidence indicates a close, even intimate, personal bond.[32] Each would use his drama satirically to suggest the limitations of the other's art but neither doubted the other's genius for a moment. And Shaw had put down the challenge that he was a dramatic Nietzschean.

> My business is to fight for the Grand School — the people who are building up the intellectual consciousness of the race. My men are Wagner, Ibsen, Tolstoy, Schopenhauer, Nietzsche, who have, as you know, nobody to fight for them.[33]

The shrewd Scot who had, from his earliest days, committed himself to 'a worthy craving to be the heaviest author of his time' [34] was unlikely to have read less widely. That Nietzsche's ideas were known to him would seem a very strong premise without the evidence of *Sentimental Tommy, Tommy and Grizel* and the three journeyman plays to support it. Is it simply a coincidence that the dramas appeared at the very moment when Nietzscheanism reached the height of its popularity in Britain?

> Nietzsche began to receive serious recognition in England in about 1902. Indeed, it is clear in retrospect that 1902 marked the opening of the 'Nietzschean decade' in English literature.[35]

Can Barrie's name really be added to those of Nietzsche's established literary debtors — Shaw, Moore, Pater, Symons, Davidson, Yeats and Wells? Where, within the many-world structure of *Quality Street* would the evidence of the Nietzschean Weltanschauung reveal or deny itself?

If the world of Fantasy is introduced to counterpoint the Street in Act 3, for primarily Romantic purposes, the remaining three Acts allow a succession of invasions from the outside world into the blue and white room. There, if anywhere, Barrie can direct our reactions to the clash between Christian spectator and Nature. There, too, he can justify his random choice of Phoebe — not *after* making it as a man, but *through having made* it, like a God-creator. The elected character *must be* unique in order to glorify the writer's art and explicate his dramatic universe within the terms of its pre-determined purpose. This purpose is to serve as a 'case'; to be at once the finest product of the street in terms of genteel Christianity and the least blinded against the empirical evidence presented by the outside world.

In Act 1, the Recruiting Sergeant is the first to break through. The remarkable image he faces is of the ladies on their knees.[36] All except Miss Phoebe then exit and there begins a discussion on Napoleon. Now, Napoleon was Nietzsche's main exemplar of the unconventional man of energy who, in his strength, forced the weak into obeisance. Like Darwin, Nietzsche began with an image of Nature as uncompromising battle:

> Life itself is *essentially* appropriation, injury, conquest of the strong and the weak, suppression, severity, obtrusion of its own forms, incorporation, and at least, putting it mildest, exploitation.[37]

He went on, however, to situate that greatness in heroes rather than creeds, noting that 'Goals are lacking and these must be individuals' [38]

If Napoleon was the major type of such an individual, his polar opposites were the weak, banded together in adherence to religious creeds. By turning into virtues the characteristics which defined their weakness (timidity, modesty, mercy), they proved *en masse* a real obstacle to the relentless advance of the race. Their very servility became their greatest power:

> The problem these men pose themselves is intimately related to this one: how can the *weaker* tribe nonetheless dictate laws to the *stronger*, dispose of it, regulate its actions so far as they affect the weaker? [39]

The weak also wilfully ignore the evidence of Nature to draw it into service on their terms, 'to impress upon it a regularity and rule of law which it does not at first possess.' [40] For Nietzsche, the creed which most clearly advocated this type of 'surrender, of sacrifice for one's neighbour . . . and all self-renunciation morality' [41] was Christianity. To it his opposition was implacable. Nor did he find a lack of support in late Victorian England. Indeed, as Peter Keating argues (citing Winwood Reade's *The Martyrdom of Man* (1872) in support), 'Few British writers in the 1880s and 1890s needed Nietzsche to inform them that God was dead':

> The following facts result from our investigations — Supernatural Christianity is false. God-worship is idolatory. Prayer is useless. The soul is not immortal. There are no rewards and there are no punishments in a future state . . . I undertake to show that the destruction of Christianity is essential to the interests of civilisation; and also that man will never attain his full powers as a moral being until he has ceased to believe in a personal God and in the immortality of the soul.[42]

The opposition between Christianity and the new evolutionary discoveries must have been known to Barrie; it is the precise nature of his images, hero-types and literary assumptions which argues for Nietzsche as a particular catalyst for his own (ultimately original) views.

Critics working on naturalistic assumptions find the 'kneeling cameo' unlikely and 'justify' it in terms of forced farcical effect. Surely, however, it was conceived as an economically witty symbol of subservient Christianity bowing before a mere bit-player in Napoleon's drama before running away from his evidence? Symbolism is the decorous language of Reality and any oddity on the narrative level points us to allegorical interpretation as Hugh of St Victor taught.[43]

Phoebe remains to listen. Her own incipient rebellion against Christianity is betrayed first in her 'ungenteel' interest in details of warfare. This is an instinctive belligerence absolutely opposed to her Quaker bonnet as even the stolidly unperceptive Valentine Brown later notes:

> VALENTINE: Your demure eyes flashed so every time the war was mentioned; the little Quaker suddenly looked like a gallant boy in ringlets.
>
> (p 285)

The bonnet of pacifism battles with the ringlets of youth and instinct. And when instinct speaks to the Recruiting Sergeant, it hurtles into unconscious heresy as wildly as Burns's Holy Willie:[44]

> PHOEBE: Oh, sir, I pray every night that the Lord in His loving-kindness will root the enemy up. (p 279)

Phoebe's very next words, however, reveal bondage to protective moral mythologising. Napoleon is 'the Corsican Ogre' who 'eats babies'. He is also, for her, 'The Man of Sin'. Such simplifications are based on non-evidence within a morality whose premises do not, for Nietzsche, stand up to empirical observation. Napoleon is the 'synthesis of the inhuman and the superhuman' in an interpretation which substitutes 'weakness' for 'evil' and 'strength' for 'good'. Phoebe may be hungrier for 'truth' than the other Street-dwellers, but her premises remain Christian. That must be; she is not a 'case' for Nietzscheanism but a Christian 'case', facing two contradictory interpretations of life's variety.

The second meeting of worlds in Act 1 is between Valentine and the sisters. In actual terms, this lustless lover has not yet proved himself in warfare any more than Andrew Aguecheek. But, symbolically he has made the absolute transition to the outside world the moment he took the King's shilling. Look at Barrie's ingenuity on this level. It is Brown's movement out of the street (based on a belief in Phoebe's instinctive belligerence) which makes a *strong* man out of him and dooms the sisters' hopes that social servility may creep into coition according to the code of Pauline condonement. In Christian terms, Phoebe's reaction to her disappointment IS heroic. Her suffering is real and its depths relate, comparatively, to her greater passion and correspondingly more horrific frustration. Nietzsche would have accepted that and noted it as a mark of her potential power. But he would have urged that suffering as a reason for pride: 'The intellectual haughtiness and loathing of every man who has suffered deeply. It almost determines the order of rank, how deeply men can suffer.' [45] Symbolically, the marriage of Valentine and Phoebe represents the union of a man who has learned the lessons of warfare and a woman who has proved her spiritual strength. Phoebe will also rebel against timidity and her first rebellion will follow — immediately — on the stoical acceptance of her lost hopes:

> PHOEBE: You dreadful man, you will laugh and say it is just like Quality
> Street. But indeed since I met you to-day and you told me you had
> something to communicate we have been puzzling what it could be, and
> we concluded that you were going to be married.   (p 287)

This reply is offered by one frozen into passivity by the tenets of Christian morality refined by the social ethics of the 'Quality' (the genteel).

Every available weapon open to her in the war of the sexes she here scorns. Mercy and politeness combine to silence the wholly justifiable revelation that Brown's incapacity to understand women matches his inability to assess the Stock Market. (The worthless shares he urged on the sisters have ruined them.) Indeed, the most daring gesture Phoebe makes towards an honest expression of emotional outrage is to turn herself (*as a servant of Quality Street*) into the butt of pitiful laughter; and in so doing to state as falsity the most intimate of truths. Nietzsche had warned over and over again that while religion might limit, the social morality deriving from its premises constricted the power for honest vision to a state approaching blindness.[46] However heroic the suffering of such as Phoebe, hers is the weakness of gentility superimposed upon the fiat of turning the other cheek:

> The fatalism of the weak-willed embellishes itself surprisingly when it can pose
> as 'la réligion de la souffrance humaine;' that is its good taste.[47]

Not only is this, the denouement of Act 1, an exact dramatic translation of quite a specific Nietzschean view, it represents an astonishing authorial ability to think through an allegoric translation of narrative argument.

The obviously tragic personal conclusion becomes, allegorically, the nadir in the pilgrimages of Brown and Phoebe. Those pilgrimages are clearly distinguished. Symbolically, Valentine has chosen the Napoleonic path, Phoebe the Blue Room. In the extremity of their different blindnesses at that moment, however, lies a single dramatic hope for vision. The callous Brown has had one true insight. He noted Phoebe's love of *physical* aggression. It is possible, therefore, to see him travelling the journey of action on her behalf. Phoebe remains within the room for the *spiritual* pilgrimage without geographic change.[48] The enactment of her moral paralysis has, however, shown her the degree of abdication which purity-gentility implies. The Phoebe we meet in Act 2 is determined to be mistress of her own fate. So much could be taken from *Everyman*. But the controlling symbol (comparing while separating) is not that of the journey into joy but the Nietzschean battle never-ending:

PHOEBE: [*more firmly*] A woman must never tell. You went away to the great battles. I was left to fight in a little one. Women have a flag to fly, Mr Brown, as well as men, and old maids have a flag as well as women. I try to keep mine flying. (p 328)

And the last word of Act 1 is not theological in reference but restrictively social. Phoebe regrets not her lost happiness but her betrayal of the first rule of the Street — 'I have been unladylike.'

In case it is assumed that this analysis is an example of a Medievalist anachronistically drawing later material back into his own favoured period and its modes of analysis, I should argue simply that Barrie is treating the Real not the real and that allegory is the language of the Real. The fact that he is doing so specifically to question rather than reaffirm Dante's harmony results not in a rejection of allegory but an adjustment of the methods of allegory. Instead of each veil[49] being removed to reveal consistently reinforcing truths, the veils reveal a series of counterpointed (sometimes even mutually contradictory) visions and a Truth of many believed 'truths.' The craft of Barrie in its desire to involve rather than alienate the audience, begins with the known in art. The relationship of this to his views on the audience and the purpose of his writing will be examined shortly. At the moment, I suggest that revised techniques of allegoresis are part of Barrie's growing skills as a dramatic Journeyman.

If this is accepted, then the emphasis on caning throughout Act 2 and Act 3 supports a thesis of Nietzschean philosophy rather than necessarily adding sado-masochism to paedophilia and Oedipus complexes as possible character traits! Any attempted use of text to assess the nature of its creator must, at least, properly define the conventions and mimetic intentions of that author before taking the dangerous leap backwards from art to psychology. Nietzsche's 'morality of the whip' is itself imaginatively conceived, a poetic means of representing the master-slave relationship which results from the 'morality' of domiance. If there was one feature of Nietzsche's thought which was generally known, it was this belief in superiority and subservience:

> We want rather, to perceive or divine how the next man outwardly or inwardly suffers from us, how he loses control over himself and surrenders to the impressions our hand or even merely the sight of us make upon him . . . There is a long scale of degrees of this secretly desired domination and a complete catalogue of them would be almost the same thing as a history of culture.[50]

The 'caning' material in *The Little Minister* is probably an anticipation of the wider Nietzschean influence, appropriately set within a supportive Darwinian context.

In *Quality Street* the ability to cane marks you out as a member of the outside world. The boys and girls who invade the Blue and White room in Act 2 are from that world. Their representative takes his name from the Duke of Wellington (Arthur Wellesley) as a type of 'hero' in the game of dominance. If the room becomes a class in which the sisters strive to teach, the schoolroom also represents a learning experience for Phoebe and Susan. Arthur teaches Phoebe the way to cane (handle the outside world) because she is eager to learn. Susan remains untaught because, once more, she gives up. Her 'whipping' remains in the world of dreams and is either directed against the man who invented algebra or towards past students (Blades). In the first case she opposes science or empiricism; in the second she lies to herself, so perpetuating her blindness in Act 1.

The major invasion of Act 4 is once more Valentine's. The learning process of Act 2 having led to the changed personality of the Ball, Phoebe is almost ready for union with the man whose lost hand marks him out as a pilgrim from the cruel land of Nature. One remaining Christian scruple remains — her guilt.

> SUSAN: Why not marry him? If only we could make him think that Livvy had gone home. Then we need never know.
> PHOEBE: Susan, you pain me. She who marries without telling all — hers must be a false face. They are his own words.   (p 327)

Now, Nietzsche saw guilt as a further excuse for weakness within the religious creeds. If an artificially high moral or theological goal were set, the failure to achieve it would incapacitate those who, already, were taught to hold themselves unworthy. By squeezing guilt out of such an unlikely 'sin', Phoebe returns to type and nearly remains within Quality Street. But of even more significance is the 'social' and 'historical' context given by Nietzsche to moral conscience:

> I regard the bad conscience as the serious illness which man was bound to contract under the stress of the most fundamental change he had ever experienced — that change which occurred when he found himself finally enclosed within the walls of society and peace.[51]

Quality Street is the most exact enactment possible of the oppositions between enclosure and openness, peace and warfare, society and wild Nature. The second 'case', *The Admirable Crichton*, adds a time dimension, taking its socialised Loam family back to a wilder past. The *Quality Street* debate is given origins and a future.

Successive breakthroughs from the outside world dramatically reveal Quality Street society as the last bastion of attitudes opposed to Life and Joy. A creed of genteel Christianity cocoons its inhabitants against harsh truths by encouraging in them wilful distancing, wilful blindness, minimal passion, maximal guilt and a simplistic mythology at odds with Nature's complex evidence. Phoebe increasingly distances herself from the others. Her cameo with the Recruiting Sergeant reveals instinctive aggression; the discussion with Brown underlines frustrated passions; the schoolroom interlude uses her desire to cane as an objective correlative for her 'worldly' longings. Then, first in fiction (the ball) and finally in fact (marriage), she leaves the street for a fulfilled emotional life. Her transition implies a moral as well as a romantic choice of the sort imagined by Nietzsche in *Thus Spake Zarathustra*:

Once you had passions and called them evil. But now you have only your virtues: they grew from out of your passions. You laid your highest aim in the heart of these passions: then they become your virtues and joys.[52]

Inevitably, however, Barrie does not present either a complete break or a straight philosophical preference. Susan is part of the agreement; all ties are not broken.

Quality Street: Perspective, Fantasy and Utility

One further key feature of Phoebe's rebellion remains. She discovers that both imitation of a single perfect theological ideal (Christ) and the social refinement of that ideal through gentility imply consistent presentation of character. Like all major Barrie heroines she finds this limits her, for she is many people at once. It is not the loss of Valentine which urges her towards the creation of Livvy; it is the need to fill, through spontaneity, her 'other existences':

> PHOEBE: Susan, I am tired of being ladylike. I am a young woman still, and to be ladylike is not enough. I wish to be bright and thoughtless and merry. It is every woman's birthright to be petted and admired, I wish to be petted and admired . . . Ten years ago I went to bed a young girl and I woke with this cap on my head. It is not fair. This is not me, Susan this is some other person, I want to be myself.   (p 299)

There are three important premises behind this, all relevant to *Quality Street,* to Nietzschean influence and to Barrie's theory of art. Phoebe's 'self' involves different personalities with different perspectives. Not all of these are consistent and some are contradictory. The lady who forgives in Christian spirit, concealing outrage behind a smile, is at the opposite pole from the one who bitterly denounces Blades:

> LIVVY: And you offer to her, not from love, but because you are so deficient in conversation.   (p 316)

Yet Phoebe contains them both. Secondly, Phoebe triumphs by way of a fiction; a fantasy. It is her imaginative creation of a new self which frees her. This at once proves the power of fantasy while underlining the tragedy of those lacking this gift. Only by a device of creative fancy can Valentine be brought to his senses and a second chance be forged. Only by ceasing to be a lady in a play within a play can the genteel spinster escape from a constricting male definition of womanhood. The sadness of the Street is enacted by the aging spinsters and indirectly voiced by Phoebe after the freedom of the ball:

> PHOEBE: A little happiness has gone to my head like strong waters.   (p 312)

Finally, she uses the greater freedoms of fantasy to manipulate her rather obtuse audience. Blades and Charlotte she simply destroys; Valentine she educates through Livvy's brash clarity. First she makes him conscious of the superficiality of his love/youth equation; then she forces him into jealousy through flirtations which mirror his own behaviour. Her utmost triumph comes when she steps out of her youthful persona briefly to deny the romantic possibility of that victory over time which currently (as Livvy) she is sustaining:

> VALENTINE: Instead of growing older you shall grow younger. We will travel
> back together to pick up the many little joys and pleasures you had to
> pass by when you trod that thorny patch alone.
> PHOEBE: Can't be — can't be.   (p 323)

As single, genteel personality. Phoebe grew older in suffering and shocked Brown by the contrast between actuality and the non-changing picture of his individuality-denying imagination; as dual personality Phoebe/Livvy grows younger in joy and uses her contrasting identities to trap him into acceptance of the facts of time and an assessment of her genuine worth. For Brown, life encouraged selfish mythologising; fantasy taught the truths of life and love.

To highlight perspectivism first: this involves noting that while Nietzsche was one of the first popularisers of a world picture built from interpretations, Barrie had been, from his earliest days, an aggressive disciple of such views. Quite certainly, he would have been a perspectivist without Nietzsche, though (arguably) his theorising would not have developed precisely as it did. Looking back to his journalist days, he often reminds us of this capacity for changing personalities. He adopts in 'Anon', and 'McConnachie', alter-egos to express the same idea. His major literary persona in the Novels, Tommy Sandys, shares this ability and laments the complexity of vision implied:

> 'It's easy to you that has just one mind,' he retorted with spirit, 'but if you had
> as many minds as I have!'
>
> (*Sentimental Tommy* p 380)

Barrie's letters reveal that it was this multi-personality which led him from the freedom of the novel to the stricter forms of the theatre:

> In a play you can keep yourself out much more easily as the characters have to
> do it all themselves.[53]

In making this 'genre' – transition, however, he still accepted the responsibility of mirroring accurately the fractured world he saw. All the evidence suggests that he sought to control basic structures ever more rigidly (simple story types; changes of mode coinciding with changes of Act) in order to permit an ever-redefining universe to be interpreted by ever-redefining characters. He knew that the moment you accept a Phoebe one simplicity of vision goes; and when you permit Phoebe to condition her own fictions, you enter the hyper-faceted world of poor Corp in *Sentimental Tommy*. Changing factual rôles, you will remember, troubled Corp quite enough. Imaginative existence as self-creator and rôle-receiver threatened to destroy him:

> This made Corp more confused than ever, for he was already Corp of Corp, Him of Muckle Kenny, Red McNeil, Andrew Ferrara, and the Master of Inverquharity (Stoke's names), as well as Stab-in-the-Dark, Grind-them-to-the-Ground-Mullins and Wary Joe (his own), and which he was at any particular moment he never knew, till Stroke told him.
>
> (*Sentimental Tommy* p 251)

The creative and metaphysical problems faced by Corp are not dissimilar to Barrie's. Indeed, every structural simplification seems to imply its own complexity. Allegorical patterning clarifies but there being no accepted harmonious world picture the levels cannot cohere and complement as for Dante; instead they must oppose or counterpoint; appear in order to re-assemble. From this point of view it is no coincidence that Schlueter's description of that other dramatic identity-searcher (Pirandello) is wholly apt for *Quality Street* and the three major plays which follow it:

> We can find the artist skilfully operating on multiple planes, teasing the mind by alternately concealing and revealing images, exposing his art even as he creates it.[54]

Barrie's dilemma from this point of view lies in having the desire to mirror the ultimate at a time when the ultimate had become relative.

As the essential perspectivism of Nietzsche is not a matter of contention and as the case for particular influence on Barrie lies in their development from this common base, I shall simply restate the philosopher's metaphysical ground rules. The following quotation from *The Will to Power* is of especial value for it economically comprehends the perspectivism of viewer and viewed, man and Nature:

> Continual transitions forbid us to speak of an 'individual' etc; the 'number' of beings is itself in flux. We would know nothing of time or of motion if we did not, in a crude fashion, believe we observed 'that which is at rest' beside 'that which is in motion'. The same applies to cause and effect, and without the erroneous conception of 'empty space' we would never have arrived at the conception of space. The law of identity has as its background the 'appearance' that there are identical things. A world in a state of becoming could not in a strict sense be 'comprehended' or 'known'; only in so far as the 'comprehending' and 'knowing' intellect discovers a crude ready-made world put together out of nothing but appearances which, to the extent that they are of the kind that have preserved life, have become firm — only to this extent is there anything like 'knowledge': i.e. a measuring of earlier and later errors by one another.[55]

It is safe to say that had Barrie read this passage, he would have accepted its interpretative definition of the world and of multi-faceted personality. But he would also have agreed with the refusal to descend further either into the nihilism of 'nothing can be known' or the extreme relativism of 'all opinions must be equally valid'. Had Barrie moved to either of these positions, art would have become pointless or careful art unnecessary. His own answer of maintaining a pattern from which to deny ultimate patterning; presenting character to deny consistency of character is absolutely at harmony with this part of Nietzschean metaphysics. He agreed with Nietzsche that 'the fact that other points of view are possible does not by itself make them equally legitimate.'[56] But his nature and artistic ambitions had led him to such assumptions before he was likely to have encountered *The Will to Power*. What Barrie would have discovered (and I believe did discover) in Nietzsche was a sympathetic voice, whose views on Fiction and art as Utility made themselves particularly attractive to him because they issued from a shared point of origin.

Both then move forward, in rather different ways, to claim that the artist may now be the only accurate metaphysician. So long as Nature is held to mirror a 'truth', then reason or faith may lead. But once that premise is questioned so is the unchallenged right of scientist, philosopher or theologian to claim prime teaching power. Neither Barrie nor Nietzsche could urge, with Carlyle, that the highest vision involves seeing 'through the shows of things into *things*,'[57] because they had blurred the distinction and doubted the end. Nietzsche replaced reason with the Urvermögen menschlicher Phantasie (prime faculty of human fantasy), the distinctive quality of the creative artist. He was at times hesitant. For example in *The Birth of Tragedy* he relates this belief to the *possibility* of dreams being more worthy than life but does so only *to mention it*. The logic behind such probing remains constant, though:

> We have done away with the real world: what world then remains? Perhaps the apparent one . . . But no, we have discharged the apparent world with the real one.[58]

Similar beliefs underlie much modern thinking. Todorov, for example, is facing the same problems when he comments:

> Literature is not a discourse that can or must be false in contrast to the discourse of the sciences; it is a discourse that, precisely, cannot be subjected to the test of truth . . . it posits meaning ceaselessly to evaporate it.[59]

So, in ages of metaphysical doubt, Art becomes the only mimetic hope.

Todorov's quotation happens also to be a fine description of the techniques of *Quality Street*, where clear but contradictory views are set up to clash and evaporate; to frustrate our reason but then re-form in vague, unresolved patterns which haunt the mind. Increasingly, too, Fantasy plays a major part in Barrie's drama. *Walker, London, The Professor's Love Story* and *The Wedding Guest* are highly imaginative but they turn away from Fantasy *per se; The Little Minister* has fantastic moments intertwining with the main Romantic plot. But all the plays from *Quality Street* to *Peter Pan* have central fantastic movements, where ideas are radically reassessed by using the greater artistic freedoms of that mode.

If Phoebe uses the ball scene to manipulate her adversaries, so Barrie uses it to manipulate his major themes. Only through Fantasy can he make the older and the younger woman the same person and so show Valentine's initial preference for appearance in all its shallowness. Only a 'split' Phoebe can utter as 'niece' the views her 'aunt' had been taught to despise. This permits the character within the play to offer explanations provided variously in the novel by the narrator, by Tommy and by Ailie in her notebook. Here, too, the link between Fantasy as proper mimetic answer to Perspectivism joins with Fantasy as Utility in necessary relation to the audience. Phoebe/Livvy at once provides a means of mirroring multiple personality and simplifying through clear structures, this time at the character level. Her double identity polarises major ideas within the complex debate for the benefit of the viewers.

Nietzsche unites the loss of the unified Real with Utility over and over again. Danto sums up his position:

> That some of or concepts should have collapsed in the light of science would hardly have dismayed Nietzsche: they are all false anyway, and essentially are subject to challenge on grounds of greater utility.[60]

From this a vital conclusion arises for any student of Barrie. If Art is not justified in terms of truth (there being no single truth) then it can only be justified in terms of serving its audiences with ideas which aid them, at their given level of intelligence, in the continuing life process. Nietzsche writes:

> The falseness of a judgement is to us not necessarily an objection to a judgement . . . The question is to what extent it is life-advancing, life-preserving, species-preserving, perhaps even species-breeding; and our fundamental tendency is to assert that the falsest judgements . . . are the most indispensable to us, that without granting as true the fictions of logic, without measuring reality against the purely invented world of the unconditional and self-identical, without a continual falsification of the world by means of numbers, mankind could not live — that to renounce false judgements would be to renouce life, would be to deny life.[61]

The superiority of the Medieval Pearl Maiden overpowering the mind of her father and strict Theological arguments justified by their Truth gives way in the early twentieth century to gentle assessment of audience capacity and Myths refined to their needs.

All this is vital for an understanding of Barrie because a failure to accept his view of Art must result in the reader either condemning me for hubris or Barrie for bad art. Who else has read Barrie in this way? Nobody. Surely, then, either I must be the victim of my own proud ingenuity or Barrie the worst communicator the world has ever known? These questions and assumptions, however, are based on a mimetic view of art. My case is different. Barrie, from his earliest days, conceived of Art as mimesis *in relation to the needs of his audience*. At precisely the moment when Nietzsche's ideas became popular, he formulated 'Art as Utility' and 'Art as Power' into something approaching a comprehensive policy.[62] The most direct evidence for this is presented in *Sentimental Tommy* and *Tommy and Grizel*. Tommy is drawn to Art because he can use it to aid the lives of others. The romantic vision of Thrums is not, as Blake believes, poor art as falsified reality, it is therapeutic art making present suffering bearable:

> 'That's it,' Tommy cried. 'I tell yer, everybody dreams on it!' and Tommy was right; everybody dreams of it, though not all call it Thrums.
>
> (*Sentimental Tommy* p 26)

Writing for Mrs Sandys, is also utilitarian. In her letters she denies the horrific facts of her life to impress, with fiction, a chosen audience:

> 'Rich folk like us can afford to be mislaid, and nothing's over braw for my bonny Jean.' Tell Aaron Latta that.   (*Sentimental Tommy* p 35)

This comforts her and provides, through lying, the strength to endure. Tommy writes his letters to help lovers; the Painted Lady keeps hers to preserve 'what she might have been'. Tommy has a brief flirtation with the 'Art for Art's Sake' school but rejects it as he moves towards artistic maturity.

This emphasis on Utility and Utility in relation with Power turns Tommy, even more enthusiastically then Nietzsche, to the most Godlike art — Fantasy. He does not debate this conclusion. Sometimes he sees his preference actively:

> 'I believe it was!' Tommy exclaimed. He had not thought of this before, but it was easy for him to believe anything. (*Sentimental Tommy* p 195)

Sometimes he sees it passively:

> He had told the truth, and if what he imagined was twenty times more real to him than what was really there, how could Tommy help it?
>
> (*Tommy and Grizel* p 77)

But always he believes the capacity for free imaginative inventiveness draws him closer to genius than those who need experience as a base. That is why, when the topic for the essay turns out to be on a church theme, he gains more joy from not having attended church than those regular attenders who compete with him.

> 'A day in Church' was announced, and . . . Tommy who had missed as many as possible, looked calmly confident.   (*Sentimental Tommy* p 418)

Like Nietzsche, too, he held that sophisticated societies lost as much in over-nurturing as they gained in comforts.[63] This line of thought is more fully explored in *The Admirable Crichton* where Fantasy permits the delicate products of Victorian/Edwardian England to meet the tests of primitivism. But it underlines his approach to the audience in ALL works from the Journeyman period onwards. A gentle, comfortable audience will turn away from direct contact with a harsh truth. (*Little Mary* will treat that theme subtly but forcefully) Tommy learns this when he seeks to show to the future characters of *Quality Street*[64] the primitive artistic vision of Punch and Judy. Only once it has been refined out of all recognition can that early artistic translation of Nature's cruelty be shown. In one of the funniest passages in the book, Barrie recounts at length, how little of this 'truth' was left for the comfortable audience. I confine myself to a single example from this *Punch Moralisé*:

> Punch did chuck his baby out at the window (roars of laughter) in his jovial time-honoured way, but immediately thereafter up popped the showman to say, 'Ah, my dear boys and girls, let this be a lesson to you never to destroy your offsprings.' (*Sentimental Tommy* p 398)

Similarly, the plays of Barrie offer a clear, Romantic plot for those who do not wish to be directly challenged. But the sub texts — the art allegorical; the art poetical; the structure and the revisions are all aimed at disturbing us indirectly while offering a complex, radical view of life to those ready for its message.

Quality Street: The Linguistic Perspective

Nietzsche did not move the concerns of philosophy only into the realm of aesthetics. He was, inevitably, concerned with language too. The fullest statement of this argument has been reserved for *Peter Pan*, because that play deals in depth with the necessary linguistic corollaries of perspectivism. At the moment, it is enough to note that, like Nietzsche and for practically the same reasons, Barrie was drawn to poetic usages of language and to an interest in the perspectives provided by words themselves. Indeed, both held to the view that if truth is only illusion justified by usefulness, no sentence can literally be true. All writing, therefore, begins by being poetic. Once settled and accepted, however, the metaphors become stale and a new poetics must supplant them. The artist's fiction is the source of these new metaphors, sustaining fresh illusions by drawing attention to the use of language itself.

> In a sense this presupposes a modest view of language's power: The language-maker was not modest enough to realise that he had only given designations to things. Instead, he believed that he had expressed through words the highest knowledge of things.[65]

But it also implies supreme care over word-choice; an acute awareness of the word's symbolic power and of the need to define the range of meaning.

For, although words must to some degree distort and deceive, belonging to a different (semantic) order than the illusions they seek to describe, only the greatest precision in their usage will limit the tendency towards misunderstanding inevitably built into their separateness. (As Tommy notes, the most important things are, after all, 'unsayable'.)

Barrie's pessimistic perfectionism in linguistic matters is a theme to which he often returns. He set his most famous play, *Peter Pan*, in Bloomsbury because 'Mr Roget once lived there.' Tommy Sandys lost the essay competition but proved himself a genius by refusing to write on until he found the one word closest to the meaning he sought:

> He had wanted a Scotch word that would signify how many people were in church, and it was on the tip of his tongue but would come no further. Puckle was nearly the word, but it did not mean so many people as he meant. The hour had gone by just like winking; he had forgotten all about time while searching his mind for the word.   (*Sentimental Tommy* p 337)

Barrie's obsessive revisions for the names of characters is also explained when related to a linguistic theory concerned with the limitations of the word as symbol. Noticeably this concern intensifies in the more allegorical dramas. A name, after all, represents the simplest kind of symbolic meaning. Even the neutral names in the novel *Sentimental Tommy* — John Maclean, Miss Ailie, Miss Kitty — signify individuals and, since subjectivity or personal identity is coincident with and constituted in language, any disturbance or slippage in language involves modification or destabilisation of identity. To a writer obsessed with changes of rôle, names must be as precise as possible in order to limit the inevitable tendency towards diversity. So, Barrie changes and re-changes names until he finds one that pins down the intended character. When, as in *Quality Street*, the name has an allegoric or symbolic force, so becoming an instrument of thought, it becomes even more essential that it define the most crucial feature of the character's rôle. This may be done through contrast — 'Valentine Brown' signifies at once the romantic perception of the ladies, and his actual, drab, conventional self. 'Phoebe Throssel', on the other hand, is a name which remains only on the ground lexically. She is one bird added to another, filling her garden with song, fleeing from the earthy restraints of genteel convention. Frailty, idealism and the desire to fly off are simultaneously suggested. In the same way, 'Thrums' becomes 'Quality Street' — a village becomes an attitude of mind, a social code and a further restraint on romantic freedom.

It follows, also, that if the totality of possible interpretations demands expression through multiple plots, so maximal verbal precision implies the examining of all possible senses of, at least, key words. In *The Genealogy of Morals*, Nietzsche addressed this problem of the synthesis of meanings by defining punishment in no fewer than eleven different ways. He concluded:

> We can still see how, from one situation to the next, the elements of the synthesis changed their valence and reorganised themselves in such a way that now this element, now that predominated at the expense of others. It might even happen that in certain situations a single element (the purpose of *deterring*, for example) absorbed the rest.[66]

In *Tommy and Grizel*, in particular, Barrie had used precisely this approach to demonstrate the complexity of meaning contained in the word 'sentimental'. Critics, he must have been amused to note, defined both Tommy and Barrie himself as sentimental in the single sense of wallowing in feeling. Yet, in the first chapter of the novel, we are directly warned that the only way to approximate towards full sense is via a dictionary (*Tommy and Grizel* p 10). There, the meaning of words past and present jostle for our attention. Tommy and Barrie *are* sentimental in the first sense but their sentiment comprehends all the other possible nuances cited in the Oxford English Dictionary. Tommy is the embodiment of sentiment, implying refined and elevated feeling ('I shall probably soon be putting on some grand airs again' (*Tommy and Grizel* p 380); arising from aesthetic emotion (' "Did you like the first words of it, Grizel?" he asked eagerly. The lover and the artist spoke together.' (*Tommy and Grizel* p 234); appealing to tender emotions, especially love ('True love . . . must be something passing all knowledge . . . something not to fight against but to glory in.' (*Tommy and Grizel* p 203); arising from feeling rather than thought (' "I think you could do most courageous things," she told him, "so long as there was no real reason why you should do them." ' (*Tommy and Grizel* p 102); pertaining to one's own feeling ('a human heart was laid bare, and surely that was fiction in its highest form' (*Tommy and Grizel* p 303) and refusing to grow up ('In a younger world where there were only boys and girls, he might have been a gallant figure,' (*Tommy and Grizel* p 117)).

In this sense *Quality Street* is at once a 'sentimental' drama and a drama which considers the multivalence of such a description. The romantic plot confirms the prime meaning; but as it is one 'story' among many, so romantic sentiment is one verbal meaning among many. Word and form 'say' simply but suggest with a complexity related to the different refractions encouraged by Barrie's determination to fill both diction and plot with meanings direct and indirect; obvious and oblique. Concentrate on surface plot or meaning and Barrie will not chide but he will pity your blindness, while accepting it in the name of Utility. Through names, symbolism, romance form and mythic logic he has produced a controlled structure which holds together what is, in all other ways, an expansive, open-ended work. Poetic use of diction, multiple definitions of words and characters; multiple plot-lines conjoin within a clearer form to a subtler effect than in any of his earlier plays.

Quality Street does end with an excess of feeling, but its inhabitants strive heroically for the high sentiment of refined emotion; the sisters in their school prefer sentiment as emotion to exact science and reason (algebra); Miss Phoebe in particular views sentiment as love and tender feelings while exactly that sense of sentiment which equates it with sustaining youth in age dictates her creation of a niece. In so doing she finds herself by releasing her diverse, unfulfilled personalities, matching the diverse plots and meanings she inhabits. This is the sentiment of knowing one's own beliefs. Finally, and most crucially, both she and her creator use the values of the dream world to proclaim the supremacy of aesthetic emotion; for Miss Phoebe as a means of discovering herself and teaching others; for Barrie as a means of revealing only what his audience was ready to learn.

THE ADMIRABLE CRICHTON

Barrie's planned assault on the English theatre took the form of four apprentice dramas, followed by four major plays — *Quality Street* and *The Admirable Crichton* in 1902, *Little Mary* in 1903 and *Peter Pan* in 1904. Each of these attacks from a different angle the self-satisfied commercial values, which he is still thought to embody. This was done while highlighting different aspects of a forward-looking view of literature's rôle in life.

With the first performances of *The Admirable Crichton* almost all critics accepted that Barrie was attempting something different and quite serious. The first difference centred on sources. Barrie had conceived a plot solely and immediately for the stage. True, the idea of a fantasy island had first appeared in *When A Man's Single* but there was no extended connection with any of his novels. If R L Green is right, the basic notion may have been suggested by Conan Doyle during a conversation at Kirriemuir, in 1893. The creator of Sherlock Holmes had then argued that 'if a king and an able seaman were wrecked together on a desert island for the rest of their lives the sailor would end as king and the monarch as servant.' [67] Another likely suggestion for the argument comes from the growing practice, in certain 'radical' aristocratic houses, of encouraging masters and servants to mix occasionally on equal terms or even to change places. A gossip columnist, for example, drew attention to such procedures in the house of Lord Aberdeen:

> Once a week they changed places with the servants and waited upon their domestics at dinner.[68]

Certainly, Lord Aberdeen was convinced that Barrie's satire was directed at him. An icy but inconclusive correspondence followed with Barrie never totally disclaiming knowledge of this updating of the 'Boy Bishop' principle.[69]

Such suggested sources, however, are only hints towards action, not fullscale narrative patterns. Moreover, the evidence of the Notebooks, while introducing another example on Aberdeen lines, confirms the specifically theatrical focus of the Crichton story:

> Play. Scene. Servants entertained in drawing room by mistress + master à la Carlisle family.[70]

The reference here is to Rosamund, Countess of Carlisle, sister of Lady Airlie. A fearsome lady, her effect on others is memorably summed up by MacKail, when he comments that she combined her 'advanced radical principles with a manner which terrified members of every class.' [71] On human dramas such as these, Barrie built the drama of Crichton.

If, in this instance, he forsook the tried practice of working from novel to play, the evidence of the Notebooks unearths a further divergence from his normal methods. Usually Barrie moves very slowly towards a total vision, adding details here and there. The extended and detailed plot outlines, which follow the initial ideas for the play, substantially support MacKail's claim that, for *Crichton* 'and only once more — but then much less clearly — Barrie saw the whole story and the whole shape in one lightning glance.' [72]

This conclusion should not be confused with immediate literary satisfaction on the dramatist's part. Barrie only saw the narrative outline and approved *that* immediately. The relentless process of revision continued as usual, focusing first on title and names. Early titles, which appealed, included *The Island* (drawing attention to the central fantastic movement) and *The Case is Altered* (a direct statement of one of the play's major messages). Interestingly Crichton was originally to be called Graves, so nominally emphasising the tragic potential, which Barrie wished to stress:

Ending. Butler a rather tragic figure.[73]

The change to *The Admirable Crichton* is consistent with Barrie's growing interest in names as figures of thought noted in *Quality Street*. The reference is to James Crichton (1560-82), a Scottish hero of the martial sort admired by Nietzsche and belonging to rougher days before authors had to concern themselves with the sensitivities of the highly civilised.

Crichton is also a literary figure. In an extended section of Sir Thomas Urquhart's *The Jewel* (1652) he became the Romance type of chivalric perfection and of eloquence:

Him who, for his learning, judgement, valour, eloquence, beauty and good-fellowship, was the perfect result of the joynt labour of the perfect number of those six deities, Pallas, Apollo, Mars, Mercury, Venus and Bacchus that hath been since the dayes of Alcibiades.[74]

The association of Barrie's character with the historical and romantic figure of Crichton at once suggests a martial, literary superman of the sort idealised by Nietzsche and by Sentimental Tommy. In opting for a title which recalls both man and myth, history and art, he calls attention to imagination and heroism in another time. In replacing the name of Graves, he emphasises victory over the odds rather than melancholy seriousness; comedy rather than — but not necessarily without — tragedy.

A third innovation was inadvertently exposed when the carpenters went on strike directly before the first London performance on 4 November at The Duke of York's. Admittedly, this was a difference of degree rather than of kind for even in the early days of *Walker, London* Barrie had shown an inclination for pushing stage techniques and effects to their limits. In *Crichton*, however, he demanded so much that at least one section of the backroom boys cried 'Enough'. The subsequent delays meant that the performance did not finish until well after midnight.

Why did the stage crew rebel? Irene Vanbrugh explains:

> It was a production full of mechanical difficulties. In one scene there was the clearing of a patch on a desert island. The lighting of a log fire, a pot to be brought to the boil at a given moment, all needed very careful timing. The properties were extremely original and had to be made with the greatest care in every detail to give the true impression of hand-made effort.[75]

If one thinks precisely of carpentry, the hut made by Crichton in Act 3 poses major construction problems both in terms of initial building and stage assembly. It contains a vast variety of implements and is the setting for an eccentric electrical light apparatus at a time when all electrical effects were in their infancy. Further, Barrie's popularity made lavish productions possible. In this case both economy and the play's circular structure dictated that Acts 1 and 4 should be set in the same room. 'Not good enough for Boucicault and Frohman at the Duke of York's. Two different rooms must be shown in Lord Loam's London residence.' [76]

Contemporary illustrations reveal how ambitious were the sets for each. It is fair, therefore, to suppose that the carpenters' exasperation grew from a combination of the playwright's aggressive theatricality, the director's ingenuity and the liberality of the backer.

That said, there is much truth in Barthes' claim that

> There is no great theatre without a devouring theatricality — in Aeschylus, in Shakespeare, in Brecht, the written text is from the first carried along by the externality of bodies, of objects, of situation, the utterance immediately explodes in substances.[77]

In just this sense of theatricality lay one of Barrie's greatest strengths. Now, freed from the novel as source, Barrie produces a play which broadcasts that theatricality. Indeed it is, perhaps, surprising that only the carpenters went on strike!

The lighting effects demanded were also very ambitious for the state of the art.[78] During Act 2, for example, the floats, battens and lengths were full up, providing a general illumination conveying sunlight within the orange range. Barrie then wanted the orange gradually to fade, leaving the blue to give an effect of night drawing in. He also asked for lemon, orange and black transparencies on the back of the cloth to give a sky of reddish orange; for a complex ripple effect involving the use of a rotating dish and for a slate reflecting the light to convey the impression of the moon. Arcs provided general illumination on the island but at the end of the act the beams narrowed to pick up individuals crouching on the rocks around Crichton while a red gleam melodramatically lit up the butler's face.

This extravagant theatricality is consistent with Barrie's unchanging desire to emphasise those effects unique to his chosen genre. The advance is one of degree. Even more than in The Wedding Guest he uses pantomimic methods at moments of tension. When the lights narrow at the end of Act 2, it is to reveal 'one of the most memorable pantomimic vignettes in all of

Barrie's work.'[79] As darkness engulfs the island, Crichton stands motionless over a pot. In this way the power of Nature — the smell of food — is conveyed solely by the action of the butler leaning forward to stir the mixture. Obedient to its power but in complete silence, the aristocrats return, weakest first, and squat animal-like, round the blaze.

How economically these visual effects express ideas which Shaw might have argued out or Wilde witticised upon! The student trying to recreate Barrie from a book must always imagine how the work is being presented on the stage. Otherwise he will do a great disservice to one of the most essentially theatrical talents of his day or any other.

The last major innovation represented by *The Admirable Crichton* is, from the point of view of critical reaction, the most important. The main plot itself directly conveys a theme of some philosophical and political significance. This is a departure from Barrie's habit of using a superficially light surface text to attract attention for (or sometimes divert attention from) more subtle messages conveyed by subtler means. It would be extremely difficult to miss the fact that this play deals with Nature and social order, for it is announced regularly and stridently. Lord Loam hilariously attempts to introduce the appearance of democracy into his household while personally retaining every advantage of hierarchy. He holds Nature's lesson to be one of equality:

> LORD LOAM: Can't you see, Crichton, that our divisions into classes are artificial, that if we were to return to Nature, which is the aspiration of my life, all would be equal. (p 354)

Crichton, with equal passion and more honesty, supports a ranked order changing according to Nature's dictates:

> CRICHTON: The divisions into classes, my lord, are not artificial. They are the natural outcome of a civilised society. (To Lady Mary) There must always be a master and servants in all civilised communities, my lady, for it is natural, and whatever is natural is right. (p 354)

From this angle, all that follows consists of a proof that Crichton is correct and Loam wrong. Transference to the desert island naturally creates another hierarchy in which butler moves towards king and Loam descends (happily) towards minstrel/fool. Return to England produces, at least on the surface level, the status quo.

Barrie builds a series of challenging ironies into this dramatic 'case',[80] which follows *Quality Street's* Romance structure. Loam praises equality while cherishing a protective aristocracy; he claims to long for the island which, initially, he loathes. Support for the master/servant relationship comes from the servants and is called into question by the masters:

> CRICHTON: No, my lady; his lordship may compel us to be equal upstairs, but there will never be equality in the servants' hall. (p 354)

The hypocrisy of the democratic argument is wittily conveyed by Loam's egocentric desire to apply it only to others:

> LORD LOAM: My views on the excessive luxury of the day are well known, and what I preach I am resolved to practise. I have, therefore, decided that my daughters, instead of having one maid each as at present, shall on this voyage have but one maid between them.   (p 356)

For Loam, democracy equals continued mastery for him and some diminution of the service owed to his children. What is enacted is a social code, then generally accepted and practised, which presents the powerful as discontented, useless parasites and those they dominate as having the virtues of dynamism and clearsighted philosophy. Yet it is Crichton, the man with the most dominant will who disclaims man's power over Nature:

> CRICHTON: That may mean, sir, that Nature is already taking the matter into her own hands.   (p 381)

It is Loam, the man with no strength of will at all, who upholds man's superiority over outside forces. All these ironies convey one of the most radical messages which any playwright had ever dared to set before a Victorian or Edwardian audience.

Crichton: Power in Government

Once Barrie brought his philosophical 'sources' nearer to the dramatic surface, his critics began to identify them. *The Times Literary Supplement* links *Crichton* with Darwin in advocating 'the perfect adaptation of organism to enviroment.' Act 3, in particular, is seen to have 'real philosophical significance.'[81] Moult perceptively moves from evolution to the implication that life must be a continuous striving towards more advanced stages of creation: always a bridge and never a goal. The play, in enacting this, represents 'an excursion into Nietzscheanism.' [82] Walkley, in *The Times,* is less excited about Crichton as Hero and more intrigued by the counterpointing of advanced society and primitive world. Inevitably this leads him to Rousseau although his oft-quoted comparison is hedged around by modifications and appeared only in the first edition:

> But [the play] deals with that subject in a whimsical, pathetic, ironic, serious way which would have driven Rousseau crazy.[83]

Once Walkley had time to prepare his thoughts (after one of the longest theatre nights in modern times) he dropped Rousseau entirely.

Walkley's difficulties derive from Barrie's ultimate comic originality. It is one thing to note that the playwright's ideas are in harmony with those of Darwin and Nietzsche, Rousseau and Carlyle; quite another to suppose that he is passively led by any of them. His use of 'authorities' was always first of all creative. Rather like Wordsworth,[84] he preferred philosophical

3   J M Barrie in his Library.

'schemes', which explained to him his own genius; Nietzsche and Rousseau in this sense are themselves employed as utilitarian myths.

As Barrie's interests are literary and his motivation instinctive, he is drawn to thinkers who are themselves to some degree *intuitive*. Grimsley's assessment of Rousseau could stand for Nietzsche, for Carlyle *and* for Barrie:

> The main principles of his 'system' were not derived primarily from reflection or a critical reaction to other thinkers' views — although these obviously played an important part in the elaboration of his thought — but in a personal response to the basic intuitions of his own inner life.[85]

The Scottish playwright was a voracious reader, as his early biographical accounts and the photographs of his library reveal. But his Notebooks, the accounts of his own intellectual growth, are his major text.

Finally, he employs authorities *eclectically*. Walkley is right to feel unhappy about his philosophical parallel even after the tonal differences have been noted. If Barrie in *Crichton* starts from Rousseau's questions concerning the dubious advantages of civilisation over primitivism, he develops them differently. He places Loam and company in a state of Nature analogous to Rousseau's 'happiest and most stable age' — that of the Première Révolution.[86] But, through fantasy, he creates a 'case' which Rousseau philosophically discounted:

> Human nature does not go backward and we never return to times of innocence and equality when we have once gone away from them.[87]

Or — to view the disparity from a different angle — if Rousseau accepted that 'L'état de nature est une fiction imaginée pour éclairer le sens de l'histoire',[88] Barrie enacted the fiction of that fiction to explicate an understanding of history in society and art.

That is one aspect of his electicism. The second concerns the use to which he puts the 'case' politically. Both Rousseau and Barrie believe that Nature determines political systems as, essentially, a compromise ('the only way of escaping from perpetual strife'), within a world where God has, at best, effectively veiled himself. Both believe that Natural Law will dictate different precise political answers at different times. But only Barrie believes that those answers must be variations on hierarchy. Rousseau accepts the inequality of individuals,[89] but moves from psychological empiricism to political idealism.

> Anything less than a democratic sovereignty means that society lacks a proper foundation.[90]

The more rigorous mind of Barrie allows 'Circumstances (to) alter Cases' only to the extent of giving Crichton covert control within his own hierarchy after enjoying overt control in Loam's.

Indeed, the single consistent line of enquiry emerges from *The Little*

Minister (synchronic counterpointing of civilised against primitive; battle for power, romantic) through *Quality Street* (synchronic counterpointing of civilised against barbaric; battle for power, social) to *Crichton* (diachronic counterpointing of civilised against primitive; battle for power, political/artistic). That is, from Barrie's own thought. Barrie draws in, *on his terms*, not only Rousseau but Carlyle. In *The Greenwood Hat* he confirms his acquaintance with the 'Sage of Ecclefechan' but also his own somewhat cavalier attitude to authorities in general:

> In our Scottish home the name that bulked largest next to Burns was Carlyle . . . indeed he was the only writer I ever tried to imitate.[91]

Even that imitation was principally stylistic, although it seems certain that the idea of the Hero (and especially the Artist-Hero) was encountered by Barrie in *Heroes and Hero Worship* before Nietzsche provided him with a darker world-view and a more sophisticated literary argument. Barrie may have admired Carlyle's style; he may have been introduced to Napoleon and Rousseau as themselves 'Heroes' via Carlyle;[92] he certainly shared Carlyle's belief in the superiority of metaphysical quests in literature and life as governed by utility and *epoch*:

> The hero will not, however, be directed only by the more salient pressures of men but by the great, unseen mystical need of men. He discerns 'truly what the Time wanted,' and leads it on the right road thither.[93]

But a pessimistically rigorous vision and a determination to mirror Nature as he perceived it drew Barrie away both from Rousseau's comfort in man's innate goodness and Carlyle's in God's benevolence. He might, like the latter, accept that 'this so solid-looking material world is, at bottom, in very deed, Nothing,' but he could not join that justification of the allegoric method to his fellow-Scot's Christian optimism. The world was not, for him, 'a visual and textual manifestation of God's power and presence.' [94] The mode of Dante thus being closed to him, he instead accepted that (in this age) his literary duty was to reflect a fractured world through a fractured medium and a fractured personality. The structures of allegory could control. But they did so as conscious simplifications or as counterpointing perspectival possibilities. This 'world upside down', governed by belief, not in a deity but in the therapeutic value of Art is close to Dionysius's image of 'veils of difficulty' as related to an audience's capacity, profitably, to understand.[95] The power being revealed or concealed, however, is not God's but the artist's: the reflection not beyond to Truth but returned either to Self or Text.

It is in this sense and context that *The Admirable Crichton* can be seen as a study of the Will-to-Power (and the limits of that Power) for both character-ruler and creator-artist. The simplest way to demonstrate this is to relate the play to four key Nietzschean ideas, noting from time to time, those instances in which the clearer statement belongs to earlier texts, later revised/refined in recognition of the audience's limitations.

The Will-to-Power as the key to individual heroism is judged by Nietzsche in relation to changing social conditions. There were periods when the social climate permitted the passions to remain strong; there were others when liberalism pertained. Although, therefore, the Hero is defined by his ability to overcome, he is still striving; the Übermensch has not yet arrived and, until that time, different societies will provide different challenges and present different limitations.[96] Crichton is such a hero.

The two episodes, which most clearly demonstrate this, are the conclusion to Act 2 and his winning of Lady Mary in Act 3. In the first case, the single red light shining on his face reveals, according to the stage-directions, 'a strong and perhaps rather sinister figure,' (p 382). His subjugation of the others is shown more clearly in the earliest known draft, where the proudest of the aristocrats, Lady Mary (absent in all later versions) enters last, squats down with the others 'and buries her face in her hands.' The butler's control over his past masters, now reduced to near-animalism, is complete.

That Barrie wished to give the dominating Crichton an even higher profile is revealed when the stage history behind his proposal to Lady Mary is examined. Even in the text known to us, he takes pleasure in watching the degree to which the earlier haughtiness survives yet is controlled:

> CRICHTON: Frown at me, Polly, there you do it at once. Clench your little
> fists, stamp your feet, bite your ribbons.   (p 384)

Like Babbie in *The Little Minister*, Mary at once shows rebellion and a love of being cowed; accepts male strength and is willing to turn her own strivings for sovereignty into an act at her master's pleasure. Irene Vanbrugh, however, reveals that originally Barrie had wished for an even harsher effect with Crichton treating his wife as 'a pretty waitress'. 'The play,' she adds, 'had become so full of humanity that this treatment seemed to strike a wrong note.' Barrie was urged to rewrite by Boucicault and, the next day, 'brought to the theatre a scene full of fancy and true romance.' [97]

While most critics see Crichton's movements towards Kingship[98] in psychological terms judged against Christian morality and so condemn him for pride, I am sure that Barrie wished to suggest that this was the logical direction in which his benevolent despotism was moving. (Loam and the others do not resent his increasing lordliness; Crichton himself accepts it, almost sadly, as 'the voice of Nature', p 397.) His ultimate moment of heroism, when he fires the beacons is not, primarily, a welcome return to humility. It is the acceptance of the Nietzschean 'conscience'. Positively, conscience is, for Nietzsche, a sign of man's most significant movement away from the bestial. ('That change which occurred when he found himself finally enclosed within the walls of society and of peace')[99] Negatively, it is a sign that, until the Superman arrives, the hero has to serve as bridge to the next social order. He eases transitions by acting as both master and minster, rather than being himself the next evolutionary goal.

> Man is a rope, fastened between animal and superman . . . What is great in man is that he is a bridge and not a goal.[100]

Only on this reading does Barrie's crucial stage direction make any sense.

> Then comes the great renunciation. By an effort of *will*[101] he ceases to be an erect figure; he has the humble bearing of a servant. (p 403)

This is not humility linked to a negating of self; it is a stoical reinterpretation of the Hero's rôle within the evolutionary process. Only by fulfilling his potential to its fullest on the Island has Crichton found the means to signal a return to Edwardian England (the beacons). He now suffers intensely, as the Nietzschean Hero must.[102] He accepts the rôle of servant; he even wills on himself a physical change suggesting a reversion to primitivism/servility; he sacrifices his opportunity to mate at the highest level of 'natural selection' with Lady Mary. Indeed his obedience to the mysterious process of Nature is as unquestioning as any Saint's submission to the believed will of God. He knows, though, that he will not return to a world unchanged. Just as the Romance form of the play dictates that knowledge gained in the fantasy world will condition the audience's response to 'London re-visited', so evolution dictates that the Hero is the catalyst of progress. Crichton merely waits to see what his new function may be; that he will have such a function, he does not doubt.

If Nietzsche's treatment of Will and Conscience helps to define Crichton's actions in relation to society, the German philosopher's thinking on lethargy and comfort accurately focuses the latest instalment in Barrie's continued assault on the smugness of effete Victorian/Edwardian society. Given that the Will-to-Power was the root of all effective energy, it followed that the weak or powerless were characterised by sleep and lethargy.[103] In Act 1 the ladies in particular — even Lady Mary — are comically presented as victims of these non-powers:

> ERNEST: [*a little piqued, and deserting the footstool*] Had a very tiring day, also, Mary?
> LADY MARY: [*yawning*] Dreadfully. Been trying on engagement-rings all the morning. (p 347)

Nor is it irrelevant that the last, mimed sequence of this Act involves Mary falling asleep while her sisters Catherine and Agatha rest. Crichton delivers these sad victims of a sick society from the misery of drawing-room dominance to the excitement of service in a more active world. The ladies move from undifferentiated lethargy to fulfilled healthiness in rôles varying from Mary's hunting to Agatha's domesticity. Crichton himself, moves not from servitude to kingship but from vicarious to actual power and finally to threatening non-alignment. Loam only *appears* to rule in England. Actually, Crichton controls on his behalf. The extent of his Lordship's abrogation of real power is finally revealed when Mary appeals to him to restate the old hierarchy on the island:

> LADY MARY: [*still anxious*] Father, assert yourself.
> LORD LOAM: I shall assert myself. Call Crichton. (p 376)

In this brief exchange, Barrie conveys an ironic message fraught with political and philosophical implications. We confuse the medium with the message at our peril.

The opposition between will and lethargy is presented beside another Nietzschean polarity — comfort and confrontation. Here medium and message fuse.[104]

The artist-master faces the world and recreates in images fit to comfort the slave. Not only does this describe the controlling considerations behind Barrie's dramatic art; within *The Admirable Crichton* as specific text Crichton spends Act 1 confronting the difficulties posed by Loam's radicalism. Like a good stage-manager he rearranges his 'players' and adapts their speeches in order to comfort his master. The island régime in Acts 2 and 3 results from his confronting the savage power of Nature before submitting to social conscience and sacrificing his own government in the best interests of the ruled. Finally, when he is back in England and they have disappointingly returned to their old selves, he confronts acerbic curiosity in the person of Lady Brocklehurst. Once more he rearranges the world to protect the Loam household, this time through the careful use of language:

> LADY BROCKLEHURST: [*sharply*] Well, were you all equal on the island?
> CRICHTON: No, my lady. I think I may say there was as little equality there as elsewhere.
> LADY BROCKLEHURST: All the social distinctions were preserved?
> CRICHTON: As at home, my lady.   (p 416)

But if he is stage-manager, Barrie is author; if Crichton rearranges language to control yet serve the Loams, Barrie uses the full text to control yet serve us as audience.

Barrie: Power in Art

The degree to which *The Admirable Crichton* is a play about language and literature has not been adequately recognised. Yet, Nietzsche's great exemplars of the Will-to-Power were usually artists — Goethe, Beethoven, Stendhal, Heine, Wagner, David and Napoleon,[105] only gain entry after their literary credentials have been checked. Shakespeare is valued primarily for his dramatic translation of the Will-to-Power:

> When I seek my ultimate formula for Shakespeare I only find this: he conceived of the type of Caesar.[106]

Barrie, like Nietzsche, saw himself as a heroic creator of heroic fictions. In *Sentimental Tommy,* the idea that the artist alone possesses control recurs frequently.

> I have a power over you that you cana resist!
>
> (*Sentimental Tommy.* p 449)

boasts Tommy, referring to his writings. In a perspectivist world only the artist as interpreter of life's variety can, through his imaginings, manipulate the fate of others. So, Tommy's 'professional' love letters *may* help but *do* influence the love-life of their recipients:

> Betsy . . . felt so sorry for her old swain that, forgetting she had never loved him, she all but gave Andrew the go-by and returned to Peter. As for Peter . . . he carried Betsy's dear letter in his oxter pocket and was inconsolable.
>
> (*Sentimental Tommy*. p 418)

Like Nietzsche, Barrie places the mythic, fairytale artist (and thus himself) above theologians (McLauchlan), moralists (Ogilvy) and naturalist writers. In short, he invites us with Ogilvy to submit and admire the writer-genius who 'imagines' rather than directly experiences; worships the word and style:

> 'The laddie is a genius! . . . Who knows,' replied Mr Ogilvy, 'but what you may be proud to dust a chair for him when he comes back.'
>
> (*Sentimental Tommy*. p 440)

I have already suggested that, far from being the modest man created by Toole, Barrie believed he possessed that genius in even greater degree than Tommy. Later evidence has strengthened this view. It is this belief in his own genius which allows him to link a major study of power in action (Crichton) with control/manipulation in Art (Barrie). If Crichton organises on the Island, so the dramatist is overtly organising within the text.

If Crichton controls Nature's complexity through division of labour within a benevolent tyranny, so Barrie organises dramatic mimesis of Nature within his most effective dramatic structure so far. First, he develops the leitmotivs (verbal and visual) with which he had experimented in *The Wedding Guest* and *Quality Street*. These constrain the ever-expanding material of multiple texts, visions, personalities which, unrestrained, would give the (theatrically impractical) chaos of a Joycean plot. For example, the rejected title, *Circumstances alter Cases,* is used as a statement by Crichton and by Lady Mary as a question. These remarks occur at the end of Act 1 and so are allowed to linger in the minds of the audience. Then the curtain rises on The Island. There, the thesis is tested:

> LADY MARY: I wonder what he meant by circumstances might alter cases.
>
> (p 364)

Later, at the start of Act 3, Lord Loam pauses for a moment in his chirping to use the phrase as an explanation of his easy transition from misery at the top of one hierarchy to joy at the foot of another. Like Dickens, Barrie simplifies his central statement by encapsulating it in an easily remembered, often-repeated phrase.[107]

The other recurring phrase in the drama is 'to play the game'. Initially, it merely defines the philosophy of the easygoing, cricket-playing clergyman, Traherne. His ability at the sport has raised him faster in the church than his theological expertise would justify. Yet he brings the same spirit of modest endeavour to the island. The phrase is then appropriated by Crichton at the crucial moment when he has to decide whether or not to signal for the ship and by Lady Mary when she decides to confess to her fiancé. It highlights in these instances both the seriousness of the issues and the fictive context in which they are set. In much the same way Medieval dramatists stressed the word 'gomen' (game) to claim that high seriousness was not inconsistent with artistic presentations, though protected from too precise a theological judgement by that fiction. Barrie uses his version of the technique to remind us that even the most painful of personal moments remain part of a dream, fittingly presented through imaginative writing.

Following the Ibsenite example, again, he uses visual or primarily visual leitmotivs to suggest, while controlling complex ideas. Interestingly, the two most obvious examples are characterised by their dramatic non-existence. What we watch is their *not* being visible. Yet, that remains part of the *seen* experience of the play. The hairpin, which is the centre of the first major and decisive quarrel on the Island, is not there because Loam disdained to pick it up. He sees no use for it at all; the ladies define its use in terms of the order they have left; only Crichton sees a practical use for it in their new setting. Once he has established that, he builds imaginatively upon it, so proving who must be their leader:

> CRICHTON: From that hairpin we could have made a needle; with that needle we could, out of skins, have sewn trousers — of which your lordship is in need.   (p 379)

Events focus on and ideas develop from a sign that isn't where it should be.

Food is the most powerful leitmotiv of all. Act 1 opens with a tea-party at which nobody really eats and Act 4 ends with a dinner which takes place offstage. In an age of decadent luxury food is an adjunct to living. In Act 2, food either escapes those who are defeated by Nature (Loam and the turtle) or is energetically pursued and captured by latter-day hunters (Lady Mary), who contest its power. The final, wordless movement in Act 2 centres round a pot whose contents remain unseen by the actors, though it graphically symbolises Crichton's establishing his power over the others through Nature:

> Once or twice, as Nature dictates, Crichton leans forward to stir the pot, and the smell is borne westward. He then resumes his silent vigil.
>
> (p 382)

The fact that Crichton's food attracts through smell, theatrically evoked, emphasises the mystic, unseen power he serves. That power depends on a fiction within a fiction.

In Act 3 there is a real dinner-party at which Crichton proposes to Lady Mary. Significantly, she is at once the producer (huntress) of food and the server (waitress) of it. She is thus seen as the servant of Nature and of Nature's servant (Crichton). The proposal of marriage goes along with a movement away from waitress status, though not without memory of how (like Tweeny in England) she will have been raised by the Master. Many other central ideas are proposed by the presence or absence of food as highlighted by the formal patterns of the play. Act 1 has the servants receiving a small redistribution of the meal they have prepared as apparent reward for making their lives actually miserable. Act 3 has the master receiving his share of food, none of which he has provided, as a real reward for making everyone's life contented. That is one set of contrasts. Act 2 dramatises the power of appetite in a society where hunger threatens and satirises the inability of the lethargic, the uninventive and the impractical to satisfy it. Act 4 dramatises the unimportance of appetite in a society where hunger is unknown yet the lethargic, the impractical and the uninventive are provided with it. In the one case a symbolic pot stands at the centre with Crichton and draws the aristocrafts to the centre of the stage as defined by the red light; in the other case a fictive meal draws them offstage into the darkness of the wings again at Crichton's behest. Barrie, also, can 'play the game'.

This type of dramatically structured thought simplifies but also polarises. Two other devices, one visual and one verbal, confirm this method while stressing Crichton's power-position particularly. The habit of rubbing one's hands together as if washing them is used as a sign of servility by Barrie. It is a characteristc of Crichton the butler, particularly in relation to Lady Mary, the most aristocratic of the aristocrats. On the island she adopts the same characteristic when faced by Crichton the ruler. Having secure rather than insecure power, he does not need the sign of it:

> CRICHTON: Polly, there is only one thing about you that I don't quite like. That action of the hands. (p 396)

The opposing symbol of regality is Crichton's cloak, the source and emblem of his kingly longings.[108] When, finally, he accepts Nature's sea-call and resumes his servile status the actor is instructed to 'let the cloak slip to the ground' and 'make his hands come together as if he were washing them.' Here, different contexts and the same gesture suggest opposed types of master/servant relationship while that gesture, opposed to the sign of the cast-off robe, embodies the transition from real master under one code to apparent servant under another.

If, so far, the control of the Artist has been related to specifically dramatic devices, mainly drawn from Ibsen, the use of Names as economic vehicles of thought relates to literature more broadly and leads into specific echoes from other texts. And if the Names convey ideas; these references usually communicate a sense of superiority over the authors challenged.

The literary and martial qualities of the original Crichton have already been discussed. Self-evidently, therefore, the creative, visionary leader of the Island hierarchy has a glorious name suggestive of more heroic eras. That name is set against Loam. Loam or clay soil is not only literally earthbound, it is of its nature degenerate being mixed with decaying animal and vegetable matter. Nominally the two contrast in the most extreme form possible.

But names are also used more subtly. In England, the servants are defined by utilitarian nicknames ('Tweeny') or, condescendingly, by surname ('Fisher'). On the Island the domestics, formerly the aristocrats, are given friendly nicknames ('Polly'), so emphasising the benevolent side of a near despotism. Language here re-defines as well as describes. Names, also, draw in the various literary associations which suggest Barrie's belief in the superiority of his own Art. Most obviously, Ernest the superficial, witty, self-indulgent employer of the epigram links us to Wilde via *The Importance of Being Earnest*. Barrie thus calls attention in a play which uses language very precisely to a contemporary who was then regarded (fairly or unfairly) as a rhetorical dandy with a selfishly cavalier attitude to Art.[109] Logically, the artist-hero must suggest superiority over his fellow-craftsmen at least within the boundaries of his own type of Art.

Comparisons with other tales of island adventure are suggested in *Crichton*, usually within a context which reflects the Scottish author's greater literary sophistication. On Barrie's Island practical ability has much greater importance than in Edwardian England. There, literature (at first anyway) has only utilitarian value. It is, therefore, significant that the initial confrontation between Crichton and Loam, shows the former successful in work and the latter unsuccessful in applying book-knowledge to his new situation. The precise portion of dialogue is crucial:

> LOAM: Then I began to feel extremely hungry. There was a large turtle on the beach. I remembered from *The Swiss Family Robinson* that if you turn a turtle over he is helpless. My dears, I crawled towards him. I flung myself upon him — [*here he pauses to rub his leg*] — the nasty spiteful brute.
>
> LADY MARY: You didn't turn him over?
>
> LOAM: [*Vindictively, though he is a kindly man*] Mary, the senseless thing wouldn't wait; I found that none of them would wait.   (p 374)

The economic subtlety of this brief interchange shows Barrie to be moving to complete mastery of his difficult craft.

Loam cites *The Swiss Family Robinson*, one of those Christian adventure fantasies in which Nature is reinterpreted in 'other cheek' terms.[110] The experiences of primitivism not only confirm the Hero-Robinsons in their charity; the animals charitably 'turn over' to provide them with the necessary food. Not only is this theologically simplistic and sophistical (why should only the *animals* suffer and sacrifice themselves?), it is dishonest fantasy. If literature has a basic utilitarian function, then Loam has, to that degree, been unfortunate through being misled. But surely, that is to weaken the effect of Crichton's victory? Barrie covers this in two ways.

First, Loam has only to examine his own reaction to sense the invalidity of his literary exemplum. 'Though he is a kindly man', one tussle with Nature turns him to vindictiveness. He cannot learn quickly from experience. He has also misused his authorities. The example of the turtle does not come from *The Swiss Family Robinson* but from Marryat's *Masterman Ready*.[111] Loam neither understands the natural nor the literary world, a dual indictment which is savagely conveyed by making him lose out to a turtle via a misquotation of an inadequate philosophy within a bad fantasy whose relevance is misunderstood in relation both to his own conduct and Nature's. All this is conveyed to the highest level of an 'ideal' audience[112] in one speech. Every word in the interchange has value, though. The word 'senseless' reflects ironically on animal senses and Loam's lack of common sense. The trauma of Tommy Sandys, unable to find the perfect word, has not been imaginatively valueless. The perfect embodying word may exist only mystically but precision via Roget[113] remains a responsible compromise.

Inevitably, *The Admirable Crichton* also invites comparison with *Treasure Island*, the best known adventure story of all at that time. Although Barrie admired and liked Stevenson, he was conscious that the view of society advanced in *Treasure Island* was essentially static. True, Jim Hawkins shows amazing initiative; true, there are shifting loyalties but adventure rules over philosophical enquiry and, generally, Stevenson assumes that the natural hierarchy established in British society will be ruffled rather than overturned when faced with barbarism. The most extreme example of this belief is the butler Joyce, who has a rather larger part in the earlier, serialised version of the story.[114] In both texts, he retains a servility which (in some instances) threatens to verge on farcical heroism:

> 'If you please, sir,' said Joyce. 'If I see any one am I to fire?'
> 'I told you so!' cried the captain.
> 'Thank you sir,' returned Joyce with the same quiet civility.[115]

His constant need for orders marks him out as a different type of butler, unlikely to aspire to kingship in any society!

Such echoes are not mere embellishments. Barrie has evolved an aesthetic vision which assumes a new challenge for the writer — as possible understudy for an absent God. He has used such echoes before and will do so again — notably in *Little Mary*. Although in so doing he issues a witty challenge, there is little real sense of condescension. Marryat and Stevenson, he admired; Wyss he had outgrown; Wilde's strengths — particularly his comic strengths — he was aware of. Dickens he idolised but saw as focusing his genius within the novel, despite frequent reservations and flirtations with the theatre.[116] Sharing similar artistic problems and intentions, they had — through genre — moved outside direct rivalry. It is in this spirit, I am sure, that Crichton's acceptance of a servile rôle coincides with the rubbing of his hands, in a manner reminiscent of Uriah Heep.[117] Heep, it should be remembered, coveted power, using false humility as the stalking-horse of overweening ambition. ('I am very umble to the present moment. Master Copperfield, but I've got little power!'). Like the Crichton of Barrie's original intentions, he is a threatening figure with depths of darkness and the red spotlight which picks out the butler's face on his assumption of mastery at the end of Act 2 may be more than an accidental repetition of that scene when first Copperfield sees through Heep's manipulative cruelty.

> I recollect well how indignantly my heart beat, as I saw his crafty face, with the appropriately red light of the fire upon it, preparing for something else.
>
> (*David Copperfield*, Chapter 25)

If so, the literary association highlights by contrast the honesty and altruism of Barrie's hero.

These appeals to the language of Art provide further economic controls addressed to a limited section of Barrie's audience. The vexed question of language's limitations as communication is also introduced via a dramatic hierarchy moving upwards towards sophistication as it moves down the ranks of Edwardian society. The most primitive communicator is Lord Loam who plays a concertina as backing to lyrics which seem to suggest that he is 'a chickety chickety chick chick'. The fact that he barely aspires to accepted words at all and so exists at a level below the simplest of folk songs is made clear in the earlier drafts. There, his animal noises are set beside Tweeny's singing of a brief ballad beginning:

> In a little cot in a quiet spot
> About a mile and a half from town
> Dwells a maiden fair with nut brown hair
> And I'll meet her when the sun goes down.[118]

Crichton alone brings literature to the island. His choice, W E Henley, is ultimately utilitarian. Henley, like Crichton, is a Tory politically, subscribing in the words of one biographer to that brand of 'Toryism [which advocated] a broad doctrine of individual freedom within the fabric of a firm but self-reformative social structure.'[119] Victorian England had represented one type of hierarchical society but necessarily this would give way to another.

Henley also shared with Nietzsche and Barrie the belief that earlier, heroic eras had provided a better framework for the strong man's philosophy and for the master poet's ability to speak directly to an audience who could face hard truths. Longingly he looked back to the age of Homer, when all was 'energy and tact and valour and resource as became the captain of an indomitable human soul.'[120] In this sense he is not only the poet of Crichton the butler-king, whose character he might well here be describing, but also of his predecessor the Admirable Crichton. The idea of life as a struggle for power is spelt out clearly in the Henley poem which Crichton uses to introduce his proposal to Mary. 'I was a king in Babylon,/ And you were a Christian slave' are lines from Henley's 'To WA' (Echoes xxxvii). The poem argues out the view of sexual love as a relationship demanding dominance and submission, first depicted by Barrie in *The Little Minister*. It also reminds us that the social inversions we have just witnessed in the limited duration of one dramatic performance are repeated over and over again, with variations, throughout history.[121]

Loam's tunes, Tweeny's song, Crichton's poetry may trace at once a rough development in time and sophistication; all are, however, failures if judged against ideal standards. Indeed, arguably in these terms, music is the least inadequate being the least anxious to set up perfectionist claims in its mimetic relationships. Those claims were reserved for the Universal Language as aspired to by Bacon and others. Can it be a coincidence that Sir Thomas Urquhart's *Jewel*, setting for the seventeenth century version of James Crichton's adventures, is a work advertising just such a language? Copies of Urquhart's book were not exactly thick on the ground in Barrie's day but they were readily available. If Sir James had read one such, he would be aware that this most central (eponymic) literary echo of all unified the nominal, poetic and linguistic controls, so rivalling aesthetically the military and practical powers of his hero.

Urquhart's 'Logopandecteision' is a language which, he claims, possesses the largest and most precise vocabulary ever known. Further, its grammar — being based on the 250 'prime radices' [122] to which Nature's variety may be reduced — does not accidentally refer to the world but conveys it schematically:

> . . . no language ever hitherto framed hath observed any order relating to the thing signified by them; for if the words be ranked in their alphabetical series, the things represented by them will fall to be in several predicaments; and if the things themselves be categorically classed, the word whereby they are made known will not be tyed to any alphabetical rule.[123]

Given such a medium, Tommy Sandys might still have been lost for his word, but he could have deducted the area for search at once. He would also have approved of Urquhart's supreme gesture towards literature as 'utility'. The vocabulary of this language is held back. Urquhart, whose Royalist loyalties had landed him in jail after the Battle of Worcester, promised the 'dictionary' to Cromwell in return for his release. If Tommy might feel dwarfed when setting his power over peasants through love letters, against the 'key to all philosophies' offered to the Lord Protector, consolation is not entirely lacking. At least, his less ambitious aims met with success. Cromwell left Urquhart in prison! [124]

Crichton in *The Jewel* is also a master of eloquence, effortlessly defeating master-debaters throughout the Universities of Italy. It is singularly fitting that a study of Barrie's literary powers as highlighted in *The Admirable Crichton* should conclude with Rhetoric, whether we accept Urquhart's text as part of its literary code or not, for Rhetoric as a key element in writing had a longer and more consistent history in Scotland than in England. And this in its turn points to Professor David Masson, the man whose views on literature conditioned Barrie during his student days at Edinburgh

University.[125] Masson's Regius Chair was called the Chair of Rhetoric and Belles Lettres. While this points back to Quintilian and past educational ideals, it also reflects one of the many special features of Scottish education throughout the ages.[126] In Scottish schools the Higher leaving certificate still links literature and language in a manner which significantly reinforces these classical aims. Hugh Blair and others established a distinctively Scottish interest in Rhetoric whose patriotic origins can, without qualification, be traced back to James VI, the founder of the 'College'.[127] Even Robert Burns, in his letter to Dr Moore, admits that his understanding of poetry began with a necessary grounding in the principles of style:

> Though it cost the schoolmaster some thrashings, I made an excellent English scholar. By the time I was ten or eleven years of age, I was a critic in substantives, verbs and particles.[128]

If Scottish Literature has to be defined, partly, in terms of distinctiveness, this is a distinctiveness defined from within rather than outwith the discipline; from verbal rather than social or political structures.[129]

And if we seek to understand Barrie by looking at those influences which he himself admitted, then Masson and the art of prose-poetry is as sound a starting-point as any. At once, we move from absolutes to an acceptance of different, valid perspectives. Barrie's admiration for his teacher is founded on Masson's capacity to encourage and encompass views which did not necessarily harmonise with his own:

> If, as I take it, the glory of a professor is to give elastic minds their bent, Masson is a name this country will retain a grip of.[130]

This did not imply the abandonment of validity to extreme relativism. Indeed the sort of criticism to which Barrie was exposed under Masson was full of value judgements. But these were always clearly related to his sense of literary history and to an honest assessment of the misty divsions between judgement and taste. Interestingly, his perspectives and Barrie's correspond in most essentials, beginning with the belief that poetic prose is superior to non-poetic prose;[131] carrying on through the assumption that Fantasy (by granting to its practitioner the power of 'providence over the mimic world he has framed'[132]) is the highest type of imaginative art; and culminating in an acceptance that great artists will address ultimate questions — not necessarily to the exclusion of the social or particular — but in the spirit and under the hierarchical thematic arrangements of the allegorical mode. That Dickens stands at the head of Masson's queue of modern novelists could have been deduced from the following:

> While on the one hand, our novelists are striving after a clear rendering of life as it is throughout all ranks of society and all professions, on the other hand, we find in some novelists, and sometimes where this virtue of Realism exists in the highest degree, a disposition to vindicate for the novel also that right of ideality which is allowed to metrical poetry, and so to introduce in their novels incidents, scenes, and characters not belonging to the ordinary world but holding their tenure from the sway of phantasy.[133]

So far as I know, no-one has commented that this explicit praise (retrospectively) of Dickens' novels coincides with prophetic praise of Barrie's practice in the other major genre which 'descended' from verse to prose without necessarily relinquishing its claims to the poetic. This angle of approach also leads naturally to the discovery that Barrie's last artistic 'control' in *Crichton* resides in relating style 'decorously'[134] to meaning.

As the aristocrats are those most obviously altered by the return to savage surroundings, it is their rhetoric which alters most obviously. Traherne, alone, retains the same style because his unassuming nature remains unchanged. Lord Loam, by way of contrast, proposes a radical vision which not only runs counter to the wishes of everyone else but is basically hypocritical, revealing his complete ignorance of the problems he is addressing. This is reflected in a language characterised by unended sentences, usually completed by Crichton. To the ignorance of incomplete sense is added the ignorance of psychological disinterest conveyed by language of interchangeable terminology:

> LOAM: A very fine boy. I remember saying so when I saw him; nice little fellow.
> TOMPSETT: Beg pardon, my lord, it's a girl.
> LOAM: A girl? Aha! ha! ha! exactly what I said. (p 353)

Phrases are as irrelevantly interchangeable as Tompsett's offspring. This depth of unconcerned ignorance, finally, is translated by his failure even to remember a proverb, the lowest sort of received knowledge:

> LOAM: I first heard it many years ago, I have never forgotten it. It constantly cheers and guides me. That proverb is — the proverb is — that proverb was — the proverb I speak of —
> [*He grows pale and taps his forehead*]
> LADY MARY: Oh dear, I believe he has forgotten it. (p 357)

The Island experience rescues him from delusions of democracy and returns him to simple speech and music, but he resumes his old habits in word and action finally.

Ernest begins with the smug self-indulgence of the epigram, a figure of speech used as much with the intention of reflecting credit on the user as of transmitting meaning:

> LADY MARY: Tell me, what did Mr Ernest mean by saying he was not young enough to know everything.
> CRICHTON: I have no idea, my lady.
> LADY MARY: But you laughed.
> CRICHTON: My Lady, he is the second son of a peer. (p 354)

His self-satisfied hypocrisy continues with the sham of his apparently spontaneous speech. (It is prepared down to the very spot on which he will give it). On the Island, his epigrams are soaked out of him by regular immersions in a bucket but he recovers on his return to the even deeper disgrace of writing a novel, which is an extended lie and (like the epigram) justified only by misusing language in order to provide himself with undeserved praise. Every heroism on the island, it appears, has been performed by Ernest; the butler gets 'a glowing tribute in a footnote.'

In the First Act, Lady Mary alternates between commands and lethargic silences. The latter suggest a society lapsing into decadence:

ERNEST: I don't wish to fatigue you, Mary, by insisting on a verbal answer,
but if, without straining yourself, you can signify Yes or No, won't
you make the effort?   (p 347)

On the Island, silence is converted into an energetic almost breathless style,
reflecting her newfound enthusiasm for all of life's experiences:

LADY MARY: He went spinning down the rapids, down I went in pursuit; he
clambered ashore, I clambered ashore; away we tore helter-skelter up
the hill and down again.   (p 390)

Back home, her lost confidence, as she remains torn between two sets of
values, is reflected by convoluted self-questioning. It also is transmitted by
socially conventional vocabulary suddenly being invaded by the colloquial
language of the island or the echoing of Crichton as a ruler:

LADY MARY: I use so many of his phrases   (p 407)

Finally, she is faced by a series of 'truth' tests. With Brocklehurst, she moves
from principle to justified compromise; with his mother she uses language to
cover truth and lie; with Crichton she takes refuge in an embarrassed
questioning which contrasts with the haughty commands he so worshipped in
Act 1. ('Do you despise me, Crichton?' 'You have not lost your courage?').
The source of power has moved.

In different ways and to different degrees the test of language condemns the
aristocrats. What does a similar analysis reveal for Crichton? In fact the butler
who becomes king and then enigma matches these extreme changes with a style
which scarcely alters at all. On the Island, his dreams of kingship draw from
him a somewhat heightened rhetoric. But the commands of the butler,
tempered by social position, are not very different from those of the ruler. For
Crichton does not alter from slave to master at all; he moves from one position
of masterful ministry to another. In England he is defined as a servant but
controls the family he serves; on the Island he is defined as a king but, when the
moment of crisis comes, sacrifices his position for the good of those he still
ultimately serves. In every case he stoically awaits, first of all defining his
position and then maximising his Will-to-Power within it.

Of course, the Island gives much greater freedom to that will, both in its
political and its creative/artistic dimensions. The drawing rooms of England
reduce the artistic Crichton to the rôle of stage director. He does not write the
script, though he can determine Lord Loam's exits; change his dialogue;
encourage Lady Mary's contempt and applaud (while cutting short) some of
Ernest's speeches. Over the 'downstairs' cast he has much more extensive
power having earlier defined the dramatis personae, the order of their entry and
many of their lines. But on the Island he becomes in all senses the 'maker' of
the society. This comprehends the obvious sense of his devising houses,
electrical systems and being the imaginatively practical man. But he is also its
poet-maker. Characteristically, for a politician, he prefers direct doggerel-
verse, expressing his ideas clearly and memorably, or brief proverbial phrases
('Dogs delight to bark and bite.') Word power has one function for a writer
and quite another for a Prime 'Minister'.

So Crichton and Barrie are not rivals for power. They inhabit different realms. One specialises in economies of government; the other in economies of structure. The butler pursues his masterful ministry in England or Island; Barrie uses leitmotiv controls (verbal, nominal, symbolic, literary, rhetorical) to demonstrate mastery over a ministering text. But both the dramatic rule of one and the rule through drama of the other is limited. This last, crucial fact is most effectively confronted via an examination of the play's conclusion.

Crichton's Fate: Limits on Power

The ending was the sole focus for major critical dissatisfaction with *The Admirable Crichton*. There were three major grounds and I shall look in turn at each along with the reasons for assuming it. First, there are those who find Crichton's decision to leave the Loam household and the muted manner in which he conveys this compromise as an anti-climax. The Definitive Text bears this out:

> LADY MARY: You are the best man among us.
> CRICHTON: On an island, my lady, perhaps; but in England, no.
> LADY MARY: [*not inexcusably*] Then there is something wrong with England.
> CRICHTON: My lady, not even from you can I listen to a word against England.
> LADY MARY: Tell me one thing: you have not lost your courage?
> CRICHTON: No, my lady.
> [*She goes. He turns out the lights.*] (p 419)

I can understand this dissatisfaction. The unspoken critical frustration, fuelled by the Loams' ingratitude and hypocrisy, is that Crichton does not grab Lady Mary and exit Stage Left with her. The undertones (borne out by the idea of love as battle from *Little Minister* to *Quality Street*) are that Lady Mary may be hoping for just this resolution! Instead, Crichton behaves like a butler. On a personal level, it is as if Macbeth turned into the Second Servant in Act 5.

Linked to the argument from anti-climax is the argument from indecision. The Definitive ending, from this perspective, displeases because it is only one of many. Walbrook uses arch-rival Shaw and his practice to chastise the Scot:

> Altered play-endings are seldom improvements. Mr Bernard Shaw's example in this matter has been an admirable one to all writers. No eminent dramatist has written so many play-endings which have bewildered or enraged even the faithful, but the more his critics would 'rave, recite and madden round the land,' the more obstinately he has refused to alter a syllable. 'What I have written' has been the law and it is a sound one.[135]

Leonee Ormond brings her authoritative voice and perceptive critical judgements to Walbrook's aid:

> The dramatist's repeated changes to his text reflect an inherent uncertainty in his own response to the sexual and social issues with which his comedy is concerned.[136]

Again the grounds, if so defined, are secure. I have myself traced eighteen different conclusions in the many revisions of *Crichton*. Some of these are slight variations on an accepted conclusion 'type'. Broadly, however, the tonal gamut runs from the thoroughly optimistic 'Postscript' offered to a New York audience in 1931 (Crichton and Mary remain on the Island) to an almost totally sombre interpretation, also played in New York. Between these two poles, a whole variety of emphases can be adduced. Sometimes the ending is mainly personal, centring on Crichton's marriage or non-marriage to Tweeny; or treating the abandonment of Mary harmoniously, neutrally or bitterly. Sometimes the major significance is social — does Crichton site himself only negatively (away from the Loams) or does he begin to define where any future heroism will be centred (a public house; a public house called 'The Case is Altered')? Sometimes the plot appears to move towards patriotism, especially in the later war-year productions. With all this evidence, it is scarcely surprising that the most thorough analyser of the conclusions, Lamacchia, resorts to personal taste as a means of deciding which endings are 'better'. He opts for those which play down patriotism and retain a constant servility for the hero. The Berg ending is, in his terms, the best for it 'proves that Crichton's reversion to his servile self is a complete one.'[137] But Lamacchia also resorts to an assumption that Barrie must have altered his views 'about the caste system in England.'[138]

Underlying this, is the third objection. The more astounding variations include (in England) undisguised efforts to make Crichton a figure of the First World War:

> Perhaps England is in a sleep, my lady, gorged with prosperity, but it will waken again if ever the reveille calls.[139]

So Crichton addresses audiences in 1916. In 1920, with victory behind us, he becomes even more confident.

> With the rolling of the drums England will awaken.[140]

If he changes through history, he also has a geographically-defined persona. In France and America, he reflects much more darkly on England than he ever does in London. In fact, the sombre, frightening figure of dark prophecy is fulfilled most evidently in New York or Paris. Is this not the most powerful evidence so far of Barrie the opportunist, judging his artistic integrity only in relation to the Box Office?

Quite simply, that must be the conclusion if one assumes he is writing simple comedies with a philosophic topping. Given the assumption that *The Admirable Crichton* is yet another experiment in allegoric plotting aimed at dramatising the Will-to-Power in government (Crichton) and Art (Barrie), the identical evidence has to to be interpreted quite differently. I urged that the philosophy of power (as derived in part from Nietzsche, Carlyle and others) places Crichton as Hero not Übermensch. He is, therefore, still subject to Nature-in-Time. Were he to seize Lady Mary, he would for the first time be putting himself (as unchallenged Master) above the needs of society and the call of evolutionary progression. The anti-climax is necessitated philosophically. In all the variations, only once does Crichton not return and move aside from the Loams to wait the call of the future. That is in the strange 1931 Postscript already mentioned. By moving his philosophical plot to the level of surface structure, Barrie stated that this was where his integrity as an artist must be judged. So far, he has passed the first test with one minor question mark, to which I shall return and even in that instance Crichton separates himself from the established Victorian hierarchy. Only the manner in which he does this seems strange.

If the endings dramatise the limitations of Crichton's power, so they dramatise the limits of Barrie's artistic control. In the simplest sense — he knew better than any other dramatist of his time how to end effectively. No one understood more than Barrie that his ending would be anti-climactic. Thematic consistency at once narrowed his range of choice. Did he show honesty here but scrifice it through indecision before the altar of commerce?

To answer this, I must first return to the Berg typescript. Although the typed text is in many ways similar to the Definitive version, there are holograph alternatives all over it. Instead of the vague movement 'away from the Loams', Barrie writes 'in the public house', which is named 'The Case is Altered'. Tweeny is, perhaps, to be Crichton's wife. Different tonal possibilities for the relationship with Mary are introduced. Could they play the scene with mischievous grins? Should there be scorn or not scorn? An alternative final Stage Direction is also introduced in holograph:

> LADY MARY laughs, turns, sees stool R C, she vaults over it as she would have done on the island, then gives him a horrified look and EXIT R. CRICHTON stands — alone — a smile slowly comes to his face — he checks it, and EXIT R. In the manner of a perfect butler. (B)

Barrie is not, in short, changing his mind as time passes; he is charting out the various hypotheses presented by his story *before it is performed*. All of these hypotheses will be fed out in different permutations later on. The text reveals not an indecisive mind but a perspectivist facing up to one of the major limitations of art — the temptation to suggest a false simplicity through the 'inevitability' of having a single written conclusion.

If Crichton comes finally to accept the limits of his power-in-ministry as King-butler, so Barrie enacts the limits of his own power-in-ministry as Writer-therapist. Any students of his early revisions from *Walker, London* onwards could have deduced this. He sees, as later authors have confirmed, that the end in ink must always be a perversion of the end in thought:

> The writer's desire to finish is fatal to the truth. The End unifies. Unity must be established in another way.[141]

He concentrates his revisions on key positions within his own 'ordering' and of all these the 'end' is (inevitably) the most important:

> A good book may have three openings entirely dissimilar and inter-related only in the prescience of the author, or for that matter one hundred times as many endings.[142]

This, along with emphases on communication and structure, would place Barrie in modern terms on the side of the Deconstructionists. Derrida's views are, in this area, practically identical to his and arise from facing the same dilemma:

> Structuralism necessarily leaves out of account the excess of meaning over form, the fact that certain elements (of 'force' or 'signification') must always escape its otherwise lucid vigil.[143]

The evidence of Berg strongly suggests conscious perspectivist recasting rather than doubt, aesthetic or philosophical.

The reason for different versions being presented to English audiences as the century wore on resides in the peculiar rôle of Crichton. He is not *any* hero. He is the Waiter-hero; the leader awaiting his time. If History proves Barrie's premises — as it did — then the assumption of power by Crichton is not opportunistic but an enactment of prophecy fulfilled. The butler's tragedy in 1902 was that he *had* to take a side-step as the Loams still held power. Like the heroines in *Heartbreak House*, who heard 'Beethoven in the bombs',[144] he welcomes war neutrally as an event (for Nature so wills) but enthusiastically as a man (for the hour is now his). The darker treatment of English society to French or American audiences was only 'unpatriotic', in the sense that Barrie felt that post-revolutionary societies were in advance of our decadent élitism. To these audiences he preached as to the converted. The nature of the minds receiving his multi-layered message provided yet another control; another restraint on authorial power. Those minds were, like Crichton's, conditioned by the societies which embraced them and by the stage of evolutionary development represented by those societies.

Two further pieces of evidence are necessary for my case. The first concerns that strange performance in New York (the last supervised by Barrie himself). When I mentioned this earlier, I intentionally withheld the information that it was a single night and a single performance which witnessed the two extremes of the tonal spectrum. Barrie signalled the circle of personal closure in a variety of ways. The younger Gillette played Crichton in so tragic a fashion that *The New York Times* journalist commented:

> By the time the Third Act has ended you are likely to fly to the text to discover whether Barrie was writing comedy or a lucubration of the woes of the world.[145]

The curtain fell. There stepped forward Gillette the elder (Crichton in the first American production) [146] to read a 'happy ending' as provided by the author in a letter. Crichton, it seemed, wishes to stay where he was. A splash offstage interrupts the reading. 'Who can it be?,' Gillette wonders aloud. The cast still being there after taking their bows begin to discuss the issue. Tweeny presumes it must be her. But no; it is in fact Lady Mary, Gillette informs them from the letter. He then, *in propria persona*, tells the audience that (if they are nice) a place on the Island remains for them.

Here is one of the most ambitious extensions of Barrie's artistic views.

The genre is being expanded in a whole variety of ways; the blockages between experience in word and theatre are being alternatively broken down and re-established. The characters are not only in search of an author, they are discussing indirectly the nature of characterisation and authorship. To that one audience, Barrie offered the polarities of perspectivism and did so in such a way that proximity in time highlighted the crucial question of where relativism ends and invalidity begins.

Barrie's own tragedy remained. Everyone continued to read him at the simplest level and, having cast one veil aside, began their criticisms. Given a perspective view of history, any play can refer to any time and can validly be revised so to do. Barrie believed this and did it over and over again in the face of criticisms from even his most sycophantic supporters. MacKail, for example, found the 1919 American version of *Dear Brutus* gratuitously idiosyncratic:

> And then it becomes even odder. *Dear Brutus*, it continues is an allegory. Dearth is John Bull. Margaret, the might-have-been, is America. The play shows how on the fields of France this father and daughter get a second opportunity for coming together, and the nightingale is George Washington asking them to do it on his birthday.[147]

It should be noted that this extreme movement of perspective is also suggested in a letter from the author; read aloud; at the end of only one performance. In these cases Barrie presents the total drama as a valid retrospective message. He would not, I think, have seen much value in attempting such an ambitious diversion of application within the text as continuously experienced.

The second relevant version of *The Admirable Crichton* continues this sub-theme of generic ingenuity. More and more Barrie sees artistic freedom in relation to the breaking down and re-defining of generic divisions. When he was asked to adapt his play for the cinema, he therefore welcomed the challenge.[148] Every suggestion he makes is related to the unique opportunities of this new form. Time can be defeated much more convincingly and so can space. He, therefore, proposes yet another ending. Visually, he can now present the various choices open to Crichton and Mary as superimposed possibilities. ('We might see Crichton and Mary reflecting island memories. We see one of the island pictures and Mary waiting on Crichton. Then we return to Hall and get final pictures as it is.' [149]) Use is made of time transcended: memory from the *past* of the film becomes in the *present* a *future* hypothesis. Dramatic time is also exploited: one moment we see a wide range of options; the next, action forces a single, inevitably imperfect decision. Such ideas will be developed in the various genre-perspectives on the *Pan* myth. At the moment, every available piece of evidence points towards the multi-endings of *Crichton* as consistent translations of a perspectival view of history translated into allegoric Art rather than the failure of naturalism to understand its own simplicity.

4 Cartoon: Pages from my album of bores: The man who *will* tell you the plot
of *Little Mary*.

LITTLE MARY

If Barrie's critics had hoped he would now, consistently, use the narrative line for direct philosophical comment, they were about to be cruelly disillusioned. *The Admirable Crichton* gave way to *Little Mary* and a surface plot so meagre that cartoonists parodied its pointlessness.[150] It is difficult to blame them. This bizarre story opens in a chemist's shop. A peer of the realm (Lord Carlton) meets a twelve-year-old girl (Moira Loney) who divides her time between mothering a crèche and studying her chemist-grandfather's three volume thesis on the ills of the English upper classes. When next we meet this unlikely pair, six years have passed. Moira — with the Irish apothecary's books as her 'medium' — is now a notorious practitioner of alternative medicine. She enters Carlton's family to cure his niece (Lady Millicent), who has gone into a decline following an unhappy love affair. She succeeds against competition from an eminent specialist (Sir Jennings Pyke) and manages to introduce the whole family to healthier living. At the heights of her triumph, however, she disobeys her grandfather's advice and tells her hosts the source of their illness — the stomach. They refuse to accept this diagnosis and turn away from her. Only Lord Carlton remains. He proposes and an apparent tragedy is diverted into marriage.

Small wonder that most critics damned it with faint praise or no praise at all. *The Times,* which was growing blinder to Barrie's faults, dismissed it as 'little more than a *jeu d'esprit'*.[151] *The Scotsman*, which by way of contrast was growing blinder to his strengths, called the work — 'a piece of humbug.'[152] Even Hammerton, whose assessments verge on the sycophantic, could only maintain his eulogistic tone by discounting content entirely:

> The play was stuffed with such a liberal supply of Barrieisms that the thinness of the plot did not interfere with the enjoyment.[153]

William Archer foresaw theatrical failure on the grounds that the play depended for its effectiveness on the audience not knowing the nature of the cure. Once the word 'stomach' had been uttered on the first night.

> the playwright can by no means count on keeping [such a] notable trick or device, a secret from the generality of the audience.[154]

This angle had also occurred to the outraged *Scotsman* journalist, who genuinely felt that Barrie was insulting his intelligence:

> Mr Barrie has misused his great powers by writing a play which operates as a practical joke upon the audience, a joke whose whole point lies in a surprise only possible upon the first night audiences.[155]

There are so many problems centring around *Little Mary*, that it is a matter of relief simply to move Archer to one side by indicating that he was wrong. Walbrook, not without puzzlement, records that:

for months crowded audiences received the dénouement with laughter almost as boisterous as that of the first night.[156]

Archer's judgement was not only faulty in the gauging of effect; it was also faulty in supposing that Barrie wanted to keep his 'stomach' hidden! A lavish booklet was provided at later performances. There, the plot was retold and the conclusion revealed.[157] Nor was the voicing of the word itself so theatrically 'naughty' as Darton supposes:

> That horrid organ had never been mentioned in the Nineties. In the Bible or in a famous fable you could use the noun as a verb. But even in 1903, it is alleged, you could not stomach the word itself.[158]

But it *had* been used in the 1890s — by Barrie himself! Nancy in *Walker, London* may have found the noun 'disgusting' but Andrew McPhail had managed to utter it 511 times without falling foul of the censor. In 1903, before *Little Mary* began its run, the same word was being used openly in *Punchinello* at *The Grand*, Fulham.[159] Finally, a study of earlier versions of *Little Mary* reveals that Barrie had not even considered it necessary for audiences to hear the word at all. In the earliest known draft, a gesture had conveyed the idea behind the Irish thesis:

> MOIRA: [*who had been calm, now agitated*] I hate the name as much as you do, but I must say it — just once. There is no other way — oh dear —
> LORD CARLTON: Can I help you Moira? [*Whacks his stomach three times.*] [160]

If the dramatic highlight were the voicing of a forbidden word as clue to a riddle, then this miming alternative would defeat the play's purpose; the publishing of the booklet would have been taboo; the audience would have dwindled and the word could not have been in current theatrical use.

If someone as theatrically sophisticated as Archer can be taken in by this Riddle-play, then it is wise to move carefully. Can *Little Mary* be anything more than a witty detour on the major path of Barrie's thought? Surely it cannot work on a variety of levels when it barely appears to work on one? Where is the heroism in gentle Moira Loney? And if we are faced with another radical experiment in form, surely it must be of the simplest sort when the play's meaning can be summed up in the single word 'stomach'?.

Little Mary: Personal Romance and Social Satire

The romantic plot bristles with oddities. Geduld, naturally, stresses its Oedipal element. Carlton meets Moira when she is acting as mother to widowers' children; he confesses his own continued childishness and turns into a son, when proposing to her. ('Then stay with me, mother, and try and make a man of me.') The fact that he is old enough to be her father accentuates the peculiarity of the relationship. For Geduld, any idiosyncrasy of this sort becomes evidence of Barrie's subconscious, driving him on to the creation of a text whose deepest meanings he does not understand. What the author himself intended is 'simple':

> He shows himself, like Shaw, to be an advocate of the simple solution; but Shaw at his crankiest would never have perpetrated anything so ridiculous as Grandpa's panacea.[161]

He may be right in this; certainly his conclusion meets with general critical approval. On the other hand, Jolles' definition of the Riddle emphasised difficulty and understanding only by the privileged few — 'To answer a riddle is to gain admission to a circle of initiates.' [162] When Tommy Sandys' tutor solved the riddle of his pupil's genius, he triumphed alone and did so as the unique reader of a complex code:

> 'You are right sir,' replied Mr Ogilvy, mysteriously, 'the joke is on my side, and the best of it is that not one of you knows what the joke is.'   (p 440)

It remains possible that the obvious riddle of *Little Mary* conceals other jokes, directed against our own gullibility.

But if, like Leonee Ormond, we move from personal to social, from romantic vein to satiric, only another obvious solution presents itself. Barrie's famed ingenuity seems to have failed him. After all, the conflict between upper and lower classes, lethargy and activity, gluttony and moderation is a rerun of *Crichton*, of *The Professor's Love Story* and *The Wedding Guest*. Dr Ormond detects this repetitiveness:

> *Heartbreak House, The Admirable Crichton* and *Little Mary* proceed upon the same assumption; that idleness is destructive, not only to the individual but to society.[163]

But is it possible that we, like Mr Ogilvy's rivals, are still looking at the riddle of genius in the wrong way?

Usually, Barrie's dramatic ingenuity has been structural rather than thematic. Extreme experiments with form and genre have been his specialisation. It is, therefore, sensible — before solving or abandoning his riddle — to understand its framework. The moment one moves from meaning to mode the astounding audacity of the author is revealed. In *The Admirable Crichton*, two 'naturalist' movements framed the central fantasy of the Island. In *Little Mary*, we begin with fantasy at its most challenging — with a chemist who has associations with Merlin, a girl mothering children in coffin-beds and an Irish panacea for the ills of those English who seem least sick. These premises underlie all that follows in the 'naturalist' world of the Carltons. In *The Admirable Crichton*, the surface plot had been weightier than any hitherto composed by Barrie. It is succeeded not just by a light story but by one which is told to you in a booklet available at the Box-Office on entry. If ever critics had been warned to study the 'medium' rather than the 'message' in its simple form, then they were so warned with regard to *Little Mary*. But even Moult, who had detected Nietzsche's voice behind *Crichton*, could not 'stomach' *Little Mary*, dismissing it as trivial 'vulgarity'.[164]

Perhaps if they had been awake to the story-types employed in Barrie's drama, they would have seen the possibility of a more subtle challenge than the one they were addressing. After all, when Jolles came to define the Riddle, he did so in terms of meaning concealed:

> The consciousness that underlies riddling is closely related to mythic consciousness . . . Riddling also focusses on the ability of the riddler to veil his knowledge and of the decipherer to unravel this linguistic veil.[165]

In this context, *Little Mary's* 'stomach' cannot be a riddle in the fuller dramatic sense because the audience is both told the answer prior to and then within the performance. Their intellects are not involved. Is this not strange when Barrie has proclaimed his determination to emphasise the unique communicatory powers of the genre in their most demanding form at each level of understanding?

Another factor should be taken into account. Within the branch of literature associated with allegory and the veil, lack of an overt dislocation between narrative and the simplest form of reference could be a more difficult intellectual challenge rather than no challenge at all. John MacQueen, in his analysis of Henryson's *Morall Fabillis*, distinguishes between the clear dislocation of story and moral in *The Cok and the Jasp* and the much subtler 'veil' of *The Uponlondis and the Burges Mous*, where only a few phrases signal the need for further enquiry.[166] *Little Mary's* easy answers may not demand this sort of complex response, but if not, why does Barrie turn the form of *The Admirable Crichton* both upside down and inside out? Why does he proclaim *greater* difficulty within a *concealing* story-type? Why does he call it a problem play if the problem is solved for us?[167] Why is it named an 'Uncomfortable Play' if our only discomfort concerns its puerile theme? Barrie's dramatic art, as so far established, justifies us in seeking other interpretative levels; these legitimate questions encourage the hope that such searching may not be in vain.

Little Mary: Religious Allegory and Historical Polemic

The quest for further meaning in Barrie has, in the past, been aided by close study of names, earlier texts and attention to odd details in characterisation. Terence Reilly, the Irish chemist, is one of the most mysterious characters he has created to date. The first anticipation of Lob in *Dear Brutus*, he is in a sense the author of the drama, having written a book called *The Medium*, whose nickname ('Little Mary') in turn becomes the title of Barrie's text. As artist-creator he has Godlike powers but uses them for specifically national purposes. ('We are doing it for the good of the dear Saxons. For England, Moira, from the grateful Irish,' p 436). His own Irish nationality is stressed over and over again, suggesting a political as well as a theological range of reference.

Suspicions of this sort are supported by the evidence of the earlier drafts. These reveal that Barrie did want to maintain both national and metaphysical associations. The question of how to balance these, focuses on names. Here, an acute dilemma is revealed. In the early typescript with holograph additions held in Austin, Texas and in the Lord Chamberlain's text, Carlton's son is called not Cecil but Adam.[168] Already, signs of dissatisfaction manifest themselves when that name is scored out and Percy substituted. Finally Percy is deleted in favour of Cecil. In microcosm, this indicates that Barrie is at once trying to sustain an allegorical level of application with his heroine as the Virgin and a more particular historical message in which Ireland's position is related to colonisation by the great patrician families of England.[169]

The pattern is worked out with great precision in all versions from the Austin MS to the Definitive texts. The heroine is called Moira, a variant of 'Maire', the Irish form of Mary. She is initially established as a virgin whose 'motherhood' is intended for the good of the others:

> MOIRA: [*Gravely*] No, I'm not old enough to have a husband — he's my Grandpa.
> LORD CARLTON: And your parents are dead, Moira?
> MOIRA: Yes, sir, but how did you know?
> LORD CARLTON: From the way you look after your little brothers and sisters.
> MOIRA: H'sh! [*Guardedly*] They are no relation. I just take them in to mother them. They are widowers' children from near by. (p 429)

Like the Virgin she sacrifices true motherhood to give birth to the 'word' as contained in her gandfather's book. Consistently she is referred to as 'converting', not only offering physical health but salvation of the spirit:

> MR REILLY: And then you shall go out among the great ones and make converts. (p 435)
>
> LADY GEORGY: I know this — that ever since Moira entered this house I have felt the phenomena of active spiritual life stirred within me.
> (p 482)

Like Mary she becomes the key to salvation for those who believe. (LADY MILLICENT: We must not doubt her. LORD CARLTON: Somehow it is terrible to me to have to disbelieve in Moira Loney.) She does this by arousing penitential feelings (LORD CARLTON: You make me feel ashamed. p 456) Regularly she is associated with angels or cherubs and set in opposition to Beelzebub. Maternally, her problems are compared to Eve's and those of Benjamin's mother as well as Mary; while characteristically Barrie supposes that she and the Virgin must often have longed to know childbirth and the normality of family life:

MOIRA: [*Woefully*] I can do — almost anything. I suppose I am the most remarkable woman alive.
[*Smiling*] But — I don't want to be.
[*Passionately*] I should so love to be an ordinary woman.   (p 480)

Like Mary she is presented as the Universal Mother, her 'children' coming from all lands and her maternal longings being eternal. As Carlton comments, 'You want to mother the lot of us, isn't that it?' She is also seen as a worker of miracles through the power of the Word, a gift which, in its turn, is associated with her nickname, 'the stormy petrel':

LORD PLUMLEIGH: They call her the Stormy Petrel . . .
SIR JENNINGS: A worker of miracles, Topping.   (p 443)

In a play where the fullest possible meaning of words is explored Barrie seems to be referring to the original connections between that bird and Peter's miraculous walk over the Lake of Gennesareth.[170]

Moira as spiritual mother and miracle worker is associated with the Virgin rather than becoming a type of Mary. The relationship is similar to that between the fox and the Devil in Chaucer's 'Nun's Priest's Tale' in constituting part of the message for the alert reader without closing off all other spiritual possibilities. In *Little Mary* these are sometimes alternatively interpreted in terms of Christian Science with 'medium' also employed in a specifically spiritualist context.[171]

The change finally from Adam to Cecil as a name for Lord Rolfe does not imply loss of the theological level of reference. But it does suggest that Barrie preferred to point up a political irony. While the fable narrates a tale of Ireland's gratitude to England focused on over-eating, the chosen names and covert associations open up a bleakly ironic contrast. The English upper class hero bears the name Carlton. This links with the Carlton club and comfortable English upper class existence. Is it coincidence, however, that Carleton was the name of the foremost Irish novelist of the day, famed for his descriptions of the infamous Irish potato famine? His novel, *The Black Prophet*, accused the English of causing that famine for selfish political ends. It includes many passages describing the fate of the poor in harrowing detail:

Their cadaverous and emaciated aspects had something in them so wild and wolfish, and the fire of famine blazed so savagely in their hollow eyes, that many of them looked like creatures changed from their very humanity by some judicial plague, that had been sent down from heaven to punish and desolate the land.[172]

This *may* be coincidence. The major famine was now past history although there had been a more recent, less catastrophic repetition of it; Carleton's works were not widely known in England, but, as leader writer in Nottingham, Barrie became an 'Irish' expert (Appendix A). And is it also coincidence that the Irish novelist's most famous folk hero — based on an old romantic ballad — shares the surname Reilly with Barrie's chemist-author?

What seems to be beyond doubt is that Barrie consistently counterpoints the chemist's rather naive gratitude to England with persistent historical references to the Irish Land Question and the opposition between Irish starvation and English gluttony. As in *Crichton*, the starved are the mentally active; the overeaters the lethargic masters. This was currently a major news topic. *The Times*, 9 September 1902, considers it in depth, concluding that the United Irish League is a 'dangerous association' and that the Irish people still respect strong government.[173] Probably, Barrie agreed with these sentiments. By finally placing the fate of Ireland in the hands of a Moira/Lord Carlton alliance, he seems to support continued paternalism along with a more enlightened awareness of past historical lessons. His frequent 'nominal' references to the hero-politicians of the Elizabethan period provide an even wider temporal perspective. By giving Carlton's son the name Cecil, he certainly invites comparison with Cecil, Marquis of Salisbury, then Prime Minster. Barrie had some admiration for Cecil, particularly because he had announced his adherence to the same openly utilitarian approach to politics as the Scot favoured for literature.[174] In the play, however, Cecil is one of the lethargic overeaters and one might fairly assume from this that Barrie was not entirely taken in by his other pose as the benevolent, restrained paternalist in matters Irish. At the same time, the cure is placed in the hands of a wiser representative of his line. One does not sense in *Little Mary* any real sympathy with Gladstone's radical alternatives, only an appeal for more understanding Toryism. Nothing more, perhaps, could be expected from a writer whose poetic ideal is Henley.

This is to provide a framework for, not to discount the power of, a dramatic contrast between the horror of famine and the self-indulgent Saxon 'deaths' of Lady Millicent in her decline or Eleanor on the stage. (LADY GEORGY: I look on at her dying till I'm sick of it. She is good at dying, and she dies all over the house.) Barrie attempts to draw his predominantly English audience towards reconsideration of policies, which have reduced one part of the United Kingdom to poverty while maintaining luxury for another. Without espousing the view of Dangerfield that this was coldblooded intention ('Ireland was a colony where social experiments could be performed for which English public opinion was not yet ready')[175] Barrie the thinker and Barrie the Celt could not accept that 'English' solutions had always been suited to Irish needs. To transfer an English poor law, which no longer permitted outdoor relief to a country where two and a half million labourers existed in a state of semi-starvation was the sort of simplistically cruel benevolence which he sought to 'cure' in *Little Mary*. At the level of political allegory Moira and the book become the 'medium' in a strict educative sense. As a Scot, Barrie knew how often the English had failed to allow for different religious, cultural and social differences. His play urges Anglo-Catholic Tories to work through a greater sympathy with Irish Catholicism, Irish history and Irish culture. Figuratively, it translates the horror of famine into English gastronomic indulgence and side-effects such as the necessity for late marriages into Moira's own delayed alliance with a father-figure.[176]

Even Barrie with his awareness of slower minds must have been astounded at the critics on this occasion especially, for they failed to see the political relevance at all. Uncharacteristically, Beerbohm betrayed a lack of insight when suggesting that a Scottish setting would have been more convincing and that Lord Carlton should have shared the overeating. To do the one would have defeated a major purpose of the play; to present the other would have brought the saviour figure imaginatively into shared guilt. Still, Beerbohm does sense the bitterness of tone and its Celtic origins:

> I can quite sympathise with the irritation which English gluttony and stupidity must arouse in the quick-witted and abstemious Irishman or Scotchman.[177]

And he dismisses the play not as trivial but as badly planned — 'Mr Barrie does not fit his illustrations closely enough to his idea.'

Having failed to grasp precisely what Barrie's idea is, Beerbohm is on weaker ground than usual. Certainly the former is trying to achieve some unity by linking the various levels of application through diverse meanings of the word 'medium'. Moira discovers romantic love as the means of moving from isolation (Lone-l-y) to fulfilment (motherhood) but she is also associated with the divine intermediacy of the Virgin Mary and the solace offered by the medium in spiritualist séances. As interpreter of her grandfather's thesis (*The Medium*), she teaches balanced government and diet as the means of preserving Ireland and personal health respectively. Both she and Reilly are, however, first and foremost servants of the word; of language in its written and spoken forms. As such, it seems likely that they represent the culmination of a line of heroic figures, presented in the Journeyman plays. If Phoebe embodied social heroism and Crichton political heroism, only the highest form of heroism remains, that of the Artist. Interestingly, too, Jolles' primary definition of the Riddle was linguistic — it 'directs attention to language itself'.[178] Is *Little Mary's* ultimate hero, then, its own medium?

Little Mary: The Artist as Hero

Reilly writes the book, so it is logical to begin with him. The first presented detail concerns his trade. He is a chemist. If, true to the methods of the Riddle, we are looking for clues from the outset, then this is a fairly obvious one. The picture of the old-fashioned chemist plying his trade in an unfashionable part of town, while 'mother' and children share his limited accommodation, is strikingly close to the surroundings in which Ibsen spent his early youth:

> Reimann, the apothecary to whom Ibsen was apprenticed, was an amiable but unpractical man of thirty-nine whose business was on the slide. His shop lay in a poor quarter of the town, occupying part of 'a small and exceedingly humbly furnished house, with small-paned windows in both of its low storeys.' The remainder of the house . . . served as accommodation for the Reimanns, their numerous children, their two maids and their new apprentice.[179]

If we wish to discover the type of artist we are seeking, we need surely seek no further than Barrie's proclaimed master. And if *Little Mary* is composed according to Ibsenite methods, then our approach — in terms of myth, allegory and symbolism — is an appropriate one.

But Reilly's thesis is not simply entitled *The Medium*. Its full legend is *The Medium, or how to cure our best people*. The adjective suggests again the hierarchical principles behind Darwin's *Origin of Species* but the major notion conveyed is that of therapy. As a chemist cures through drugs, so the artist cures through his writings. Reilly's trade, like Barrie's, is founded on Utility. Like Barrie, too, he will go on handing out false remedies so long as the public believe that is what they need:

> MR REILLY: I understand you wish this prescription to be made up?
> LORD CARLTON: Yes, they are powders I frequently take for nervous headache.
> MR REILLY: [*The words evidently having some meaning of his own to him.*] Nervous headache, He said nervous headache — why not?
> LORD CARLTON: You don't believe in them?
> MR REILLY: [*Coming to himself quickly*] I am a chemist and druggist, my Lord — not a doctor. (p 425)

His mission is not only the finding of a cure beyond drugs but the educating of society to a stage of understanding in which they can accept that cure. From this viewpoint the play narrates his success as inventor and Moira's ultimate failure as missionary. England is no more ready for the Stormy Petrel than for the Admirable Crichton.

Little Mary's satirical power is the medium whereby Barrie seeks to prepare Edwardian civilisation for direct, harsh truth. Through fantasy he can present medical conservatism in a much more ghastly light than would be open to Shaw in *The Doctor's Dilemma*. A more naturalistic art can show greed but not someone so nominally and actually voracious as Sir Jennings Pyke: a doctor who can follow utterly false diagnosis with the seizing of a cheque for services unrendered:

> SIR JENNINGS: [*surprised to find cheque*] What, what? Ah, ah! [*twiddles it*] Well, do you know, I hardly like — after business. [*puts cheque in pocket.*] Oh, but still — accept my heartiest congratulations again, dear lady. (p 480)

As usual the visual confirms. Reilly is associated with medieval alchemy and magic. Against his mysterious, spiritual quest, the purely physical panaceas offered by Pyke in his fraudulence vanish into insignificance.

Additional satirical focuses may economically be revealed by studying in turn the revolutionary effect of Moira's teaching on Lord Plumleigh, Lady Milly and Eleanor Gray. Plumleigh as idle schoolboy is an indolent successor to W G in *Walker, London*. While W G's body was at least kept active by his cricketing obsession, his successor has just been voted 'the idlest boy in the whole school.' Not only does Moira rouse him to a life of planned action, she revives his mind as well:

> 6.30 — leap out of bed; 7 — run a mile, walk a mile;
> 7.30 — breakfast; 8 — Botany; 8.45 — Herodotus;
> 11 — run a mile, walk a mile; 12 — Latin verse;
> 2 — dinner.
>
> (p 464)

This first confirms the idea of the medium as the 'media via'. Moira is advocating the harmonious balanced life summed up by the Latin tag — 'mens sana in corpore sano' — as the personal equivalent of the middle way in government. The choice of Herodotus as single named author is also significant. Understanding at the highest level comes through the father of Fantasy.[180]

Lady Milly in her self-indulgent state of decline physically symbolises the resurrectional miracle worked on everyone by Moira. She is actually raised from her bed and wheelchair. By making her delay the publicising of this recovery, Barrie presents the contrast in its most extreme form. She does not hobble across the stage but jumps across it. Again the mode is symbolic rather than naturalistic.

If Lady Milly was characterised by one sort of false death, the actress Eleanor Gray represents another ('Dad, if you could see her die.') While Moira draws the one towards physical truth, she brings the other to a valid evaluation of her own worth. As the self-made woman, it is Eleanor who pronounces the most damning indictment on a society built on heredity rather than worth:

> ELEANOR: Your title — your wealth — they are mere accidents of your birth. I said to myself, he deserves no credit for them. The amount of sense that has come to me quite suddenly positively bewilders me, Cecil.
>
> (p 473)

This newfound sincerity underlies the changed rôles provided for all her patients by Moira. When, finally, they reject the truth about their cure, they turn back to comfort built on fraudulence.

In this connection, the very last of the introductory Stage Directions about Reilly becomes understandable. 'He is,' Barrie tells us, 'absolutely sincere.' Equally, it is Moira's sincerity which drives her to reveal the word 'stomach'. In an early discussion on the nature of Genius, Barrie defined this type of honesty as the lowest common denominator from which grew greatness. Heroism evolved through complete committedness to a sincerely held goal, whose nature depended on whether you were soldier or artist, Napoleon or Wordsworth.[181] Carlyle, whose views are brought in to this dialogue, would certainly have agreed:

> No Mirabeau, Napoleon. Burns, Cromwell, no man adequate to do anything, but is first of all in right earnest about it.[182]

Napoleon, the hero whose diminutive stature and low origins drew Barrie's sympathies, is mentioned more than once in *Little Mary*. The first two occasions set his greatness against the fatuous imitations of Cecil:

CECIL: [*folds his arms in Napoleonic manner, and speaks with biting severity. When* CECIL *folds his arms* LORD CARLTON *retreats a little in mock terror.*] (p 447)

LORD CARLTON: I can play Napoleon too. [*He copies Cecil's pose a la Napoleon*] (p 450)

These farcical mimes are played out by two men at the height of power in Edwardian England and bearing names associated with past and present English greatness. They are played out as part of a mock domestic battle over an actress, who despises their unmerited eminence and longs for revolution.

Only once is the Napoleonic parallel evoked seriously. That is when Carlton refers to Moira's final encounter with Pyke and the family as her 'Waterloo'. In the sense that this is a conflict which begins promisingly but ends in tragedy, the comparison is accurately prophetic. What has not been pointed out, is that throughout the play Moira wears a hat modelled on that worn by the Emperor. Stylised and with a large revolutionary rosette, it owes its basic shape to the headgear as worn by Napoleon in David's portrait,[183] but has its nearest analogues in the scurrilous caricatures of Gillray. The closest parallel I could find appropriately belongs to a cartoon of Gillray entitled 'Armed Heroes'. A diminutive Napoleon faces, across the Channel, the lanky figure of Addington. The latter stands, legs astride a massive cut of beef, and (as Doctor) challenges him, to deprive England of her favoured food.[184] Many of Gillray's caricatures denigrate Napoleon in a dietary context; he is also responsible for popularising the image of the Emperor as Beelzebub, used by Phoebe in *Quality Street*.[185] Barrie too was aware of his work. *The Historical and Descriptive Account of the Caricatures of James Gillray*[186] had been published in the 1850s and, whenever the playwright wished to compliment his friend Thomas Gilmour on his sketching skills, he called him by the nickname, 'Gilray' [*sic*].[187]

Whether the caricatures of the Georgian artist form the source for Moira's strange choice of hat is ultimately of little moment. Headgear has always been of major symbolic importance for Barrie as the rowan berries in *The Little Minister*, the Quaker bonnets in *Quality Street* not to mention the Greenwood Hat[188] itself confirm. Now Reilly's skull-cap with its explicit medieval, alchemical associations is set against the emblem of heroism as worn by a man whose diminutive stature and low birth drew sympathetic understanding from Barrie.

Little Mary: The Artist and Creation

The inordinate emphasis on motherhood within the play constitutes the next problem of interpretation. Whatever Barrie may *not* have been aware of revealing in Oedipal terms, he had already begun (notably in *The Little White Bird* and *The Wedding Guest*) to use the mother — Nature's vessel of creation — as a standard against which to gauge man's similar aspirations in Art. This will, in fact, be a major topic of the Pan myth. It will be fully

5   Hilda Trevelyan as 'Little Mary' wearing the 'Napoleon' hat in
Little Mary on tour 1889.

considered in the next Chapter but some comment is necessary here, not
only to chart the gradual development in thought but to remind readers that
the 'Mother' figure may loom large as a conscious key to Barrie's aesthetic
ideas rather than an unconscious sign of personal trauma.

The exact relationship between Reilly and Moira must first be
established. In *Peter Pan*, Christian myth will be used as a means of
comparing the creative powers of God and his susbstitute, the Artist.
Similarities established, differences will also be highlighted. This technique
is first fully employed in *Little Mary*, where Reilly's presentation as a
'patriarchal' figure complete with 'long greyish beard' invites comparisons
with popular conceptions of God the Father. Reilly is also the creator of the
Word, who becomes the word, 'the book is I'. As Holy Spirit and Father,
he has not a son but granddaughter whom he nonetheless sacrifices for the
good of mankind (or at least the English upper class!):

> 'My child — I am a little sorry for you, for I cannot but see in what career —
> [*Looks at cots*] — your greatest happiness would have lain. But we are doing it
> for the good of the dear Saxons . . . Self must be sacrificed.'   (p 436)

Variations in the form of inexact genealogical parallels and a narrowing of
focus alert us to those areas where the comparison becomes
'uncomfortable'.

It is possible now to see why Moira must be presented as a frustrated
Mother figure, following on from Jenny Geddes in *The Wedding Guest*.
The cot-coffins, bizarre in terms of the simple story line, are symbolically
necessary. They are signs of a Mother's rule over birth and death. Moira
and Reilly may potentially be allies in a grand therapeutic plan but they are
also rivals; rulers over birth in blood and ink respectively. Crucially, Reilly
can only gain his power as Father if he deprives Moira of her rights as
Mother. That is why, he explicitly demands of her an apprenticeship in
reading followed by a missionary existence:

> MR REILLY: I have saved money for you, my child, for six years, and all that
> time until you are eighteen you shall do nothing but read the book . . .
> And then you shall go out among the great ones and make converts.
>
> (p 435)

Without the evidence of the first scene, we should not have been aware of
Moira's natural desires to be an ordinary mother rather than an
extraordinary medium. She is asked to sacrifice precisely the years of
maternal potential whose loss will re-affirm her nominal solitude ('*Lone-l-
yness*').

As indicated earlier, this theme was one which had also concerned both
Ibsen and Strindberg. In *The Little White Bird*, Barrie had come out heavily
in favour of his heroine both as Artist and Mother. Man, deprived of the
capacity for childbirth by Nature, was the villain of that text. His selfish
claim for the primacy of the shadow in Art had been revealed as fraudulent.
Reilly is even more egocentric than the Narrator figure in the earlier

novel. He forgets Moira's birthday; he has killed both wife and daughter through using them as 'experiments' for the book and his love for the English has induced hatred (p 435) in his immediate family. The encouraged comparisons with the Christian Trinity and God's sacrifice in charity of his Son highlight the *inadequacy* of the Artist-Father who literally murders both wife and daughter for his Art. His major aim proves to be not our immortality but his own. Moira will give her youth so that he may artificially regain his:

> That is what I have grown into — in this [*the book*] I shall pass young and hale
> down the ages.[189]   (p 435)

She will forego the natural growth of the child within her to become the guardian of his child, which already has developed from a pamphlet into three volumes. And instead of the freedom over death as represented by Christ's sacrifice on the cross, she will be offered eternal imprisonment:

> MOIRA: [*in agony*] . . . I have been imprisoned in the book all these years!
>   Oh, Grandpa let me out.   (p 485)

Every detail is important. Hers is the agony of Christ but suffered because of a selfish father; the Trinity of the three books is her mystic origin but not her justifying end. She is not even permitted the dramatic centrality of Christ on the cross for she is only a spectator at the birth of Reilly's word.

Christian myth within the new dialects of Darwinian doubt is neither rejected nor accepted by Barrie any more than Napoleon is presented as all-Hero or all-Villain. Each is used as a type against which to explore the re-defining of ultimate questions. I sense that Barrie had lost his own religious faith but regretted the forfeit of certainty; I sense that he worshipped Napoleon as self-made manikin[190] as a type of action and obsession; as the product of power born on revolution while accepting many of the reservations of Gillray's patriotic vision. But his aim was not to convey his own opinions but to transmit the nature of the new questions facing thinking people in an age of doubt. His major problem, nowhere so radically dramatised as in *Little Mary*, was a fear that God's death had coincided with the demise of the enquiring spirit:

> CECIL: Thank goodness ours is a healthy-minded public, and declines to
>   think.   (p 452)

If Barrie's major assault on Art as creation is reserved for *Peter Pan, Little Mary* at once depicts and embodies the enigma of dramatic communication.

Little Mary: The Artist and Communication

The unrivalled dramatic communicator of the age was Shaw. If there were doubts about his theatrical talents, there were none concerning his rhetorical power of persuasion. Just as *Little Mary* proferred an easy solution as dietary drama, so it presented superficial symptoms of being a Shavian satire. Its descriptive sub-title — 'An Uncomfortable Play' clearly parodied and sought to diminish the high seriousness of Shaw's *Plays Unpleasant*. Its opposition to English eating habits suggested, for most, 'roast beef' and so it was linked with vegetarianism. Shaw, the best known vegetarian of his day, accepted this and called Reilly's treatise, 'a vegetarian pamphlet.' [191] The old alchemist's strident references to his Irish origins also invited comparison with Shaw — much to the latter's advantage in the eyes of the critics. Only one riddle within this riddle out of a riddle remained. Shaw took the challenge very seriously and wrote his Irish play, *John Bull's Other Island* less than a year after *Little Mary* was first performed.

Arguably, only someone who had seen the serious line of national satire would have felt the necessity to answer in this way. Had Shaw, like other commentators, glimpsed in Reilly nothing more than an eccentric octogenarian of accidental Irish origin, his latest patriotism would scarcely have been disturbed. And this in its turn leads to a singular piece of evidence for the *Little Mary* riddle. As the Shavian quotation in the introductory section of this Chapter implied, it was *Little Mary* which proved to the Irish writer Barrie's true quality. In a letter to Forbes Robertson, he judges it — 'a didactic lark compared to which my most wayward exploits are conventional, stagey, & old fashioned.' [192] He calls attention to two other factors — first Barrie's tremendous comic power. He 'brings the house down.' Secondly, everyone is laughing in a state of almost complete bafflement — 'at such incomprehensible stuff.' Shaw, I am certain, understood Barrie at the higher levels of the riddle's enigma and took pleasure from the intellectual satisfaction provided. That said, he ended his comments to Robertson by noting the Scot's popularity — his ability to please the many while instructing the few. Shaw weighed all his words carefully and when he calls *Little Mary* a 'didactic lark', adjective and noun have equal force.

If once accepts that the play, like any sophisticated riddle, is ultimately about communication, then the reason for directing us towards the Preface of *Plays Unpleasant* becomes obvious. Dramatic communication is the major theme of that Preface. It concerns itself with the unique quandary of transmitting a message via so many theatrical intermediaries to as many differing types of audience. Characteristically, Shaw's inclination is towards authorial tyranny. He regrets being unable to take all the parts himself and wishes to convey 'full content.' But he sees the opposite pole.

> It is quite possible for a piece to enjoy the most sensational success on the basis of a complete misunderstanding of its philosophy: indeed, it is not too much to say that it is only by a capacity for succeeding in spite of its philosophy that a dramatic work of serious import can become popular.[193]

Little Mary proves the validity of that remark within an opposed theory of Art. Shaw's overt Fabianism had the effect of narrowing his audience to those who wished to hear but there was no doubt about what they were hearing. Barrie chose the more dangerous path of appearing to address all but offering a text, so open and so 'maniefalde', that it could instantaneously broaden and exclude. *Little Mary* was so trivial that it drew in the music-hall audiences but it was also addressed uniquely to the other dramatic genius of that age. (The next step would be *Peter Pan*: a play for adults and children written for Barrie alone.) The quotation which heads this Chapter must be weighed carefully. Sentimental Tommy spells out both the ideal and the frustration of Barrie's Art when he laments:

> How wretched the lot of him whose life is cast among fools not capable of understanding him! What was that saying about entertaining angels unawares?   (*Sentimental Tommy* p 377)

This is a proud form of artistic benevolence. It is written after Barrie had become obsessed with verbal multivalence. 'Angels', therefore, conveys both the higher vision of spiritual being (Superman) and the limited understanding of Angles (English). Unawares, therefore, has four different references at least.[194] To a generation brought up in the shadows of Naziism, such pride is uncongenial. We have seen how this frame of thought can, politically, be perverted. Shaw and Barrie were, however, products of the dawn of Darwinianism. The former, even in his Vegetarian writings, clearly distinguished between the genius (for whom careful diet was necessary) and the ordinary man (for whom it was not).[195] It should be remembered that Shaw even hoped for a Superman, who would digest all waste matter inside himself! The image of beefsteak, used as a type of English greatness in Gillray's caricatures, was for Shaw as for Moira Loney, a poisonously deceptive image.

> He reminded those Englishmen in whom the superstition persisted that 'by eating a beefsteak he can acquire the strength and the courage of the bull', that the bull (like an elephant) was vegetarian. Some vegetarians, he added, were bulls.[196]

It would seem that *Little Mary* may be a fuller and more particular response to Barrie's major rival than has been suspected.

On this general level, Sir James is maintaining the perspectivist belief that no 'full answer' can be honest unless it admit its incompleteness. *Little Mary* is full of maximally interpreted messages, verbal and visual:

> MOIRA: The neighbours go like this. [*Taps her head*].
> LORD CARLTON: And what do they mean by that?
> MOIRA: They mean what an intellect Grandpa has.[197]

Lady Milly's physical symptoms suggest two hourly feeding and complete rest to Dr Pyke; constant activity and practically no feeding to Moira. Prior to her revelation of the true nature of 'Little Mary', all the patients guess what 'she' may be and guess differently. This is a double-barbed challenge.

It reframes the advice of Pym who drew Tommy from journalism to artistry:

> Analyse your characters and their motives at the prodigious length in which you revel, and then, my sonny, cut your analysis out . . . Stop preaching . . . Nineteen and you are already as didactic as seventy.
>
> (*Tommy and Grizel* p 20)

Monistic didacticism is not only (as Nietzsche had argued and Jesperson would later support)[198] deceptive mimetically, it is inferior art. The latter implication was picked up by Beerbohm, who chose the run of *Little Mary* as an opportune moment to draw his own comparison between Shaw and Barrie:

> The other way is to have no innate sense for the art from which you select and to disdain any effort at mastery of it. That is Mr Shaw's way. If Mr Shaw tried to be artistic, he would assuredly flounder and go under and be lost to view. Luckily he does not try. But, supposing that Mr Barrie's self is as remarkable and delightful in its way, as Mr Shaw's, one is bound to place Mr Barrie on the higher pedestal.[199]

Beerbohm was attracted to poetic fantasy and so is already instinctively on Barrie's side. But the issues are precisely those raised by Shaw in the Preface to *Plays Unpleasant* and answered by Barrie in *Little Mary*.

The debate has a more particular focus. Pym called himself a 'literary chemist' (p 9); Ibsen had been a chemist's apprentice; Reilly was not only a chemist but one whose dress was intended to remind us of 'an alchemist of mediaeval days'; Shaw's explicit assessment of Ibsen had been called *The Quintessence of Ibsenism*; it was a secondary focus of the Preface to *Plays Unpleasant*; and the panacea sought by the alchemist of old was the quintessence. Essentially, as has been earlier noted, Shaw used his *Quintessence* to narrow Ibsen into the realms of social and political comment:

> His heroes dying without hope or honour, his dead forgotten, superseded men walking and talking with the ghosts of the past are all heroes of comedy: their existence and their downfall are not soul-purifying convulsions of pity and horror, but reproaches, challenges, criticisms addressed to society and to the spectator as a voting constituent of society.[200]

But he was aware that Ibsen had metaphysical interests as well and that these were poetically or mythically addressed. Shaw openly admitted he was highlighting the ideas in Ibsen which most appealed to him. What he really objected to, was not the nature of Ibsen's message but its lack of clarity. What, he asked, was the point of labouring for two years over a play when the result is 'mysteriousness of effect' but 'intellectual obscurity'.[201] That was also the focus of Archer's objection to *The Quintessence*, 'You have throughout reduced the poet's intentions and the motives of his characters to a diagrammatic definiteness.' [202]

Unlike Barrie or Nietzsche, Shaw was unwilling to face the possibility of chaos mimetically translated into the Art of the non-answer or the shifting question. Of Nietzsche's many statements on this topic, I have chosen a section from *Human All Too Human*, which bears on a number of the interlinked issues addressed in *Little Mary*, but highlights this central problem:

> SORROW IS KNOWLEDGE — How greatly we should like to exchange the false assertions of the priests, that there is a god who desires good from us, a guardian and witness of every action, every moment, every thought, who loves and seeks our welfare in all misfortune — how greatly we would like to exchange these ideas for truths which would be just as healing, pacifying and beneficial as those errors! But there are no such truths; at most philosophy can oppose to them metaphysical appearances (at bottom also untruths). The tragedy consists in the fact that we cannot *believe* those dogmas of religion and metaphysics, if we have strict methods of truth in heart and brain: on the other hand, mankind has, through development, become so delicate, irritable and suffering, that it has need of the highest means of healing and consolation; whence also the danger arises that man would bleed to death from recognised truth, or, more correctly, from discovered error.[203]

Both Shaw and Barrie accept the first premise. Shaw seeks to cure by finding a new political 'religion', which he explicitly dramatises then further explains in Prefaces outwith the drama. Barrie questions all but the premise, writing progressively enigmatic plays, which maintain their comic popularity but are simultaneously growing more élitist. *Little Mary* could easily be regarded as a cryptic allegory of the above passage, farcically celebrating the tragic spiritual and intellectual death of those who applaud it.

The idea of civilisation encouraging fragility of body and cowardice of mind is addressed by both Barrie and Shaw. Each turns to the Renaissance as the welcome counterpart of adventurousness in life and words. Each turns to Shakespeare as the dramatic supremo of that era. With this we move to another major clue in Barrie's riddle. Shaw in his Preface to *Plays Unpleasant* convicted Shakespeare of the same crimes as Ibsen. In an age which welcomed genius and heroism, Shakespeare has all the advantages of being 'unsurpassed as poet, storyteller, character draughtsman, humorist, and rhetorician' but, like his Norwegian successor, he 'has left us no intellectually coherent drama.' [204]

Shaw finds the greatest promise of modernity in the unpopular Shakespeare; in plays such as *Measure for Measure, All's Well* and *Troilus and Cressida*. In the sub-plot of *Little Mary*, Cecil's gratitude that Edwardian audiences refuse to think is followed by the proposal that they perform another of these plays:

> LORD CARLTON: A play something like 'Much Ado about Nothing'.
> ELEANOR: Yes, that's a pretty little play.   (p 452)

This sub-plot, variously seen as extraneous and/or ridiculous by those who read *Little Mary* according to naturalist pre-suppositions, is actually crucial to the Riddle as posed. Its farcical presentation of the father/son relationship further emphasises the importance of motherhood. Eleanor at once embodies the artistic equivalent of 'false dying' and represents the lower-class work ethic in opposition to heredity and lethargy. As heroine of this hypothetical performance, however, she provides the last part of the answer to Shaw's thesis on dramatic communication.

As always, a simple reason is explicitly provided within the text. *Much Ado* is a tragedy with a happy ending designed to please an unthinking audience. The obvious parallel here is Shaw's championing of tragi-comedy as the mode appropriate for the age and exemplified in his *Plays Unpleasant*. The first satiric barb, levelled within that field of understanding, concerns the forcing of an ending on to apparently intractable material and the sudden triumph of the comic spirit over a plot which has progressively revealed humanity's most tragic inadequacies. Shakespeare can do this because he is not trying to present a neat, intellectual thesis. Nietzsche had argued that earlier, adventurous ages such as the Renaissance felt no need for the distortions of simplification. Only with civilisation did there come both the loss of openminded ambiguity and the reduction of metaphysical to social which characterised Shaw's *Quintessence*:

> It is the mark of a higher culture to esteem more highly the little, unapparent truths, established by strict method, than the dazzling, happifying errors, which metaphysical and artistic epochs give rise to.[205]

Barrie, in his turn, offered a play which only at its lowest level (and as a red-herring) offered neatness. Each veil, lifted by the enquiring mind, revealed not deeper truth but further paths of enquiry. The social, the national and the political were not ignored but comprehended; not offered in terms of didactic solutions but against an ultimately aesthetic and linguistic background of dominant and recessive questioning.

If one moves beyond this, to ask what *Much Ado* might mean to Shaw and the wider audiences for *Little Mary*, the full extent of Barrie's wit is uncovered. What might seem to us a relatively minor Shakespearean offering was, in 1903, necessarily at the forefront of theatrical attention. Ellen Terry starred as Beatrice in Gordon Craig's lavish 1902-3 Lyceum revival of the play. As she had earlier (1891) played the same part opposite Henry Irving's Benedick, she had *become* the play rather as Reilly had *become* his book. In her turn, she was already known as Shaw's 'Little Mother'. Nina Auerbach's comment on the relationship between actress and playwright suggests other elements of this personal relationship, which make Barrie's use of particular theatrical associations within a metaphysically framed satire seem nothing less than inspired:

> After 1890, lovers of Ellen Terry were delighted to applaud a mother who was at the same time unchangingly young: her stage childhood had allowed her to leap over the boundaries that enclosed the lives of proper little girls, but her stage motherhood shut her out of the life cycle. Shaw was only the most articulate of the sons who adopted her as their all-powerful, baby-talking Madonna.[206]

Moira as little-mother, as virgin, as challenger of time, as type of 'Baby B'
Napoleon is confirmed by an outside commentator, concerned only to
define the most salient features of Terry's public image, as it impinged on
the life of the 'great communicator'.

Terry was, of course, the heroine of the main plot. Significantly, as a
comment on *Little Mary*'s study of artistic heroism, the Shakespearean sub-
plot concerns Hero as heroine. Terry had herself played Hero at the
Haymarket when she was 15. Then, as for subsequent performances, a
surprising amount of literary energy was devoted to criticism of the
frequency with which Hero fainted. 'I had suggested that Hero fainting
twice is awkward, and that she had better fall once for all' records the
author of *Alice in Wonderland* in his *Diary*.[207] To note that these faintings
have parallels for both supporting (!) female leads in *Little Mary* draws us
down another path of wittily relevant associations. Lady Millicent faints
frequently as part of her false illness; Eleanor faints frequently to imitate
artistic death. Charles Dodgson was one of Barrie's proclaimed literary
heroes. Unsurprisingly, his noted objection was part of a sustained satire on
naturalistic criticism falsely applied to fantastic art. Five days after the
diary entry cited, he composed a famous letter to Miss Terry exposing the
fatuity of such an approach at length. The method may be appreciated from
the following extract but the full text should not be missed:

> If only there had been a barrister, to cross-examine Beatrice! 'Now ma'am,
> attend to me, if you please: and speak up, so that the jury may hear you.
> Where did you sleep last night? Where did Hero sleep? Will you swear that she
> slept in her own room? Will you swear you do not know where she slept? Etc.
> etc., I quite feel inclined to quote old Mr Weller, and to say to Beatrice at the
> end of the play (only I'm afraid it isn't quite etiquette to speak across the
> footlights), 'Oh Samivel, Samivel, vy vorn't there a halibi?' [208]

Associations of this sort would have been obvious to anyone in 1903, had he
but identified the Riddle's code. Barrie, it seems to me, has used one of his
own literary heroes to voice (within what Ellen Terry herself defined as a
letter-puzzle)[209] an enigmatic comment on a drama-riddle concerned with
heroism and false literary interpretations. Indeed, his own reputation and
Ibsen's at that stage were threatened primarily by the same naturalistic
blindness here parodied. And if Shaw were not guilty of so doing himself,
critical contributions such as the *Quintessence of Ibsenism* raised the Irish
dramatist's reputation by encouraging lesser minds in the directions of
simplistic didacticism, surface plotting and the illusion of life as a riddle
with meaning.

To turn finally to *Much Ado* itself, is to reaffirm immediately the belief
that dramatic communication is the principal aesthetic concern of *Little
Mary*. Then and now it is celebrated as the Shakespearean text which most
welcomes differing interpretations. If the Victorian and Edwardian
audiences had failed to notice how often characters misinterpret what they
see and hear; consciously or unconsciously offering alternative interpretations of action or language,[210] then the radically different Beatrices of Sarah

Siddons against Ellen Terry or the quite contradictory Benedicks of Henry Irving and Oscar Asche would, within living memory, have driven Shakespeare's non-message home. That no other single text could more appropriately have been chosen by Barrie as a hidden justification of literary perspectivism is borne out by this recent critical assessment of the work:

> Thinking about Shakespeare's *Much Ado About Nothing* led me to thinking about messages and the process of interpretation imposed by the delivery of messages. The play takes up this perfectly ordinary, everyday activity and subjects it to comic scrutiny. In doing so, the play highlights the act of message-sending itself, as well as the subsequent act of interpretation or, more often, misinterpretation . . . The play ends as it began, with a messenger . . . But the framing of the action of the play by these messengers signals more than that. It suggests that the 'jeu de signification' (Derrida's term) exceeds what is signified, that *Much Ado* as a whole, is itself a play of signification.[211]

Indeed, Barrie's next conveyed irony is that while Shakespeare's audience had laughed at Dogberry because they understood his inadequate handling of language at its simplest, Barrie (like Moira Loney) was faced with an audience which did not wish to understand language at its most precise. When the patricians turn away from her because they do not wish to hear an unpalatable truth, Moira is evidently a type for Barrie himself. And her explicit contrast between Victorian cowardice and Renaissance courage is not accidental, nor is its specific literary focus:

> MOIRA: [*wheedling*] Please, please, and now we need never mention it again. Let us call it the organ. Oh, and let us all look our organ firmly in the face, and dear England will once again be invincible as in the great Shakespearean days. (p 484)

Barrie has not shared her error. He has not, directly, told us anything. Like Reilly, he knows that his audience cannot face an 'uncomfortable fact'. 'It would startle them too much. These noble ones must be saved by stealth.' (p 436). Fittingly, as creator of both Moira and Reilly, he understands more than either, for Reilly finally (like Shaw) does present us with a truth. *Little Mary* presents us with the fatuity of believing there is any metaphysical equivalent of 'stomach'. Stomach should, itself, mean only what you choose to understand by it.

Indeed research reveals that originally Barrie had conveyed this too. I sincerely doubt whether any modern writer with all the advantages of deconstructionist thought at his service has concluded a creative work so subtly as Sir James did in *Little Mary*. The play ran its London course; it went on tour. Barrie then withdrew his answer as his creation — Reilly — had counselled and his other creation — Moira — had enacted. It alone of his post-apprenticeship full-length[212] dramas was not given authorial permission for inclusion in the Collected Works. Its non-appearance, if I understand the convolutions of Barrie's proudly-modest hyper-intelligent mind correctly, answers to two intensely felt personal reactions. As literary theorist, he could not take pleasure in the thought that the one drama primarily concerned with the impossibility of accurate literary mimesis must itself disappear. As a rather insecure man, who needed popularity and applause, that withdrawal also enabled him in covert fashion to signify his regretful conclusion that the audience did not deserve his benevolently-intended art. If they wished to search, the acting text and the earlier manuscripts remained. If they did not, so be it.

That is not all, however. Should anyone care to trace the play backwards through its inky evolution, he would discover that a major compromise on signification had already been made in an effort to include rather than alienate the theatre-going public. If one looks for 'stomach' as single solution in the earlier texts, one will not find it. Reilly's 'truth' had not — initially — been so simple. The Austin MS reveals the original First Act discussion on Reilly's 'panacea' to have read as follows:

> MOIRA: [*reading*] Phreen: or How to Cure our Best People, a pamphlet by Terence Reilly.
> MR REILLY: When I began it I meant it to be a pamphlet.
> MOIRA: What is Phreen grandpa?
> MR REILLY: [*secretly*] It is the medium by whose help you are to cure them.[213]

During the third Act, Carlton gets on the correct track:

> [*Exit* ADAM L. LORD CARLTON *who is up stage takes the Greek dictionary from books and consults it quietly.*]
> LORD CARLTON: . . . the mind — also used to mean the hum — ha! strictly, it is neither the one nor the other but the connecting link between them — the connecting link — the medium — Little Mary.[214]

The Edwardian audience did not fail the enigma in its original form; almost certainly the director and actor failed that, on their behalf, at rehearsal.[215] They failed a simplification of the Riddle, whose solution had first been intended to reside in a Greek interpretation of the organs of consciousness expressed in a word whose meanings were themselves legion.

Even the source for Barrie's knowledge of the phreen can be uncovered. The relatively recent appearance of *The Times Literary Supplement* guaranteed any book reviewed in its pages the widest possible intellectual audience in England. The edition for 8 May 1903 covered at length a major study of Greek thought, which contained a lengthy introduction by Frank Jevons, one of the foremost classical scholars of the day.[216] There the 'phreen' or 'phrén' was the topic of two sections, the first covering its Homeric and the second its Sophoclean use. Briefly, I shall relate these comments to the different layers of Barrie's literary puzzle.

The 'phreen' refers first of all 'to the diaphragm, the muscle that separates the heart and lungs from the lower organs.' (p 293) As such it is, physically, the stomach and so can appropriately be used for the social and dietary level of *Little Mary*. Within it, however, the Greeks placed all the emotions we now connect with the heart, in its romantic rather than strictly anatomical sense (p 293). 'Phreen', therefore, covers all the feelings of love, anger and grief which are experienced by Moira in her romantic quest.

It also stood for 'intelligence, thinking-power, memory and will.' (p 293) As such, Sophocles stressed, it was generally shared and not the possession solely of heroes or great men — (p 421) 'not to one favoured figure alone'). This impinges on the question of heroism, while reminding us all of the duty to use our minds actively. Citing Plato, Sophocles further reminds us that the 'phreen' permits the 'moral judgement [which] distinguishes right from wrong' and so 'constitutes the very basis of political freedom' (p 421). The relevance of this to the political and nationalist sub-strata of *Little Mary* could not be clearer. In the Lord Chamberlain's text there is even an overt discussion on the topic of political freedom, later excised. At the highest level of all, 'phreen' has a spiritual connotation. It comprehends the 'noblest part of man' (p 294); Homer is quoted using the word in the sense of 'spirit' (p 294) and so the anagogical connections between Moira and the Virgin, Napoleon and Beelzebub have a single linguistic referent as well.

The meanings and connotation of 'phreen' are equally apt when referred to the question of artistic communication. In terms of authorial purpose we are reminded that the duty of the writer in those days was to be 'first and last, the great teacher.' (p 295). The message being conveyed was, in its broadest sense, a religious truth ('The dominant thought and feeling of the whole work is religious' p ix). But it was a complex, not a neat truth; a challenging not a comforting truth as the later narrowing of 'phreen's' idealogical complexity into the neater opposition between body and soul suggested. It was conveyed to a past, adventurous age partly re-enacted on these shores during the Renaissance, when Greek thought was discovered again. And the word itself is an example of language used poetically (p 421), poetry being the only means of transmitting the highest truths.

If the word links the crucial idea of literature as communication which form the major artistic quest of *Little Mary*, *The Makers of Hellas* reminds us also that this was an age which believed in an ordered, benevolently-created Universe:

> No people ever more clearly recognised the Divineness of order, or showed more of what we call a 'law-abiding spirit.' Their language itself shows this; the universe to them was a kosmos or divinely *ordered* whole, in which each separate part performs its own function in subordination to the general well-being of every other part. Their myths tell the same story.   (p 421)

Barrie was faced with a different world-picture[217] but the problem of creation (natural and artistic) was once more broached. *Peter Pan* — a work concerned with creation myths — would follow. Barrie, in it, would wittily affect to conceal the identity of its author. *The Makers of Hellas* was composed by E E G, recently dead according to Jevons' Introduction, and unwilling to have his name known. (p ix). Finally, Reilly's fear of losing identity in death and his subsequent attempt to recreate himself through his book is given added poignancy by this Greek context. Few Greeks were held to keep their 'phreen' (or spirit) after death. The Greeks of the Homeric age viewed life's end with abhorrence, for it meant 'the loss of his or her real self . . . The only soul in Homer who retains the *phrenes* is that of Teiresias, the blind Theban seer?' (p 295).

The subtlety of Barrie's literary text is astounding. Perhaps it was too subtle, although Shaw clearly saw a good deal of what remained obscure for others. The accompanying booklet did give the theatre audience further written evidence to pursue the questions opened up in the speedier context of dramatic delivery. Indeed, the logic was not Archer's 'once seen, all revealed,' but 'once seen, the need to see again.' Two bleak ironies remain — one for the Edwardians, the other for us. The clearest clues on the allegoric level were erased in naturalist smugness by those who could not see. Their success in blinding not only themselves but future generations is most vividly exemplified by the non-recognition at Yale that the Beinecke Library houses the major manuscripts of a daring forerunner of deconstructionist art. There may be a certain poetic appropriateness that the leading academic exponents of the 'non-existent' text are (like Pan with Hook) refusing to recreate these texts though lack of interest.[218] Whether Barrie, with his earnest belief in the resurrection of his true message by the best intellects of a future age, would have found this situation so amusing, is quite another matter. Certainly *Little Mary* with its five levels of application *quintessentially* fused by diverse usages of 'medium' and 'phreen' in the original intention of its author, not only taught but enacted the impossibility of communicating with those who do not wish to hear.

CHAPTER FOUR

The Master and The Myth

I *Peter Pan and the Pan Myth*

All Barrie's life led up to the creation of Peter Pan, everything he had
written so far contained hints or foreshadowings of what was to come.

R L GREEN

Peter Pan — the tale of the boy who never grew up — remains Barrie's
masterpiece. It is the culmination of his thinking over many years. As such,
it serves as a convenient means of drawing together the various lines of
argument advanced in the earlier chapters. I believe that it also provides the
final justification for moving the balance of critical attention away from the
psychological to the metafictional; from simplicity, sentiment and escapism
to complexity, the will to power and the reality of the archetype. It is one of
the most ambitious works ever contemplated, with even more drafts than
usual.[1] It is also the fullest and most profound of Barrie's enquiries into
art's place in the world. If *Walker, London* heralded his apprenticeship to
Thalia;[2] *Quality Street* his initiation as a journeyman; it was *Peter Pan*
which proclaimed his mastery and after it his interests were to move into
other areas.

(i) *Theatrical Enthusiasms: Critical Condescensions*

A return to the starting point of this enquiry — Barrie's loss of critical
reputation — reveals this play to be the one work regularly remembered
even by those who condemn him out of hand. Often it is cited only to be
dismissed as the childish creation of a childish mind. Nor does it figure
largely in most Histories of English Literature where its author has, in any
case, usually been relegated to a list of minor figures. One might, however,
have expected that the paucity of the dramatic tradition in Scottish
Literature would have guaranteed prolonged discussion. If this were,

indeed, the hope then the latest assessment in the Aberdeen History will come as a disappointment. In a studiously neutral sentence, it informs us that:

> Although *Peter Pan* is essentially a story for children in it can be seen Barrie's attraction to the power of a world beyond the material one, a world of dreams and fantasies.[3]

There is only one earlier Scottish drama which lays claim to the sort of theatrical primacy which *Peter Pan* boasted and that is David Lindsay's *Ane Satyre of the Thrie Estaits*, first performed three hundred and sixty-four years earlier. However great the current animosity to Barrie in his homeland, it is surely astounding that a universally known work, a theatrical perennial, the generator of brand names in commerce and 'types' in psychology can be so briefly summed up. Even complete silence (given a clear explanation of the grounds for canonical exclusion) would have been preferable.

It must, of course, be admitted that in its own day the play did not originate in a spirit of critical adulation. Indeed, Barrie, fearing it might be a box-office disaster, justified it rather in terms of intense personal commitment to a 'dream-child.'[4] He stressed that the artist in him demanded that it be given expression whatever the misgivings of his business sense.[5] So, when it was refused by directors, and Beerbohm Tree gave it as his opinion that 'Barrie had gone out of his mind',[6] he persevered. Ironically, he used the supposed commercial promise of *Alice Sit-by-the Fire*, now nearly completed, as a means of encouraging entrepreneurs to take a chance on this dream as part of a two-in-one package. The history of the play thus subverts the personality myth of Barrie as businessman first and artist second, while *Alice*'s brief run and the 'dream's' huge success for once revealed a failure to assess his audience's tastes accurately.

It needed a man with Barrie's own enthusiasm and romantic turn of mind to take a chance on *Peter Pan*. In Frohman he found someone who possessed both. As his biographers note:

> There is a prevalent impression that Charles Frohman is a hard-headed American man of business . . . On the contrary, he is the most wildly romantic and adventurous man of my acquaintance . . . Charles Frohman became a famous manager through his passion for putting himself in the way of being ruined.[7]

He also had complete faith in Barrie. Indeed, at every level of production and direction, *Peter Pan* drew to itself talents who joined admiration of its creator with complete commitment to his fantasy. Boucicault directed with manic enthusiasm:

> Boucicault worked himself almost to death over those rehearsals: he knew every line of the play, could act every part, demonstrate every step of the dances — and became indeed the human repository of the *Peter Pan* tradition.[8]

In this he was matched by the playwright:

> Rehearsals made me realise that the finished article of the play owed almost as
> much to Barrie the producer as to Barrie the author. There was no part he
> couldn't act — or, at least, show how it should be acted.[9]

In this age, when *Peter Pan* seems safe and conservative, it is difficult to put
oneself back into the cast of mind necessary to appreciate the act of faith
shown by those willing to devote their time to a play which was not a play;
in a genre not yet defined or understood; at the instigation of an author,
himself intent on prophesying its failure. With an original cast-list of over
fifty, with five sets and every dangerous piece of business then known or
introduced especially for the occasion, any sane man would retreat rapidly
from the playwright. But Barrie did not finally convince the conventional.
Rather, in Frohman and Boucicault, he discovered like spirits for whom the
magnitude of the challenge proved its greatest appeal. Who else would have
become involved in:

> a combination of circus and extravaganza; a play in which children flew in and
> out of rooms, crocodiles swallowed alarm-clocks, a man exchanged place with
> his dog in its kennel, and various other seemingly absurd and ridiculous things
> happened.[10]

Yet Histories of the British Theatre, like the Literary Histories earlier
mentioned, pass such efforts by in silence or in a parenthesis devoted to
children's drama. One would have thought that its technical ingenuity alone
warranted more than this. Surely also the question of why Barrie succeeded
in drawing so many audiences for so long into his strange, imaginary world
deserves more serious and prolonged study than is usually now afforded to
Peter Pan? After all, it broke almost every box-office record then available.

The list of Pans, to whom Bonnie Langford provides the most recent
addition, reads like a *Who's Who* of actresses. It includes Nina Boucicault,
Pauline Chase, Maude Adams, Zena Dare, Fay Compton, Gladys Cooper,
Eva Le Gallienne, Jean Forbes-Robertson, Elsa Lanchester, Anna Neagle,
Anona Winn, Barbara Mullen, Ann Todd, Phyllis Calvert, Dinah Sheridan,
Margaret Lockwood and Joan Greenwood. For decades it was the most
coveted part in the most coveted play, awarded at the end of the season as a
type of Oscar. Eva Le Gallienne admits this enthusiastically:

> At last I was to play Peter; I had looked forward to it for years.[11]

Characteristically, Gladys Cooper was more circumspect in her acceptance
of the honour:

> People say that every actress wants to play Peter Pan and, although I was
> tremendously keen to do so in my turn, I fear I was not very tractable about
> the part.[12]

It was also the goal of ambitious juvenile leads:

> In November I satisfied a long-cherished desire to be in *Peter Pan*, which was the Mecca of all child actors.[13]

The observation came from the young Noel Coward who played Slightly in 1913-14 to Pauline Chase's Pan. In so doing he followed A W Baskcomb and preceded such modern masters of farce as Charles Hawtrey, Michael Medwin and Kenneth Williams.

The parts of Hook and Wendy were also coveted by the finest acting talent of the day, attracted to the virtuoso rôle of the one and the subdued subtlety of the other. Gerald Du Maurier's terrifying demon was succeeded by other powerful interpretations of the gentleman pirate, notably the dark lowering shadow of Harwood[14] and the freer, burlesque treatment by Alastair Sim. As Wendy, Dorothea Baird was followed in the part by actresses of the quality of Marie Lohr, Zena Dare (one of the few to move from one principal female rôle to the other) and Violet Coleman. Du Maurier's sister Angela, who also played Wendy, accepted that she became, in so doing, part of a theatrical myth. Though never one to launch into unnecessary raptures, she confessed that she did not need to learn the words as she knew 'Wendy and the whole play backwards.' [15]

If *Peter Pan* attracted more great names in its hey-day than any other play in Britain, it also moved from theatre to theatre with an energy matching that of Wendy's house.[16] Between 1904 and 1928 it had London presentations at the Duke of York's, the Adelphi, the Gaiety, the Garrick and the Palladium, with tours covering the country from Southampton to Aberdeen. In the States it had a Washington opening in 1905 before moving to New York Empire. Other major revivals included those at the Knickerbocker (1924) and the Civic Repertory (1928). There was also a memorable trip to Paris in June 1908 when, with the aid of a twelve page explanatory booklet, Barrie introduced the other half of the Auld Alliance to 'L'Histoire de Peter Pan, ou le petit garçon qui ne voulait pas grandir.'

Of course, one can cite a play's continued popularity yet leave the question of its literary worth unanswered, and the history of *Peter Pan* demonstrates nothing more clearly than Barrie's continued power to invoke opposed assessments of his work. What was evidence of madness for Tree argued genius to Boucicault. The drama of which Mark Twain wrote:

> It is my belief that *Peter Pan* is a great and refining and uplifting benefaction to this sordid and money-mad age; and the next best play is a long way behind it.

is the same play which Kenneth Tynan so obviously loathes:

> The only adult thing about Barrie's play is its unctuous sentimentality.[17]

Yet, I should contend that the greater and wider the appeal of any work, the more carefully a critic should look before rejecting it from a personal, evaluative canon. Equally, a literary historian should, with that much more care, define the canonical grounds on which it is excluded.

(ii) *Building a Definition*

This refusal clearly to define has been an unconscious leitmotiv in many studies of the playwright. It applies to all his dramatic writing but is particularly and crucially noticeable in the case of *Peter Pan*. That this play is unique, most thinking people agree, but what — precisely — is it?

No more complex question will be addressed in this enquiry. The answer could be expanded to fill an entire volume but, in the shorter space available, I shall begin with the Notebooks to discover how the initial idea was established and developed. It seems that Barrie wished to create a new *MYTH* based on classical material. The validity of this approach is confirmed by Morton Bloomfield, who also stresses the value of using the pagan gods to combine universal attributes with personal associations:

> Myths could be seen as the original and poetic vehicle of speculative philosophy, of all ideal discourse concerning nature and its first cause . . . Classical mythology had at last symbolised its more self-conscious introspection.[18]

Barrie was concerned with the first cause as his early attempts at a title in the Notebooks prove (e.g. 'The Great White Father').

Two lines of classical myth emerge in particular. Foreseeably, one of these concerns Pan:

   18)   Peter Pan.
   19)   Peter Pan as sprite inveigling children away from nanny.
   20)   Peter Pan as sprite whom all mothers fear because of his drawing away
         children.[19]

Although this seems a clear motif, it is ultimately ambiguous. Pan, the pagan god, has the name of the first disciple, type of the church. Pan, in Greek, means Everything and the associations surrounding him conflict as often as they confirm. Variously he can represent the goat-footed god dying at God's crucifixion or the Romantics' spirit of growth and ecstasy;[20] be the embodiment of evil in the old earth or the kindly rural deity, son of Hermes and Dryops.

The other god to appear in the Notebooks, as *Peter Pan* evolved, is Cupid.[21]

    2)   Cupids teaching girl to fly away.
   51)   Cupids shooting arrows into Prince.
  134)   Cupids playing Blind Man's Buff.
  204)   Cupids bring back children.

These functions will be performed by a range of characters. Peter becomes the flying teacher; Tootles plays the part of bowman and Wendy collects the children for their return to Bloomsbury. In some versions of the drama, Blind Man's Buff is played in the Never Land by the Lost Boys. The underlying Cupid-theme, that of Love, will be enacted directly through Pan and the contrasting sexual approaches of Wendy, Tiger Lily and Tinker Bell.

The first narrowing of definition, then, is to move from myth — one of Jolles' basic story types and so a development of Barrie's usual structuring techniques — to *CREATION Myth*. In one sense, this ambitious theme is a concomitant of the type:

> Myth is a revelation of the way things are, of the cosmos seen as unchanging, world without end, as it is now and ever shall be.[22]

To say that myth reveals universal problems, however, is not to deny the huge task implied. And the first major problem is how to embody 'world without end' — or, indeed, from Barrie's agnostic position, world without known beginning.

A glance at the Dedication provides us with Sir James's first answer. There is, he stresses, immense confusion over the authorship of the work:

> Some disquieting confessions must be made in printing at last the play of *Peter Pan*; among them this, that I have no recollection of having written it.
>
> (p 489)

In true perspectivist fashion, he discusses a number of possible interpretations of the evidence. Perhaps the play originated mystically, quintessentially[23] from the Llewelyn Davies children:

> I always knew that I made Peter by rubbing the five of you violently together, as savages with two sticks produce a flame.   (p 489)

Other possible 'authors' include a depressed stage-painter (p 491) and the youngest actress:

> Little Miss Ela Q May came before the curtain as if she were to speak a prologue, and retired without a word . . . and at the end thanked us as author, and next explained that her friend Mr Barrie was not in the house.[24]

These are all conscious fictions; Barrie had revised his plot over and over again;[25] he had attended rehearsals obsessively. And indeed that Dedication, after stating alternative possibilities, concludes that probably he did create it 'in the usual inky way'. The programme also grants Ela Q May authorship in the list of dramatis personae but Barrie's name still dominates. No serious doubts are cast on his authorship. He only stands aside as part of a witty attempt to invite consideration of all the implications of dramatic creation.

If man's rôle in the creative process is suggested first of all by questioning authorship, it is also advanced through the oppositions, the repetition and variation of the culture myth pattern used in *Gawain and the Green Knight*. Just as the seasons oppose one another but are repeated with the renewing of the year, so the characters in *Peter Pan* are polarised — Wendy against Tink against Tiger Lily as types of the female — or recur re-defined in domestic and fantasy plots — Mr Darling and Hook. The seasonal movement is also broadly suggested by the alternation between nursery and Never Land, while almost all the endings proposed have some element of optimism through anticipated regeneration. The clearest example of this is the conclusion (or Epilogue) to the 1908 Revival. There, Wendy looks forward to an endless series of younger selves influenced by the unchanging Pan:

> WENDY: Don't be anxious, Nana. This is how I planned it if he ever came back. Every spring cleaning except when he forgets, I'll let Jane fly away with him to the Darling Never Never Land, and when she grows up I hope she will have a little daughter, who will fly away with him in turn and in this way I go on and on for ever and ever dear Nana, so long as children are young and innocent.[26]

Though this is an explicit answer through regeneration, the possibility is usually referred to more obliquely. In the Definitive version, Wendy's final speech includes her half-thought parenthesis. 'If another little girl — if one younger than I am —'. The alternative religion, therefore, finds some reassurance in the pagan consolation of Nature.

Further precision of definition involves the mimetic approach and moves us to a *PERSPECTIVIST Creation Myth*. This has already been implied both by the varied interpretations of authorship and reference to the multiplicity of endings. Indeed *Peter Pan* has more endings than even *The Admirable Crichton* and for, essentially, the same reasons. In a sense this series of open endings is the logical dramatic mirror of a perspectivist belief, which stops short of complete relativism. For any writer, concerned with the failure of a single form to convey multiple meaning, the conclusion must be of prime importance. Brian McHale comments:

> Endings constitute a special case of self-erasing sequence, since they occupy one of the most salient positions in any text's structure. Conventionally, one distinguishes between endings that are closed, as in Victorian novels with their compulsory tying-up of loose ends in death and marriage, and those that are open, as in many modernist novels. But what are we to say about texts that seem both open and closed, somehow poised between the two, because they are either multiple or circular?[27]

Barrie's perspectivism as practised in *Peter Pan* is much more ambitious than the much-lauded experiments of many modern writers. Depending on the 'Pan' text you are consulting or even the revision variations within a single text, you have every possible permutation from Peter staring in at the nursery window, rejected, to Wendy returning hopefully to the Never Land to be eliminated by his lack of memory; from stress on the impossibility of real life in the tree-tops to a determined playing down of the differences; from the highlighting of Wendy's age (through her height and difficulty in flying) and sacrifice of virgin-motherhood to pretence that this is possible with Peter:

>PETER: Are you glad, glad, glad mummy, that I'm your son?
>WENDY: Peter I consider it such a privilege.   (MS Scene 6 p 6)[28]

The greatest challenge, however, is yet to come. For Barrie, the only possible glimpse of truth was that presented in art. He therefore attempted a specifically *ARTIFICIAL*[29] *Perspectivist Creation Myth*. This implied translating all the methods so far analysed into their literary or artistic equivalents. The fact that authorship is veiled in mystery and variety becomes an emphasis on the variety and antiquity of the literary sources from which *Pan* grew. First, there is variety of source material. Barrie is anxious that we know the degree to which his childhood reading of penny dreadfuls, adventure narratives, fairy tales and nursery stories influenced *Peter Pan*. Recent suggestions of debts to George MacDonald and S R Crockett would have delighted him[30] as he did not fear plagiarism but had a positive classical attitude to Imitation and Invention.[31] From the referential point of view, he implied, the only happening is a linguistic one, so the textual history of his play and his virtuoso adaptation of it become necessary centres of attention.

Jacqueline Rose realised this[32] but *The Case of Peter Pan* does not deal with Barrie's earlier writings and the growth in subtlety of Barrie's ideas. Certainly the full import of the drop-curtain introduced for the 1909 revival has not been appreciated. This curtain had the appearance of a giant sampler. Embroidered on it was the author's thanks to 'Dear Hans Christian Anderson', 'Dear Charles Lamb', 'Dear Robert Louis Stevenson' and 'Dear Lewis Carroll'. At the top there was the alphabet and near the bottom children carrying off a group of captured pirates.

I have not seen it pointed out that a sampler is a means by which the sewer may show off his art, calling attention to skill and artifice. Nor has it been noted that the letters of the alphabet[33] are the code by which the writer mediates his understanding of the signs of the outside world. The sampler, like *Peter Pan*, is a virtuoso display of the artist's power within his chosen medium — threads or words. This sampler refers to a further skill, the echoing, in a Creation Myth, of the play's *literary* parents. Stevenson, as one of the additional 'Fairy' Notes reveals, provided a major source for Hook in Long John Silver. Those Notes also prove that — at least in intention — Anderson's influence was so great that his appearance as a character had been seriously considered.[34] The debt to Carroll comes via Moira in *Little Mary*. As the dramatic character, closest to Wendy in conception, her name and her 'angelic' allegorical force provide Miss Darling with her second and third names — Moira Angela. But where does Lamb stand in all this? Less than two years before *Peter Pan* was first produced, a small volume appeared. It was a reissue of two essays from the

Elia stories — 'Dream Children' and 'The Child's Angel'.[35] Both consider the conflict between the freedom to create a literary child and its factual non-existence. This paradox is set against the pains of motherhood — the limitations yet actual existence of children who grow and die. By definition, this must be the central theme of an artificial creation myth. Moreover, Lamb anticipates Barrie in calling the children of art 'might have beens' and in facing up to the sad truth of barren bachelorhood:

> And immediately awaking, I found myself quietly seated in my bachelor arm-chair, where I had fallen asleep, with the faithful Bridget unchanged by my side — John L (or James Elia) was gone for ever.[36]

Antiquity of sources joins to variety of sources through the frequent references to Punch and Judy shows and to the Harlequinade. In *Sentimental Tommy* and *Tommy and Grizel* these traditions loomed large for they represented the ancient origins of literature, poised between silence and voice.[37] In the Notes, their importance for Barrie's presentation of the Pan myth is clear:

> 198) Children having origins in Harlequin (Peter), clown, columbine, girl.[38]

There are references to both in the later texts of *Peter Pan* but the degree to which Barrie originally intended this literary equivalent of the theological 'Word' to be stressed remains hidden from those who have not consulted the earliest versions of the play. Both the Lilly MS and the early Beinecke texts have a lengthy scene in Kensington Gardens. This follows the return to the Nursery but precedes the tree-top conclusion. It shows Hook as schoolmaster, surrounded by the characters of the Commedia. All the boys are disguised as clowns. With increasing desperation, Hook unmasks everyone except Peter. Nurses, girl-children and school-mistresses dance around him as columbines. Even babies in their prams look like clowns.[39] The critics reacted with anger to this scene, denouncing it as pointless. In fact, it was necessary for Barrie, being the literary equivalent of origins in Nature and the textual equivalent of authorship disappearing into mystery.

What integrity, then, does he show in allowing this important element to be diminished so extremely? The arguments of Art as therapy, advanced for *Little Mary*, apply here also. If myth has the force suggested for it by Lévi Strauss — 'a pleasing narrative form' existing 'precisely in order to make palatable certain truths about the human situation which men have always found it difficult to contemplate,' [40] then a confused audience reaction implies that the author substitute more oblique strategies. But another fact is relevant. The harlequin material did not simply disappear. It moved beyond the structure of *Peter Pan*, becoming the one act play *Pantaloon* (1905) and the ballet *The Origin of Harlequin* (1905).[41]

It is striking how often the elements of *Peter Pan* usually referred to as signs of Barrie's oddity, in fact prove to be necessary implications of his advanced critical thought. Even the regenerative myth has its theatrical translation. The pagan consolation is rooted in the idea of continuity through procreation, through unbroken patterns eternally repeated with variation. Barrie, it may be remembered, was passionate in his insistence that *Peter Pan* should not be regarded as having first one run and then another. It runs continuously and is ever the same but renewed through revision.[42] Other related traditions include the refusal to change the original costumes long after they should normally have been renewed. Angela du Maurier recorded her horror at their filthy state:

> No new wardrobes for a hardy annual like *Peter Pan*! My diary quotes that my senses revolted at 'clothes dreadfully shabby, ghastly old shoes.' [43]

The ancient constumes would even regain their power after the determined innovations demanded by Gladys Cooper. She wore shoes and old flannel shorts but the stylised Robin Hood shorts and boots returned immediately afterwards.

To translate concept into artificial presentation of that concept would have been more than enough for most artists but even MacDiarmid accepts Barrie's tireless perfectionism. A last move is necessary. The creation myth has become artificial but there is no equivalent yet in art for the interpretative variety implied by perspectivism. It need not be further stressed at this stage that Barrie equated literary perspectives with the variety of approaches permitted by alterations of mode or genre. That had been a major feature of his apprenticeship with its many experiments in treating the same theme in different forms. The choice of mode is, for Barrie, itself an act of interpretation and he moved from prose narrative to drama because he recognises that the rigorously structured form demanded by the theatre imposed its own necessary control on the complexity of his artistic vision.

To view first *Peter Pan* and then the Pan myth from this angle is to face in proper humility the vastness of Barrie's aesthetic philosophy, as stated *and* enacted. *Peter Pan* is in itself a meeting place of modes. It relies more than any previous Barrie play on mime; its characters have musical cues; in the original MS space was left for twenty songs; acrobats double for Peter; dance is a major element throughout, attracting ballet experts such as Anton Dolin to it;[44] the drop-curtain becomes a piece of embroidery and Barrie even astounds traditionalists by asking a portrait painter to design the costumes.[45] While, inevitably, this thoroughness must seem to most people a bit eccentric, perhaps even flashy, to someone who has followed the slow evolution of Barrie's ideas it follows naturally.

So far, I have confined myself carefully to *Peter Pan*, the play. But it is only one of a whole variety of different modal interpretations of the myth. These may be listed as follows:

1) Hypothesis within Novel. Tommy Sandys' next work will be about a boy who does not grow up.   (*Tommy and Grizel*, 1900)

2) Photograph Collection, with headings after the style of Marryat. Based on the real 'Pan' games with the Llewelyn Davies children. (*The Boy Castaways of Black Lake Island*, 1901).

3) Episode in Novel. Later published separately as *Peter Pan in Kensington Gardens*, it forms the centre structurally of an adult novel which on one level charts a bachelor's attempt to steal a boy child from its mother but on another continues the opposition between mother and artist as creator figure, explored in *Little Mary*. (*The Little White Bird*, 1902).

4) Full length Play. This presents the myth in a constant state of re-definition and in a mode which stresses the variety of other artistic forms which can be used in the theatre. The re-definition is constant and (theoretically) infinite. Three groups may conveniently be distinguished: a) Early Dramatic Texts containing the Harlequinade and/or Mother Identification scenes b) Later Dramatic Texts omitting these scenes c) Later Reading Texts — Collected and Definitive Editions — containing the Introduction and longer, explanatory Stage Directions.

5) One Act Play. It explores the logic of the Commedia dell' Arte, adapting it to the new post-Nietzschean view of life in art.
(*Pantaloon*, 1905).

6) Ballet. It follows both the narrative logic of *Rosy Rapture* and the aesthetic demands of *Peter Pan* without the Harlequinade. It deals with a gift of clothes leading to false pride and so, in a Scottish context, takes up a theme earlier treated by Holland in *The Buke of the Howlat*.
(*The Origin of Harlequin*, 1905).

7) Children's story. Barrie for the first and last time wrote it for a children's audience alone, in so doing betraying his inability to keep adult concerns and references out of his work.   (*Peter and Wendy*, 1911).

8) Scenario for Film. Barrie's keen interest in this new form had resulted in his parody of *Macbeth, The Real Thing at Last* (1915). His inventive scenario was, disastrously, ignored by Hollywood but reveals a great deal about his advanced thinking on genre. (Film Scenario, 1920)

9) Short Story. Barrie is defeated as playwright by his child prodigy who approaches the problem of words as code from a startling, new angle. (*The Blot on Peter Pan* in *The Treasure Ship*, ed Cynthia Asquith, 1927).

10) Speech. The idea of justifying Hook's Latinate and public school credentials came to Barrie first in short story form, preceding 9). In the end he delivered it to the first hundred at Eton.   (*Jas. Hook at Eton*, 1927).[46]

There is much more to come but the essential structure for an artificial, perspectivist updating of the creation myth has been laid down with an intellectual rigour which I have not personally encountered elsewhere in my reading.

(iii) *A Childish Play?*

The claims I am making may still seem suspiciously overambitious to many. Before analysing the creation myth further, therefore, I shall counter the most frequent dismissive arguments, beginning with the assertion that 'It is only a child's play.' There are two implications in this which must be separated. The first is the belief that those who write for children in whatever fashion are, themselves, childish. C S Lewis cleverly turned this contention on its head:

> When I was ten, I read fairy tales in secret and would have been ashamed if I had been found doing so. Now that I am fifty I read them openly. When I became a man I put away childish things, including the fear of childishness and the desire to be grown up.[47]

The key to maturity of response lies not in the topic but in the manner of approaching that topic. Barrie always refuses to make the distinction between adults and children which dictates that the former talk down to the latter. This does not mean that he denies differences but that he strives for a form which comprehends rather than divides. In *Notes on the Acting of A Fairy Play,* which introduce Beinecke 1904/05B he asks us to suspend our disbelief in order to participate in a secondary creation where naturalness follows acceptance of this first step into the extraordinary:

> In short, the cumulative effect of *naturalness* is the one thing to aim at. In a fairy play you may have many things to do that are not possible in real life, but you conceive yourself in a world in which they are occurrences, and act accordingly.[48]

We move into *Peter Pan,* adults and children, via a mutual act of complicity demanding difference only in the conceptions of reality which we abandon.

The second condescending charge is based on the contention that *Peter Pan* has no serious adult content. Certainly, it is aimed, at least in part, at an audience of children. To captivate them, Barrie first of all ensured that it would be a tremendous spectacle. Complex lighting effects, the flying of the children and the building onstage of a house for Wendy are only three among many visual surprises. Secondly, Barrie knew the importance of actually involving children in what was going on. The most obvious example of this is Peter's cry at the end of Act 4 for the children in the audience to save the dying Tinker Bell by clapping. More subtly, the opening scene with its firm establishment of children as heroes and the childish vision as the norm lets his younger viewers know that the piece is *for* them as well as *about* them. To this he adds variety not only within individual scenes but also from Act to Act. The curtain rises and before a word is spoken the clock strikes six; a dog springs up and prepares the bath; Mrs Darling enters and Peter's face is silhouetted briefly against the window-pane. Later, the setting changes rapidly from Bloomsbury to the Never Land, from underground house to lagoon to ship, from redskins to lost boys to pirates to fairies — a fascinating diversity, which must hold even the shortest of attention spans.

Not all children will enjoy it. Why should the success of a play for children depend on universal acceptance when we do not demand such unity of reaction for adult drama? Inevitably, too, its appeal will tend to lessen to the degree that social specificity is part of its formula. The following facts remain. When the *Scotsman* critic prophesied that 'It ought to be exactly the thing that will appeal to children,'[49] even he could not have forecast that it would captivate London every Christmas from 1904 until 1939 when the Second World War did what the First could not and interrupted its continuity. Eva le Gallienne records that most children found it hilarious. She wondered if this was in any part due to parental presence until first she performed for a Christmas matinée. The audience was composed solely of unaccompanied, non theatre-going youngsters. She comments:

> The children did not know ordinary applause, and they simply *yelled* their approval.[50]

Shaw was also impressed and again set about a rival production. *Androcles and the Lion* is witty and by no means a box-office failure but the children clearly preferred *Peter Pan*.[51]

Is this because Barrie presented a sentimental view of children? Hardly — he had no illusions about the drawbacks of childhood innocence. He had, after all, accused the Liewelyn Davies boys of bringing him to cynicism at an early age. Peter Pan as a 'type' of eternal child possesses all youth's attractive qualities — the energy, imaginative freedom, beauty and wit. But, behind him lies fear — the fear of innocence invaded by sexuality; liberty by responsibility; youth by age. Irresponsible egocentricity also has its villainous side and anyone, who wishes to see how darkly Peter issued from Barrie's imagination, should consult the 'Fairy' Notes.[52]

Nor should we allow the lighter, parodic treatment of Hook, which has grown in popularity since the days of Alastair Sim, to blind us to the fact that Barrie wished that character to embody the most extreme horror possible to the childish imagination. So he was to be played and Du Maurier eagerly obeyed:

> When Hook first paced his quarter-deck in the year of 1904, children were carried screaming from the stalls, and even big boys of twelve were known to reach for their mother's hand in the friendly shelter of the boxes. How he was hated, with his flourish, his poses, his dreaded diabolical smile! That ashen face, those blood-red lips, the long, dank greasy curls: the sardonic laugh, the maniacal scream, the appalling courtesy of his gestures . . . He was a tragic and rather ghastly creation who knew no peace, and whose soul was in torment.[53]

Peter Pan addresses children but it treats childhood neither sentimentally nor as a condition divorced from adulthood. The essence of myth, as Tolkien saw, is to face up to the harsh truths of real life:

> Creative Fantasy is founded upon the hard recognition that things are so in the world as it appears under the sun.[54]

Peter Pan, by highlighting the cruelty of children, the power-worship of adults, the impossibility of eternal youth, the inadequacy of narcissistic and bisexual solutions, presents a very harsh view of the world made palatable by humour and held at an emotional distance by wit and the dream. J C Trewin is surely right in pointing us to the 'thorn under honeysuckle', the essential cruelty of Nature as viewed by the Scottish playwright.[55]

If honesty is the essence of myth, so comprehensiveness is the first demand made on a creation myth. As this applies to audience as to all else, it follows that *Peter Pan* would *have* to appeal to children as well as to adults.

From the beginning, the vast majority of critics and actors accepted this. True, the 1904 *Scotsman* reviewer thought it childish but all the other major newspapers prophesied success for maturer minds too. *The Times* and *The Illustrated London News* both understood that Barrie chose to inhabit the vision of a child for primarily adult purposes:

> There has always been much in Mr Barrie's work, of the child for whom romance is the true reality and that which children of a larger growth call knowledge. Insofar as the play deals with real life, we think it a bit cruel.[56]

True, A E Matthews somewhat cynically accepts the definition of 'a play for children'[57] But he played Mr Darling and used that character's involvement in first and last act alone as an opportunity to gamble in the interim at the Duke of York's Club, thus never seeing the drama he so confidently defines! Gladys Cooper, who thought about the play a great deal, is a sounder witness and she has few doubts:

> I am inclined to hold and maintain that *Peter Pan* is really more of a play for grown-ups than for children.[58]

Anyone who sees *Pan* as part of the progression of Barrie's thought and practice can have no doubt that Miss Cooper is right.

I shall now look in turn at sources, themes and form, to prove that the dual audience addressed in the play is, in fact, a natural consequence of the type of myth chosen. Those who have seen Barrie gradually refining his dramatic methods in order to meet various grades of intellect without estranging any, will be ready to accept that the involvement of children as audience is a logical step forward: a difference in degree and not in kind. Those who have read *The Little White Bird* (the play's major prose source) and the dramatic drafts will likewise be prepared for a serious, adult line of thought.

Indeed, *The Little White Bird* is not only a novel for grown-ups but for grown-ups interested in an eccentrically imaginative handling of the basic questions surrounding the idea of creation in nature and in art. Geduld sums up its essential message perceptively:

> The main narrative is not so much a love story as a conflict of shadow and substance, a rivalry between the Creator-Artist (the narrator) and the Creator-Mother (Mary), in which a writer's literary fantasies are unfavourably contrasted with reality represented by a living child.[59]

The links here with *Little Mary* and the Reilly-Moira conflict will be obvious. Is creation in Nature or in Art superior? Real children actually exist while fictive children are, ultimately, illusions. In the novel, the bachelor narrator's attempt to steal Mary's real child via tales of a literary child is a vehicle for exploring these ideas directly; the Chapters on Peter Pan are the mythic translation of that argument. The fantasy world throws the emphasis on to the ideal rather than the natural while permitting (as in *Quality Street*) some problems to be probed from daringly imaginative angles. The narrator, for example, uses his own fiction of a pre-natal, birdlike state to assert his prior claim on Mary's real son through having met him, before birth, in the nest. These are the ideas which continue into the play; dramatised creation myth carries on the concerns of *Little Mary* and *The Little White Bird*.

Generative research also reveals the gradual excision of explicitly adult dialogue from the earlier drafts and its replacement by poetically ambiguous exchanges.[60] In the Lilly MS and Beinecke 1904/05B Wendy, Tiger Lily and Tippy (Tinker Bell's name at that stage of literary evolution) make direct sexual assaults on Peter's innocence. Each represents a different type of feminine resource. Wendy, for example, holds him through her motherliness but is always aware that she wants him to transform her into a real mother. In Beinecke 1904/05B, when he fails to understand her advances, she retorts with the marriage vows:

> PETER: Very well — that's really wishing to be my mother. [*They stamp feet.*]
> WENDY: No, no. What I want, Peter, is to love, honour and obey you.
>
> (II/3. p 58)

Tiger Lily's part is much longer in these early texts and she offers herself to Peter in an aggressive manner, echoing the idea of sexual battle first sounded in *The Little Minister*. ('Squaw means somebody to whack.') In Scene 3 of the Lilly MS she even suggests that, literally, she may throw herself at him:

> TIGER LILY: Suppose Tiger Lily runs into wood — Peter Paleface attack her — what then?
> PETER: [*bewildered*] Paleface can never catch Indian girl, they run so fast.
> TIGER LILY: If Peter Paleface chase Tiger Lily — she no run very fast — she tumble into heap what then? [*Peter puzzled. She addresses Indians.*] What then?
> ALL INDIANS: She him's squaw.   (MS Scene 3 p 2)

When, in Scene 4, she comes to accept the impregnability of his ignorance her fury is that of a passionate suitor spurned. Bitterly, she abandons him to his fate:

> TIGER LILY: Then Tiger Lily leave you here — you starve, or else wild beasts come eat you little bit here, little bit there.   (MS Scene 4 p 3)

Tippy (Tinker Bell), being of fairy size, cannot represent any real sexual threat. She is nonetheless represented in a more overtly sensual way with frequent references to her dancing around in her negligée and being 'a very woman'. Peter even uses this shamelessness to manipulate her. ('Tippy, if you don't get up and dress at once I shall open the curtains and then we shall all see you in your negligée.' 1904/05B, Scene 3 p 8) She is, on her own evidence, a completely free spirit, able to indulge her abandonment with Peter imaginatively. In yet another passage erased in later texts, Wendy furiously confronts Peter on the subject of her tiny rival:

> WENDY: It isn't for a lady to tell.
> PETER: [*huffing*] Oh, very well. Perhaps Tippy will tell me.
> WENDY: [*with spirit*] Oh yes, Tippy will tell you. She has no scruples — she hugs you openly — though she can't go a twentieth part of the way round — Tippy's an abandoned little urchin! [*Tippy darts about.*]
> PETER: She has been listening! [*TIPPY rings.*] She says she knows she's an abandoned little urchin and that like a true woman she glories in it. I suppose she means that SHE wants to be my mother (*TIPPY rings 'You silly ass' which the audience can now understand for itself.*)
>
> (MS Scene 3, p 5)

The much more intense enmity amongst the three; their clear desire to attract Peter sexually and their distinct modes of approach as mother, mate and mischievous flirt respectively, are distinguishing features of the earliest texts. Soon Barrie would tone down the sexuality and markedly reduce the rôle of Tiger Lily in particular. Yet his original intentions are plain, providing further evidence of the drama's deeper concerns.[61]

If the argument from sources strengthens the case for a dual audience, so does closer consideration of the theme of youth. The idea that children possess in some way a deeper or purer knowledge, being closer to the mystic creative source, is after all a myth within a myth. Defined as such it is known to most readers of English literature through Wordsworth. Barrie follows the Romantic poet in claiming greater imaginative freedom for Peter, while in *The Little White Bird* he even argues for youth being more revered in the fantasy land. 'In fairy families, the youngest is always chief person.' (p 152)

For a writer who believes in his code as an end in itself as well as a means of interpreting the changing shapes of the outside world, imitation of myth within myth is appropriate and justified through invention. In this, Barrie follows Wordsworth only sharply to differ from him. For the latter, the child held a brighter 'candle' to the 'sun' of a benevolent first power teaching lessons of harmony in either Christian or pantheistic terms. Barrie's child, by way of contrast, both saw and embodied the idea of life as battle, manipulation and the search for power. Similarly, while the authors come together in distrusting the 'prison house' of the schoolroom with its demand for early acceptance of the limitations on time and place, only Wordsworth idealises the lost vision by referring it to spiritual truth and the constants 'of moral evil and of good.'[62] Lacking the consolation of the patterned universe, Barrie does not pit youth against age, as ideal against lost vision; he invites us to consider the fantasy of eternal youth as an impossible, flawed but attractive, view of the human dilemma and thus highlights, by contrast, the equally flawed reality of mutability and death.

Finally, a study of form proves that Barrie was intent on devising a structure which combined the demands of an artificial, perspectivist creation-myth with those of a drama addressing both adults and children.

The earliest analysis has shown the care he lavished on form and on the development of 'domestic'/'fantastic' alternations. In the Definitive text of *Peter Pan* one can detect the same movement from the home into the world of the imagination and out again, which lay behind *Quality Street* and *The Admirable Crichton*. The first noticeable variation is that the Darling household with its dog-nanny, its child-father and rather adult children is well on its way to fantasy before it is invaded by Peter and Tinker Bell. It took the sharp eye of a Chesterton to see this. He did not approve:

> It seemed to me to be inartistic, strictly speaking, that the domestic foreground should be almost as fantastic as the fairy background.[63]

In using the structure of *Quality Street* and *The Admirable Crichton* as a norm against which to assess *Peter Pan*. Chesterton forgot the new section of the audience. In *Notes on the Acting of A Fairy Play*, Barrie reminds us that the Nursery Scenes are imitations of reality as understood 'by a child in deadly earnestness'.[64] This reality, therefore, must contain elements which (to an adult) will seem fantastic.

The later texts work through variations on a simpler linear pattern:

Domestic setting — Never Land — Domestic Setting/Never Land.

But major complexities lie beneath that surface. The method, as in *The Admirable Crichton*, is to create a 'reality', draw the characters from that 'reality' into a dream world and then return them to the original setting, in order to see how they have been altered by the dream experience. In *Peter Pan*, however, the 'hero' is a creature of dream and the heroine a child whose reality is partly dream. The neat structural pattern must be blurred to accommodate this. There is, therefore, an element of fantasy throughout — as in *Little Mary*. Also, while it was adequate in *Quality Street* or *Crichton* to return to the street or Loamland, the dual return is necessitated by our loss of a clear reality/dream distinction. Both Nursery and Tree-Tops must be re-defined because they are merely different emphases — dream in reality or reality in dream. Two types of Nature (adult/child) and of vision (rational/imaginative) are, in this way, embraced and re-examined in the light of the Never Land. The strengths and weaknesses of each are exposed and a merciless truth spelt out. Acceptance of one vision implies loss of the other.

The earlier versions have a more complex structure. The Scene division of the Lilly MS is as follows: Scene 1 The Night Nursery; Scene 2, Scene 3, Scene 4 Adventures in the Never Land; Scene 5 The Night Nursery; Scene 6 Kensington Gardens and Harlequinade; Scene 7 Never Land. The new feature here is Scene 6 and the existence of a scene explicitly representing the myth in art. For the child, therefore, the dramatic experience moves from the game of life via two different extensions of that game as 'play' to an ending where life and play unsuccessfully try to accommodate their separate logics. For the adult the movement is through fantasy as childhood reality via fantasy as childhood dream and fantasy as early dramatic art to a conclusion which accommodates the real as fantasy for young and old. In this final movement, a pessimistic view of the actual world is obliquely presented by enacting the incompatibility of the 'dream' not only with the 'real' but with the 'Reality' of artifice.[65] Clearly this was the originally favoured scheme because, for Barrie, 'artificial' was as important a definition of his creation myth as 'perspectivist' or 'eternal'.

Two questions follow. How far was the variant structure of Lilly and Beinecke 1904/05B the sign of a different argument from that advanced in the texts known to us? And if the additional Harlequinade was intended to translate the — necessary — artificial aspect of the myth, was this sacrificed or was it reinterpreted using a different dramatic means?

It is most convenient to begin by thinking again of Barrie's Art in relation to levels of interpretation. The presence of a third formal level of fantastic reality[66] permits characters to exist on any or all of these levels — Bloomsbury, Never Land, Kensington. Barrie favours some characters with triple existence (Wendy, Peter), others with dual identity (Hook) but confines a further group to one setting (Mr and Mrs Darling). Mr Darling is especially interesting for although he is confined to Bloomsbury, he creates for himself an inversion fantasy distinct from those of the Never Land or Kensington Gardens. He carries the sign of this (his kennel) into the real world of the office which exists outside the play's parameters. As the early texts are also unique in bringing Nana, as the mother of her puppies,[67] into the Never Land conclusion, these versions alone set the ultimate sanity of a dog-nurse in a world of fairies against the ultimate madness of a man-dog businessman in London.

Mr Darling, indeed, not Pan headed the list of dramatis personae in the early programmes and had much more dialogue in the earlier texts. At the end of Scene One he returns to provide the final comments after the children have flown off and in Lilly Scene 5 his kennel exploits are analysed at much greater length. To this must be added the important contribution he makes to the mother-recognition scene when he finds his home suddenly invaded by women ('Twenty! There are thousands of them!'). At the end of the play he usually accompanies Mrs Darling to the little house and gives his views on the proposed arrangement.

The original structure of the play may have been more complex in having an extra world but it was simpler in being more balanced and more explicit. The first productions were not nearly so Peter-dominated; Mr Darling was not only in a sense Hook's alter-ego, their parts were roughly similar in length. In short, as Pan came to dominate all, so Hook grew at the expense of Mr Darling and Wendy at the expense of Tiger Lily. Hook was also much more clearly the successor of the schoolmaster Pilkington in *The Little White Bird*, a rôle he played in the Kensington harlequinade:

> HOOK: Keeper, I am a schoolmaster, and I know there is a boy in the
> gardens who never goes to school. It's against the law. I want that boy.
>
> (Beinecke 1904 Act 3 Scene 6)[68]

This represents the most extreme extent of Barrie's 'Russian Doll' [69] structure. If, for convenience, we label the real world outside the play (A); Bloomsbury (B); the Never Land (C) and Kensington (D) — then Hook is a creature created entirely within (C) who longs for the world of (B) but has now become a type transported from (A) to (D). He is more completely the opposite of Pan and more clearly his creature than in the later texts. As Pan is a creature of (A) who has chosen (C) so Hook is at once a creation of Pan and (C) who, for that reason is unable to choose even (B) but longs for (A). The ultimate irony behind Hook's speech to the Keeper in Kensington Gardens is that the only way he can obey his one master (Time) is to allow his other master (Pan) to kill him within Pan's own fantasy lands and according to their rules.

Barrie probably departed from his original plan reluctantly, in response to his awareness that neither the dramatic form nor the Edwardian audience could be overstretched. One answer was *Pantaloon* which permitted him to argue out the problems posed in Kensington Gardens in detail. The other solution was to make Hook much more obviously a 'literary' villain. He, instead of Kensington Gardens, reminds us that this is an artificial myth. The pirate's conscious use of all ranges of language and of Latin quotations are additions in these later texts. If anyone was associated with this form of literary and linguistic self-consciousness in the early drafts, then it was Mr Darling.

In the 'Fairy' Notes, he was viewed as a philosopher (141) and reader of French novels (148). Given to Latin quotation, he would conclude the First Act with a cry of 'Mea culpa' (123). This last intention was translated into the Lilly MS

> MR DARLING: [*full of remorse*] My fault, my fault; mea culpa — my fault! Mary, from this hour until my children come back Nana and I change places. She becames head of the house and I go into the kennel.
> [*He goes into kennel, sits with head out. Nana comes down and stands looking at him.*]   (MS Scene 1, p 20)

Another favoured phrase of his in Lilly and the Beinecke texts is 'Sic transit gloria mundi' [70] But he is to lose his place as rhetorician and classicist to Hook and, as his part diminishes, so the pirate gains those literary soliloquies which are, for actors, the highlights of that part. None of these — not even the most famous one — appeared until Kensington and the clowns had been entirely banished. It is therefore only the fullest rhetorical compensation for those lost Harlequins:

> HOOK: How still the night is; nothing sounds alive. Now is the hour when children in their homes are a-bed; their lips bright-browned with the good-night chocolate, and their tongues drowsily searching for belated crumbs housed insecurely on their shining cheeks. Compare with them the children on this boat about to walk the plank. Split my infinitives, but 'tis my hour of triumph! And yet some dusky spirit compels me now to make my dying speech, lest when dying there may be no time for it.

> All mortals envy me, yet better perhaps for Hook to have had less ambition! O fame, fame, thou glittering bauble, what if the very . . . No little children love me. I am told they play at Peter Pan and that the strongest always chooses to be Peter. They would rather be a Twin than Hook; they force the baby to be Hook! The baby! that is where the canker gnaws. 'Tis said they find Smee lovable. But an hour agone I found him letting the youngest of them try on his spectacles. Pathetic Smee, the Nonconformist pirate, a happy smile upon his face because he thinks they fear him! How can I break it to him that they think him lovable? No, bi-carbonate of Soda, no, not even . . . Quiet you dogs, or I'll cast anchor in you! Are all the prisoners chained, so that they can't fly away?   (p 560)

A character defined by multiple ironies (a rhetorical mode which can only be released in multi-level codes)[71] Hook assumes new complexity when he becomes the major repository for the lost literary world of Kensington.

Far from being a childish play, then, *Peter Pan* proves to be a daringly ambitious attempt to find a structure and tale capable of transmitting the various myths of the real and the Real simultaneously to all. But if it is not childish in this sense, may it not, still, be immature — the product of a mind which had not developed into adulthood?

(iv)   *A Maimed Psyche*

Let us begin by accepting that, in some ways, this play does draw more closely on Barrie's personal experience than any other. Andrew Birkin reminds us of the dramatist's trauma when his elder brother David died in a skating accident on the eve of his fourteenth birthday; of his doomed attempt to console his mother by acting out the part of David dressed in the dead boy's clothes and of his enduring sense of being an inadequate substitute for that 'immortal' boy.[72] That Barrie had a mother fixation is not in question, but he was aware of it; *Margaret Ogilvy* proves that. The idea of the bachelor author competing with natural mother and father for a child is not only the controlling narrative for most versions of *Pan*, it is part of Barrie's life as the Quiller Couch and Llewelyn Davies families could record. Time and again too my study of form has involved looking outside the play to a real world biographically defined. When Geduld comments on the play's 'psychological substructure',[73] I have no quarrel with him.

Is there not some inconsistency, however, in arguing for the universality of myth while accepting so particular, so intimate an origin? One of Barrie's contemporaries did not think so, although he provided no justification for his view. Alfred Noyes found the union of personal and metaphysical the major strength of the play:

> Like all masterpieces of art [*Peter Pan*] is a revelation and incarnation of things eternal. It embodies a personality so completely that you might almost vow you had a section of the author's soul before you on the stage.[74]

More strikingly, later commentators on myth are agreed that this, the most *universal* of story-types, demands that very intimate contact with *personal* life, which might at first sight seem to be inimical to it. Eric Gould emphasises the way in which myth depends on the personal and the subconscious:

> The structural facts about myth as a type of speech are first noticeable for their challenge to the interiority of readers. There is a dialectic between the transparent but significant order of language, and the transparent but significant order of the reader's unconscious becoming conscious in reading.[75]

Myth's classical origins in Psyche are not accidental but necessary, and Barrie wholly justified in proclaiming that his universal tale is the addressing of subconscious via subconscious-explicated. Barthes expounds the reasons for myth at once approaching the universal obliquely through poetry but also bringing the worlds of personal experience and ontological exploration sharply together. Myth misses out a referential step. By synthesising concept and image into a single signifier it brings the worlds of actuality and fantasy most sharply together. His essay on 'Myth To-day' has importance for the proper understanding of Barrie because it explains why right wing writers are usually attracted to the mode and defines the way in which myth may be political in one sense yet depoliticised in another. Above all, however, he gives a linguistic explanation of the paradox with which we are faced:

> Myth is a peculiar system, in that it is constructed from a semiological chain which existed before it: it is a second-order semiological system. That which is a sign (namely the associative total of a concept and an image) in the first system, becomes a mere signifier in the second.[76]

Myth is not *opposed* to the intimacy of personal experience; it *invites* it.

To accept that *Pan* deals with problems acutely experienced by its author is one thing; to suggest that these are its sole theme and interest is another. The invalidity of trying to define any literary work solely in terms drawn from another discipline with the implication that limitations defined by the latter must argue for limitations in the former need not be stressed. For Barrie and for *Pan* the issue is more complex. The Oedipal theme in *Pan* is curious, not because it is hidden, but because it is advertised so clearly. Jacqueline Rose notes this:

> In point of fact it is too easy to give an Oedipal reading of *Peter Pan*. The father, Mr Darling, is humiliated — he plays a joke on Nana the nurse (the Newfoundland dog) which falls flat and then challenges the family: 'Am I master in this house or is she?' (Beinecke 1904-5B, Act 1, p 13). The children fly off and he crawls into the kennel out of shame. On the island, the children meet their father in another form, symbolically murder him through Peter Pan and return home. Whereupon Mr Darling crawls out of the kennel and the children can grow up.[77]

Barrie's cold view of life included a remorseless Freudian analysis of his own maimed emotional state. In *Pan* — the work most concerned with authorship — he has to define his own nature and does so with frightening honesty. It is part of his belief that our sense of truth is built up from interpretations. Art, which selfconsciously considers this aspect of creativity, must begin from an accurate awareness of the vision which controls the code; the creator of the secondary world — Barrie himself. If it is absurd to use the methods of the dream as described by a partly discredited psychiatrist to explain a work of words, then it is surely even more dubious to suppose that arguments for the subconscious can describe a work which starts from those very ideas made conscious.

If there is irony in one of the most psychologically 'aware' of writers becoming a victim of crude Freudian criticism, then there is further irony in Barrie falling before generalisations based on author/text equations when he had himself so carefully warned against such an approach. If the earlier evidence has proved anything, it has shown Barrie emphasising personality as constant re-definition with everyone containing within himself different, conflicting types. It has also shown that, far from assuming the author to be of peculiar importance in the face of his work, he has only the prominence of shaping interpretations through structured thought. Even this power is limited by his chosen code and subject to re-creation by audience/readers. Jacqueline Rose sees this clearly:

> In fact it is virtually impossible to place Barrie in relation to his text — which makes it all the more striking that *Peter Pan* has come to be dismissed in almost exclusively biographical terms. When Barrie is presented as the creator of his work, he appears, as we have seen in the form of a disturbance of intention and voice. Where he is not present, it is precisely because he has been displaced, and someone else is writing the story.[78]

Barrie, after all, moved to drama because he found it the mode most suited to his beliefs in the multiplicity of personality and the importance of subsuming authorial primacy in a team effort directed towards the closest possible audience involvement.

There *is* a psychological line in *Peter Pan* but, following *Little Mary*, it exists as part of a 'maniefalde allegorie' which also contains social, theological and aesthetic levels of interpretation. Nor can it be properly understood if one begins from the Pan-Barrie stance. Indeed, if one accepts the writer's own evidence that the play is 'clipped' down from *The Boy Castaways*, then the one major character with whom identification is NOT encouraged is Pan. Barrie's preference for his photograph volume partly derives from its closer relationship to biography; its use of a more open code and its allowing his rôle to alternate between maker and player. Following this, within the 'book' he is Hook[79] and advancing from the book as the new, upsetting influence he is Wendy:

> Wendy has not yet appeared, but she has been trying to come ever since that loyal nurse cast the humorous shadow of woman upon the scene and made us feel that it might be fun to let in a disturbing element.   (p 499)

Among psychiatrists, Grotjahn and Skinner approach the text with the assumption that Barrie IS Peter and tend to use the drama to confirm psychological beliefs proposed at a distance from the text.[80] By way of contrast, Meisel looks carefully at the play first then at other versions of the legend. He notes that on the only occasion Barrie specifically identifies the mind and the Never Land, the mind is Wendy's and the mother figure is identified as the agent of repression.[81] He might have added that the Russian Doll structure of the play becomes, itself, an emblem for Wendy's mind, when Barrie uses that image to explain female psychology at the start of *Peter and Wendy*:

> Her romantic mind was like the tiny boxes, one within the other, that come from the puzzling East, however many you discover there is always one more.[82]

From 'the start it is Wendy's feminine narcissism that is flattered and then given full expression in her adventure.' [83] Psychologically Barrie takes his own repressed masculine pesona as an accepted fact and, in *Pan*, explores its female equivalent. Nothing remains simple, not even that generalisation. The one character may embody both male and female fears when faced with the issues of sex, aging and death. Meisel's analysis of Hook confirms that *Pan*, as ur-text,[84] addresses all (children/adults) through types which necessarily define, but may transcend, gender (male/female):

> Hook not only has the elements of a forbidden oedipal father, he has many feminine aspects as well and is likened to Peter in his narcissistic stance. He is an adult with wishes to be a child, with great energy and hatred of the children who have mothers . . . He is a damaged bisexual figure who represents the competitive and dangerous aspects of the parents as seen by the child. At the same time, he represents the degraded and weak parts of the child projected into the other parent in the face of the powerful idealised mother.[85]

Here, in one character, child and adult, male and female mix.

Meisel's analysis confirms the view that Barrie is in no sense an escapist. Starting from a careful analysis of the various texts, he accepts the dramatist's own definition of the world as a totality of interpretations. He sees Barrie, the author, as one interpreter with an everchanging identity and he confirms the bleakness of the underlying ideas. We are not presented with easy answers to the ultimate problems of existence. Children are faced with the unknown terrors of the adult world, its sexual awareness and responsibilities; adults are confronted with their own oversimplifications of type and gender as well as the dangers of doomed shortcuts which lead to narcissism and bisexuality.[86] The pessimism comes from Barrie, the openendedness from the chosen form. A creation myth composed by a creature has to present the widest range of possibilities, while defining the polarities of available choice. This is the 'inexplicable simpleness of dreams' as explained by Lamb in one of Barrie's sources, 'The Child Angel.' [87] Literary works based so closely on mythicity cannot explain themselves;

they must always remain ambiguous. Barrie understood this both rationally and, I think, instinctively. Only by using a mode which offered the surface attractions of comedy, sentimentality and even levity could he introduce the Edwardian theatrical audience to a philosophy so modern (post Darwin; post Nietzsche) and so uncompromising. In 1920, writing for *The Bookman*, Sheila Kaye-Smith was one of the first (and the last) to see that the medium was artfully being employed at once to present and to conceal the message:

> He has been inspired to see that the greatest tragedy of human life to-day is that its tragedy cannot be faced, that it can only be shown us by a trick — the trick of Laughter.[88]

In *Pan*, the directness of psychological assault is matched by open criticism of protective, upper-class society in the play. Continuing its author's hatred of lethargy and mistrust of positions unearned by endeavour, *Peter Pan*, as social satire, takes off where *The Admirable Crichton* and *Little Mary* had ended. True, Barrie found families such as the Llewellyn Davies's, extremely attractive on a personal level. But his envy (insofar as they represented another magic world) was mixed with cold superiority (insofar as he remembered the crowded poverty of Kirriemuir). For once the critics were quick to appreciate his intentions and the distinctive culture which sharpened his tone:

> Barrie's world, a little like that of Shaw but in a different sense, is the English world analysed by an un-English spirit.[89]

> [*Barrie*] probes into the subconsciousness of a psycho-neurotic society.[90]

> He came of parents who could not afford nurseries, but who could by dint of struggle send their daughter to boarding-schools and their sons to universities.[91]

Socially, Barrie is concerned that the Edwardians cosset their children with Nannies and oppressive motherliness for so long that they will be unfitted for the cruel battle of evolutionary competition described by Darwin. To make them aware of this is his purpose in *Pan*, as it was Reilly's in *Little Mary*. Both act out of love but neither underestimates the seriousness of the illness being diagnosed.

From this point of view, Barrie, in *Peter Pan*, demonstrates how adults may use children to extend for themselves a false ideal of innocence and so create for their children a debilitating, unnatural environment. It is seldom realised that, in the opening scene when Mr Darling's guilt is so melodramatically displayed, Mrs Darling disarms the children as effectively as he does the dog:

> MICHAEL: Can anything harm us, mother, after the night-lights are lit?
> MRS DARLING: Nothing, precious. They are the eyes a mother leaves behind
>   to guard her children.   (p 514)

Though, we are told in the Stage Directions, she will go and warn Liza, her constant short-term strivings to falsify into innocence a world of savagery leave Wendy and the others vulnerable. Nor, it should be remembered, are the Darlings part of the aristocracy like Lady Mary or Lady Millicent. They are working-class parents mimicking the ways of their 'betters'. Wendy, John and the others will have less time to adapt to the world outside, being temporarily sheltered by youth alone and not by caste.

Peter Pan adds to its psychological and social levels of interpretation a number of associations relating its major protagonists to the eternal battle between good and evil. In particular, we are often encouraged to see Hook as Satan and Pan as Christ. This level of application, as in *Little Mary*, is not carefully built into a consistent allegorical message. The parallels are often comically intended; they are briefly suggested and then bypassed. In a sense, therefore, Christian patterns of thought and history are evoked in order to be subverted. The childish vision may at times polarise Peter as light, as birth, as bird of dawning against Hook as darkness, death and tempter (hook). But it can also equate them, making the one play the other's part; highlighting their shared love of power; attributing to Pan the sin of pride — flaw of the Devil.[92]

In general terms, Hook for all his gentility and brief moments of generosity proves himself a worthy successor to the evil but heroic devil depicted in *Paradise Lost* and revered by Robert Burns.[93] Pan, as Christ, is notoriously self-concerned, causing Humphrey Carpenter to wonder whether Barrie was remarking on 'the overwhelming pre-occupation of the Christ of St John's Gospel with his own nature.'[94] He may or may not have had this in mind but certainly he would have accepted Carpenter's interpretation as a valid extension of the theological focus, encouraged by associations and parallels within the text. Hook is no more a type of the Devil than is the fox in Chaucer's 'Nun's Priest's Tale'; Pan is no more a type of Christ than Chauntecleer of Adam. But in each work an essentially light-hearted approach encourages us to ask more serious questions and to some degree controls the theological formulation of those questions. Barrie and Chaucer share this openness; where they separate is in the Medieval author's ultimate acceptance of a divine truth against Barrie's determination to subvert belief and the certainty it implies.

In blurring the rôle between Pan and Hook, by sometimes giving his 'villain' more generous impulses than his 'hero', Barrie breaks down the absolute theological and moral patterns. By stressing that they are both fictive creations made possible by the conventions of fantasy, he distances them from any claim to be Truth. In short, he subverts both the infallibility of the Word and the word. He strongly suggests that, in his alternative religion, the ideal world is not only a creation of dream literature but is itself a dream; not as higher Platonic reality but as Platonic illusion. So, when Anthony Hope made his oft-quoted appeal for 'an hour of Herod',[95] he revealed himself to have 'understood' *Peter Pan* only at the most superficial, naive level. In fact Barrie consistently plays Herod to his own world and, in particular, to its allegorical configurations.

Only those who understood the structure of *Little Mary* as a 'maniefalde allegorie' adapted to the doubts of the twentieth century, would assume that any psychologically-based definition of *Peter Pan* could describe even part of a world where multiple interpretation is not confined to the visions of author and of characters, but refracted through both linear and layered form. As in *Little Mary*, we have traced psychological, social and spiritual levels of application. Indeed, only the historical line, so important to the Irish play, is missing from *Peter Pan*. This is not surprising; it is a concomitant of *Pan* as myth. The earlier discussion on *The Little Minister* showed how myth is opposed to history; *Peter Pan* is not only a myth but, specifically, a myth about the defeat of time through art. As such it inevitably highlights narrative pattern in preference to direct literary imitation of linear chronology. As Barthes puts it:

> To understand a narrative is not merely to follow the unfolding of the story, it is also to recognise its construction in 'stories', to project the horizontal concatenations of the narrative 'thread' onto an implicitly vertical axis; to read (to listen to) a narrative is not merely to move from one word to the next, it is also to move from one level to the next.[96]

In myths such as *Peter Pan* recognition of these 'stories' is not only a guide to understanding, it is an emblem of the type of exploration implied by the chosen form. That form is opposed both to consecutive experiences as life and consecutive community experiences as history. Synchronicity and universality are at once its logic and its end.

(v)   *To Sum Up*

As some of the arguments I have advanced in this section are at once radical and complex, I believe a brief summation may have both a synthesising and a memorial value. Nietzsche is not, after all, the most likely influence to find in a nursery!

To say that *Peter Pan* is only for children implies a view of childhood which is at once condescending and falsely idealising. As such it is opposed to the sympathetic yet realistic vision it seeks to describe. We are concerned with the rehandling of Wordsworthian myth in another mythic form whose universality *demands* that children as well as adults be addressed. To claim that there is no adult content is at once to deny that universality and to ignore all the source evidence from Notebooks to early dramatic MSS; from *Sentimental Tommy* to *The Little White Bird*. And ultimately a theory which makes sense through accepting all available evidence must have more validity than one which excludes what it does not want to see or of whose existence it is ignorant. *Peter Pan*, as a creation myth addressed to us all, grows naturally out of the structural experiments of Barrie's earlier dramas and their movement from one story 'type' to another; in these terms the complicated linear alternations between domestic and fantasy worlds are yet another advance in structured thought.

Likewise, the peculiar belief that one can describe *Peter Pan* by revealing the psychology of its author does more than reveal a reductivist view of art; it is hypocritical in the sense that it claims to discover facts which Barrie has been at pains to broadcast on his own behalf. It fails to meet his own challenge that all art is a code only definable in terms of the conventions, according to which — specifically — it is operating. If your author is arguing this, how do you justify 'accounting' for literary myth via largely discredited analyses of the psyche? Moreover, if you are seeking to discover the personality of this author, he challenges you to do so in the self-contradictory, constantly redefining terms of Pirandello rather than the usually favoured static definition of 'mother-fixation'. These are problems usually evaded by the biographical and Freudian critics. In so doing, ironically, they appear to be erecting the very comfort-justified myths which Barrie attacks in *Pan*. The advantages of viewing *Peter Pan* as creation myth is that such a theory *implies* these apparently insuperable factors. A layered allegorical drama presented by a multiply defined author and with rôle-playing characters is a logical way of mirroring the unordered flux of Nature.

II *Peter Pan and Creation*

'By the banks of the River Pison is seen, lone — sitting by the grove of the terrestrial Arch, whom the angel Nadir loved, a Child; but not the same which I saw in heaven. A mournful hue overcasts its lineaments; nevertheless a correspondence is between the child and that celestial orphan, whom I saw above.'   Charles Lamb, 'The Child Angel.'

(i) *The Background*

The complex structure of *Peter Pan* permits a series of creation conflicts to be explored. As 'prime' [97] author of the drama, Barrie places himself in a position analogous to that of God above Time. In turn, Pan (a Creature-God) challenges both deity and dramatist through his claim to perpetual existence. Finally, within chronological time, Wendy as Creature-Mother throws down the gauntlet of 'real' birth to the dreams of Barrie and Peter. A brief outline of the major issues, in terms of Fantasy, Time and Power, will help to clarify where this stage of the 'Road' may lead.

A return to Wordsworth and *The Prelude* reminds us that, although *Pan* is a particularly sophisticated and selfconscious example of power exercised over the Unities, such Godlike control is assumed by all writers of fantasy or fairy-tale.

Ye whom Time
And Seasons serve; all Faculties to whom
Earth crouches, the elements are potter's clay,
Space like a Heaven filled up with Northern lights;
Here, nowhere, there, and everywhere at once. [98]

Power, Tolkien stated openly, is an attribute of God rivalled in this mode:

> When we can take green from grass, blue from heaven, and red from blood, we have already an enchanter's power upon one plane; and the desire to wield that power in the world external to our mind awakes . . . Man becomes a sub-creator.[99]

The ultimate problems besetting man can only, fittingly, be handled through myth:

> Myths could be seen as the original and poetic vehicle of speculative philosophy, of all ideal discourse concerning nature and its first cause.[100]

Peter Pan celebrates the artist's victory over a wide range of human limitations. Characters escape from spatial restrictions through flight; shadows are given shape and ironed; fantastic hybrid animals of colossal size and astounding colour wander around. Wendy's house anticipates Mary Rose's island in being and not being. In the Never Land, Peter and the others change identities with bewildering rapidity. Lighting effects alter colours in just the manner described by Tolkien. Look at Barrie's directions prior to the major battle scene:

> The stage directions for the opening of this scene are as follows: 1 Circuit Amber checked to 80. Battens, all Amber checked, 3 ship's lanterns alight, Arcs: prompt perch 1. Open dark Amber flooding back, O.P. perch open dark Amber flooding upper deck. Arc on tall steps at back of cabin to flood back cloth. Open dark Amber. Warning for slide. Plank ready. Call HOOK.
>
> (p 559)

The exaggeration of both darkness/shadow and warmth/light visually embodies the polarised non-naturalistic methods of the fairytale.

But the crucial Unity, in all Barrie's versions of *Pan*, is that of Time. Wendy, despite her flirtations with the Never Land, chooses Linear time. She will age and die. Peter, with his refusal to age and Barrie with his claims for artistic control, challenge in different ways the divine monopoly of Time as 'perpetual presence' and 'instantaneous transcendance'. Aquinas, in *Exposition Perihermenias*, analysed these distinctions explicitly.

> Now God is wholly outside any system measured by time; he dwells at the summit of eternity in a duration entire and complete all at once. The whole system of things below him falls under his single and simple regard. With one glance he sees all the events that take place in time, and he sees them just as they are in themselves. The casual order is appreciated, but events are not seen as past or future to him. They are eternally in his presence and he sees them, to whatever period they may belong, as we see a man actually sitting down, not merely going to sit down.[101]

St Thomas's immediate purpose is to deny any assumption that the concept of divine foreknowledge implies loss of free will for man, but in so doing he crucially distinguishes linear from both perpetual and transcendant time. Among the most convenient confirmations of this framework are those in Boethius' *De Consolatione Philosophiae* and Augustine's *De Civitate Dei*.

For these communicators in an Age of Faith there was a clear distinction. Linear time was ours; perpetual and transcendant time were God's. The whole mirrored a single, benevolent (if mysterious) Truth. Barrie, writing in an Age of Doubt, blurred the divisions; proposed creatures as claimants for the higher temporal dimensions; and replaced the statement of single all-embracing Truth with a series of questions on what (if anything) Truth might be. The result, however viewed, is a sad echo of the joyous Medieval triumph. Whether the creative power be Barrie's own or the audience's in resurrecting Tinker Bell, it remains a shadow power. Whether the victory be Pan's over death or Wendy's in motherhood, it is gained at the cost of a concomitant sacrifice (fatherhood/imaginative freedom).

The majestic confidence of much Medieval art arose from a view of individual and historical harmony. *Peter Pan*, in its perspectivism, necessarily introduces and even emphasises the Darwinian view of life as conflict. On the simplest level, it is a play about battles. In Bloomsbury Mr and Mrs Darling fight for the love of their offspring. In the Never Land, the Redskins fight the Pirates; the Pirates fight the Lost Boys. Cruelty dominates. Hook, for all his gentility, has Wendy 'driven up from the hold and thrown to him', before tying her roughly to the mast. The climax is a prolonged struggle in which Peter finally defeats Hook.

At this point, it is important once more to remember that, although Barrie saw himself as a literary follower of Darwin, Nietzsche and Roget, he was not a quiescent disciple. He rejected Darwin's clear male/female distinctions, preferring to explore ideas of mixed sexuality. He developed Nietzsche's general thesis that different societies produced different 'truths' into a particular opposition between the Edwardian and Renaissance periods in England. He refined Roget's views on language through explorations of linguistic limitation in relation on the one side to universal language and on the other to primitive codifying. The Road to the Never Land will lead us to each of these areas of concern but it comes to each via Sir Francis Bacon.

There is no doubt that Barrie had read Bacon. He always refers to him authoritatively, usually in a comparison with Shakespeare.[102] Bacon's thought had assumed new importance in the post-Darwinian period because he anticipated a number of the biologist's ideas.[103] As a result, his works were republished during the 1880s. This was the time when Barrie was reading voraciously in order to cope with his journalistic duties in Nottingham. In Bacon he found not only a scientific alternative to theological certainty but one which, in *New Atlantis* (1624), was set on a fantastic island hidden away from the corrupting influences of the world.[104] Barrie's linguistic concerns were also anticipated in the Renaissance philosopher's quest for a Universal Language. Most specifically of all, Bacon had handled the Cupid and Pan myths perspectively, not as convenient Pagan complements to Christian truth but in darker questing terms:

> PAN: Pan, as his name imports, represents and lays open the All of things, or
> Nature. Concerning his origin, there are only two opinions that go for
> current: for either he came of Mercury, that is, the Word of God,
> which the Holy Scriptures without all controversy affirm, and such of
> the philosophers as had any smack of divinity assented unto; or else
> from the confused seeds of things. For they that would have one
> simple beginning, refer it unto God; or if a material beginning, they
> would have it various in power . . . But as touching the third conceit of
> Pan's origin . . . it points to the state of the world, not considered in
> immediate creation, but after the fall of Adam, exposed and made
> subject to death and corruption.

> CUPID: They absolutely bring him in without a father, only some are of
> opinion that he came of an egg which was laid by Nox, and that of
> Chaos he begot the gods and all things else . . . This fable tends and
> looks to the cradle of Nature, Love seeming to be the appetite or desire
> of the first matter, or (to speak more plain) the natural motion of the
> atom, which is that ancient and only power that forms and fashions all
> things out of matter of which there is no parent — that is to say, no
> cause, seeing every cause is as a parent to its effect.[105]

Here, many of the problems, contradictions and oppositions embodied in
Peter Pan are foreseen and related to the very myths which dominate the
Notes for 'Fairy.'

Even the 'bisexual' bias in Barrie's play is supported by Bacon's strictly
logical interpretation of chaos as 'confused matter':

> *PAN:*   Nature is also excellently set forth with a biformed body, with respect
> to the differences between superior and inferior creatures . . . This
> description of the body pertains also to the participation of species,
> for no natural being seems to be simple, but as it were participating
> and compounded of two. As, for example, man hath something of a
> beast; a beast something of a plant; a plant something of an inanimate
> body; so that all natural things are in very deed biformed — that is to
> say compounded of a superior and inferior species.[106]

Barrie, in *Pan*, considers this problem from both evolutionary and sexual
angles. Hook's bisexuality is at once a natural and an immature stage of
development as Meisel saw.[107] Progression into adulthood demands
equating one's 'nature' with either male or female; on all levels, practical
living demands the assumption of fictions as truths; simplifications as facts.

Unlike James VI and I, who likened Bacon's thought to the Grace of God
in passing all understanding, Barrie admired but did not revere the
Renaissance philosopher. Not only did he have reservations about the rights
of a legal mind to claim genius; he shared Sir Francis's own inductive
conclusion that, given equal gifts, the later mind would be superior as
'Every act of discovery advances the art of discovery.'[108] Nonetheless, the
Road to the Never Land passes through *New Atlantis* and the *De Sapientia
Veterum Liber*. To aid my own passage through the labyrinth of Barrie's

thought, I shall look in turn at the three central creative conflicts within the drama. The other treatments of *Pan* will be drawn in whenever comparative evidence proves necessary or helpful.

(ii) *Creative Conflicts: Artist – God and the Film of Pan*

The moment one approaches the play from this angle, all the 'oddities', which have puzzled critics throughout the ages become understandable. The very first words after the *Dedication*, for example, are an aggressive statement of artistic freedom with an apparently idiosyncratic focus:

> The night nursery of the Darling family, which is the scene of our opening Act, is at the top of a rather depressed street in Bloomsbury. We have a right to place it where we will, and the reason Bloomsbury is chosen is that Mr Roget once lived there.   (p 503)

There are further, specifically linguistic reasons for making the play an act of homage to Roget; these will be discussed in the final section of this Chapter. As composer of the *Thesaurus*, however, he is the refiner of the literary word. As God voiced us into existence ('And God said, Let there be light; and there was light' [*Genesis* I/3]), so Barrie voices his creation into existence by calling attention to verbal precision. As God embodied the Word ('In the beginning was the Word, and the Word was with God, and the Word was God,' [*St John* I.1], so Barrie invokes in Roget the embodiment of the word as an instrument of philosophy. The context is also important. The Dedication has been concerned to minimise authorial power in the service of the audience and the greater good. The dramatic text reminds us that it is not necessary for an author so to behave. Freed from a sense of responsibility, he can do precisely what he wishes. This will, by no means, be the last instance of Barrie celebrating gratuitous creative ascendancy.

> A vision of LIZA passes, not perhaps because she has any right to be there; but she has so few pleasures and is so young that we just let her have a peep at the little house.   (p 536)

The motivation *happens to be* benevolent; the premise is one of complete power.

The opening game in Act 1, while an accurate depiction of one type of childish play, translates this idea of the creating word into the youthful world of Pan and its comically serious tone.[109] Statement brings identity but can also deny it:

> WENDY: I am happy to acquaint you, Mr Darling, you are now a father.
> JOHN: Boy or girl?
> WENDY: [*Presenting herself*] Girl.
> JOHN: Tuts.
> WENDY: You horrid.

JOHN: Go on.
WENDY: I am happy to acquaint you, Mr Darling, you are again a father.
JOHN: Boy or girl?
WENDY: Boy. [*JOHN beams*] Mummy, it's hateful of him.
    [*MICHAEL emerges from the bathroom in John's old pyjamas and
    giving his face a last wipe with his towel.*]
MICHAEL: [*expanding*] Now, John, have me.
JOHN: We don't want any more.
MICHAEL: [*contracting*] Am I not to be born at all?
JOHN: Two is enough.   (p 506)

Already the egocentricity and gender jealousy of children is lightly touched upon, but the imaginative centre of the game is the creative power of the word. Barrie does not seek to assimilate artistic and deistic powers. His purpose is to counterpoint honestly, so John introduces this dialogue with the double reminder that 'We are doing an act; we are playing.' Wendy underlines this by asking him to 'pretend'. One statement to this effect would have been naturalistically satisfying; *three* are signs of a deeper purpose and meaning. The gap between the 'real' world and that of artifice is also forced upon us at the end by Michael who moves outside the pretence to gain comfort from his actual mother:

MICHAEL: Nobody wants me!
MRS DARLING: I do.
MICHAEL: [*with a glimmer of hope*]. Boy or girl?
MRS DARLING: [*with one of those happy thoughts of hers*]. Boy.   (p 506)

The notion is thus conveyed that she has to console him dually; as natural creator but also as participator ('happy thought') in the imaginary world.

If this scene suggests the creative act, how does Barrie transpose the continuity of perpetual presence? If the artist is to claim God's throne (however hesitantly) he must meet aesthetically the idea that a supreme being:

. . . dost in time precede times; else thou shouldest not precede all times. But thou precedest all times past, by high advantage of an ever present eternity: and thou goest beyond all times to come, and when they shall come they shall be past: whereas thou art still the same, and thy years shall not fail.[110]

In part, Barrie has met this by using the most ancient of literary and non-literary sources. Structurally, he has imitated the continuous seasonal cycle. He has also opened the question of authorship to accentuate its mystery and provided a continuous series of varied endings. In addition, however, he made strange, peremptory claims about the drama itself; claims which can only be understood if it is seen as an emblem of perpetual creation. The first of these is noted by MacKail, Green and others. Barrie demanded that it be revived as if it had never stopped running; as if it were a constantly evolving child whom the audience chanced to meet at certain stages in its progression:

When the play re-opened on 19 December 1905, at the Duke of York's Theatre, it did so as a continuation of the previous run and not as a new production, and according to this tradition, *Peter Pan* has been running ever since.[111]

I am sure this was what Barrie was privately stressing when calling it his dream-CHILD. The play was eternal and perpetual within his mind; actors might embody its creatures at specific points within an ever-changing story; audiences might come and go but artistic creation cannot be reduced to slices of time; it is perpetual.

Another ritual which contrasted the eternal unchanging nature of the Artist-Creator and the perpetually modifying pattern of his Dream against the limited vision and mutable nature of lived reality, is described briefly by Anton Dolin:

On re-applying . . . [Mr Boucicault asked] whether I remembered my part and if I had grown.[112]

and at greater length by Pauline Chase:

Every December a terrifying ceremony takes place before *Peter Pan* is produced, and this is the measuring of the children who play in it. They are measured to see whether they have grown too tall.[113]

There are two lines of thought here. First, the continuity of creation within the mind of an ultimately benevolent Maker may yet produce specific cruelties within its pattern. Secondly, the peculiarity of Myth's direct relationship with reality permits a shortcircuiting of the mimetic process. *Peter Pan* is at once aggressively artificial and capable of invading the actual as if it embodied rather than imitated at one remove.

Before consideration of the rituals embodying transcendant rather than perpetual dimensions of time, the Fathers may once more be used to define and distinguish. God exists perpetually before, after and during the life of his creations (alpha and omega). He also, however, sees the complete pattern instantaneously while his creatures, necessarily, perceive relatively and disjunctively. Aquinas uses the analogy of a General (God) reviewing a marchpast of soldiers (humanity) from a podium. Cleverly this image contains within it a Creator's freedom from the Unities of Time, Place and Action. Vitally, though, each soldier can only see the back of the man immediately preceding him.[114]

Barrie carefully provided a ritual to mirror transcendance as well. Hilda Trevelyan records her astonishment at receiving, not a script nor a detailed account of rehearsal arrangements but only a card bearing the cryptic message, 'Flying, 10.30 a.m.' [115] The members of the first cast were not given texts of the full play. They were not even handed a personal script confined to their character's words and cues. Instead this method was further broken down. They got an individual script but it was confined to the immediate scene or immediate piece of action. In this way their indi-

vidual 'fates' were successively handed out to them and the limited vision of
Aquinas's soldiers' re-enacted. As Actor-Creatures, they knew neither what
was to come nor what effect their words might have. Here was an exact
dramatic emblem of our own blindness as we live out a text which exists
complete only in the consciousness of its Creator.[116]

It should never be presumed that Barrie viewed the Artist's conflict with
God optimistically. *The Little White Bird* had earlier suggested that he felt
motherhood a superior state; it was not the quality of Godlike vision which
he questioned, it was its essence. Only if God had abdicated, must the Artist
painfully and inadequately assume His rôle. And even if he could translate
deistic vision mimetically, he could not escape from his own death. That
problem is addressed on every level of *Pan* and never joyously resolved. The
author, for his part, can imitate Reilly in *Little Mary*, becoming his book
and living through it. But this is an answer which involves re-defining the
problem; its success is as real and unreal as Pan's existence. Another
compromise develops from the premises of the Dedication — that the
'immortal' author is the one readiest to share creativity with the onlookers.
In their reaction, they can change the whole spirit of a production. The
Dedication to *Peter Pan* records how one man's enthusiastic reaction made
the first night of *Ibsen's Ghost* successful:

> On the first night a man in the pit found *Ibsen's Ghost* so diverting that he had
> to be removed in hysterics. After that no one seems to have thought of it at all.
> But what a man to carry about with one!   (p 491)

The opportunity granted to the spectators through silence to kill Tinker Bell
or through applause to raise her is an even more daring example of the same
belief. The specific context has, of course, been manipulated by Barrie as
creator but our free will is appealed to nonetheless.

The success of this attempt to transfer the recreative power to us has been
greater than even Barrie could have presumed. Many, many parents send
their children to *Peter Pan* or accompany them. Having themselves been
introduced to it when young, they seek at once to recreate the childish
wonder in their offspring and relive/reassess it for themselves. Ironically,
the first clear statement that *others* knew this to be a key feature in the
transmission of the text came just after Barrie's death.

> If Barrie had the power . . . of compelling successive generations to invent his
> story afresh, to tell it to themselves and in their own terms . . . criticism may as
> well throw its pen away, for then *he is immortal by election* and there is no
> more to be said about it.[117]

To me, this is among the most perceptive remarks ever made about Barrie
and his Art. In one sense, he has elected himself for the reasons advanced by
Voltaire, when arguing that the death of God would have to be followed by
re-invention of his mythological status. In another, he has triumphed
through his words, in perpetuating the book of his mind from beyond the
grave. The major questions and sadness remain. He is dead; father only of

words; and — most galling of all — words which are, for the most part, only interpreted at their most superficial communicative level and misinterpreted at all others. That may provide some ironic parallels with Christ; Barrie might have sacrificed those parallels for rather more praise and critical effort.

The most valuable complementary evidence from within other versions of *Pan* comes (fittingly) from a work which exists only potentially. Barrie, with his interest in translating genres through extreme emphasis on unique characteristics, could not but be attracted by a form which emphasised the visual and provided means of defeating the Unities. Already, he had provided A E Matthews with a film-script for *Macbeth* which contained so little dialogue that it could all be set down on two sheets of notepaper.[118] In March 1916, the final version was granted a Royal Command Performance. On every level, it was a radical experiment in confronting the new genre with the conventions of its predecessors. A burlesque, it explored how Hollywood might exaggerate the subtleties of Shakespeare, turning a spot of blood into a sea of gore. The cinema was set up with Stage Doors through which the distinguished cast passed before 'becoming' their reflections on the screen or, as Matthews put it:

> The effect which Barrie intended was for the audience to see the flesh-and-blood actors and actresses before seeing their images perform.[119]

When Paramount Studios asked Barrie for a *Peter Pan* scenario, one can imagine the enthusiasm with which he set to work. At last his ideas could be presented to a wider audience via a medium, adequate for his godlike fantasy. He quickly sent off:

> Twenty thousand words of the most carefully re-written scenario, with all the sub-titles, and a mass of fresh visual detail which to anyone but a film producer and his attendant experts must surely have seemed like a gift from Heaven.[120]

In his introductory notes, he highlights over and over again how drastically he wishes to move emphasis away from words to music and the visual. 'The music of the acted play, as specially written for it, should accompany the pictures. Thus there is the music which always heralds Peter's appearance — the Tinker Bell music — the pirate music — the redskin music — the crocodile music etc . . . The aim has been to have as few words as possible. There are very few words in the last half hour or more of this film, and there are also about fifteen minutes of the lagoon scene without any words.' [121] These preferences were ones towards which he was moving in *Peter Pan* itself. Musical signatures and mime sequences there reached the limits possible within the play form. Study of the Scenario shows how eagerly Barrie seized the freer world of the camera, already praised in the Dedication with regard to *The Boy Castaways*, to maximise the strengths of the new mode.

The most important of these was the greater range of imaginative power offered. In the opening scenes he plays havoc with chronology. A child is taken within the space of seconds from cradle to manhood. The technique was one Barrie had noted during one of his own cinema outings:

> The idea is to apply to the growth of a child from babyhood to manhood the same sort of cinema treatment that is sometimes given to illustrate the growth of flowers and plants.[122]

Space too loses its power to him. The flight to the Never Land is routed via the House of Commons, the Atlantic Ocean, the Statue of Liberty and the Pacific Ocean before close-ups of old-fashioned maps merge into our first view of the Fantasy Island. To this Barrie adds the control of God as potter. The boys get stuck in trees as they land so Peter has to make them fit the new topography:

> John is being held down, while Peter flattens him out with a rolling pin. He is flattened out too much. He is flattened out on the ground till he covers quite a large extent — as if a hundred barrels had rolled over him.[123]

Finally, he is wrapped up like a carpet and manipulated by Peter until he adapts to his environment.

Colours are much brighter than in the world. The ground, for example, is a 'rich green'. Size is as flexible as shape, with Barrie always suggesting not only effect, but the techniques which might achieve that effect. When the boys grow up and move into offices in the city, he recommends a tiny office set with minute furniture. Even sounds are not free from imagination's control. When Smee stamps on a twig, the music stops so that this noise may be emphasised; then the short crack is repeated against backdrops of different island areas. Pan's capacity for multi-identity is also developed. When he 'turns into' Hook, the cinematic mode permits him to change clothes and have a smaller hook.

Small wonder that the refusal of his Scenario shattered Sir James. Few writers of his time were so equipped to aid the newly established cinema industry. Successive refusals to understand why he considered 'snapshots of the theatre' an insult to his Art resulted in his final withdrawal in a spirit of injured cynicism. The fact that the only major author of the day who, arguably, had thought out the unique, defining features of the new genre and was equipped, radically, to develop them, should be rejected by practitioners intent on minimising these differences is a sad one, however viewed. Latterly, Barrie refused even to attend cinematic '*translations*' of his plays because they were precisely that.[124]

(iii)   *Creative Conflict: Character — God and Pantaloon*

Before moving from the power of Barrie to the power of Pan, it is helpful to return to the opening scene and John's definition of what the children are doing.

JOHN: We are doing an act; we are playing at being you and father.

(p 506)

There could not be a more abrupt call to recognise the world of the play as one of artifice. In looking at Pan as a power figure within a battle, one is forced to remember that he is an artefact within a fantastic development of an artifice. While this aids analysis of his rôle, it is also a necessary implication of the artist's new position. In rivalling God or seeking to replace him, the artist must call attention not only to new realms of potential control but the limitations on them. One of these is that, necessarily, he transmits his message through a limited code. That was a subject which exercised Barrie a great deal and will be the topic of the final part of this study. The other is that control within a perspectivally defined (or undefined) Universe must necessarily lose some of its force through not being the voice of unified Truth and some more through having to substitute self-contemplation for presentation of a clear message in which that self is embodied. This is the root-cause of Metafiction:

> The fictional content of the story is continually reflected by its formal existence as text, and the existence of that text within a world viewed in terms of textuality.[125]

The clearest way of demonstrating Barrie's approach is to look at Pan. Peter is consistently viewed as an embodiment of pride and power. That, we learn explicitly, in the short story, is 'The Blot on Peter Pan' (1927). It is the desire to dominate through art which causes the boy Neil to destroy Barrie through his own power-source, the drama. Granted by Fairies the gifts of Beauty (love of Art); Showing Off, Mimicry, Sharp Practice and the power to Dish his Godfather, Neil is a mythic recreation of Pan, who destroys Pan's original creator by re-defining the dramatic character in a superior code.[126] Peter in *Peter Pan* is also driven by the Will-to-Power. Most obviously, he loves to be called captain, and, in that rôle, attempts to destroy Mr Darling;[127] in the Never Land he issued commands with the certainty of the Stage Director which, in a real sense, he is.

This leads us to yet another instance of critical incomprehension. In the original production the defeat of Hook is followed by a tableau in which Pan appears, dressed as Napoleon (MS/p 9). Granted the Nietzschean philosophy behind Barrie's thinking, this is almost inevitable. The type of Power, having the power to change identity, chooses the first of all Nietzsche's heroes. The transmutation grants universality to the particular dramatic battle. Dramatically, it was an effect gained at the expense of a good deal of trouble for Peter had to be given time to change. That Barrie believed it worthwhile to undergo this proved how essential the effect was for him.

Nor could Peter turn into any Napoleon. If art must reflect itself, he had to become a representation of Napoleon in art. It was not just a case of letting Peter slip off with perhaps the use of a double to cover for his absence. As Fig 6 shows, the Act ended with a tableau mirroring the

6   Act 5, Scene 1, *Peter Pan*. Tableau mirroring Napoleon on the *Bellerophon* as painted by Orchardson.

Corsican on the *Bellerophon* as painted by Orchardson.[128] Foreseeably, all this was much too subtle for journalists convinced that they knew their author and determined to keep him in his kailyard. And when Barrie introduced another type of dramatic self-reflection, using the first front-cloth scene as an opportunity for Hook to mimic the great pirate actors of the past, some gentlemen of the press lost their patience entirely:

> We have unfortunately to endure a 'front-scene', as meaningless and as exasperating as it is paltry. The only excuse for its introduction, if excuse it can be considered, is that it affords Mr Gerald du Maurier an opportunity of imitating the bearing and style of Sir Henry Irving, Mr Tree and Mr Martin Harvey: but that Mr Barrie should have fathered an interlude so unworthy of his brilliant talent is wholly and entirely incomprehensible.[129]

All the evidence suggests that this scene was needed for practical reasons. The Home under the Ground had to be constructed. But Barrie's particular choice of action is consistent with the Notes[130] and the desire to make 'literary' as well as 'actual' time perpetual by returning to past sources, regressing into mystery. *The Daily Telegraph* may have found this incomprehensible. Students of Metafiction and the Lilly or Beinecke texts would not.

If Barrie dispensed with memories of Irving without a struggle, he clung tenaciously to the Napoleon association. He was under a good deal of pressure to obliterate it but refused so to do. The idea originated in the Notes[131] and although the full tableau would disappear, Pan's link with the Corsican at the moment of greatest triumph remains in some form whatever version you are consulting. This being the case, I turned with interest to find what effect Barrie suggested at the equivalent stage of his Film Scenario. I anticipated an underlining of literary or aesthetically defined heroism. Once more my expectations were outdone. Peter's part in the conflict is defined as 'heroic'; he is described as 'a figure of fate' twice; and he takes on not only the personality of Hook and Napoleon but of Wendy. This 'Avenger', this 'dealer out of death' confirms the youth's Pan-personality and the idea of gender-transition as anticipated by Bacon.[132]

Structurally, Pan as secondary creator dominates the inner world of the Never Land. Just as Barrie encourages us to see his own creative powers framing the whole play, so Pan stands perpetually on the outskirts of Bloomsbury. He is first seen looking in at the window and last seen, again outside, playing his Pan pipes eternally:

> He plays on and on till we wake up.   (p 576)

The fact that he returns to close resemblance of the pagan god is not unimportant. The circular pattern once again mimics divinity above time. And his existence in an eternal present is an inadequate but adventurous attempt to match Divinity in instantaneous, superior vision:

> WENDY: Fancy your forgetting the lost boys, and even Captain Hook
>   (p 576) [133]

The fact that Pan's synchronicity highlights personal egoism rather than universal benevolence is another mark of the creative 'fall' implied by lost theological certainty. Barrie translates not only to encourage parallels but also to highlight differences.

As perpetual governing presence within time, Pan dominates his world in two different fashions. First, he has in a sense created the Never Land in his own image. Barrie's associative techniques permit us at one and the same time to see it as having an objective distance (it is, after all, before us in all its particularity) and as being an extension of Peter's imagination. The latter logic lies behind the Stage Directions at the start of Act 2, encouraging the actors to present a world whose activity depends on the boy's arrival:

> The whole island, in short, which has been having a slack time in Peter's absence, is now in a ferment because the tidings have leaked out that he is on his way back.   (p 523)

> They (the Lost Boys) are like dogs waiting for the master to tell them that the day has begun.   (p 525)

If *Peter Pan* encourages us to watch a writer contemplating his own creativity, so the Never Land shows us a character doing precisely the same thing at one fictive remove.

The emphasis, so far, has been 'presence' as dominant, 'governing' as recessive. Altering the emphasis, we find that Peter proves in all senses an imperative creator. Characteristically, his opening remarks on his return are an exclamation and a rhetorical question serving precisely the same rhetorical function:

> PETER: Greeting, boys! [*Their silence chafes him*] I am back; why do you not cheer?   (p 531)

Particularly in battle contexts, he moves from one command to another ('Ahoy there, you lubbers! / Set her free. / Cut her bonds, or I'll plunge my hook in you.') The fact that he is here speaking in the voice of Hook reminds us that he also governs by omnipresence, moving from one dramatic rôle to another. ('Peter . . . has a perplexing way of changing sides if he is winning too easily.') If this characteristic demonstrates Barrie's belief that we all have many conflicting personalities, if it represents the greater imaginative potential of the child — it also mirrors the necessity for the creator to permeate his creation in both time and space. And, if God was presented as the unchanging force amidst the altering faces of his creation, then Pan mingles the capacity for eternal variation *within* his textual world (the Never Land), with the constancy of never-altering youth — meeting the generations as they share that stage then pass out of it. Although this aspect is most forcefully dramatised in the versions with emphatically regenerative conclusions (such as the 1909 *Epilogue*)[134] Barrie always stresses it to some degree:

> Wendy looks a little older, but Peter is just the same. She is cloaked for a journey, and a sad confession must be made about her; she flies so badly now that she has to use a broomstick. (p 575)

As with Peter transcendant, Peter perpetual presents a rather depressing rival to divinity. His powers within time, though impressive, again have a base in personal limitations rather than universal comprehensiveness. He endures as a stage of life artificially held, not as All-Life mirroring the ages of man. As a simplification of experience used to 'explain' the problems of life within a literary and self-reflexive world he is also appropriately an emblem of the method of structured drama as understood by Barrie. Just as the practical limitations and formal clarity of mythic theatre offered an attractive mechanism of control with which to face the multiplying complexities of Nature in a world of doubt, so Pan's divine simplicity could at once create and reflect upon the worlds of life and art.

As such, he is also inevitably the greatest fantasist within the Never Land. He it is who speeds up the time processes of his domain, which do not (as most critics report) pass as quickly as filling a jug at the well. Barrie tells us only that they '*may*' so pass. Like all the other 'natural' laws of the island they obey a ruler who can either confirm or suspend their action. Just as Barrie confirms the artist's power over time, space, shape and colour, so Peter re-confirms those powers. He does so, however, within an even more self-consciously artificial world. Battles in the Never Land are not fought according to the rules of war but according to the rules of Peter, and if he wishes to initiate a conflict, he allows the pirates to break those rules:

> Hook has basely broken the two laws of Indian warfare, which are that the redskins should attack first, and that it should be at dawn. (p 554)

The redskin laws are those refracted through Peter; their defeat permitted to draw Hook on to defeat by Peter. In a startling new sense we see Nature manipulated to enact the greater glory of the godhead. Even the most hallowed law of all, the refusal of a mother to desert her young is contravened at the end of Act 3. Already Peter has denied two fundamentals of his own world. He claims that he and Wendy need a kite to escape from drowning when in fact they can both fly[135] and when, as the stage directions remind us, 'if it can lift her it can lift him also.'

The sole purpose of all this is to present Pan with a suitable melodramatic conclusion to an Act in his own play. He achieves this at the expense of revealing every one of his own inadequacies. To give the appearance of martyrdom for Wendy's sake he deprives her of her share in the dramatic climax; a mask of real sympathy conceals the truth of an actor's selfishness. He claims to be worthy of the mother-figure in the play through tricking a mother bird into entrusting him with her eggs. His cavalier placing of those eggs in Starkey's hat shows the egoism which sustains him. The bird's pathetic acceptance of this substitute next suggests, as in *Little Mary*, the imaginative artist's cruel power in persuading women to subserve his interests rather than their own; to rank art above nature. Viewed from another angle, Pan manipulates true maternal love in order to celebrate, in game, the one adventure not open to him — death. Only within the control of his chosen world can he allow himself to experience really the fear which dictated his cowardly evasion of life. In a dream within a dream he does feel that chill but Barrie at once demonstrates in his 'hero' that self-consciousness which was his own greatest artistic strength and, arguably, his greatest human failing.[136] 'A tremor runs through him like a shudder passing over the lagoon; but on the lagoon one shudder follows another till there are hundreds of them, and he feels just the one.'

So, when he exits 'naked and victorious,' it is not on a note of unambiguous triumph. How could it be when he celebrates his bravery in terms of an impossibility ('to die') born out of fear? That is, in fact, the one adventure he does not dare to face. The Notes confirm the intention to present Pan as flawed 'hero'; indeed on occasions, they suggest that he might have vied more obviously with Hook in villainy.[137]

These discoveries, when adapted to the 'allegorical' conflict between Good and Evil, are consistent with the earlier contention that the Pan/Good — Hook/Evil polarity is suggested only to be blurred. Ethical clarity is inappropriate for an Age of Doubt. Even more than Hook, Pan possesses the Devil's sin of Pride; neither has any real claim to Christ's defining virtue 'Mercy' but Hook at least shows a greater sense of pity; each longs to be the other rather than rejecting his opposed type. And, of course, rather than being serious representations of Reality within a Primary Myth, these miniatures of Christ and Satan are game figures within a text composed by a writer who is determined never to let his audience lose sight of either the element of play or of Play. Once more the lost patterning of divinity has sombre implications for those who sense its dissolution.

The most striking parallel here relates to the Theology of Guile according to which the Devil was tricked intentionally by Christ over the matter of his divine identity.[138] Barrie sets up a contest which is a non-contest and is so for the very same reasons and with the very same effects as those assigned by Peter Lombard and others to Christ's conflict with Satan. In neither case can the non-divine figure win; in each case he has really been created by his opponent and doomed by that opponent for exemplary reasons within a comprehending scheme. Interestingly, in Medieval exegesis and iconography, the image of the 'hook' is used to recreate for the visual imagination the essential trick of hidden divinity.[139] In Barrie's creation-myth Hook, like Satan, only becomes aware of his impotence finally ('some disky spirit compels me now to make my dying speech') and dies because his creator wills it:

> [*Where is* PETER! *The incredible boy has apparently forgotten the recent doings, and is sitting on a barrel playing upon his pipes. This may surprise others but does not surprise* HOOK. *Lifting a blunderbus he strikes forlornly not at the boy but at the barrel, which is hurled across the deck.* PETER *remains sitting in the air still playing upon his pipes. At this sight the great heart of* HOOK *breaks.*]   (p 568)

This stage direction is of the utmost importance. Only if Barrie (who knew his Bible with Presbyterian thoroughness) was thinking in theological terms has the phrase '*but does not surprise* Hook' any meaning. Likewise, Pan's movement from battling child to hovering god translates dramatically his dual nature. As Christ overthrew Satan by holding back revelation of his divinity so Hook only finally realises that he has pitted himself against his own creator.

Barrie does not invite parallels with the certainties of Nature as Biblically interpreted to pronounce the superiority of his own Myth. In some ways his purpose seems to be the opposite of this. Those among his audience who follow his associative leads are invited to share Barrie's own regret that these comforting myths of belief and of moral view have been challenged so powerfully. The Scottish playwright's own nostalgic return to days when the Minister ruled shows his emotional preference for belief. *A Window in Thrums, Auld Licht Idylls* and *The Little Minister* convey this nostalgia directly; in *Pan* the inadequacy of either writer or literary hero as rivals to God conveys his regret indirectly. But one cannot force the intellect to believe simply because faith comforts. The duty of the artist remains the imitation of Nature, so he will shape the images perceived through the window of his Art. Barrie saw a bleak Nature, deprived of God, which he had obliquely to introduce to an audience which determinedly refused to think beyond the benevolent illusions of the past. This awareness had already been stated and discussed in *Sentimental Tommy*, where the Nietzschean, utilitarian justification of art is argued most extensively. Barrie's movement into the theatre from this point of view is a courageous advance to the front line, literally facing his patients with their cure (*Little Mary*).

If he is aware of intellectual change with regard to the source of creation, however, he does not descriptively change his view of Nature. The idea of a competitive, cruel world in which all species strive for domination is for Barrie, a fact. And if the loss of a loving God proves regrettable for all the reasons advanced by Voltaire, the evolutionary solution at least provides stronger intellectual justification for that understanding. In Thrums, let us remember, the idealising vision was not the reality but the comfort against the reality; in *The Little Minister* the characters believed in God but did so in the face of accepting (and even enacting) life as battle. Christians have always found particular difficulty in equating a personal, loving Godhead with Nature red in tooth and claw. The honest among them have striven to gather this evidence into a theocentric metaphysics rather than deny it. Sadly, Barrie had concluded that their sincere views were not adequate accounts of Nature as he understood it. By way of contrast, everything that Darwin recounted confirmed his personal views so fully that he felt bound to slant Reality in terms of Christianity questioned and Nature re-defined.

Every version of the *Pan* myth shows life as battle. In *The Boy Castaways* and *The Little White Bird* the author figure challenges the mother; in *Peter Pan* and *Peter and Wendy* this conflict exists along with the artist's challenge to divinity; in 'The Blot on Peter Pan' the author is finally conquered by his own creation. The clearest enactment of life as cruelty, however, is reserved for the true continuation of the 'children's' play — *Pantaloon*. Here we have the fourth 'world' of the original Lilly and Beinecke MSS, now a one-act drama in its own right. Each version enacts the belief that the closer we come to art's origins, the more cruelty defines mimesis of Nature. One should not forget, either, that the villainous Clown is the embodiment of Peter, deprived of his charm, in the fourth world.[140] As such, he does not only defeat Pantaloon, he humiliates him. He forces the old man as father to accept his impotence. He cannot buy his daughter and her husband out of poverty:

> CLOWN: I know about them. They go starving like vagabonds from town to town.   (p 591)

As artist, he not only stresses and re-stresses his own popularity against Pantaloon's forced retirement:

> CLOWN: Yes, I heard you was dead, Mr Joseph. Everybody knows it except yourself.   (p 591)

but relates that death to the loss of public interest. Pathetically, Pantaloon himself admits this:

> PANTALOON: Joey, they don't know me even at the sausage-shop. I am just one of the public.   (p 592)

As Hook is destroyed by Pan's lost interest, so the Clown dies an artistic death (becoming his own audience) through the lost interest of the paying public. And though, as in the full-length play, there is some hope offered through regeneration, the fact that his grandson is a clown tragically places that optimism in the very values of domination which have destroyed him. (What real joy is there in contemplating a continuation of hell?) Presumably both Darwin and Barrie would have answered in terms of evolutionary advance and the superman who, like Crichton, would combine the Will-to-Power with the Will-to-Minister.

Indeed, the further we move from divine-creator to literary-creator, the crueller the vision becomes. Barrie, the humane Nietzschean, is much more generous than Peter but much less so than the Christian God. Clown — the creator figure within the text of Peter's fantasy — is the least humane of all. In a sense, of course, it is foolish to ask that he be humane, for he is a *type* of an *aspect* of the *literary* personality. He is, therefore, at three removes from naturalistically presented humanity. He is an allegorical figure, presenting an unrelenting vision of Truth. Barrie uses Clown to convey all the essentially egotistical motivations of the artist. Most of these are obvious — the obsessive interest in self, justified in terms of perfecting the artistic vision; the love of praise, justified in terms of effective audience rapport; the desire to break up youthful love, justified in terms of Art's superiority to Nature.

As usual, however, changed premise produces a different perspective. Viewed, not personally but metaphysically, Clown can be seen as the successor of Moira Loney presenting the naked truth to an audience nursed on illusions. It may be sadistic to glory so much in his victories but the protective lies he uncovers when analysing Pantaloon's character ('it's you that lie now . . .') are not invented. Clown is the type of the new artist and an example of his unwelcome rôle. The 'realist' may write of economic advance but the 'Realist' has to chart a new Universe; in this sense only the fantasist can destroy fantasy. The dislocation of the Harlequin episode from the original plan of *Peter Pan* enabled these points to be made at greater length. That gain, regrettably, was at the expense of a magnificently complex literary irony. In Lilly and Beinecke, myth is condemned through Barrie's re-creation of a character from the mythic origins of drama, placed within a mythic game at the centre of a mythically presented world created by a mythic author with a view to commenting on the ultimate creation Myth. Barrie's claim that he could not expect to be understood does not suggest humility; it does not necessarily imply false pride either.

(iv) *Creative Conflicts: Artist, Mother and The Little White Bird*

If the rival creative power in terms of Time Transcendant and Time Perpetual is God, so the rival creating power in terms of Linear Time is the mother. This is the AUTHORIAL reason for Barrie's mother fixation, and it is that LITERARY reason, when allied with Barrie's belief that a perspectivist must clearly define the limitations on his own vision, which demands that his mother be described to us. All writers who start from this standpoint see honest clarification of artistic viewpoint as the essential premise of integrity. Chaucer, for example, in his study of art as transmission (*The House of Fame*), defines (or more accurately undefines) at each stage the perspective from which we see. It could be argued that no fewer than seven controlling perspectives are established in the opening section of Chaucer's poem. After all, the dreamer (i) sees via a vision (ii) of a temple whose decorations (iii) illustrate an interpretation (iv) of Virgil's version (v) of the Trojan Wars as represented in one chosen episode (vi) designed to please Venus (vii). But we begin with an honest assessment of the mind of the narrator persona. Obsessively given to book learning and lacking experience of the world, his mental slowness is intensified by a type of melancholy, which was believed to freeze the brain's activity. Even his one strength, his knowledge of authorities, is used further to diminish our reliance upon him. His reading of Macrobius and others has enabled him to list dream-types thoroughly but it highlights his complete inadequacy when it comes to interpreting them. His admission, with regard to his melancholy, that:

> Suche fantasies ben in myn hede
> So I know not what is best to doo.
>
> (*House of Fame*, 28-29)

applies also to the many dreams of which his own is one.

The Chaucerean parallel is an important one. Here is both the complexity of perspective and the clear announcement of textual artifice later to be embraced by Barrie. Fantasy exists within fantasy within dream uncircumscribed. In each case the intention is to focus on the power and the inadequacy of the word as written and spoken. The one difference is that the Medieval writer in composing a dramatic poem for recitation, presents a fictive persona. Barrie, in both novels and dramas, starts from an honest attempt to interpret his own psychology. This was necessary for him; unnecessary for Chaucer. Ultimately the latter believed that accurate delineation of the limits of code or personality were only necessary to highlight the constraints on art as mimesis. The Primary Author would turn all to good and use even the most limited servant as a means of glorification. ('God turne us every drem to goode!') [141] Jupiter seeks only to extend the dreamer's vision; he does not condemn his rôle as artist. (II/609-668) Only Good *needs* definition and so, in the Middle Ages, the complexity of art was related to the difficulties implied in comprehending the Deity. In post-Darwinian metaphysics, the more seriously an artist claimed to be God's substitute rather than His messenger, the greater became the need to describe really who the new claimant was. Barrie could not retreat behind a fictive personality as that would imply misleading the audience. If they did not know where the artistic mind came from, then they would be misled and unable to create their own valid perspective because of the invalidity of the initiating vision. Many artists were thinking along these lines in the Edwardian period. Few forced themselves to accept the logical conclusion that, the more intimate the experience, the more essential it was to reveal it. Barrie as man must have known that it was cruel to let the world know of the sexual failures within his marriage to Mary Ansell, yet as artist he deemed them essential, so Tommy Sandys outlines them in *Tommy and Grizel*.

His confession in the same book that, 'I have to assume a character, Grizel, and then away we go.' (p 306) does not negate this conclusion — only puts it at one literary remove. A creation myth such as *Pan* may use personae but the mystic nature of the arch-creator remains crucial. Insofar as the printed text with full narrative comments and Dedication expands this dimension in particular, there are strong grounds for adding it to the list of ten modal interpretations as being different in kind. Both prose commentary and poetic drama combine and all major genres fittingly unite in a trinity to explain the implications of moving the metaphysical mystery from message to medium.

Within the normal processes of chronological time, creation lies with and defines the mother. Dramatically, Barrie's fullest exploration of this fact had, so far, been *Little Mary*. The discussion of *The Boy Castaways* in the Dedication to *Peter Pan* revealed its camera-creator to have shared many of Terence Reilly's motivations and problems.[142] After all, his photograph-album narrative is 'a last desperate throw to retain the five' (p 490) by creating a world of play from which women, and especially mothers, are excluded. But without doubt the fullest consideration of this battle is reserved for *The Little White Bird*. The narrator, knowing that the facts of life are against him, seeks superiority through the divine power of the imagination. First, he stresses his power to uncreate; to consign real children back to the oblivion from which they came:

As I enter the club smoking-room you are to conceive David vanishing into nothingness, and that it is any day six years ago at two in the afternoon. (p 10)

Knowing that Linear Time will always give the victory to the mother he tries to diminish its power by claiming greater ones. Thus, he suggests that his knowledge precedes the act of creation. His art, in the form of a letter, brought the mother and father together after a quarrel. In that sense his 'Word' pre-created:

'You don't seem to understand, my boy,' I said tartly, 'that had I not dropped that letter, there would never have been a little boy called David.'   (p 18)

But his imagination has also created a pre-natal myth. Children originate not in the womb but in the land of birds. From there, they are despatched to the mothers by the bird-god, Solomon Caw:

Solomon Caw . . . thought at first that it was the usual thing, a message from the lady, saying she would be obliged if he could let her have a good one. They always ask for the best one he has, and if he likes the letter he sends one from Class A, but if it ruffles him he sends very funny ones indeed.   (p 135)

The myth, which both Barrie and Mrs Darling deliberately encourage, derives from a false equation between adult pre-existence and divine perpetuality. It appears to young children that their parents have existed for all time and so claim power because of their inhabiting a superior dimension of time and understanding. Inevitably, this claim will be exposed as they grow older and see that their elders obey the same laws of mutability as they do.

Another symptom of this rivalry and its basis in a wilful confusing of Linear and Perpetual Time is explored in *The Little White Bird*. There, the Narrator admits that he is trying to 'burrow under Mary's [the mother's] influence with the boy, expose her to him in all her vagaries.' To do this, he creates his own mythic boy. Timothy, who can enjoy all freedoms of the imagination. He also emphasises to David the limitations of his natural parents. As the contest exists (a) *actually* as a debate on who creates (b) *imaginatively* as a debate on who may create (c) *psychologically* as a study of different kinds of illusory consolation and (d) *theoretically* as a study of what art's claim to reality may be — the conclusion has to address a variety of concerns simultaneously. It does so, not to provide the ambiguity enacted in *Peter Pan* but to deliver the victory clearly to the mother. Her triumph in time is represented by the proof that her second child was 'conceived' three weeks prior to his book. Psychologically she demonstrates that his 'artistry' is a desperate myth erected to protect him against the knowledge of age, sterility and love sublimated ('I have stored within me a great deal of affection with nobody to give it to.') Her answers on the other two levels are inextricably linked. They involve a restaging of Plato's argument in *The Republic* in order to explain to the Narrator the different possible definitions of reality and to accuse him of wilfully confusing them in order to steal, through sophistry, an apparent victory. We are told that the mother intended to write about the dream child. She also explains to the Narrator that he only thought he was writing about her son. His book, she tells him, was clearly a celebration of *his* 'Timothy' and not *her* 'David.'

The justification for this scenario is that the defence of an author with Barrie's beliefs when asked to leave the Republic of philosophers is identical to Dante's. He is not imitating the shadow of the shadow, naturalistically seeking to give an image of one table. He is seeking directly to imitate the Idea of tableness. His literary child is a Timothy and not a David. What the mother is demonstrating is first that an author who believes he is achieving the lesser goal while seeking to justify himself in terms of the greater, has no right to claim anything. But, even if he were making the claim in its more reputable fashion, he is still the master only of a shadow, even if it be the Idea of a shadow. She has, at least, a child, limited by its nature but a proper object of love and concern.

> 'But it is I who have the substance and you who have the shadow, as you know very well,' said she.   (p 273)

It is of prime importance to understand that the mother claims complete victory in *The Little White Bird* because she is faced with dishonest artistry. In *Peter Pan* the author figure does not deceive himself about why he is writing; he does not deceive himself about the sacrifice involved in giving himself to words rather than woman; he does not deceive himself about the limitations of his medium. The Narrator in *The Little White Bird* deceives himself both wilfully and unconsciously in all three areas. His final sad recognition of his pathetic position is poorly conveyed by Barrie, who allows it to become a brief Moralitas to an extended fable-debate. Charles Lamb in one of Barrie's acknowledged sources, 'Dream Children', portrayed the same complex dilemma more briefly and more powerfully because he relied on his art to convey without explication. His Narrator awakes as the shadows of his literary children disappear:

> 'We are not Alice, nor of thee, nor are we children at all. The children of Alice call Bartrum father. We are only what might have been and must wait upon the tedious shores of Lethe, millions of ages before we have existence, and a name' — and immediately awaking, I found myself quietly seated in my bachelor arm-chair, where I had fallen asleep, with the faithful Bridget unchanged by my side — John L (or James Elia) was gone for ever.[143]

In *Peter Pan*, Barrie, like Lamb, ruthlessly admitted all his personal inadequacies. He clearly confessed his complete commitedness to art and his awareness of the human losses implied by that choice. By so doing, he guaranteed a more evenly balanced battle than in *The Little White Bird*.

Barrie's sophisticated understanding that any successful Creation Myth must deal with both human and divine aspects of time is confirmed by modern writers. Gould, for example, argues that such myths must convey a systematic attempt to grasp the world as fact and metaphor, as a synchronic and diachronic whole.[144]

In its turn this implies that Linear Time, framed by mysteries every bit as much as Perpetual or Transcendant Time, will pose major problems of origin and conclusion.

Let us return once more to the first scene of the Definitive Edition. Already analysed as 'creation game', it proves to function equally effectively as a literary substitute for the sexual origins of childhood.

WENDY: Now let us pretend we have a baby.   (p 506)

The audience is at once asked to suspend its belief and so enter into this childish, literary translation of the facts of life. Here is the dramatic equivalent of the letter[145] in *The Little White Bird*. When we move deeper into the dream, however, Peter seeks to re-define the world of the children, so a new metaphysical system must be erected with a new objective correlative for birth. Fittingly, this world is born in myth and metaphor. In their flight, Wendy and the Lost Boys 'become' the pre-natal birds of *The Little White Bird*. Their downfall through Tootles' arrow (in Barrie's *Notebooks* the archer was Cupid)[146] symbolises male procreation, drawing Wendy into the womb of the little house. The carefully orchestrated ecstasy and apparent surprise when she exits from its protection are justified not by narrative but by allegory. On the story level, they have already met her; as a type of birth her identity must only now be revealed:

PETER: [*with his hand on the knocker*]. All look your best; the first impres-
          sion is awfully important. [*He knocks, and after a dreadful moment of
          suspense in which they cannot help wondering if any one is inside, the
          door opens and who should come out but* WENDY! *She has evidently
          been tidying a little. She is quite surprised to find that she has nine
          children.*]
WENDY: [*genteelly*] Where am I?   (p 535)

Given the allegorical focus of interpretation and the associations between Peter and Christ, the exaggerated paradox of virgin birth coinciding with maternity is probably intended to suggest Mary. Like Moira Loney, she is compared, on one level of the text's message, to the Virgin Mother of an 'eternal' son. Though these associations are always part of a game, they are also an extension of the theological character-patterning against which the pagan myth is set.

As the later versions of the drama work only on two structural translations of mythic consciousness (Bloomsbury/Never Land), they only need the two poetic versions of creation just discussed. In Lilly and Beinecke, however, the additional level of life-in-art became the world of Harlequin and Kensington. Peter merged into Clown, and another visual image of creation became necessary. That is why, before the transition occurred, Nurses walk around checking that none of their children are likely to fall out of their prams. As in *The Little White Bird*, the idea of a pram-womb is sustained.[147] In Lilly, Scene 6, Wendy's house stands centre of stage in Kensington Gardens while the nurses walk around it. Wendy, the house and the pram are different translations of birth relating respectively to the worlds of Bloomsbury, Never Land and Kensington and time as understood via experience, imagination and literary (aesthetic) history. Exits from the nursery-widow, from the Wendy-house and the pram are oblique representations of the same idea at different levels of representation and understanding.

Inevitably, these different logics demand different conclusions, confronting Barrie with the problem of imaginative narrative's refusal to accept the pressure exerted jointly by the Unity of Action and the patterning of structure. The latter urge neatness and, at least, the appearance of finality. The fomer imply that such neatness is itself a myth, offering comfort sophistically through a simplified aesthetic form. Of course all allegories face the first part of this problem. But the author who seeks to represent both variety of ontological interpretation and a metaphysics of doubt faces an even greater problem when trying to make 'sense of an ending'. A comparison with Morality Drama will highlight this difference economically.

In *Everyman*, the central narrative (like *Peter Pan*) is developed through different consistent metaphoric logics. In ignorance the protagonist sees life as a journey towards death as a tragic end. The logic is negative; his bad deeds are set in a reckoning or account-book before a landlord God whom he can, by definition, never pay. As he learns of salvation, so the journey becomes a pilgrimage and death changes from being a dark end to being a new beginning. This world ceases to be visualised as 'hostelry' and becomes the 'prison' from which death releases him. The reckoning is not paid in economic terms under the rule of law but is offered in spiritual terms to a God of mercy. Finally, Everyman rises into joy with God. Potential variety and tragedy remain with us, as audience, on the playing area for we are not yet saved and may not share his glory. That potential, however, is subsumed beneath the accepted truths that our true end is not here and that God sets us clear tests, acceptance of which must result in eternal life.

For Barrie, the truth (so far as it could be said to exist at all) lay in the variety of human potential. He could not present any joyous answer, for his understanding convinced him that no certainty lay beyond the temporal interpretations of journey and reckoning. He sought, therefore, to maximise the questioning without denying that any individual choice for one type of freedom involved accepting another prison. Embrace eternal youth with Pan and you deny yourself the joys of adult love and parenthood. Welcome the latter with Wendy and you lose the imaginative freedom which is the joy of child and artist.

As his only hope was evolutionary rather than personal, he chose to end with variations on a future in which Wendy was changed by time and Pan remained constant within time. These sometimes stressed Pan's isolation, sometimes Wendy's age. Sometimes they presented a hopeful pattern by emphasising an easy movement from Wendy to her children as substitutes. Sometimes they struck a painful note by instead 'panning' in on an aging Wendy in a land of perpetual youth. Sometimes the stark oppositions between Bloomsbury and Never Land could be underplayed by making the Darling parents accept the new arrangements in terminology suggesting a house removal, complete with furniture van. Sometimes the stark nature of choice would be highlighted through giving Wendy broken wings or a broomstick or showing her outgrowing her clothes. Sometimes Peter would make the easier transition, welcoming Wendy as if she had never been away and urging her to complete a story she had begun two years ago. Sometimes Wendy would be ready to tell that story but Peter had forgotten its existence, not to mention her own. The variations are, if not infinite, at least sufficient to keep a dramatist, intent on multiple conclusions, at work for years. I know of over twenty variant endings to the dramatic story and do not presume to have tracked down all Barrie's revisions.

Behind this determined ingenuity lay another image whose logic Barrie wished to explore. In *Little Mary*, Moira had claimed that her grandfather *was* his book. In *Tommy and Grizel*, Tommy had identified his book with Grizel, its evolution with hers:

> 'Ah, Grizel,' he declared, by and by, 'what a delicious book you are, and how I wish I had written you! With every word you say, something within me is shouting, "Am I not a wonder!" '   (p 185)

Tommy also saw himself as an extension of his own fiction:

> But she kissed the manuscript. 'Wish it luck,' he had begged of her; 'you were always so fond of babies, and this is my baby.'   (p 295)

It is important to realise that, although Barrie was by nature a compulsive reviser, he had also moved towards a view of art which demanded revision as a means of shadowing the many views of the perspectivist world. With *Peter Pan* he moved one further step towards equating instinct with necessity. In a diachronic study of life as art, the work as created becomes the child, its potential as varied as the child's growth. Joyce, in *Ulysees*, may have seen his task as imitating the diversity of detail contained within a single day; Barrie saw his as the dramatic translation of growth in life. Evolution, with its emphasis on change (or progression) from statically achieved states or species, suggested the obvious rhetorical method — that of repetition and variation but carried out on an ambitious scale. Barrie does not alter the ending of *Pan* for every Production or at different stages within the same Production in order to please the box office or because he could not make up his mind. He changes his dream child constantly because that is *the nature of a dream child*, capable of extension in time and beyond time. No definition can contain him any more than any definition could contain David and Timothy in *The Little White Bird*. The many versions of *Peter Pan* within its unending run are no more and no less than Barrie's emblem, in art, of life's potential (actual and imaginative) within eternity.

And what of life within the frame? Inevitably, this question has to account for the aesthetic dimension. Life refers first of all to nature with the mother-creator at its centre and secondly to art with the fiction-creator at its centre. In both areas the sustaining metaphor of battle (already firmly established in the earlier study of strife among Wendy, Tinker Bell and Tiger Lily; or between Peter and Hook) is confirmed. It is logical, therefore, to begin with Mrs Darling, the only childbearer in the play.

Mrs Darling, in the early drafts, had almost as important a part as Wendy; Mr Darling as Hook. Successive revisions reduced their rôles. In the earlier versions of the play, the parents returned to round off Act 1; were involved in much longer discussions on parenthood in the last movement and were often brought into the final scene to add their perspective to the problem of continued life in the Never Land. This did not make the earlier performances better. In many ways the less analytic treatment preferred in the later drafts played to the work's dramatic strengths and imaginative power. Knowledge of performance history here provides a guide to initial authorial intention; no suggestion of a fall from the grace of artistic integrity.

As Wendy is the 'make-believe' mother of the Never Land so Mrs Darling is the real mother in Bloomsbury; and once more the artistry and multiple functioning of the opening scene reveals itself. First it acts as a bridge between the worlds. We begin not with Mrs Darling as mother but with Wendy acting her part. More insidiously, however, Mrs Darling encourages her children's ignorance and does so to luxuriate in her own delight in them as 'sweet objects'. When Michael moves uncomfortably close to asking about the true facts of birth, she encourages his ignorance the more lastingly to retain his innocence:

> MICHAEL: [*growing solemn*]. At what time was I born, mother?
> MRS DARLING: At two o'clock in the night-time, dearest.
> MICHAEL   Oh, mother, I hope I didn't wake you.
> MRS DARLING: They are rather sweet, don't you think, George?   (p 508)

If, in *The Little White Bird*, the Narrator's attempts to discredit motherhood were seen as kinds of artistic dishonesty and set against his rival's purity. Here, in *Peter Pan*, Barrie sets fallible motherhood against a less jaundiced view of art. If the artist is tempted to sweeten truth in order to be loved by his audience so is the mother tempted to alter truth in order to maintain dependence. Just as the craft of the artist moves him into rivalry with God, so does the mother's nature. The crucial test for each is how that rivalry is presented to their audience. Mrs Darling, no less than Peter, claims too great a kinship with the idea of God. In so doing, she wilfully misleads and disarms her children. Most critics, in blaming Mr Darling for his irresponsibility, fail (as was noted earlier) to see the complementary selfishness of his wife. He may chain up the dog; but she disarms their minds ('Can anything harm us, mother?' 'Nothing.')

The economy with which the counterpointed images of kennel and night-light suggest different types of parental betrayal reminds us of Barrie's ability to use the unique powers of the theatre as a substitute for rhetoric. The polarised views of the family as haven and exclusive society presented in Act 1 centre on another image — that of the window — with Wendy arguing for the first simplification and Peter for the second. The issues surrounding parental responsibility in this sense were much more fully developed in the earlier texts. In this instance, Barrie showed good sense in excising the scenes where Peter and Mr Darling debated such problems and the lost boys faced a sort of adoption-auction.[148] These movements not only demanded twenty additional actresses, they were unnecessary for the precise aspect of 'creation' — 'parenthood' under dramatic and philosophic consideration. The power of mother or author in *Pan* relates to the principles of creation and not (other than parenthetically) to the empirical development of those principles.

This, in turn, leads us to look at the crucial rôle of Wendy. If practical parenthood had been the issue, she should have given dramatic precedence to her mother. Instead she assumes the maternal rôle in the Never Land and succeeds her mother as teller of tales.

Wendy, as Meisel noted, is a complex and elusive creation. She is not in any important sense the passive figure parodied by Tinker Bell. Indeed, in the first battle — that between the rivals for Peter's affection she is the most devious of the three. While Tiger Lily and Tinker Bell play the coquette and the Very Woman in Barrie's division of the female mind, Wendy, like the heroine of *Seven Women*, can assume whatever rôle gives her greatest power.[149] No sooner is she out of her house (i.e. born into the Never Land) than she moves from one persona effortlessly to another:

WENDY: [*not to make herself too cheap*]. Ought I? Of course it is frightfully fascinating; but you see I am only a little girl; I have no real experience.

OMNES: That doesn't matter. What we need is just a nice motherly person.

WENDY: Oh dear, I feel that is just exactly what I am.   (p 535)

It is this chameleon-like power which keeps her in control of the family and endears her to Peter. But, as the opening to Act 4 illustrates, her tendency with the former is to move towards the all-powerful but ultimately selfish control enjoyed by her mother. In the opening dialogue she assumes first a dictatorial then a father-conscious voice before, like Mrs Darling in Act 1, sacrificing nature to an egocentric delight in contemplating 'sweet things':

MICHAEL: Wendy, I am too big for a cradle.

WENDY: You are the littlest, and a cradle is such a nice homely thing to have about a house.   (p 548)

With Peter she will subsequently act as aging mother, domestic drudge and passionate girl. Alone, she has the power to match his arbitrary changes of mood and person with the rôle best suited to them. But she does so with as much self-interest as he does. After all, it was not Peter who took her into the fantasy land, it was she who stopped him flying off by suggesting herself as substitute for Mrs Darling (p 520). She it is, also, who decides to break up the family (p 551). So the crucial movements into and out of fantasy are dictated by Wendy; Peter plays the passive or manipulated rôle.

And when does she opt out? When she loses interest in Pan as potential husband; when he yet again proves that he does not understand the concept of motherhood in its true as opposed to fantastic definition. Like Tink she comes to see him as a silly ass (p 550) so she rejects his world with just as murderous a disinterest as Peter would affect for Hook. This central conflict between the two youthful figures is, essentially, the conflict between Nature and Art, between real and make-believe. Though for a time they come together and share a type of love, Wendy is always the force of acceptance deriving her power from the real world. She aims to draw Peter back to Bloomsbury as a true father. For her the Burns' folk-song 'John Anderson my Jo',[150] which she sings to Peter in Act 4 is not an ideal but a reality which she seeks to impose upon him. For Peter it is one fiction added to others, part of the Never Land in which he seeks to possess her.

Nature against Art; Bloomsbury against the Never Land; sex against platonic images; youth-sacrificed against youth-maintained — the polarities are many. But the desire to dominate and draw your lover/ antagonist into your private definition of fulfilment remains constant. Like all the lover figures in Barrie, each seeks a worthy opponent but strives to overpower him. The impotence on one side of Mr Darling and on the other of Hook are servile extremes, the achievement of which would be as destructive as the impasse which in fact results. But they remain goals, towards which the energies of Wendy and Pan, unconsciously, pull each other. As creatures of opposed worlds they can never find the near-matching compromise of Babbie and her Little Minister or accept domination/servility rôles like Crichton and Tweeny. But they remain — wilfully or wistfully — unaware of their doom.

If, dramatically, their battle focuses on definitions of motherhood, their separateness reflects opposed views of death. Peter denies its existence, an option only possible through fantasy; Wendy accepts its existence, an option only possible through denying Peter. Here too Barrie uses his oblique pessimistic references to lost Christian certainty with great force. What is lacking in *Pan* but present in *Everyman* is the idea of life as death. To accept the reckoning as payable and to convert journey into pilgrimage, the protagonist in *Everyman* had first to accept into his personal history the myth-hero Christ. Only once he saw death defeated in the crucifixion did his world upturn into joy. His prison is not cessation of life; his prison is the belief that life necessarily *ends* in death. In his evolution myth, Barrie does not mirror certainty beyond this life but uses that certainty as an inadequate structure forcing us to return into doubt and the text itself. His predominantly Christian audience are given images of imprisonment which issue from the mind of a pagan god within the drama, and deliver their innocent inhabitants into the jaws of evil (the house underground), or achieve for a world-defined child-god who fears death, a sophistic escape through self-serving melodrama (the rock in the lagoon).

While Everyman looked beyond the shadow of death to the single joyous promise of salvation, even the 'heroes' of evolutionary progression must look to a future stage and to the Superman for such a hope and synthesis. True to his Ibsenite principles, Barrie uses one overarching dramatic conceit to mirror the pessimism of avoiding one prison only by entering another.

That comprehending dramatic image is the barred window. Opened, it permits the disruptive entry of Pan and so suggests the failure of motherhood; barred it is used by Pan to emphasise the failure of motherhood in faithful patience. So significantly, it is employed with opposed associations to highlight Mrs Darling's indecision. Finally, Pan will decide to shut it in order to keep Wendy out but find that he needs to re-open it again for his own escape. ('Doors, however, are confusing things to those who are used to windows.') As in the power struggle, their inability to reconcile conflict is enacted. And even the final 'window' act, the barring of it by Mrs Darling, does not resolve the irresoluble. For all the apparent certainty of the Stage Direction with its redoubled verbal force — 'Mrs Darling closes and bars the window' — she neither closes the action, having just consented to the spring-cleaning compromise; nor the philosophical argument, having merely confirmed the division between two limited worlds. Even the symbolic meaning remains 'open' for Peter will only see her act momentarily as a sign of failed motherhood, continuing to seek for and value the very qualities he professes to despise.

Barrie's imagistic openness, supported by his perspectivist beliefs, raised for critics the problem of defining the area where permissible ingenuity ends and invalidity begins. I should myself add to the 'prison' imagery the dark cabin of Act 5. The black interior, Pan's constant crowing, Hook's confusion and the overall motivation of freeing the heroine suggest to me a parody of the Harrowing of Hell. Medieval iconography, recently re-popularised in Victorian and Edwardian England, provides the imagery of the Devil with hook against Christ as bird (sometimes specifically as cock, the herald of the new age). If this be accepted, we once more have a clear narrative of joyous triumph for Virtue being replaced by a much less hopeful picture. Now it is the Christ figure who inhabits the darkness and the Devil figure who enters with the 'light' ('With a lighted lantern in his hand [Hook] enters the cabin.') Instead of the 'saved' guided out of darkness by Christ, they are thrust into darkness by Hook ('Here is a notion: open the cabin door and drive them in.') Nor do we have the resolution of the last battle with the Devil; instead the 'harrowing' precedes that battle reduced to game form. Certainly, this associative leap seems more likely once one has accepted the strongly visual power of Barrie's drama and *Pan* as a myth which seeks to rival Christianity by using images (the hook) and symbols (crocodile; crow) drawn from the art which sustained those earlier beliefs.

Within Linear and Theological Time, then, the central conflict between Peter and Wendy is fought out with determined egoism against a background of thought and image suggesting irresolution or exclusion. In addition, consistent as ever, Barrie moves the argument into the literary arena. Hook may be the master stage-manager but Wendy is the bard, the storyteller. There are two important lines to this transition. First, in terms of power, the bardic rôle is crucial.[151] Wendy does not go to the Never Land as girl or mother. She goes as storyteller. Peter needs someone to satisfy the deep imaginative needs of his Lost Boys but is, on his own evidence, as helpless as they are:

> PETER: None of us knows any stories.   (p 519)

This is inevitable. Peter only exists for himself and in the present. Stories as repositories of past knowledge provided for the benefit of others are outwith his range. Wendy, seeing this, invites herself as visiting narrator:[152]

> WENDY: Don't go, Peter. I know lots of stories. The stories I could tell the boys!   (p 520)

She exerts this power in the Never Land over pirates and redskins as well and for the same reasons. Then, just as she 'told' her way into the fantasy realm, so she 'tells' her way out of it.

Her manner of doing so is interesting. In dream vision poetry, the narrator figure had, usually, to pass through each stage or level of the dream before returning to the natural world. Wendy, having seen that Peter will never make her a natural mother, turns to the boys and evokes in them a powerfully emotive image of forlorn parenthood:

> WENDY: Now I want you to consider the feelings of the unhappy parents with all their children flown away. Think, oh think, of the empty beds.   (p 552)

Barrie has gone out of his way to tell us that Wendy had not, until this point, given a single thought[153] to the misery of her parents. This is tactical use of the power of the word to withdraw from a world which she discovers irrelevant to her own search for fulfilment. But she does not begin with the direct and the particular. Instead she begins with the general ('A gentleman'); then she fights off, but does not deny, the children's Never Land imagination:

> WENDY: They were married, you know; and what do you think they had?
> NIBS: White rats?
> WENDY: No, they had three descendants. White rats are descendants also.
>   (p 551)

In story she makes the transition through fantasy towards fact but does so in a way which manipulates everyone away from Peter into her world. In Lilly and Beinecke this power through art is contrasted with the most impotent figure in the natural world, Mr Darling. Specifically, we are made to see that he lacks the controlling force of narrative:

WENDY: Father and why are you in the kennel?
MR DARLING: It's a long story Wendy, but —
WENDY: If it's very long, father, we'll excuse you telling it.

(Lilly MS Sc 5 p 8)

One thing is, therefore, clear. If, as Barrie believed, the Will-to-Power at its highest was held by the artist, then Wendy is the heroine of *Pan* in a deeper sense than Pan is its hero.

In an evolutionary myth, power must not only be defined aesthetically but be seen as part of a continuous and developing process. Again, once the correct question is asked, Barrie can be seen to have faced it. Peter does not come for Wendy as myth purveyor, he comes to Mrs Darling to hear her version of *Cinderella*. Judging from the emphasis both he and the Lost Boys place on the fairytale, Mrs Darling is also a manipulator through words. She clearly highlights the happy ending, the prince and the slipper rather than the more troublesome elements of failed parenthood and manipulation verging on sadism. But that is only the literary equivalent of the falsely secure home world Mrs Darling is intent on erecting. Wendy usurps her rôle not only as mother but as bard. She then experiences a world unknown to Mrs Darling and has to explain it to her mother. Characteristically, she does so *as bard* descriptively rather than judgementally:

MRS DARLING: I thought all the fairies were dead.
WENDY: No indeed! Their mothers drop the babies into the Never birds' nests, all mixed up with the eggs, and the mauve fairies are boys and the white ones are girls, and there are some colours who don't know what they are. The row the children and the birds make at bath time is positively deafening. (p 574)

The transition is complete. Now the mother listens to the child-bard telling of a new world and its mythology. If Mrs Darling, through age, still controls Wendy ('I have got you home again, and I mean to keep you'), it is Wendy as artist who initiates her escape, her return and her claim to greater narrative knowledge.

In returning to the conflicting claims of mother and artist, already considered in *Little Mary* and *The Little White Bird*, Barrie does again award the victory to the female. Wendy as artist-controller makes a choice for potential motherhood and so gains the same double victory enjoyed by Moira Loney and David's mother. The difference (and there is a marked difference) resides first of all in the more balanced nature of the battle. Dramatically, Pan overshadows Wendy; he rules his world with mystic, godlike confidence even if that world is ultimately sterile and fictive. But Wendy's own world is darkened by the loss of innocence and the failure of man to embody her ideals or match the altruism of her love. As such it is also incomplete. The patterns and images of Christianity may diminish Pan but they also mock Wendy's expectations.

Indeed, at all levels in *Pan*, the only victories are gained in the face of greater, tragic defeats. And this applies to the only true hero and heroine of all — to Barrie and Wendy. For the former, artistic greatness is claimed at the expense of a pitiful existence in this world. The creator of the transcendant dream[154] is also the pitiful figure imagined by Lamb in the Elia of 'Dream Children.' By contrast, Wendy triumphs as power-figure in life and life-in-art but she does so in sad acceptance that this is the best that the real world can offer and knowing that she has left for ever that imaginary and imaginative kingdom whose sad embodiment is Peter, whose sadder creator is J M Barrie but whose saddest exile of all is her past self and the pure imaginings of incipient womanhood.[155]

III *Peter Pan and Language*

'CALIBAN: You taught me language and my profit on't
            Is. I know how to curse.'
                                    William Shakespeare, *The Tempest*

(i) *Artist, Word and The Boy Castaways:*[156]

As a perspectivist Barrie did not believe there was an objective reality to imitate in Art. In this, as in so much else, he anticipates Postmodernist thinking. On a general level he deduced from this that his myth had to be a selfconscious exercise in artifice. For if the world becomes text and the norms and conventions of the world become textualised it is obvious that the code must itself become the major focus of attention. And in a recursive structure, imitating the Russian Doll mind of Wendy, each alteration of narrative level involves a consequent change of world and message.[157] It must be remembered that the Scottish playwright did not have the advantage of being part of an accepted movement with accepted beliefs formulated by critics and philosophers. As an innovator he impresses not only by the extraordinary breadth and depth of his conclusions but by the ambitiousness of his literary experiments. For *Pan* he uses not only clearcut forms as foregrounding but moves through the conventions of ten different modes; these are his aesthetic norms within a textually *various* world. He then explores within each genre the features which define and separate it from others; here are the ideals.

   That he is thinking through the whole situation with precision is revealed by the frequency with which he anticipates not only single ideas presented by the accepted avant-garde of literary theorists but whole patterns of argument. For Barrie, the idea of the author's death is inevitably linked to the death of objective reality. Superficially, one might find this puzzling when the author also appears to be rivalling God. But, as Barthes will later argue:

> As soon as a fact is narrated no longer with a view to acting directly on reality but intransitively, that is to say, finally outside of any fiction other than that of the symbol itself, the author enters into his own death.[158]

Peter Pan, a comically tragic lament on the loss of God-controlled reality, opens with a witty murder of its author as the most economical method of announcing these literary beliefs and their tonal accommodation in drama to the more serious audience who wished to read as well as see the work.

In some Postmodernist works attention focuses more particularly on the limitations of the available codes themselves. This aspect of *Peter Pan* first becomes noticeable in the Dedication. It is indirect for it works through Barrie's assessment of the picture collection in *The Boy Castaways*. That strange gift to the Llewelyn Davies youths is used to lead in to the drama in a variety of ways. It anticipates the idea of an author trying, through his art, to steal children from their mother; it also anticipates the pre-creation birth of Pan.

> We first brought Peter down, didn't we, with a blunt-headed arrow in Kensington Gardens?   (p 489)

In the play, variation will produce a different natal myth for the hero and use this one for Wendy but both have to defeat time and sex through the artistic imagination. Next it anticipates the Christmas Pan-tomime as alternative religion by widening the myth to draw in Biblical associations. The male paradise of Eden is invaded by evolutionary imagery though not, as yet, by Eve:

> One by one as you swung monkey-wise from branch to branch in the wood of make-believe you reached the tree of knowledge.   (p 490)

Age would eventually bring them out of the writer's fantasies, but Wendy is anticipated as the catalyst which never reached Black Lake Island:

> Wendy has not yet appeared, but she has been trying to come ever since that loyal nurse cast the humorous shadow of woman upon the scene and made us feel that it might be fun to let in a disturbing element.   (p 499)

Verbal reliving of experience, visually recorded, skilfully creates a series of intelligent expectations for the next theatrical development of the myth.

The analysis of the means of transmitting this myth also begins on Black Lake Island. Barrie reminds us that this was a work of photography, not composed 'in the usual inky way'. And of the two he wishes us to believe that he prefers the former. All his comparative metaphors stress the play's more confined nature. In *The Boy Castaways*, 'We had good sport of him [Peter] before we clipped him small to make him fit the boards.' Why, he wonders, did they decide to rework the photographic material into 'the thin form of a play?' It is difficult, knowing Barrie's tremendous enthusiasm for *Peter Pan*, to take these judgements entirely seriously but they do lead logically from certain firmly held beliefs.

The first is his distrust of the word. From the moment Tommy Sandys laboured throughout his essay competition for the one exact phrase which escaped him, Barrie consistently argued both for the necessity of verbal perfectionism and the ultimate futility of such a search. If, in macrocosm, Art could only approximate to Nature, so, in microcosm, the word was sought in perfection to demonstrate its own referential limitations. The image which describes Peter being 'limited' into the play continues by equating that restriction with writing. And behind this comment, I sense a personal bleakness of spirit. To believe that your work must involve constant labour only to issue as a second rate form of silence misunderstood by its audience is not the most cheerful motivation to send a man hurtling into his study. Yet, this was a powerful part of Barrie's complex vision of his Art:

> Cold they are to me now as that laughter of yours in which Peter came down into being long before he was caught and written down.   (p 491)

The perverting nature of the word is pursued through consideration of the brief notes beneath the photographs. On the plenitude of the visual image they impose one meaning. This may be deceptive: 'Thus in a scene representing Nos 1 and 2 sitting scowling outside the hut it is untruly written that they scowled because "their brother was within singing and playing upon a barbaric instrument." ' Or it may introduce an extraneous and totally inadequate piece of erudition: ' "It is undoubtedly," says No. 1 in a fir tree that is bearing unwonted fruit recently tied to it, "the *Cocos nucifera*, for observe the slender columns supporting the crown of leaves which fall with a grace that no art can imitate." ' By falling thoughtlessly into a parody of the style favoured by *Guidebooks to the Forest*, No. 1 is made unwittingly to demonstrate the truth of his last remark. The full imaginative truth of the picture is held in the minds of the participators alone. Words serve only to distort or delimit.

In a further sense, they are unnecessary. There are only two copies of this text. Its only supposed audience is No. 4. The photographic code is held superior to the drama for these reasons as well. *The Boy Castaways* is celebrated as 'the best and rarest of this author's works.' In retrospect Barrie affects to regret having given part of the experience through *Peter Pan* to others at all. 'That which had been woven for ourselves alone' was not a gift to 'give to the public'. Stressing the autobiographical nature of the shared experience, he reminds us that language only operates to the degree that it is shared and transmits accurately. Black Lake Island is embodied for the participants through the pictorial and the memorial; to that degree words are unnecessary. When directed towards No. 4 they convey inadequately; when addressed to us as a wider audience they open up a sphere hallowed by privacy.

Just as the author of *Peter Pan* is wittily presented through a variety of possibilities so the camera is variously celebrated as concealing and revealing the identity of Barrie; as an instrument behind which the artist lurks but also a means of bringing him into the game, the object of his own vision:

> In *The Boy Castaways* Captain Hook has arrived but is called Captain

Swarthy, and he seems from the pictures to have been a black man. This character, as you do not need to be told, is held by those in the know to be autobiographical.[159]   (p 497)

It presents an apparently objective reality but this conceals secrets known only to those who were on the island ('Hullo, Peter rescued instead of rescuing others? I know what that means and so do you, but we are not going to give away all our secrets.)' Equally, its neutrality permits the eyes behind the camera and the games in front of it to strengthen their mythic nature:

Are these again your javelins cutting tunes in the blue haze of the pines; do you sweat as you scale the dreadful Valley of Rolling Stones, and cleanse your hands of pirate blood by scouring them carelessly in Mother Earth?   (p 496)

The value of the camera over words lies finally in its power completely to embody not the exact image but that image as harboured imaginatively by those who secretly shared it.

All the ideas here raised will be reconsidered through the different lens of a drama drawing much of its appeal from ballet and pantomime. *Peter Pan* is clearly intended to show us a playwright frustrated at the impossibility of mirroring non-existent Nature through constantly changing definitions of self and turning to contemplate the further imperfection of the mirror itself. Barthes is the modern writer who shares Barrie's interest in the photographic comparison most closely when facing this problem. It is striking that, while his analysis is not in all ways similar, he does reinforce most of the Scot's major contentions. Particularly he prefers the camera as providing an image which embodies its reality rather than presenting it at one remove:

The photography professing to be a mechanical analogue of reality, its first order message in some sort completely fills its substance and leaves no place for the development of a second-order message.[160]

But, the glory of Black Lake Island lay also in its secrecy; and photographs maintain intimacy. Barthes comments:

This purely 'denotative' status of the photograph, the perfection and plenitude of its analogy, in short its 'objectivity,' has every chance of being mythical . . . Thanks to its code of connotation the reading of the photographs is thus always historical; it depends on the reader's 'knowledge' just as though it were a matter of real language.[161]

Despite the inevitable differences in bias, it is clear that Barthes is thinking through the artistic implications of holding, in an image, memories and emotions. The picture, while apparently open and objective, has this completeness only for the few; those who, like us, see the Island from beyond its shore are actually shut out from the full actuality or even deluded by the apparently public nature of an essentially private code.

(ii)   *Sounds, Silences and The Origin of Harlequin*

Barrie had first learned the importance of the silent and the visual through Ibsen. His very first unaided dramatic offering to the London theatre, *Ibsen's Ghost*, may have parodied successfully the Norwegian dramatist's use of pregnant pauses but that satire was born out of something approaching reverence[162] for the artist whom Barrie was satirising. Shortly afterwards, it will be remembered, Toole explained to him the value of cutting soliloquys to allow for gesture and mime. That lesson, practically conveyed during *Walker, London*, led to further experiments throughout the apprenticeship period culminating with the visual and miming emphases in *The Wedding Guest*.

But Nietzsche, too, laid great emphasis on the power of imagery. Just as he believed that the greatest manifestation of the Will-to-Power lay in the intellectual achievements of artists and scientists and philosophers, so he stressed that its power lay in their ability to impose not only ideas but *pictures* on the minds of others.[163] The plays of 1902 continue Barrie's experimentations with sound and silence, action and extended mime. The dance scene in *Quality Street* as well as the farcical removal of the non-existent Miss Livvy involve extended miming moments. *The Admirable Crichton* goes further, especially on the island. A device to be repeated in *Peter Pan* is, for the first time, fully employed in the two central Acts. Each opens and closes with an extended movement broken only by occasional sounds.

Such photographic moments are in part the result of a simple desire to let the audience drink in the complex sets. It must not be forgotten that the London theatre, then as now, was famed for its technical expertise. The underwater scene in *White Heather*[164] was only one instance of all this skill being brought to bear on fairly slight works. Barrie delighted in sharing his skills with those of painters, joiners and lighting engineers. So the opening to Act 3 of *The Admirable Crichton* has an even longer introductory silence, this time focusing on Tweeny as she plucks the feathers from a bird. It is broken only by Lord Loam's concertina song. Even this is rebuked by Crichton's 'Silence' card, so that the audience may see every detail of the wooden house lit by onstage electricity. The celebrated conclusion to Act 2, as the aristocrats creep in one by one to congregate around Crichton's pot, is also characterised by a 'great stillness' broken only by one sound, that of 'the indescribably mournful' surf, while the tableau of Crichton as 'noble hero', at the end of Act 3 anticipates Pan as Napoleon. In this last case, the silence is disturbed by two words — 'My Lady' — described in the Stage Direction as the speech of Crichton's life.

Peter Pan is the most overtly visual of all, however. When you entered the theatre for the first run, your introduction to the myth took the form of proferred postcards. Available at the entrance to the theatre and presumed to be a product of commercial enterprise, they nonetheless gave you a frozen pictorial image to contemplate before the live theatre began. You could look at 'The Arrival of Peter Pan'; 'The Building of the House'; 'The

Pillow Dance'; 'The Approach of the Indians'; 'The Defeat of the Pirates' and 'The Tops of the Trees' before these became part of a live production.

Then, every single Act is framed by mime and contains intermediary mimes and tableaux. The silences do not only allow us to appreciate the visual wonders of Bloomsbury and the Never Land; structurally, they work via circles and parallelism in a manner which further reinforces the seasonal patterning of the play. My earlier reference to *Gawain and the Green Knight* as romantic fertility myth was made with this in mind. In *Gawain* too, highly visual descriptive passages alternate with action; the structure contains smaller circles of time within the overall seasonal pattern of the year and a day defined by the quest; but it also parallels winter and spring to suggest contrasts contained by time. Working within the same traditions and with the same aims Barrie adopted a very similar structural solution.

The clearest example of cyclical form emphasising contained time occurs in Act 2 of *Peter Pan*. This act opens with darkness; white (fairy) dots are then superimposed and the one sound of tinkling bells introduced. In silence, the major inhabitants of the Never Land appear in turn — the shadows of beasts; the mermaids; the pirates; the lost boys. Slightly's whistle (like Loam's concertina) finally breaks the silence and dialogue begins after about seven minutes' playing time. Further mimes expand on the nature of the Pirates and introduce us to the Redskins. Finally, however, the pattern retreats into circularity. The noise of the Pirates' carousing lessens, the lights dim; only the fairy lights remain; total darkness. A Never Land day is over.

The mimes enclosing Act 3 takes us from moonlight to moonlight and focus on the lagoon. Here there is variation — the rock becomes smaller; the opening escape is effected by the Mermaid on hearing the crowing sound while the concluding escape is effected by Peter to the sound of bird cooing. Act 1 begins with the Nursery and the exclusion of Peter in a protracted mime broken by one piece of dialogue. It ends with the Nursery and the exclusion of the Parents in a briefer tableau. But these circular structures contain oppositions — just as the day contains light and darkness or the seasons contain cold and heat. Barrie may show summer on trees co-existing with winter on the river (Act 2) or direct the action so that Wendy against the mast becomes Peter; Hook appearing to defeat both Pan and Crocodile gives way to Hook defeated by the one and consumed by the other (Act 5). Thus the contrasts of Nature and the sudden turns of Fortune's wheel are suggested visually by an author-creator who orders his material with aggressive virtuosity. If the Dedication to *Peter Pan* argues for the superiority of camera over pen, *Peter Pan* itself draws heavily on the strengths attributed to the photographer and does so in order to emphasise the power of the not so secret identity behind the theatrical lens.

It is important to remember that Barrie did not only emphasise the visual because of positive theatrical or structural reasoning; he did so because he wished to question the value of the word. Rather like Rousseau, who at one and the same time appreciated verbal excellence but defined the preferred natural state in terms of silence,[165] Barrie had become obsessed with the limitations implied by the metaphor of Art as mirror. If the mirror were by definition flawed what could Art's value be? And Barrie feared that it must be flawed so long as words represented things accidentally rather than necessarily embodying them. The more and more frequent recourse to silence and the pictorial, culminating in one sense with the Napoleonic Orchardson tableau in *Peter Pan* was only a part of his dramatic reaction, though an important one. In another sense it culminates with his film scenario via *Pantaloon*, a one-act play which runs for well over half an hour on the strength of about five minutes dialogue.

Barrie's ballet, *The Origin of Harlequin*, takes the power of silence even further. Here, he uses as base a theatrical form whose conventions deny speech entirely. It is interesting, then, that he cannot refrain from introducing one or two minor pieces of dialogue, designed to show the literary context of the major characters. Nonetheless, a stern warning at the head of the manuscript establishes his consistent desire to reinterpret, while conserving the unique powers of his chosen mode. Yes, he has introduced 'a little talking' but 'just enough to explain the action.' [166]

The other reaction consists of a full presentation of the ways in which language may develop, emphasising its simple foundation in sound, its essentially social and conspiratorial origins and its relationship to the Will-to-Power. As all of these approaches move away from ideal conceptions of language as philosophy or language as exact science, Barrie forces us to see our sound-code critically without explicitly needing to use it to say so. And, after all, what would be the use of employing the means whose power he is questioning to convince us, when the whole point he is making is that it lacks conviction? These concerns had surfaced more naively in *Sentimental Tommy* and *Tommy and Grizel*. Dramatically, they were side issues in *The Admirable Crichton* and *Little Mary*. In *Peter Pan* they come to centre stage.

Barrie's Never Land, like Prospero's island,[167] is a more natural and ancient society than ours. It is fitting, therefore, that communication often works simply through sounds rather than words. The significance of these sounds differ. For example, we hear the sewing-machine ('the only sound to be heard') at the opening of Act 4 and that sound conveys at once a reassuringly domestic side to the character of Smee and 'a touch of domesticity to the night.' The effect for us as audience is to introduce comedy and lessen the horrors of the stark setting. Usually, however, the signs are used primarily as signifiers *within* the dramatic conflict.

Barrie starts with a clear and simple relation between sign and signified. The crowing of Peter is explained to Wendy by the boy himself, 'I can't help crowing, Wendy, when I'm pleased with myself.' The sound of tom-toms represents an Indian victory. The ticking of the crocodile reminds Hook of his lost arm in an earlier battle but acts directly as a warning:

HOOK: Smee, that crocodile would have had me before now, but by a lucky
         chance he swallowed a clock, and it goes tick, tick, tick inside him; and
         so before he can reach me I hear the tick and bolt.   (p 528)

We start, therefore, with economically effective codes.

Given, however, the combative and perfidious nature of man, these sounds only work in the positive manner intended so long as they remain secret communications within one group sharing similar interests. The Pirates, Barrie stresses in a stage direction, both know the Indian code and scorn the ethics of fair-play:

> Hook has basely broken the two laws of Indian warfare, which are that the redskins should attack first, and that it should be at dawn. (p 554)

Most people tend to assume that the Pirates defeat the Indians because treachery out-thinks honesty. This is not the case. The belief in these laws fairly followed is Peter's alone. The Indians, we are told, have used every stratagem they can think of, including another sound-message — imitating the call of the lonely coyote. They are just as devious as the Pirates, hoping that their sound-sign will lull Hook into a sense of false security. Hook is not deceived and triumphs over them because he reads the sound correctly as a false signifier. His use of the tom-toms follow the cunning methods of the Redskins but is honestly, and therefore falsely, interpreted by Peter:

> PETER: Hst! If the Indians have won they will beat the tom-tom; it is always their signal of victory.
>
> HOOK: [*licks his lips at this and signs to* SMEE, *who is sitting on it, to hold up the tom-tom. He beats upon it with his claw, and listens for results.*]
>
> (p 555)

Simple codes at once become complex through entering into the warfare of Nature; the struggle of the Will-to-Power.[168]

Another problem arises when the sound, used inappropriately, works as sign differently within the code of another character. For Peter, the crowing sound is a sort of joyous signature tune. Inappropriately voiced when he is trying to catch a mermaid, it simply acts as a warning noise. A much more complicated development of this centres on Hook and the ticking crocodile. In a sense, the Pirate anticipates his own tragedy.[169] A sign which acts as warning comes to be relied upon. If it does not 'signify' clearly on any one occasion, that reliance is translated into the unreadiness which precipitates disaster:

> SMEE: [*sombrely*] Some day the clock will run down, and then he'll get you.
>
> HOOK: [*a broken man*] Ay, that is the fear that haunts me. (p 528)

The prophecy is realised but not before an opposed complication is introduced. The sign mimicked by Peter will produce real fear in relation to danger imagined and turn Hook into a comic figure for Bergsonean reasons.[170] The boy has only to *sound* like an approaching clock for Hook to give the hysterical reaction appropriate to the arrival of death.

Another type of complexity is introduced by emphasising the *audience* as recipient of the message embodied in the sound. Sometimes, Barrie uses this new dimension simply to contrast the superior knowledge of sharing the code against the ignorance of not knowing the signification of a particular sound. So, *we* know that the crowing sound in the dark cabin is the sign of Peter but the Pirates, for the sake of the game, do not. This is another way in which communication is of necessity an act of power. True, if one knows the code, it is possible to manipulate it in order to come out on top; but not to know it all implies (and will always imply) impotence. In this sense the word not only creates but implies the Fall as the first act beyond creation. Paradise is silence; sound introduces confusion and combat.

More subtly, Barrie uses a technique very similar to the 'signing' of typological signification through narrative oddity. In the Miracle Cycles, for example, an unusual addition such as the introduction of concern for Isaac's mother prior to his being sacrificed by Isaac acted as a 'sign' to the audience. This detail was absent in the Biblical version. Why had the narrative been changed? That question led the listener to interpret at a different level of signification. In this case the typological link is between Abraham's sacrifice of his son and God's sacrificing of Christ. The oddity guides us to a parallelism between the suffering of Abraham's wife and the Virgin Mary. For the audience, the tick of the crocodile not only factually is a warning sound; it is a sound which symbolises Hook as the victim of Time against Pan as the victor over Time.

Often, details in *Peter Pan* are justified only in representational contexts. Why does Hook stress that once he heard the clock within the crocodile strike six, if it is not to take us back to the opening of the play and the emphasis there on the clock striking six — the very first *sound* in the play? That first sound suggested security but it has been a security threatened and destroyed; now for Hook it is both a sign of reassurance and of future doom. The sound, interpretatively, has moved from the 'meaning' of character and situation to the 'meaning' conveyed by structure and myth.[171]

The highest and most essential level of significance in *Peter Pan* is what, in medieval terminology, would be called anagogy; the exploration of final mysteries such as death and salvation. If the preceding analysis has revealed Barrie dramatically examining the necessary complications of the sound as accidental sign in a world where communication is part of a power struggle, then all applications bar the anagogical have been covered. Nor is it ignored. First, it is approached through the music of the Pan-pipes. These define Pan both in his assumed power as God and his actual, diminished power as Pagan Godlet under Nature.

It is noteworthy that Pan always plays the pipes whenever he has withdrawn himself from the action of the play in childish huff or creative boredom. He retreats to them after his decision to let Wendy return; after the death of Hook; after his own flight from Bloomsbury and (as the last, unending sound of the play) when Wendy leaves after springcleaning:

> With rapturous face he produces his pipes, and the Never birds and the fairies gather closer, till the roof of the little house is so thick with his admirers that some of them fall down the chimney. He plays on and on till we wake up.
>
> (p 576)

On all levels, bar the anagogical, the sound of the pipes conveys nothing directly and everything indirectly. On that highest level, they are at once a sign of his rejecting the outside world and strengthening his rule within the Never Land. Often, their music is also part of an attempt, literally, to rise above his own creation. As he plays, he flies (p 575) or hovers (p 568) or moves to an elevated position on the stage (p 576). Despite the harmony and the elevation, despite the power and the personal joy, Barrie does not allow us to see in the raised Pan either triumph or answer.[172]

Just as Pan's victory over time has been won at the cost of a retreat from humanity and death, so the pipes proclaim a lonely victory. Their sound embodies perceived identity at the same time as taking that identity away from comment. They glorify Pan at the very moments when the limitations of his rule and his loss of control over humanity are most stressed. It would be nice to see in Pan a solution to our problem but, in the end, he is a creature of the dream world, ruling in that world alone; a useful tool for metaphysical enquiry but a useless rôle model.

If we begin with a hopeful, easy equation between sound and signification but are led into increasing confusion by the drama, so the first sound of the play encourages and the last troubles our dreams. The nursery clock striking six offers us an enclosed, protected world within time. This domestic harmony will soon be disrupted from outside and questioned from within but it opens as a comforting image of this world. The last sound of the eternal pipes of Pan is a disturbing image of the spiritual world in which the hope of salvation has been replaced by a fantastic youth mimicking pagan harmony; God become man to teach man, replaced by god unlike man rejecting man to glorify self. Disrupted domestic harmony followed by disrupted spiritual harmony. All this is not, of course, explicitly stated. But it is part of Barrie's gentle imaginative guidance. His character attempts to sidestep the logic of the action and claim the highest type of Will-to-Power mystically. If the plot had supported that claim, Pan would be Truth. But Barrie has gone out of his way to contextualise that 'victory' in such a way that we see the youth satisfying only himself, in one of his many rôles, momentarily. For us as audience the only reliable spiritual truth is that we can conceive of such harmony and realise inadequate claims to it. Beyond that, doubt rules darkly in a world of multiple identity facing complex, combative Nature under the rule of linear Time.

The second mystic use of sound contrasts with the Pan-pipes in two ways. The mystery is fictive in form and in reference rather than in form alone; and it is triumphant tonally both for characters and for audience instead of character alone. I refer to the famous incident where Peter asks us whether we believe in fairies.

This incident has, briefly, been discussed earlier. It is, in terms of the power struggle, one of the clearest dramatisations of Barrie's own imaginative control. That control, like Peter's, is limited to his own world — the world of the literary myth. But it also transcends Peter's and contains it. There is again a narrative oddity which 'signs' this to us. For the first and only time in the play, Peter acts altruistically, forgetting himself in the desire to save Tink. The motivation for this is not primarily psychological. Here, at the end of Act 4, Barrie suspends the natural laws of this world in order to provide himself with a melodramatic climax emphasising his own power; this balances the end of Act 3, where Peter had done exactly the same thing for exactly the same purpose. Peter's pretence that he cannot fly and his pretence at self-sacrifice on the rock demonstrates his absolute rule in the Never Land; the actual self-sacrifice is used to explore just how far the powers of the fantasist may extend.

Let it not be forgotten, this request to save a character defined by sounds (bell-language) through sounds (clapping) could have been a dreadful failure and would only have been attempted by a writer profoundly sure of his ability to entrance.[173] Barrie shows his awareness of this in the Stage Directions, where he notes that 'Many clap, some don't, a few hiss.' He was, after all, asking for an audience containing many adults to proclaim their belief in the world of 'faery' as represented within a child's fantasy by effects of light and sound alone. Could staid Victorians either abandon themselves to such sentimentality or permit their children so to do?

Barrie's success in controlling, through Art, the reactions of others is, therefore, set against the lost power of God and gods. The temerity and the degree of his sovereignty is demonstrated not only by directing sympathy at a collar of bells and the reflection from a spotlight,[174] but doing this at a point in the drama where failure would have been catastrophic; audience silence would have ruined the entire Act. One should also remember just how addicted to the voyeurism of proscenium-arch theatre his audience was. Pan's cry of 'Do you believe . . . ?' was a daring challenge to established theatrical convention, as well. Something of the audience's astonishment on the first night is conveyed by Marcosson and Daniel Frohman in their biography of Frohman senior:

> It registered a whole new and intimate relationship between actress and audience, and had the play possessed no other distinctive feature, this alone would have at once lifted it to a success that was all its own.[175]

Such directness also conveys Barrie's claim for heroic stature within the combative Darwinian world. Wendy seeks to rule; Peter seeks to rule; even poor Mr Darling seeks to conserve a domain of power — but the obsessed and obsessive Scot overrules them all and, here, flaunts his superiority. In *Little Mary* he had done so almost secretly, in riddle form. In *Peter Pan* he does so with a frightening, Iago-like, enjoyment in making things difficult for himself so that his glorification may be the greater. Sentimental Tommy had rejoiced in a similar artificial heightening of tests of the Will-to-Power;[176] his creator now reveals, openly, that personality trait.

> He loved to play the manipulator, to be God to other people; to shape their lives, arrange their friendships, make them as dependent on him as he possibly could.[177]

His silent, unexplained appearance between Peter and Wendy at the end of the 1908 Epilogue was also done with the intention of confirming the sinister, shadowy side of his public personality as described by Cynthia Asquith.[178] As the Gods relinquish benevolent power so the artist seizes it.

(iii) *Language, Power and Roget*

As an exploration of art and anagogy, *Peter Pan* laments that language is an imperfect medium and regrets that lost theological certainty prevents the text conveying truths beyond that medium. As yet another expression of the Darwinian battle of life, however, it presents a sustained and subtle analysis of the power of the imperfect word in an imperfect world. Modern English readers have been introduced to the political implications of this idea by Orwell.[179] Darwin was equally clear. The evolution of the species was matched by an evolution of sound-codes:

> I cannot doubt that language owes its origin to the imitation and modification of various natural sounds, the voices of other animals, and man's own instinctive ones, aided by signs or gestures.[180]

As man's intellect developed, so these patterns of significatory sound became more complex:

> Through his powers of intellect, articulate language has been evolved; and on this his wonderful advancement has mainly depended.[181]

Within the cruel world of evolutionary conflict, mastery of this code inevitably implied the ability to manipulate others less well versed in its subtleties. But Darwin saw language not only as a tool within the warfare but as an emblem of the battle itself:

> A struggle for life is constantly going on amongst the words and grammatical forms in each language.[182]

Just as the hero rises above the mass and survives, so the word lives and dies according to its capacity to adapt and impress:

> The survival or preservation of certain favoured words in the struggle for existence is natural selection.[183]

Pan as Napoleon; Wendy as bard and Hook as proud possessor of a Thesaurus[184] fight their battle within the field of the text just as really as they face each other on the decks of the Jolly Roger.

Before this argument can advance, however, the full implications of a text conducted under the aegis of Roget must be addressed. One of the truly remarkable gaps in Barrie studies is the failure to see either how closely Roget's life paralleled Barrie's own or to relate Roget's thinking to *Peter Pan*. Peter Roget, like the Scottish dramatist, had attended Edinburgh

University; like Barrie he had spent his apprenticeship in the North of England but decided that his destiny lay in London:

> He had learned in these years, that if one wished anything more than a mediocre success, one must seek it in London.[185]

Not only was he influenced by Darwin; he mixed socially with him. This is less surprising than it might seem on the surface because Roget was not, primarily, a linguist but a doctor and anthropologist, who achieved his version of Barrie's 'self-made' triumph, when he was elected Fullerian Professor of Physiology at the Royal Institution in 1834.

His *Thesaurus* is not only a 'literary tour de force but the culminating effort of a lifetime devoted to discovering a way of presenting the unity of man's existence.' [186] Its categories are based on the Zoological phyla and are an attempt to reconcile the apparent opposition between the validity of ordering forms and the continuum of nature as re-defined by Darwin, Monboddo and others. He had a more optimistic view of God's existence than Barrie, advocating a kind of sequential creationism. Crucially, however, all his work was aimed at solving the ultimate problems of life and death. His *Thesaurus* (like Urquhart's Universal Language) was conceived as an instrument of thought:

> None but those who are conversant with the philosophy of mental phenomena can be aware of the immense influence that is exercised by language in promoting the development of our ideas, in fixing them in the mind, and detaining them for steady contemplation.[187]

That instrument must cope with the complexity of interrelations within the natural world as defined by Darwin:

> It is by such analysis alone that we can arrive at a clear perception of the relation which those symbols bear to their corresponding ideas, or can obtain a correct knowledge of the elements which enter into the formation of compound ideas, and of the exclusions by which we arrive at the abstractions so perpetually resorted to in the process of reasoning, and in the communication of our thoughts.[188]

Even if the task be impossible in ultimate terms, the struggle for maximal perfection was necessary, both in theory and in practice:

> A misapplied or misapprehended term is sufficient to give rise to fierce and interminable disputes: a misnomer has turned the tide of popular opinion; a verbal sophism has decided a part question.[189]

Like Barrie he would have applauded the refusal of Tommy Sandys to put pen to paper so long as the belief that he had failed to find the most precise word haunted him.

Barrie worked with the *Thesaurus* always on his desk. His antiquarian interest in Edinburgh and his knowledge of the full range of its faculties had been displayed in *An Edinburgh Eleven*. It is tempting to connect Roget's own horror at discovering how few students graduated from the medical faculty with *Walker, London* and the dilemma of poor McPhail. It is more persuasive to see the use of 'phreen' in *Little Mary* in relation to the origins of the *Thesaurus*:

> Characteristically, he begins with the etymology of the word *physiology*, finding that its Greek progenitor had a much wider signification than the modern word.[190]

But it is in the wider context of lives lived in dedicated pursuit of the ultimate mysteries that Roget and Barrie are proven soulmates. It is the excess of meaning over form which haunted Roget from 'physiology' on; it is the excess of meaning over form which haunted Tommy Sandys and the dramatist of multiple endings. It is the need to explore how far categorisation can go before validity turns into comforting myth, which underlies the *Thesaurus*. The same motivation leads Barrie from novel to drama, and within drama to the story-types of Jolles. The 'dedication' of *Peter Pan* to Roget is not as playful as it seems. It is fitting that, in his major work and his major dramatic analysis of the origins of life and language, the Scottish dramatist confesses his debt to the Swiss doctor who shared with him so much more than a few years spent in Edinburgh's Old College.

(iv) *Names and the Seizing of Power*

The extent to which *Peter Pan* and Barrie's treatment of the *Pan* myth is a study of the means of human communication is a topic of labyrinthine complexity.[191] I have chosen to highlight first, the power of Names and second, the linguistic version of Darwin's battle for survival. Each major character is 'master' of a different type of communication code and uses it or abuses it to gain his ends within the drama. Thirdly, Barrie's short story, 'The Blot on Peter Pan', will complement and confirm these arguments.

Barrie's obsessive interest in names was one of the first discoveries I made when studying his draft-texts and revision techniques. Every one of the dramas prior to *Peter Pan* reveals names being cancelled, changed, re-called and changed again as Barrie strove to find the one form which harmonised with the character's personality or expressed exactly the most important level of representational concern.[192] In *Peter Pan*, the reasons for this part of the Tommy Sandys dilemma assume thematic force.

The Christian God's power, as embodied in the creative Word, has already been identified as a necessary starting point for *Pan* as Creation Myth. A fuller reference to *Genesis* may remind us of how clearly the Bible relates Naming to essence, knowledge and control:

> And God called the light Day, and the darkness he called Night . . . and God called the firmament Heaven . . . And God called the dry land Earth; and the gathering together of the waters called The Seas; and God saw that it was good.
>
> (*Genesis* I, 5-9)

For us, the naming follows the act but theologically they must be instantaneous, being a demonstration of an infinite Being, in whom all knowledge and power exist eternally as alpha and omega.

The expression of mystic beliefs through letters, words and names is not unique to Christianity. Barrie's interest in Africa (evidenced in the Novels and especially *Walker, London*) had been encouraged by the anthropological writings then in vogue. The unique linguistic status of the Name — a category of Language, rather than a category of speech — links it with primitive cultures and so, appropriately, with both *Genesis* and the Never Land. A modern writer sums up the situation thus:

> It is indeed inconceivable that any human society, however primitive, should have lacked a word for 'name'. This term belongs to the pre-grammatical stage of thought, to a time when people had no interest in words for their own sake, but thought of them solely as a means of speaking about the things of the external world.[193]

A literary creation myth should, therefore, not only embody structurally the great plan or non-plan; it must pay attention to the apparent detail of the letter and to Names in particular.

As the ideas culminating in *The Origin of Species* developed, so anthropologists became more and more interested in the magical powers associated with naming in primitive societies. There is evidence that Barrie read some of these articles but they had, anyway, been synthesised by Sir James Frazer in *The Golden Bough*, two years before *Peter Pan* was first produced. Frazer attributes to the 'primitive savage' Peter's own simplistic faith in Name-as-magic:

> Unable to discriminate clearly between words and things, the savage commonly fancies that the link between a name and the person or thing denominated by it is not a mere arbitrary and ideal association, but a real and substantial bond which unites the two.[194]

One further authority may be cited before I move to the audaciously thorough treatment of this area of linguistic metaphysics in *Peter Pan*. This adds the necessary dimension of knowledge-power as personal confrontation. It also completes another time circle, uniting one of the most radical modern writers with one of the most ancient:

> A name, in the narrow logical sense of a word whose meaning is particular, can only be applied to a particular with which the speaker is acquainted, because you cannot name anything you are not acquainted with. You remember, when Adam named the beasts, they came before him one by one, and he became acquainted with them and named them.[195]

The writer is Bertrand Russell; the satisfactory drawing together of material cyclically is not mine but a necessary consequence of Barrie's brilliance.

In *Peter Pan*, the battle of names is introduced at the earliest opportunity with Peter's first question to Wendy:

PETER: What is your name?
WENDY: [*Well satisfied*] Wendy Moira Angela Darling. What is yours?
PETER: [*Finding it lamentably brief*] Peter Pan.
WENDY: Is that all?
PETER: [*Biting his lip*] Yes.
WENDY: [*Politely*] I am so sorry.   (p 515)

This is the nominal equivalent of a knock-out in Round One. The length of her name impresses the primitive imagination, which equates brevity with insignificance. Wendy's surname is also the sign of her stability within a loving ('Darling') family unit. Each of the three Christian names, which she leads before delivering this uppercut, have emerged from a long process of rejection and election within the *Notebooks*. Wendy is decided upon quite early (see Nos. 300, 416 etc), and is — as Birkin reminds us — itself a coinage, derived from the attempts of W E Henley's daughter to name the playwright.

> Margaret christened Barrie 'my Friendly', but because she couldn't pronouce her 'r's' it came out coyly as 'me Wendy' — a non-existent name at that time.[196]

It is absolutely appropraite that the heroine of a play about creation should have a created name; it is also fitting that an author who wishes to join his inspiration to the minds of young children (Dedication pp 489-92; 497-502) should choose a name, originating in this way.

Of the other names, Moira is, in the Lilly MS, Maria: Angela is Elizabeth. Maria Elizabeth joins the ideas of virginity and power through associations with the mother of Christ and the Virgin Queen. Moira Angela has the same force but the references are allegorical (Angel) and textual (Moira Loney) rather than specific and historical. For a work which reflects on its own words, this choice is apposite. By contrast, Peter is not only brief but contains irreconcilable contradictions — pagan against Christian; God against Child; non-meaning through multiplication of meanings against single meaning as evocation of divine truth.[197] There is a sense in which that name, for all its tragically contradictory but uncancelled visions of self and Nature is much more in the spirit of the post-Darwinian age. Indeed, the title *Peter Pan* can be seen as Barrie's most economical coding of what Septimus Smith would later see as one of literature's saddest functions — 'The secret signal which one generation passes, under disguise, to the next, of loathing, hatred, despair.'[198] But the comfortable Bloomsbury setting allows Wendy to control the terms of the debate and evade, for the time being, the question of whether 'Wendy Darling' is itself a comforting myth.

Act 2 presents another form of nominal diminution. If Peter is bested by Wendy in debate, Hook's name is itself a sign of his subsidiary rôle. Given to him by Peter, it refers to part of his appearance. Anthropologists had noted that nicknames of this sort were common among savages. Frazer distinguishes between 'real or primary names' and these 'secondary names'.[199] 'Hook,' therefore, belongs to the realm of the shadows, to a secondary world imagined by Pan. Within that world, however much he may boast of a hook's superiority to the hand, the major emergent fact is that he has been maimed by his creator:

> HOOK: Most of all I want their captain, Peter Pan. 'Twas he cut off my arm.
> I have waited long to shake his hand with this.   (p 527)

Appropriately he reacts with an impotent desire for vengeance reminiscent of the devil, whose 'hook' was itself a sign of his inability to accept the implications of omniscient divinity.[200]

When Hook does confront Peter in Act 3, therefore, the outcome is pre-determined. Again the central focus is the act of naming, this time with particular reference to identity. What follows is the assumption by Peter (logically) of Hook into his own essence by re-claiming his name. This is done as part of the trickery, which characterises the game-battles on the island. The seriousness of the underlying meaning is 'signed' both by Hook's piteous readiness to accept and his extreme tonal horror:

> PETER: [who is only too ready to speak] I am Jas Hook, Captain of the Jolly Roger.
> HOOK: [now white to the gills] No, no you are not.
> PETER: Brimstone and gall, say that again and I'll cast anchor in you.
> HOOK: If you are Hook, come tell me, who am I?
> PETER: A codfish, only a codfish.
> HOOK: [aghast] a codfish?
> STARKEY: It's lowering to our pride.
> HOOK: [feeling that his ego is slipping from him] Don't desert me, bullies.

'Codfish' and 'gills' provide the last detailed insult. Hook — part-name, part-creation, part-devil is now drawn into the fishlike state of primitive evolutionary development. As such, he fulfils the evidence of the anthropologists, who observed the vulnerability of the savage imagination to the magic of names.

> Magic may be wrought on a man just as easily through his name as through his hair, his nails, or any other material part of his person.[201]

If naming creates, then un-naming dissolves.

If impotence can be related to withdrawal of a name, it also may be mirrored through the inability of a character to relate name and identity accurately. The most aggressive claim to self-knowledge is, in this sense, Smee's (It's me.) But, as Hook notes, that pirate has a notoriously false sense of his own nature:

> HOOK: Pathetic Smee, the Nonconformist pirate, a happy smile upon his face because he thinks they fear him! How can I break it to him that they think him lovable?   (p 560)

Even more serious is the error of Slightly, who grants himself a false name, drawn from misinterpretation of motherhood:

> SLIGHTLY: My mother was fonder of me than your mothers were of you. [*Uproar*] Oh yes, she was. Peter had to make up names for you, but my mother had wrote my name on the pinafore I was lost in. 'Slightly Soiled'; that's my name.   (p 525)

In short, Pan makes sure that his own sense of impotence within Barrie's text is transferred to the shadow realm where he holds sway. The names he confers consistently define identity in relation to his overarching power or misdefine identity in relation to origin and nature.

The final major problem relates to naming in relation to objective reality. In the Never Land there are different orders of 'shadow'. Pirates and Redskins are created within the game by Peter. Over them his power is complete; he can name and un-name, confer and withdraw existence with impunity. Wendy and the Boys (of both Bloomsbury and Lost varieties) exist outwith the dream in the sense that they can escape into the outer frame of *Peter Pan's* dramatic structure. So long as they are in the Never Land, they share Pan's ethereal nature without abrogating their humanity. This crucial distinction between dream-fiction and realities imported into the dream is skilfully translated into the 'naming drama' through discussion of the most basic needs of the body. As in *The Admirable Crichton* food becomes the centre of mimetic concern.

Peter, it is suggested, no longer needs to eat. Wendy and the Lost Boys do. For them the 'pretend meals', therefore, present a unique problem.

> The pretend meals are not Wendy's idea; indeed she was rather startled to find, on arriving, that Peter knew of no other kind, and she is not absolutely certain even now that he does eat the other kind, though no one appears to do it more heartily. He insists that the pretend meals should be partaken of with gusto, and we see his band doing their best to obey orders.   (p 547)

The command context is important for it once again enforces Peter's Napoleonic absolutism within the fantasy realm. But its effect is not absolute. He can control action but he *cannot* ordain the associated emotion. They will obey by eating nothing; they will not, and cannot, do so with 'gusto'. Here, animal need or particular reality dictates and that is outwith the influence of Pan. The opening words of dialogue, backed up by the playwright's parenthetic comments, underline this:

> WENDY: [*her fingers to her ears, for their chatter and clatter are deafening*]. Si-lence! Is your mug empty, Slightly?
> SLIGHTLY: [*who would not say this if he had a mug*]. Not quite empty, thank you.   (p 547)

The conventionally polite reply of the most confused Lost Boy of all is still a triumph over the demands of the mighty Pan. His gusto remains inviolate.

It will only be inspired when the name refers to one real mug filled with real poe-poe. Until he has won him away from his humanity entirely, Pan cannot command the least of the Lost Boys in the way he can the mightiest of his pirates. The nicety and exactitude of the linguistic struggle cannot be coincidence. It has been worked out by Barrie in advance. So, Pan makes sure that his own sense of impotence within Barrie's text is transferred nominally to his own creations in the Never Land.

(v) *Codes and the Limitations on Power*

In the Edwardian period, Shakespearean criticism held *The Tempest* to be the bard's finest work.[202] Barrie, in his own great dream play, returned to many of the issues faced on Prospero's island. Here again are the ideals of youth and intellect faced with the compromising and corrupting effects of real power. Once more, a primitive land is invaded, disrupted and deserted — the practical problems of colonisation set against the grand ideas of innocence, mercy and justice. Crucially, however, both Barrie and Shakespeare focus attention on the conflict between real and ideal in language as well as action. Just as the creature can never know God, so the Universal Language does not exist. In the shadow of these failures man plays out a tragi-comedy, inadequately explaining it to himself and others through shared but imperfect conventions of sound.

This implies that we too must move from silences, simple sound signs and names to language as code. *Peter Pan* takes us through the various evolutionary stages of language mapped out by Darwin. So, too, had Shakespeare. Appropriately the primitive earth-creature Caliban communicated via animal sounds:

> PROSPERO: I pitied thee,
> Took pains to make thee speak, taught thee each hour
> One thing or other: when thou didst not, savage,
> Know thine own meaning, but wouldst gabble like
> A thing most brutish, I endow'd thy purposes
> With words that made them known.   (1/2/355/60)

But if he lacked words to transmit messages directly, the same Caliban is shown to have both poetry in his soul and a type of amoral innocence suited to his rôle as Aristotle's natural man.[203]

In this he resembles Pan with regard to code and Hook with regard to status. Like the pirate, Caliban has been given a marred name which defines his impotence (Cannibal) in the power game of art. Like Pan, he has come to speak in words but is uniquely defined by his power over the less precise and more mystic language of music, which can suggest either divinity or savagery, depending on perspective. For Pan, as for Caliban, this talent is related to control within the primitive or dream world. Peter understands and can reproduce all the secret codes of the Never Land:

> The answer comes as of a tinkle of bells; it is the fairy language. Peter can speak it, but it bores him.   (p 515)
>
> Peter, who knows the bird language, slips into the nest.   (p 545)

So, within that confined realm, an imported language will only have value for its importer, as Caliban explicitly tells Prospero.

Prospero and Barrie, however, move the dialectical goalposts, conducting their argument in ideal metaphysical terms. So long as there is the Idea of a perfect form of communication embodying rather than referring to the vast complexity of the observed world, the code must widen and refine in order to match that advanced vision. The linguistic corollary of Peter's refusal to accept Death, is his knowing acceptance of a limited code. When Barrie tells us that he can *only* play 'fairy music on his pipes', he is using that restricted range as a mirror of Pan's personal limitations. In the late fifteenth century, Robert Henryson had used Orpheus' harp in a similar significatory fashion. Spiritual ignorance translated itself into lost musical power; complete divine knowledge enabled him to control all levels of existence through music. But Orpheus, like Pan, knew an intermediary stage where innocence had not yet become ignorance. At that stage his harp charmed the natural world alone:

> Him to reios, 3it playit he a spryng,
> Quhill all the foulis of the wod can syng,
> And treis dansit with thar leves grene,
> Him to devoid of his gret womenting.
>
> (*Orpheus and Eurydice*, 144-7)

Communication is related to identity, understanding, status and perceived purpose.

While Shakespeare *states* that language is process and a process, which can exclude as well as embrace, Barrie uses Peter to *enact* this argument for the benefit of audience and fellow-players. Following the belief of Victorian and Edwardian anthropologists that the earliest sounds were associated with differentiated emotional states, he allows his eternal child to explain the significance of varied patterns within Tink's bell language. Stage Directions connect distinguished sounds with joy, frustration, shrill anger and so on. That information is closed to the theatregoer until Peter begins to interpret a limited number of bell-phrases such as 'silly ass'. Soon the sound will come without the explanation; the audience has moved into a state of superiority. This demonstrates not only the essential secrecy of language but its power; should someone arrive after the interval he will be excluded from the shared understanding.

If Peter and Tinker Bell are primarily associated with the mystic and primitive powers of language; Wendy is the mistress of English both as bard figure and representative of the 'real' world. Frequently, her more advanced understanding of language as explication results in her becoming, like Prospero, the teacher of the innocent and the unsophisticated. Once more, limitations of code and man's nature come together. If words embodied the objects they signified according to some logic, teaching of that code would be the limit of Wendy's or Prospero's power. As it is, each comes with her or his peculiar vision of truth, conveyed within a body of sounds conventionally established and unsustained by any necessary referential principles. The temptation to manipulate proves irresistible for both. Prospero, like the rulers in Havel's *The Memorandum*,[204] uses language as an instrument of power over Caliban and Ariel. He also employs it as a means of limiting Miranda's[205] understanding to the comforting myths perpetuated by Mrs Darling. Worst of all, he has denied to her a true understanding of her identity and origins:

> PROSPERO: . . . thee my daughter, who
> Art ignorant of what thou art.

(1/2/17-18)

As a consequence of the fact that the bard figure rules Shakespeare's Island, while Peter as stage-director controls Barrie's Never Land, the equivalent lesson is again played out rather than revealed in the later work. The kiss/thimble dialogues are first of all illustrations of primitive against sophisticated communication through words:

> WENDY: I shall give you a kiss if you like.
> PETER: Thank you. [*He holds out his hand*]
> WENDY: [*aghast*] Don't you know what a kiss is?
> PETER: I shall know when you give it me. [*Not to hurt his feelings she gives him her thimble.*] Now shall I give you a kiss?
> WENDY: [*primly*] If you please. [*He pulls an acorn button off his person and bestows it on her. She is shocked but considerate*] I will wear it on this chain round my neck.   (p 517)

> WENDY: Peter, you may give me a kiss.
> PETER: [*cynically*] I thought you would want it back. [*He offers her the thimble*]
> WENDY: [*artfully*] Oh, dear, I didn't mean a kiss, Peter, I meant a thimble.
> PETER: [*only half placated*] What is that?
> WENDY: It is like this. [*She leans forward to give a demonstration, but something prevents the meeting of their faces*]
> PETER: [*satisfied*] Now, shall I give you a thimble?
> WENDY: If you please.   (p 519)

Wendy's superiority is established, when Peter replies to her accurate use of English ('kiss') with a gesture revealing ignorance ('He holds out his hand.') The generous protective impulse which makes her replace correct word with false object (thimble) nonetheless grants her potential power within a language system, which she knows she can manipulate with some impunity. Soon, altruism will give way to self-interest. Moving the kiss to her finger also reflects primness and gives her a breathing space. In the second exchange — as the bracketed stage directions reveal — she simply exploits the eternal boy. So great, indeed, is her success that he is about to disobey his own stated rules and let her lips touch his.

That is the simple message of the verbal battle, released by the accidental relationship between signifier and signified. Carried to extremes, it permits the chaos of interpretation, tragically noted by Peter in the Beinecke 1904/05B text — 'You see you all mean different things,' (Scene 3, p 58). If that is possible when agreement on word and reference is accepted, how much greater may intellectual anarchy become when the medium is itself used to deceive and to perpetuate part visions. But Wendy's linguistic power lies within the realm of naturalistic narrative and is limited to explanation of the 'real'. Does the 'kiss' dialogue 'mean' differently, when related either to the primitive or the allegorical use of language?

The first exploration is by far the easier. Peter, in his naivety, clearly hopes there is some referential logic behind language. Once a kiss becomes a thimble, he seizes on the semantic property of 'comparative slightness' [206] and so substitutes an acorn button. The irony here is that his simple honesty provides him with a weapon against Wendy. Her desire for a true kiss is now opposed by the idea of slightness, which she had herself introduced as an interim means of keeping her distance. If she had hoped to manipulate language freely, she is hoist on her own metaphorical petard.

There is, however, another range of linked meanings. In Victorian slang 'button' and 'thimble' were associated with confidence trickery of precisely the sort which Wendy is linguistically perpetrating. The 'button' was the accomplice of the 'thimble ringer' or pickpocket. 'Thimble', according to this code, meant 'watch'.[207] Given Barrie's intellect and ability to convey economically, can one confidently deny the possibility that here the sub-God is unconsciously revealing the ultimate truth of the Darwinian battle at a textual level? Can one definitely reject the intention of using the lowest, most devious type of code, indirectly to convey the highest ontological problems? Can one discount the possibility that Barrie had carefully concealed, as in *Little Mary*, the answer to the subtlest riddle of all, when that answer proves to be the very object (watch) which in its *comparatively larger* form (clock), is at once the symbol and the fact of the drama's most obvious theme — Time? According to his own literary theory, of course, the problem of intention is ultimately irrelevant, the text being capable of opening up a meaning beyond its authorially conceived significances. But, anyone who has followed his perfectionist mind, logically pursuing the different implications of layered meaning and imagistic openness from *Walker, London* through to *Peter Pan*, may be forgiven for preferring an answer in terms of self-conscious authorial genius.

There is no exact parallel for Hook's linguistic 'impotence in versatility' on Prospero's island, because Shakespeare was not concerned to call into question the real existence of the outside world as such, or the Real patterning of that world by a deity. Hook is, as we have noted, the most subtle of orators. His problem is that he has no audience. A creature of words, created by a creation of his author's, he ultimately rants to himself within the prison of his text. If Peter and Wendy demonstrate the limitations of language, there is a sense in which Hook IS that limitation.

Once more, his language defines his nature. As the representative of the lost aesthetic world of the harlequinade, all his references are to that aesthetically defined realm. His, then, is the language of the artifice, whether that be understood as mimicking the style of past actors (Irving etc.) or of past dramatists. At times he can sound like the arch-trickster in Jonsonean comedy:

> HOOK: Brimstone and gall, what cozening is here?   (p 541)

at others like the blackest of villains in a Victorian melodrama:

> HOOK: So you like it, do you! By Caius and Balbus, bullies, here is a notion: open the cabin door and drive them in. Let them fight the doodle-doo for their lives. If they kill him we are so much the better: if he kills them we are none the worse.   (p 565)

Sometimes, as when 'he capers detestably along an imaginary plank and his copy-cats do likewise, joining in the chorus', he is the much less frightening villain of music hall or pantomime. But always he is referred to or refers himself to literary and dramatic types.

The most subtle literary echoes encourage us to associate him with Shakespearean heroes. In the Stage Directions we may, as readers, note that 'he cannot give the quietus' and so think of Hamlet or refer his end to Lear's because Barrie writes that his 'great heart . . . breaks.' In the theatre, the pirate's dialogue more often reminds us of another, more villainous, hero — Macbeth.

> HOOK: All mortals envy me, yet better perhaps for Hook to have had less ambition!   (p 560)

For the most part, Barrie does not work with passages lifted from earlier texts, preferring to use more oblique methods.

Fittingly, his final speech is full of literary associations:

> HOOK: Back, you pewling spawn. I'll show you now the road to dusty death. A holocaust of children, there is something grand in the idea.   (p 568)

'Pewling' evokes the cynicism of Jacques in *As You Like It.* In the first of his seven ages of man, that cynic cites the infant 'mewling and puking in the nurse's arms';[208] Barrie's coinage combines the two participles. 'Spawn' indicates an even earlier pre-birth stage, evolution having related man's development to fish and amphibians. One remembers his despair at 'becoming' a codfish and associates this farcical misery with the many humorous verses on this topic, then current:

> 'When you were a tadpole and I was a fish
> In the Palaeozoic time,
> And side by side in the ebbing tide
> We sprawled through the ooze and slime'.[209]

Hook's first sentence, then, is a cold, satiric acceptance of creation without God, set within a farcical context.

His second sentence leaps the time to come and accepts death with the hopeless dignity of Macbeth. The echo on this occasion comes from the final act of Shakespeare's play immediately after Seyton has announced Lady Macbeth's passing.

> To-morrow, and to-morrow, and to-morrow
> Creeps in this petty pace from day to day,
> To the last syllable of recorded time;
> And all our yesterdays have lighted fools
> The way to dusty death. Out, out, brief candle!   (V. v. 19-23)

This association has also been carefully chosen. Just as 'spawn' drew us before birth, so the Macbeth context draws us past individual death into acceptance of single and multiple deaths and on to an eternity without that sun which justifies the 'brief candle'. Finally, the 'holocaust' with its reminiscences of another tragic 'fool' — Herod,[210] type of the Anti-Christ, — resurrects the devilish associations round Hook. His pride in intellect also characterised Satan and his angelic crew in *Paradise Lost*, the *Miracle Cycles* and *The Gospel of Nicodemus*. This is Hook's tragedy — seeing the folly of all life, he still dramatically models himself on the greatest fool of all: as actor he is born and, as actor, dies with form but without essence.

The crucial remaining 'speaker' is Barrie himself. The manner in which he uses the complete text of his Dream indirectly to expose the limitations of philosophical and artistic visions of the individual creations within it, has already been dwelt upon. Shakespeare had done much the same thing in *A Midsummer Night's Dream*, when setting the circumscribed views of rulers, courtiers, lovers and artisans within the highest and most comprehensive form of poetic truth. The cruellest paradox of all, however, centres round the author. For, if he speaks to both children and adults in *Peter Pan*, he is also setting the greatest literary test for the smallest group of readers via the weakest and most villainous of his characters. The theological, ethical, natural and linguistic implications of this choice have been considered; the authorial implications only touched upon.

By setting his 'autobiography' in an appearance (Swarthy), who becomes a non-essence characterised by soliloquies, Barrie restates the isolation of the author within his own communications. In *Little Mary*, Reilly was understood only when he was misunderstood; he achieved his immortality only through myths based on what his audience gained at surface level. *Peter Pan*, through Hook, reflects the truth that the most challenging topic of all, apparently addressed to the widest audience of all, is ultimately addressed to himself alone and, perhaps, to a future age. The audience's rôle, given in *Little Mary* to the aristocrats, is played in the Never Land by the most lost of all the Lost Boys.

The part of Slightly expands in the later texts. I see this as Barrie's covert condemnation of those who received his Creation myth, expressing the new metaphysical problems raised by Darwin and Nietzsche in a form honed through Shakespeare and Bacon, with the usual cries of gratified non-enlightenment. If you have been recrowned with a laurel of cabbage-leaves,[211] it is surely only human to characterise your critics as lost children, protesting the more vehemently the less they know:

> PETER: [*holding up a button that is attached to her chain*]. See, the arrow struck against this, it is a kiss I gave her; it has saved her life.

Remember, the arrow is imagined; the button did nothing; her life was never endangered; the button is not a kiss. The whole event is created by Peter to dramatise himself and by Barrie as a metaphor for the sexual act and birth. All this, Slightly feigns to 'understand'.

> SLIGHTLY: I remember kisses; let me see it. [*He takes it in his hand.*] Ay, that is a kiss.

In so doing, he enacts a major argument within the myth — that we know nothing and know least the more certain we become. Slightly calls a thermometer a glass thing much as some critics call *Peter Pan* a play for children.

(vi)   'The Blot on Peter Pan'

My emphasis on Roget should not be taken to imply that Nietzsche anticipates Barrie's central ideas less forcefully in the linguistic arena. In fact, he laments the inadequacy of language in all three of the major areas treated in *Peter Pan*. It is unable to embody truth, although some people falsely make the greater claim:

> The language-maker was not modest enough to realise that he had only given designations to things. Instead, he believed that he had expressed through words the highest knowledge of things.
>
> (*Human All Too Human* Section 11)

That failure is part of the greater poverty of signs in relation to Nature's plenitude and variety. As no language can match the fullness nor the subtlety of the world, so 'words dilute and stupidize' (*Unpublished Notes*, p 610). As words also 'make the uncommon common (*Unpublished Notes*, p 610), so they play their part in matching the inaccessibility of Truth with the staleness of the fictions, which we create to mimic our perspectives on Untruth. Danto explains the Nietzschean viewpoint clearly:

> Art consists in illusions, while 'truth', which we contrast with it (as we contrast art with nature, fiction with fact), consists in stale illusions, illusions so worn with use that they have come with time, to be accepted as expressing the rock-bottom facts of the universe. The difference between so-called fact and (so-called) fiction is virtually quantitative, that being taken as fact which has been repeated a sufficient number of times.[212]

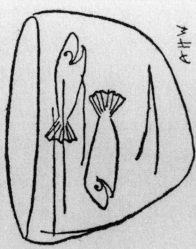

MACCD
MNO
OSAR
LMECD
LNINOCD
MAYUNOCD
MNO
R
OOOU iiii I 8 D
OG
U 8 M U I
SSS
OUINTK8
YU8MUNTK8YYY
OLNUCIMTNICMNI8M4T
4RTLRDI
4IDINTFS

7 A sample of the metalanguage invented by Neil, the hero of 'The Blot on Peter Pan'.

From this there arises the belief in the superiority of poetry and of fantasy as well as the recognition that the greatest communicators will be the least understood in their own age. As the ones who re-create the power of language through metaphor in order to employ it at the very limits, where it proves most inadequate, the first rank authors face the greatest failure. And drama, as the genre which depends most directly on popular appeal, must be the most oblique in its testing aspect, most direct in its soothing appeal.[213] All these ideas — shadowed in language — Nietzsche set down and Barrie enacted.

In this case, however, Barrie provides his own critical proof. The hero of 'The Blot on Peter Pan' (his short story in Cynthia Asquith's 1927 collection) is a little boy, Neil, who has defeated the Nietzschean staleness by inventing a new language. Using this primitive poetry he writes a curtain-raiser for *Peter Pan*. It is so successful that the audience forsake their old favourite. Both Barrie and his dream are destroyed.

As Fig 7 illustrates,[214] the text is set out so that words and picture provide alternative means of reference. This is a mirror both of Neil's primitive sense of language and of the accidental as opposed to necessary correlation between sign and signified. 'MACCD' translates 'Emma sees de (the)' and the picture provides the conclusion of 'goldfish'. Neil, like Peter Pan, seeks some logic behind the form of the words he has heard. This he supplies from his basic spelling lessons, making each letter have the value of its sound. 'MAYUNOCD' thus becomes 'Emma, why you no see de (goldfish.)'? His poetic imagination soon creates variations on this pattern. Numbers are brought into play. 'YU8MUNTK8YYY', sounds 'Why, you ate 'em, you Auntie Kate? Why? Why? Why?' with the number providing the past tense of eat as well as rounding off Auntie's name. Nor is the boy's ingenuity exhausted.[215] Lower case 'i's draw the appearance as well as the sound of letters into this primitive language system. 'Uiiii' is 'You four little ones'. The same letter, poorly printed, becomes 'You bad one' or, in upper case, 'You big one'.

In the short story, Barrie literally spells out those inadequacies of language, which permit the poetic and the primitive to challenge it. In *Peter Pan*, he had enacted the same conflict. It had, there, been related to a struggle for power. In the story, this battle is fought out at the level of authorship between the boy and Barrie himself. By identifying the crucial struggle with the battle for genius, Neil proves himself an instinctive Darwinian. It will be remembered that evolutionary theory centred on the belief that, as favoured forms increased, so less favoured forms would decrease. The boy's desire not simply to rival Barrie but to annihilate and humiliate him is equally consistent with the teaching that 'each new variety or species . . . will generally press hardest on its nearest kindred, and tend to exterminate them.'[216] The fact that Neil admires the author of *Peter Pan* and shares his dedication to words (sleeping with a dictionary rather than a soft toy in his arms!) is a condition of his enmity rather than being inconsistent with it.

If Neil's rivalry begins with personality and the medium, it continues with the message. That, first of all, is related to the idea of Art as utility. Neil's story is at once an emblem of the artist as a minister to society's ills and proof that bitter truths CAN be related to a rapturous audience. Auntie Kate commits the heinous offence of eating the goldfish. Not only does she come to realise her sin but the goldfish obediently climbs out of her stomach into the bowl again via the doctor's stethoscope! Within Barrie's own favoured form of sentimental comedy — The Doctor and Kate marry — a tale of greed and the stomach[217] is again conveyed but this time applauded. Neil triumphs where Barrie and Reilly or Barrie and Pan had failed. The world of the goldfish bowl is nasty and competitive but it is comprehended (in different senses) by both the younger dramatist and his audience. Like Reilly, Neil develops a book from a 'riddle', but unlike Reilly, he can reveal — literally — the nature of his message and the motivation behind it:

> The curtain falls and rises, with an enlarged copy of Neil's MS, pinned to it. The audience spell it out and learn how the play was written. The enthusiasm is now louder than the thunder.   (p 97)

It has been an essential part of my argument that the concerns of *Peter Pan* derive from the riddle of *Little Mary*, properly interpreted — the fact that the two 'tales' unite in Neil's triumph supports that contention.

In *Peter Pan*, the power of the author had also been related to naming. Both the magical power of the name as creative force and the importance of accuracy in relation to essence had been addressed. In 'The Blot,' these ideas are naively reinterpreted. Neil's tale does not begin with the gluttonous Auntie Kate but with the boy's own christening. The devices of Fairytale[218] are invoked but in a new spirit of empirical pessimism, appropriate to the age of Darwin. The Fairy Godmother's arrival is delayed by the evil figure of Science and the good fairies find their benevolently intended gifts perverted. Only the Bad Fairy's wish that Neil be proud (cocky) is actualised. Mimetically, this world of confusion confirms the message of *Peter Pan* that name determines nature in a world of conflict:

> There is a reason why I should describe his christening, for if it had been a different kind of christening, Peter Pan would be a different kind of boy.
>   (p 83)

Accurately defined, the 'hero' emerges with the chief characteristic of the devil in Christian mythology, and uses it to vanquish Barrie within his own text.

But does he? The final question is, as usual, capable of opposed answers on different levels of interpretation. Neil certainly wins the narrative; he wins on at least two levels of the allegory; but does he triumph in the Darwinian equivalent of anagogy? It is part of Neil's plan that he chose the Godlike rôle of Stage Director, dictating all the action of his play from the wings. Instinctively, he prefers sound and images which suggest elemental forces:

8   J M Barrie *c.* 1904.

He did not act himself (because the author did not act), but from the wings he worked the thunder and the sea and the horses. The scene was laid in the Peter Pan nursery thus taking all the novelty out of it.   (p 94)

He, therefore, takes over Barrie's rôle and seeks to emphasise the novelty of his own drama by making *Peter Pan* seem ordinary. This is a direct challenge and it is an audacious one. In arrogating to himself control over the supernatural (thunder), life (sea) and the passions (horses) he seeks to destroy Barrie completely. By claiming primacy in Time (curtain-raiser) as Youth (four year old) he makes that claim within the major theme of *Pan*.

Is the victor in this battle for creative control, Neil, who perfects Barrie's language, destroys the effect of his most cherished play and wins over the audience by an act of miraculous power translated into the images of teaching and curing? Perhaps. But who names Neil? Who is the Bad Fairy?

'And is cockiness the Blot on Peter Pan?' asks Billy.
'Alas,' said I.
'But you gave it to him. Hello, are you Peter's bad fairy?'   (p 100)

Who stands on the wings of the story, telling an 'actual' boy about this 'fictive' boy within an imaginative adaptation of the Fairy-Tale Form? Who claims that the major effect of Neil's linguistic coup is in fact the alteration of his own hero (Peter) in a time prior to his audience's knowledge? Who is the puppeteer and who the puppet?

The answer again depends on perspective although one is tempted to say that here Barrie presents his pessimistic aesthetic equivalent of the 'Fortunate Fall'. As Christian theology defined creation in a priori terms of supernatural benevolence, thus making all apparent misery, actually fortunate; so in the fictive Universe of chaos, all apparent dishonesty must ultimately be determined by the Artist in the interests of his own integrity. Both are related to and justified by understanding. But the nature of the understanding appealed to and the nature of the Universe posited are at opposed poles — truth against doubt; unity against perspectivism; Reality against fiction; God against Artist; Nature as Love against Nature as Battle. Barrie may not wish to present this vision; but as honest author he sees no option. His fantasy is justified by its honest presentation of the actual and in that world pride ceases to be the first sin. Instead, it becomes the first necessity for survival. The 'blot' on Pan is, thus, also the self-directed pride-in-genius of his Creator.

CHAPTER FIVE

The Road to the Never Land

> O voi ch'avete li 'ntelletti sani,
> mirate la dottrina che s'asconde
> sotto 'l velame de li versi strani.
> (Dante, *L'Inferno*, IX, 61-63)[1]

> Every profound thinker is more afraid of being understood than of being misunderstood. The latter may perhaps wound his vanity; but the former will wound his heart.
> (Nietzsche, *Beyond Good and Evil*, 290)

How then, at the end of the Road to the Never Land, do I evaluate Barrie? Following his own love of a circular pattern with variation, I shall return to the considerations of Chapter One. In particular, I shall consider the position of Scottish Literature and the reasons why that discipline in particular finds the author of *Peter Pan* an uncomfortable companion. I shall reassess his wider critical reception and address the complex issue of the degree to which he may offer us a deceptive or unfair Art. I shall end as I began with a consideration of Genius and his own artistic Never Land.

A Scottish Never Land

As a perspectivist, Barrie would necessarily have been concerned with the way in which he is viewed by his countrymen. He would also be dismayed for, if he is largely dismissed elsewhere, within Scottish Literature he has become an anti-hero. As a lover of definition, he would then seek to understand what Scottish Literature is. The most obvious feature is its current dynamism. During the 1940s and 1950s Scottish letters — like Scottish History — were largely ignored within the Scottish Educational system. Reaction has produced more thorough teaching at all levels, extension of the canon and critical attention throughout the world. This movement is one with which I associate myself; it was necessary and has been fruitful.

But if the nature of the discipline is changing, the means of discrediting Barrie within it have not altered much. William Donaldson's recent study of *Popular Literature in Victorian Scotland* echoes practically all the views of George Blake.[2] In four pages of literary postscripts to his valuable research in a new area he confines specific reference to the early story collections and *Margaret Ogilvy*. This narrow canon is associated with the Kailyard, inevitably characterised through its most extremely sentimental exemplar, *Beside the Bonnie Brier Bush*. Barrie is not distinguished from the writings of Ian Maclaren; indeed the group becomes 'Barrie and Co.' (p 146). He is connected only with the conservative Christian thought of Robertson Nicoll and *The British Weekly*. His message is 'simplistic' and his language 'minimalist' (p 146). Accurately, Donaldson accepts that Barrie is not naturalist but begs the question of whether fantasy be, necessarily, dissociated from the real or the Real. All this can be found in Millar or Blake. Even the latter's odd refusal to accept the poverty of Barrie's origins is repeated. Once more, the dramatist is removed to the bourgeoisie via the methods of Romance.[3] As the anti-hero's biography does not fit in with the desired message, his family are brought in as substitutes:

> The milieu of the Kailyarders was in any case noticeably bourgeois. Much has been made of Barrie's lowly origins, but his family were in fact relatively well-to-do. His mother's brother, for example, was a minister; his father was a small employer . . .   (p 147)

Why does the self-evident modesty of that tiny house in Kirriemuir matter so much within a literary argument?

The answer is that we are not really here concerned with a literary argument but with sociological judgement. This is not so improper as it may sound for Scottish Literature is a definition which crosses disciplines. The moment the word 'Scottish' is added, a genuine invitation is thrown out to those whose major concerns are non-literary. What Donaldson, like Blake before him, is doing is to set Barrie against a series of archetypes drawn from those other disciplines. The linguistic archetype is Doric or Synthetic Scots; the historical archetype is concern with Scottish history, limiting the canon to themes of this sort; the national archetype, which finds enthusiasm for England and English audiences a sign of treachery, is the recovery of Scottish nationhood; the political and social archetypes are those of the Left Wing and the working classes.

Barrie would not object to this wider audience nor that audience's enthusiasms, perspectives or mythic constructions. But he was himself first, foremost and exclusively a man of letters. Correctly, he would object to judgements which failed to take that into account or failed adequately to define his aims (the presentation of the actual through the mythic)[4] and his methods (based on those of Shakespearean Romance). Moreover, as a believer in the governing power of changing Nature, he would urge that the recent changes in Scottish Literature must imply new answers to the new questions posed by that development.

So long as Scottish Literature's greatest aspiration was the establishing of an introductory course, it was fitting that the canon favour those books which satisfied the widest range of the sub-criteria listed above. The law of literary excellence was invoked to exclude the inferior; inclusion depended on additional qualities drawn from one or other of the non-literary archetypes.[5] But the more the discipline expands, the greater the call becomes for literary criteria to be distinguished from 'Scottish'. At all times, the student must admit his own major reasons for interest. It is one thing to assess Barrie sociologically; it is quite another to appear to condemn the artist as artist because he does not meet sociologically or politically pre-determined standards. Modest awareness of this would prevent much of the belligerence which, academically, sets critic against critic when, in fact, they start from different but undifferentiated premises.

Barrie, like Moira Loney, could offer students of Scottish Literature some uncomfortable truths about our own state; like Moira Loney he has been excluded for his troubles. The master of the story-type, the 'case' and the paradigm is dismissed within a subject which is, itself, a paradigm. In establishing its distinctiveness, any sub-culture is forced into paradigmatic formulations of one sort or another. In advancing this case, R Cairns Craig argues that the major rival will tend to become the measure of contrast:

> Scotland is not compared to Ireland or to Norway, but to England and an England endowed with a cumulative, unbroken history supporting an organically growing literature.[6]

There are two strands of reasoning here, both accepted by Barrie as early as *The Little Minister*. The paradigm offers clarity in exchange for simplification and polarisation.

To gain clear ground the minority culture must further narrow its canon in terms of a tradition.[7] That analytic definition will in one sense put it at an even greater disadvantage *vis-á-vis* the major rival. English Literature will effortlessly draw in all those who write in English (Conrad, T S Eliot) but Scottish Literature will either exclude or have difficulty in accepting those writers of Scots birth and background who do not embody the defining characteristics of the paradigm. The fantasist, the metaphysical writer, the Right Wing writer, the writer in English will stand outside this initial definition, only to be drawn in again when there is greater confidence.

I cannot see Barrie objecting to the situation thus defined, although he might have found a bleak irony in his currrent situation as convenient anti-hero and anti-myth within the paradigm of Scottish Literature. After all, what other Scottish writer had thought so much about myth and paradigm? What he would have opposed is the looseness of definition which permits his status *as writer* to be falsified in the interests of that formula. His view can only be seen as simplistic and idyllic if the canon is narrowed to an eclectic reading of *Auld Licht Idylls* and *A Window in Thrums* plus a misreading of *Sentimental Tommy*. Once we do this, we are seeing the paradigm as an end rather than a means.

If we should beware canonical simplification, then, we should also beware polarisation posing as literary judgement. The usual contrast with Brown's *The House with the Green Shutters* is advanced in terms of its welcome opposition to Kailyardism. It may be that this novel deserves its current status as one of the 'greats' within the Scottish Literary Tradition in spite of its over-explicitness and melodramatic tendencies. Any such literary judgement must, however, be made in full awareness that it also fortuitously meets, positively, every one of the distinctive sub-criteria noted above.[8] How far is it welcomed as an individual work of art and how far as fitting embodiment of a distinctive myth?

If the paradigm, like the myth, simplifies and polarises it also dehistoricises. Barrie's use of the archetypal story — the case in *The Admirable Crichton;* the myth in *Peter Pan;* the riddle in *Little Mary* — was conducted in full awareness of this. To be a powerful weapon of analysis and comment it must freeze it but only in order to issue, with new knowledge, into time again. (Moira's book is only the medium; Peter Pan's choice is tragic.) If Scottish Literature allows its chosen pattern to become its own ideal (follows Peter rather than Wendy) then the underlying threat of increasing anachronism will wreak its own revenge. I shall look briefly at the question of 'dehistoricisation' as it affects the curriculum, literary history, the Real and the real.

If Scottish Literature obeys a static definition, it will escape the changing curricular demands implied by the welcome extension of its canon. Now that students can work from the twin base of four years Honours curricula and the four volumes of the Aberdeen History, a graded and defined progression becomes possible. Under this, Muriel Spark may be introduced via *The Prime of Miss Jean Brodie* but studied in depth for her literary worth at higher levels. The curriculum of the Introductory course may well concentrate on George MacDonald's Scottish novels because motivations and audience so demand; his fantasy can quite properly be presented for more advanced study. The only important caveat is that, if we choose to make value judgements, we must define the grounds on which they are made.

The value of Prospero's Island or Pan's Never Land belongs to those who return from them to this world. Diachronic definition of the discipline, therefore, leads to a similar contemplation of literary history. Here the dangers of the paradigm are at their clearest. Its formulation as myth is at odds with the changing evidence of the past. The paradigm of language looks back longingly to the Middle Scots of the makars; the paradigm of nationhood similarly looks back. Yet, the greatest makar of all — Dunbar — calls London the flower of all cities and describes his literary inheritance as deriving from Gower, Lydgate and Chaucer ('rose of rethoris all'). The first definitions of Scottish Literature to work via contrast with England are, significantly, composed by James VI and I in anticipation of the Union of the Crowns and Allan Ramsay, after the Union of the Parliaments.[9] These are both confident expressions of national distinctiveness, in no way decrying the English tradition in order to boost the Scottish.[10] If we accept a dynamic definition, the way forward may be a return to the past; the way backwards a freezing of the present.

This leads me to the third danger. Outside time, the paradigm proposes to itself an apparent Truth based on the distinctions favoured in its own day. This error, Nietzsche had eloquently described in *The Gay Science*:

> He continually invented new tables of values and for a time took each of them to be eternal and unconditional, so that now this, now that human drive and state took first place and was, as a consequence of this evaluation, ennobled.[11]

Once more study of Barrie's practice reveals his awareness of the dangers of creating such a pattern in relation to the Real and the actual. Substitute myths, holding themselves to be the mirror of Truth, are retreats into comforting simplicity. Complexity is avoided by sidestepping the metaphysical for the social, the political or the national. Unfortunately, such priorities further isolate his own art, which is falsely viewed as dreamlike when, in fact, that dream stolidly faces the Real and comprehends social, political and national satire within its multi-layered structure. From this perspective, George Blake's insistence on the social realism of *The Shipbuilders* becomes the use of naturalism to shadow forth a myth, while Barrie's dreams mirror the cruelly real within the chaotic Real.

The desire to freeze a passing phase makes it particularly difficult to distinguish when one's own beliefs cease to be accurately mirrored by the changing glass of History. Once that does happen, the honest artist can either abandon the view in the name of accurate mimesis or abandon social realism as the means of projecting his ideal. What he must not do is deny the event. Some Scottish writers and critics still cling, in the name of national distinctiveness, to that working class experience, which has been 'the only real and consistent basis for a Scottish national culture' since the 1920s.[12] Hence the desire to remove the anti-hero from that experience to the bourgeoisie. As Cairns Craig indicates, however, once

> the death throes of industrial West-Central Scotland have become the touchstone of authenticity for our culture . . . we merely perpetuate the cultural alienation in which we negate the on-going struggle of our experience by freezing its real meaning in a particular defeat.[13]

One of the most talented theatrical companies in Scotland — 7.84 — has become a victim of this very dilemma.[14]

Study of Barrie's methods suggests that Scottish Literature should cease condemning him within a static paradigm but alter the paradigm to welcome him and meet its own altering situation. Failure to do so will not only perpetuate the loose bases for evaluation hitherto but conceal Scottishness within the past to simplify Scottishness in the present. For when Blake or Donaldson describes Barrie as a working class man who — along with his family — used the broader educational curriculum and wider educational opportunities to join the dreaded bourgeoisie, they are accurately explaining what distinguished Scot from Englishman in the late eighteenth and nineteenth centuries. It is not only the rise in class implied by this Democratic Intellect,[15] which they object to in terms of the modern paradigm; it is the philosophy of right wing competitiveness, which is at odds with the idea of the left wing Scot. If one probes further, of course, one discovers that Barrie strongly satirises a society based on inherited wealth, urging the case of the man of merit.[16] Inevitably, however, his outlook as a mimetic artist has more in common with Adam Smith than Karl Marx. His intellectual inheritance is that traced in *An Edinburgh Eleven* — Scottish Darwinism, the Scottish School of philosophy, the Edinburgh school of Rhetoric and Belles Letters under Masson. We impose patterns synchronically at our peril for they may not only oversimplify the evidence of the present but obscure the testimony of History — and that testimony will contain the ethnological variations which are the grounds for so arguing in the first place.

A Critical Never Land

In Chapter One, I linked Barrie's loss of reputation in the wider critical world to the separatist tendencies of Scottish Literature[17] and to the assumption that a writer will be most generously assessed by his own people within their own culture. The insecure bases for these suppositions have now been more fully examined. The fact remains that, seeing Barrie to be an object of scorn or studied neutrality in his own land, students of literature in English have felt no impulse to reconsider his position. In the same Chapter, I noted how psychological assessments of writer and work grew more destructive, the further he moved from protection within his reputation as genius. My approach was focused on the extra-literary nature of such attacks. At this stage on the Road, it is possible to provide further defences founded on his own views of Art and authorship. How secure can a view based on personality be, when the author concerned is intent to deny or fragment personality? Is it fair to see only Oedipal limitations in an art which emphasises them honestly on grounds of perspective and highlights them within a literary theory based on creation as substitute motherhood of a child text? At the very least, such discoveries argue for subtle analysis and clear distinctions between psychoanalysis and literary criticism.

But the purpose of resting at the end of the Road is not simply to conduct a defence of Barrie in the light of revelations on the way. It is to assess his fall from critical grace. If there are many unfair reasons for this descent, there are also ways in which he invited his own doom. While valuing popularity based on the idea of a curing art, he also prided himself on difficulty — even perverseness. Along with the idea of the gentle minister goes that of the Imp who loves to convey contrary meanings; along with the kindly teacher, there is the wilful manipulator; like Hugh MacDiarmid, Barrie believed in his own genius and would have shared the former's self-justification, 'So, I contradict myself? I am great, I contain multitudes.'

The two quotations at the head of this Chapter provide an accurate framework for his situation. Loss of certainty in the Promised Land, as described by Dante, implied those changes in the nature of the quest and the means by which it could be conducted. These will be summarised in relation to Barrie's own Never Land. The current question is the degree to which he misleads as a guide, either through asking too much of his followers or by wilfully deceiving them. It is convenient to begin such a discussion by looking at the drama as experienced within the time limits of a single theatrical performance.

Barrie knew that the brevity of dramatic form had disadvantages. He accepted these because of his overriding desire to impose aesthetic order on the multiplicity of partial meaning. I have concentrated on the skill with which he provided a form capable of embodying his highest intentions and exploring the deepest thoughts. But some simple facts remain to disturb. The most obvious of these is tonal. However much he may have admired Ibsen, Barrie was incapable of sustained seriousness. *The Wedding Guest* was a comparative failure, not because it was less skilfully planned but because it lacked the dry wit which was a necessary part of Barrie's dramatic appeal. He wished his audience to learn complex, difficult truths but expected them to do so within the brevity of performance while doubled up in laughter. Nor is his vein of the acerbic kind associated with satiric purposes. It remains light and mischievous.

As the bias of this book has been towards the unrecognised and the recondite, it is salutary to remind ourselves of those moments of dramatic hilarity available even on the later, darker stages of the Road. There is, for example, Miss Susan's desperate battle with the laws of arithmetic in *Quality Street*:

> MISS SUSAN: Phoebe, if a herring and a half costs three ha'pence, how many for elevenpence?
>
> PHOEBE: [*instantly*] Eleven.
>
> MISS SUSAN: William Smith says it is fifteen; and he is such a big boy, do think I ought to contradict him? Might I say there are differences about it.   (p 292)

The unconscious wit of meekness is matched in *The Admirable Crichton* by the conscious acidity of Lady Brocklehurst's aristocratic scorn:

> LORD BROCKLEHURST: They all talk of it as true.
>
> LADY BROCKLEHURST: How do I know they are not lying?
>
> LORD BROCKLEHURST: Why should they lie?
>
> LADY BROCKLEHURST: Why shouldn't they? [*She reflects again.*] If I had been wrecked on an island, I think it highly probable that I should have lied when I came back.   (p 412)

And in *Little Mary* the two doctors provide delightful variations on the theme of crawling:

> DR TOPPING: And how angelically she bears it. I never go near her without feeling that I am in the presence of a cathedral.

SIR JENNINGS: Yes. A broken lily.
DR TOPPING: Or, better still, of a broken lily.   (p 442)

This capacity for humour is one of Barrie's greatest dramatic strengths. It gives him the power to please. The question is whether we can also be expected to think with the thoroughness desired for, say, *Quality Street* or *Little Mary*.

In posing this last question, I have intentionally omitted *The Admirable Crichton*. If Barrie is setting an unfair test, it is through an alliance of humour and brevity allied to a surface plot which appears to confirm the tone of lightness and sentimentality while using poetic and indirect means to suggest counterpointed or contrasted messages. If the apprenticeship plays lack real depth and *The Admirable Crichton* uses the main plot for direct philosophical comment, the question of deceptive Art still hovers over *Quality Street, Little Mary* and *Peter Pan*.

When Virgil led Dante onwards, he did not disguise the difficulty of the planned ascent but clearly defined the levels of interpretation demanded, giving each equal stress and adequately signing his transitions. He also provided a careful movement upwards from ignorance to knowledge aimed at a questing, if innocent, mind. For many good reasons, Barrie chose differently. He accepted that first he must please the smug, the non-seekers. He did so with a surface plot which at once met them on their own level of sentimental self-deception and did not always seek to raise them above it. True, there were many devices of symbolism, imagery, irony signalling further routes of meaning. It could be argued, however, that the immediate and most powerful dramatic appeals are to sentiment and romance. Given a wider and less enquiring group of pilgrims than Dante, did he not require a strident announcement of the tests ahead rather than an effective veiling of them? After all, if I am correct, it was not only the groundlings who were left unaware of the riddle in *Little Mary* or the linguistic implications of *Peter Pan* — it was every major critic of the day. Can Barrie consistently pride himself on this (as he did) while calling himself a literary doctor (as he did also)?

To return to the image of the veil. It is one thing to uncover mutually reinforcing but intellectually more testing truths in a genuine attempt to instruct. Within the three plays indicated — and for genuine reasons — Barrie sought also to play the Imp, the manipulator and the Superman. The Imp set representational meaning *against* straight narrative message. It is here that he may be regarded either positively (Kaye Smith), negatively (Daiches) or neutrally (Iris Murdoch) as a dramatist of the unconscious or subconscious. His signs become less clear rather than more clear for the darker truths and so, rather than teaching progressively, he enacts a subliminal form of indoctrination, which you may find threatening or mysteriously exciting, clever or deceptive. Having tended to side with the positive interpretations of Kaye Smith or Peta Lily from the mimetic viewpoint,[18] I have to admit these problems surrounding the 'affective' line in his critical thought. I also accept that Barrie's chosen form in these plays does guarantee that the least able may also be the least capable of redressing or reassessing subconscious influences through further study. Perhaps these paradoxes and contradictions merely reflect (as so often) the genius's awareness that he interprets the future to the present without being able to relinquish the desire to be celebrated by that present. Whatever the cause, some unreconciled tensions remain in even the best of Barrie's work.

The desire to manipulate as well as minister, to prove genius by ultimately addressing only the complexity of his own mind, is also part of Barrie's world view, his literary and linguistic theorising. Not only does he set himself the impossible task of reflecting innumerable perspectives on a world conceived in doubt and transmitted through inadequate signs, he tries to do so while being at once the generous Moira and the self-absorbed, proud Reilly; the medium towards acceptance of difficult 'truth' and the authorial embodiment of that perversity. But the sincerity does not cancel the impossibility nor free him from the claim that he sets up unfair tests in his more complex dramatic texts. *Little Mary*, for example, reveals its full nature only to the scholar who reconstructs a synthetic text by gathering together multiple endings and cancelled meanings.

This can, of course, be seen as an inspired extension of the belief that form must always pervert meaning through simplification in single action. In the final section I shall argue that case. But it may, equally, be regarded as the necessary translation, in terms of communicative failure, of the manipulative powers granted to the master artist within the cruel world of Nietzsche's slave morality. I believe this was the way in which Barrie 'escaped' from his dilemma, justifying increasingly 'deceptive' techniques as either a necessary part of Art's new impossibility topos or as the embodiment of the Will to Survive within a world of Macchiavellian combat. After all, language as deception and domination is given thematic status in *Little Mary* and *Peter Pan*; the world of Quality Street or Never Land is not fair but deceptively charming. Why should the text obey one law as medium and another as message?

Whether this 'solution' satisfied him or ought to satisfy the critic is another matter. What appears to have happened is that once the First World War had demonstrated the danger of extreme interpretations of the Will-to-Power dislocated from its affirmative and redemptive context[19] or the modesty of Nietzschean relativism, Barrie altered his world-view and abandoned the all-including/all-excluding Never Lands of Pan and Reilly's riddle. *Dear Brutus, Mary Rose* and *The Boy David* stand at the end of another painful and ultimately pessimistic quest but they do not 'deceive' in the same way as *Quality Street, Little Mary,* or *Peter Pan*. The honesty and perfectionism of Barrie's haunted search for salvation in Art remains but the darkness is different and he does not offer us as hostages to it.

So, while I am willing to accept the arguments on deception and wilful complexity thus framed, Barrie still seems to me primarily a victim of his own critical overambitiousness rather than a third rate writer who once, erroneously, was called great. I believe his flaws are the flaws of genius. On that topic, Ezra Pound comments:

Can you be interested in the work of a man who is blind to 80 per cent of the spectrum?

Here the answer is, curiously enough, yes IF . . . his perceptions are hypernormal in any part of the spectrum, he can be of very great use as a writer —

though perhaps not of very great 'weight'. This is where the so-called crack-brained genius comes in. The concept of genius has been carefully fostered by the inferiority complex of the public.[20]

Before it is hurriedly assumed that I have retreated to 'genius in oddity . . . without weight', the exact meaning of this passage should be distilled through careful reading. Pound uses every word and nuance with a care which Roget would have applauded.

The question, he tells us in the immediately preceding line, is a 'delicate' one. That is, it is resistant to any blanket answer unrelated to the specific case under consideration. Barrie is blind to, say, maximally 30 per cent of the spectrum — that part directly associated with adult love fulfilled. He is, however, acutely aware of the blindness and has adapted his literary methods to minimise it. His perceptions within the area he reserves for himself are original and intensified by the narrower focus.

Pound's use of the word 'perhaps' should also be noted. Such a writer need not be lightweight or crackbrained; these judgements are related to individual cases. So profound is Barrie's mind; so aware is he critically of the problem he embodies that he claims higher rank in the hierarchy of genius. Certainly, he has addressed the next problem raised by Pound. *Little Mary* is the clearest dramatic study of an audience's resistance to advanced thought but it is not the only play in Barrie's canon to raise that question.

My evaluation of Barrie is, of course, conditioned by my research and, to a degree, by my personal literary preferences. I have not written this book in the necessary expectation that it will be shared. What I do claim to have revealed is a new framework within which future assessment should be conducted. The influence of Ibsen, Shakespeare, Darwin and Nietzsche as well as Barrie's own advanced critical thought are the areas to which the writer himself directs us. Further — and of extreme importance — while the Scottish context is crucial, Barrie's hope was to be a major world dramatist. By emphasising his metaphysical leanings, I believe I have revealed a much firmer line of specifically Scottish satire than has earlier been allowed but this exists within a quasi-allegoric structure, having the same force and place as Dante's concern for Florence in the *Divina Commedia*. I am asking for Barrie to be reconsidered in relation to Shaw, Ibsen and Strindberg — again on the grounds of his own vision. His rôle within the History of Scottish Theatre is a much more 'accidental' enquiry — there being, practically speaking, no History of Scottish Theatre at this point and Barrie being unconcerned with ethnological definitions anyway.

Im summarising some of the major lines for consideration, I turn from the Never Land which critics have created for Barrie to the Never Land which he created for himself. The value of a summary at this point lies in the consistency of thought revealed. I shall outline only the major arguments, tracing first the artistic development and then the reasons for growing despondency, as it became clear that his particular Grail was out of reach.

An Artistic Never Land

The literary pilgrim who has most in common with Barrie, as I understand the latter, is the Gawain of *Sir Gawain and the Green Knight*. He carried emblazoned on his shield the sign of the pentangle, standing not only for five different virtues but their sub-classifications all interlaced into an emblem of perfection.[21] When he was found guilty of the slightest fault, therefore, he despaired because one breach of the pattern implied total failure (*'connexae sibi sunt concatenaeque virtutes'*). Barrie's literary quest is equally ambitious, equally perfectionist; his thought equally intricate and equally interconnected. Crucially, his approach is also as analytically systematic as Gawain's. His method is embodiment of critical exploration within creative experimentation of the most throrough sort. Where he differs from Gawain is in lost doubt over the single purpose behind his quest. Loss of faith imples that Barrie MUST fail on every level.

This is the reason for my finding a combination of Medieval and Modern critical ideas the most valuable approach to Barrie's Art. He seems to me, literally, to deconstruct the benevolent Christian world picture as presented most systematically in the literary methods of the Middle Ages. He does so at every possible textual and authorial level. Asking the same mimetic questions posed in the twentieth century, he evolves an aesthetic theory, which looks forward and back. Essentially, as I have earlier argued, it is at once mimetic and affective. If Nature may only be the sum of perspectives *on* Nature, then fictive 'truth' may justifiably be manipulated in relation to the perceived needs of the audience. The most ancient and the newest critical approaches here overlap.[22] Medieval writers, holding mystery to be an element of complex Truth, permitted the same duality from certainty as Postmodernists from doubt. The aim of the Miracle Cycles is not to present Divine History but the vision of it which most strengthens faith (*'ad fidem corroborandum'*). The reason for invalidating the message of Chaucer's Pardoner is not the ingenuity with which he contorts Biblical evidence to specific purpose (that was permissible, indeed praiseworthy). His words are false because he is a worthless man concealing the true purposes behind his Art.

Let us look, then, at Barrie's own pentangle as defined by his quests towards meaning, authorship, form, art and language. Why, after the clear advances charted in the Apprenticeship — Journeyman — Master structure of this book, did he only reach a Never Land?

Meaning: In William Langland's fourteenth century pilgrimage poem, *The*

Vision of Piers Plowman, Holy Church defines the end of the long quest before it begins: ' "The tour upon the toft," quod she, "Truth is therinne." ' If we follow Barrie's studies at Edinburgh University as recorded in *An Edinburgh Eleven*, we learn that the most challenging mind he met was that of the Metaphysician Campbell Fraser. The problem of the 'real' especially worried the student and he records that his notebooks were 'scribbled over with posers in my handwriting about dualism and the real.' [23] There, we also discover the breadth of his scientific and anthropological knowledge, leading to that interest in Africa which pervades the early prose and *Walker, London*. The lost truth centres, then, on the major current opposition between Christian and Darwinean theories of creation and Nature. The clearest emblem of this in his work appears as early as *Auld Licht Idyllis* (1888) with the schoolmaster comparing a ploughman's Christian texts with his copy of Darwin; thinking altruistic thoughts but seeing Nature red in tooth and claw. Thrums, too, is only sentimentally perceived as a malleable myth in the protective or manipulative fictions of those who know it (e.g. Mrs Sandys).

Barrie's choice was to continue to imitate the real within the Real, following the hierarchical topical evaluation of the Middle Ages[24] but adapting his methods to an ever-expanding dilemma in communication. Instead of Unity there was diversity and the possibility that mimesis might be a false aim. The complex but complementary methods of Dante might be suggested but they had to be replaced by Nietzschean perspectivism. And that was the problem posed only on an ontological narrative level. Already he had decided to follow Dante in comprehensiveness as well. His texts would primarily present the current world vision but as a frame for subsidiary (usually satiric) treatment of romance, society, history or nation.

I shall use only three examples to demonstrate the systematic thoroughness with which Barrie addresses the problem of meaning. Fearing loss of control consequent on Perspective usurping Unity, he consciously moved from prose narrative to drama. He did so, however, by using his first four apprentice-plays as a means of critically defining the unique features of the new form and exploring four widely contrasted forms of genre-translation. *Walker, London* draws lightly from many texts; *The Professor's Love Story* draws heavily from only one Chapter. *The Little Minister* thoroughly re-casts the story of one major novel; *The Wedding Guest* imaginatively re-defines the themes of another. Even more subtle experiments would continue in the major plays but the principle of using genre as a literary perspective had been established earlier and there is an effortlessness, a lightness of touch from *Quality Street* onwards, derived from this exhaustive preparation.

If 'genre-translation' is a leitmotiv before 1902, it is fair to say that Napoleon becomes a leitmotiv in the later plays, standing for the new 'virtues' of the Will-to-Power. If Barrie is, indeed, the sentimental Kailyard conservative, that view must counter the presence of the Napoleonic Wars as background to *Quality Street*. It must confront the presentation of Crichton as minister-Emperor. More particularly, such critics have to explain the Napoleonic hat worn by Moira in *Little Mary* as well as the Scottish playwright's stubborn refusal to withdraw the Napoleonic tableau from *Peter Pan*.

These two leitmotivs covering eight plays join to another type of analytical thoroughness. While different perspectives (philosophical, social, national) are undercurrents in the comedy presented from *Walker, London*[25] *onwards, profound metaphysical issues are reserved for the Edwardian dramas. Of these, it is Quality Street* which most clearly and exhaustively presents the major opposition between theology and anthropology. Dialogue is only one of the means employed and, indeed, social or romantic topics often dominate the surface text. What impresses is the wide range of subtle theatrical techniques, drawn into service. The setting, with its blinds and distant viewing of outside warfare, is itself an emblem for the oblique Christian vision of Darwin's world. A series of contrasted visual symbols reinforces the opposition (e.g. Quaker bonnet v. sword) as does the more general counterpointing of peace against battle, enclosure against openness. The ever-changing character of Miss Phoebe embodies Nietzschean perspectivism while the street's silent message confirms his tenet that gentility is the social ally of theological modesty in the creation of impotent servitude. The leitmotiv of the cane and the kneeling cameo in Act 1 use uniquely *theatrical* methods to present his slave morality. This message, so imaginatively and virtuosically conveyed, depends structurally on the ideas and methods of the allegoric pilgrimage being appealed to but simultaneously being withdrawn and reinterpreted. There is a sense, as Phoebe herself sees, in which she and Valentine fight complementary battles of war and peace, finally to complement one another in marriage. But the Nietzschean or perspectival background is not the only means of undercutting that joyous end. Miss Susan and the transferred wedding dress remind us even more poignantly that many remain spinsters in the Never Land and that Barrie's texts seldom mean what they say.

Author: Barrie's path towards understanding of the problems surrounding creation was a long one. In the apprenticeship period it was most fully considered in *The Wedding Guest*. Among his later works, *Little Mary* treats the topic at its highest (anagogical, allegorical) levels of application. *Peter Pan* IS a creation myth introduced by a Dedication on the same subject. The idea that this drama should run eternally, the ritual of excluding child actors on grounds of size, and the part-scripts offered to the actors are all justified by an authorial desire to translate Divine Time (perpetual and transcendant) into Art. The symbolic rebirth of Wendy as bird prior to entering the Never Land is a claim for literary defeat of Natural birth within time and had, earlier, been illustrated by the letter device in *The Little White Bird*.

As with the problem of meaning, however, Barrie's heroic efforts led him to final despair. His method of analysis, again, was the setting up of a series of patterns, this time drawn from basic Theology. Reconsideration of these within a new world of lost divine certainty where the artist advanced to rivalry with the Godhead, produced sad contrasts or confusions. This is one of the most complex areas of Barrie's thought and my chosen examples again are simplified and representative only of some aspects of some techniques.

The clear conflict of Good against Evil in Christianity is presented through the narrative of Christ's opposition to the Devil. The first dramatic suggestion of this (as of so much else) is to be found in *The Little Minister*. There, it clearly exists in the imagination of Gavin and Babbie but is transmuted into marriage in the popular ending of the text.[26] In *Peter Pan*, the clear pattern is suggested through a hero, who is son without mother, creature of light, of the day, of birth, of the cockcrow. Hook, as villain, is unsure of his origins, and a creature of darkness, the night, death and crocodile. In fact, he is created by his antagonist, just as Christ within the Trinity created Satan. Like Satan, he has no chance of victory in this re-running of the Theology of Guile within a world defined by Darwinean conflicts.

Barrie was brought up on the Bible and these basic tenets, learned in his early Kirriemuir days, were all known to his audience. He alters them to shadow a new philosophical darkness. Pan and Hook do not always stand at opposed moral poles. First, they become creatures of a game, whose rules are frequently manipulated by the 'good' figure in his own selfish interests. Pride, Satan's chief sin, is the accepted 'blot'[27] on the child of Light, while Hook is often capable of surprising magnanimity. Their different spiritual origins become blurred when they swap identities in the game or when Pan becomes Napoleon. All is 'justified' by appeal to the confused origins for the goat-god. Following Bacon, Barrie sees Pan as Nature — a definition so open as to cover changing interpretations through History. He is also 'bi-formed' — pagan or Christian; the Word of God or the Confused Seed. Appeal to such a godhead highlights lost certainty but also lost joy in this age. Christ offered certain joy in victory over Death; Pan, who has used his godhead to escape Death, can only lead artist and audience towards tragic compromise.

The idea of the Trinity is also suggested in *Peter Pan* but *Little Mary* makes more effective use of this particular system of thought. The power of God the father becomes the power of Reilly. Seeking to teach through the Word, he sends down a granddaughter rather than a Son with a Book which embodies his loving Spirit. As with Pan, Barrie suggests pride as the principle motivating power behind Reilly's love. He suspects manipulation as much as teaching. He stresses destruction of women on the temporal level rather than glorification of the Son spiritually. When the people turn away from his message finally, their ultimate blindness is the same as those at the Crucifixion but the message has been both blurred and humanised. The image of Reilly as Alchemist has almost as wide a range of potential reference as the associations surrounding Pan. Contrasted with the Doctors, he offers a Christlike cure in mystery. But his potential for good is countered by images of black magic and the ambiguous figure of Merlin.

He proffers life through his Book but has actually killed wife and daughter by the same means. The living death he assigns to Moira requires her to be without child and so leads into another conscious deconstruction. Moira is Mary in being the chosen vessel of the Word and in having a child who turns all the natural joys of motherhood into loss. She is unlike Mary in serving one who ambivalently shares the qualities of love and pride; who desires to manipulate, as well as minister; who sacrifices his offspring for self not as part of Self (Trinity). To deny the complexity and the self-consciousness of this pattern, one must counter the extensive revision evidence, the careful matching of argument to sign or symbol and the very ingenuity-in-specificity of the underlying logic.

To the conflict between God and Satan and the mystery of the Trinity, I add the rivalry between Author and Mother. To carry this line of thought to its most extreme point of development, Barrie adapted the mother/surrogate father contrast of *The Little White Bird*. In the novel, the artist lost out on all grounds. In *Peter Pan,* the mother's altruism is questioned and Wendy does not become artist, only bard. Nonetheless, this confusion proffers no joyous hope to the Artist in an age of Perspectivism. His own personal weaknesses must be highlighted to ensure honesty of intention. Barrie manipulates his own biography to highlight the qualities (selfishness, impotence, mother-jealousy) which disable him in Art. The Fantasy writer may pride himself on providing a higher fictive Truth to replace the lost Truth of God but in practice he has no Truth and may only be presenting a shadow of a changing shadow. He sees himself as curatively addressing all but he may be talking only to himself within a world of selfishness and non-communication. A mother may equally mix love and the Will-to-Power but she at least produces a real child through whom she continues to exist. Barrie's own dream child (*Peter Pan*) has innumerable potential endings because it is the laborious inky equivalent of natural, unforeseeable growth. The cold truth remains, as Lamb had described it. Ultimately the work of art is nothing. The bachelor-artist stands apart from life in jealousy, a rôle which Barrie determinedly played out with the Lost Boys and their mother. Unlike the early literary pilgrims, he has lost his purpose as Spiritual Guide through having no clear Spiritual Goal.

Form: But he has no reliable Literary Guide either. When Dante found Virgil ready to lead him, there was no need to announce the literary forms behind the *Divina Commedia*. Here was the marriage of Pagan Epic to Divine Allegory. Barrie faced the structural equivalent of lost purpose. His long experimentation with the linear model of Shakespearean Romance can be confirmed in two different ways. Chronologically, he rejected the alternatives of Classical Farce and the Shakespearean sub-plot in *Walker, London* and *The Professor's Love Story* respectively. *The Little Minister* began a careful process of refinement from which there emerged a series of variations on a circular form, with central movement into Fantasy. Different story-types were introduced, notably the Case for *Quality Street* and *The Admirable Crichton*; the Riddle/Joke for *Little Mary* and the Myth for *Peter Pan*. At the same time, this basic structure was being adapted to bear increasingly complex metaphysical and allegorical ideas. If linear structure worked against Romance, vertical structure worked against the fullest multi-level form of Allegory, modified by the mytho-poetic practice of Ibsen. *Little Mary* with its appeal to anagogic, allegoric, social, national, historical and romantic lines of thought is the most developed example of this structure in depth. But the ideas of counterpointing messages through different levels and techniques preceded Barrie's earliest works for the Stage. It is as old as his Imp and begins, however tentatively, with the Cuckoo image added to *Walker, London*.

The most obvious deconstructions of the Medieval/Shakespearean Romance form relate to Oeconomie. The circle was the emblem, in order, of infinite benevolent divine purpose.[28] None of the circular structures adopted for the Edwardian plays suggest benevolence, divinity or purpose. Rather they conclude with doubt in multi-potential. *Quality Street* is the simplest, with its final cameo capable of interpretation as romantic joy or social tragedy. With *The Admirable Crichton* comes the first truly ambitious attempt to present the deceptive appearance of structural Unity in an age of duality and doubt. The waiter-hero literally awaits Nature's dictated conclusion as it changes from day to day. That is the only truth consistent to all the revisions fed out by Barrie and the only justification for making the later Crichton a hero of the First World War. It is unfair to see changed endings as a sign of authorial insecurity. Such a judgement runs counter to the author's proclaimed intention, the hero's vision of his rôle, the witty concept of a waiter-hero, the evidence of the revisions and the very purpose behind Barrie's transition to the stage. *Peter Pan*'s many possible endings similarly embody the idea of culture myth adapted to the idea of the textual child within the ultimate logic behind extreme perspectivism. Here, the only consistency is lost joy in multi-compromise. The many ideas for a conclusion noted in the 'Fairy Notes' even suggest a return to the literary beginning and *Walker, London*.[29] Single, progressive use of the circular form is thus translated into infinite hypotheses on tragic inertia or pointless game-playing.

The allegoric model adopted by Medieval writers stressed four levels complementing one another through knowledge accumulated. The audience received the message according to their ability to cope with its veiled literary forms. As one method of adapting this system has been addressed in the 'Critical Never Land' Section of this Chapter, I shall highlight another and concentrate on *Little Mary*. In that play, Barrie did not so much alter or deconstruct the Allegoric model as stand it on its head. Where the expectation was an announcement of serious difficulty on graded levels of sophistication, he pronounced a simple riddle, gave the answer to it but allowed the audience to blind themselves both onstage and off. Where the expectation was ever more ingenious theological thought, which the few might grasp in intellectual triumph, he tempted everyone to misdefine the obvious and laugh, in their different ways, at his apparent superficiality.

While Allegory works on a clear writer-audience distinction, he blurred this division through accepting actors and audience as fellow-composers; identifying action with reception; yet boasting of having outwitted all but himself and the future. These are only three of the many inversions but they serve again to show Barrie's analytic and witty thoroughness in setting up those models, which subsequently he pulls down with comically incongruous effect in the name of honest artistic purpose.

Art: The additional dimensions of Art and Language are in themselves signs of the Never Land. Barrie felt constrained to reflect on his own code and practice only because the surer ground of shadowed Truth had been lost. The reasons for taking this step and the methods employed are consistently stated in the prose and the earliest drama (*Ibsen's Ghost*). Once the hint is taken the critic has the rare delight of being able to anticipate in advance where the evidence *should* lead. I assumed, for example, that the Napoleonic tableau *ought* to be an imitation of a picture or another dramatic tableau before I learned of Orchardson. I discovered the multiple meaning of 'phrén' because I was *looking for* a word with wider meaning than 'stomach', capable of linking the varied allegoric suggestions conveyed by the plot of *Little Mary*. The Never Land from this viewpoint is the complete failure of Barrie's contemporaries to understand the self-mirroring text or the reasons for resorting to it.

And, as a careful painstaking writer, he would not have added further layers of complexity to his ever-expanding literary world, had he not felt he had to. The first translation from Nature to artifice follows from perspective. If the literary equivalent of contrasting viewpoints is 'mode', then the uniquely defining characteristics of Drama assume a new importance. Here is the reason for Barrie's determination to become a man of the theatre; for accepting its multi-authorship convention and religiously attending every rehearsal. Here is the logic behind his emphasising the strictly theatrical powers of mime (*Admiral Crichton*, finale Act 2) and audience intimacy. ('Do you believe in fairies?') If the perspective of artifice dictates one system within genre so it suggests another across genre and mode. *Peter Pan* is an exercise in uniting specifically dramatic strengths to those of ballet, mime, painting, music, song — even gymnastics. It is also the full length theatrical treatment of a myth reconsidered as hypothesis within novel, episode within novel, photograph collection, one act play, ballet, children's novel, short story, film scenario and speech. Once more, the analytical mind of the perfectionist explores a concept by setting up a series of systems proliferating from the central point of his thought.

If modal experimentation is regarded as the equivalent in Art of personal perspective, then the various literary satires become analogues for group perspective. In parodying Ibsen (*Ibsen's Ghost*), in satirising Shaw or Wilde (*Little Mary; Admirable Crichton*) and in allegorically adapting Shakespeare (*Little Mary*) Barrie defines his own literary techniques even more narrowly through suggesting the comparative strengths and weaknesses of his literary companions. Only Wilde of these four is superficially and farcically treated. The others are satirised against a background of critical respect as part of the never-ceasing analysis of his own Art.

If the need to mirror in artifice as well as Nature were not a major concern, why did Barrie want to add to *Peter Pan* — already too long, over-ambitious technically, and monstrously expensive — the Commedia dell'Arte sequence? Why, after giving way to advice reluctantly, did he at once transform it into *Pantaloon*? Only if we assume his uncompromisingly logical mind demanding an artistic equivalent of mysterious origins can his urgency be understood. If the multi-modes of *Peter Pan* and *Pan* are the imaginative extensions of infinite perspective into artifice, so Harlequin and Clown are the mysterious creator-analogues in Art for the philosophical questions on origin, raised by the play as Creation Myth.

If the Kensington Garden episode provides a metafictional insert within the circular structure of Romance, the most complex addition to Barrie's dramatic messages in depth comes with *Little Mary*. Not content with a quasi-allegorical comprehensiveness extending over at least five levels of application, Barrie *at the most profound level*, comments on the word as book rather than (though not to the exclusion of) Word. Reilly as selfish Aunt seeks power and immortality in Art in the name of altruism. But he acts selfishly as rival to motherhood or natural creation.

Little Mary may conveniently be used to sum up Barrie's failures on this point of his Pentangle. All the effort involved in setting up these additional systems and translating them into an ever-expanding, ever-lengthening artistic quest ends with the simplest and most complex messages of that play being misunderstood onstage and off. This is done within a world picture whose lost optimism is effectively measured against the techniques of allegory. The medieval writer led his audience towards the understanding of Truth on all levels. The highest of these taught eternal salvation within God's benevolent master-text. In *Little Mary*, the most profound message conveys misunderstanding on all levels of an essentially personal message by God's weak rival, the artist. All the structural effort and metaphysical aims behind *Little Mary* finally convey only one thing without doubt — Barrie's own failure to communicate. The virtuoso variations on the Romance form in *Peter Pan* ultimately mirror only the Russian-box mystery of Wendy's mind. Allegoric method in an Age of doubt returns to the personal and the self, finding almost as many confusions there as in the outer world of Nature, whose complexity caused the reversal and narrowing of focus in the first place.

Language: There is one thing on which all critics are agreed. Barrie was a master stylist. Roget is evoked as the major proof of this, although it is evident in everything he wrote. When one seriously considers that he is of the school of Flaubert[30] and relates that fact to the exhaustive pilgrimage here chartered, his boast that he had sacrificed all life to Art, seems scarcely an overstatement.

It is remarkable that those, who accept Roget as the household-God of *Peter Pan* and describe the writer with his *Thesaurus* as constant companion, go no further. There are three clear directions. Roget stands for precision in use of language. Tommy Sandys wrote nothing for the essay because he sought the best and only word to convey specific meaning. Barrie's dramatic revisions with their constant verbal alterations mirror this nicety of practice. Positively, the most ambitious extensions of linguistic care in relation to form and meaning are the multivalent usages of 'sentiment' in *Quality Street* and 'phrén' as allegorical link in *Little Mary*. The implied failures are also obvious — nobody understood these exercises in sophisticated communication and 'Phreen' was actually withdrawn from the black riddle of Reilly.

Roget provides the key to this dilemma. He was a Zoologist; his *Thesaurus* was a conscious attempt to face precisely the same problem as that which haunted Barrie mimetically. His verbal system, based on the Phyla categorisations of his discipline, attempted analytically to match the hyper-complexity of Nature. A believer in sequential creationism, he stood theologically between Christianity and Nietzsche. Such a systematic attempt to face the ultimate in language could not but attract the similarly constituted mind of the Scottish playwright. But if Barrie found no certainty in God at the end of his philosophical trail, he found no Universal Language, no single embodying code at the end of his stylistic endeavours. The fact that the Introduction to the *Thesaurus* Barrie possessed referred to Bishop Wilberforce's failures to achieve such a language provides further evidence for his theoretical awareness of this problem. His practice — including the Nietzschean[31] consciousness that experiments in verbal multivalence may produce greater chaos in the name of systematic analysis — proves the same point.

Thirdly, language can only be the weapon of Darwinean power, given this failure. The impossibility of finding signs which necessarily embody the signified in a single code leads to the very 'struggle for life . . . amongst the words and grammatical forms in each language,' which Darwin saw as the confirmation, through the medium, of his message. The very first revision-obsession, which faces the student of Barrie's early texts is that over names. That intensity, leading as it did to coinages for characters (Wendy) and plays sometimes having more than twenty try-out titles (*Walker, London*), is based on nominal magic. *The Golden Bough* taught the power of the Name as soul-possession. Barrie carried that belief into his relationships with Mrs Llewelyn Davies, calling her Jocelyn in rivalry to her husband's Sylvia.[32] He dramatised this primitive faith in Peter's seizing of Hook's identity through claiming his name, while the battle over length of name between Pan and Wendy is another angle on the same power struggle.

The link between Darwin and Roget was widely accepted by Barrie's contemporaries; it is underlined in almost everything he wrote from *Auld Licht Idylls* to the ghastly creation of Neil, the child-tyrant who destroys Barrie as man and dramatist through re-translation of *Peter Pan* into a new code. It provides the linguistic key to *The Admirable Crichton's* study of different forms of communication through the ages from music to poetry. These evolve into fullscale conflict within those codes in *Pan*. If it were not

Barrie's intention to show language as power within a chaotic world picture, why are there no fewer than ten different codes competing within the Never Land?[33] Why does Hook (the most poetic, literate character) have the least power? Why does Pan's music suggest at once the highest type of mystic union, limited pagan dominion and primitive sounds? Why does Pan use his knowledge of the different tongues of the Never Land to manipulate Wendy? Why does Wendy use her more sophisticated knowledge of English (thimble/kiss) to manipulate Pan? Roget is not a decorative reminder of stylistic care within the work of Barrie, he is a sign of language failure, of the linguistic dimension within Darwinean theory and the maximal power of the word to convey or subvert.

Barrie did not end his aesthetic pilgrimage with *Peter Pan*. War; the rise of the Women's Movement; personal tragedies and the altered visions of old age provided further challenges in a life sacrificed to Art. Of his accepted 'major' plays — *What Every Woman Knows, Mary Rose* and *Dear Brutus* were written after *Peter Pan* But that work — at once his most personal and most metaphysical — remained his favourite. It brought him in glorious failure to his Never Land.

Barrie and the Nottingham Journal

From January 1883 until October 1884, Barrie was the leader writer for *The Nottingham Journal*. As he gained confidence he also contributed weekly columns, signed 'Hippomenes' and 'A Modern Peripatetic'. Many of the book reviews can also, with certainty, be attributed to him because of specific biographical references. This is an area of research ignored by almost everyone and I do not pretend to have covered it fully myself. As the evidence provided by a first over-view further confirms my theses, however, I have noted some of the major lines to be pursued.

Darwin and Darwinism: As leader writer, he had to be aware of the major assault on the traditional Christian world-picture. His tone suggests one of resigned regret that certainty has passed. The clearest example I have discovered is in a book review, unsigned but with a reference to the Edinburgh Professor, John Stuart Blackie, which betrays Barrie's authorship. Two articles in the journal, *The Nineteenth Century*, are his concern. Both accept Darwinism as having consigned Christian views on creation to the dustheap; the reviewer does not challenge that conclusion. Of Frederic Harrison's 'Agnostic Metaphysics' he notes that, unlike Spencer, Harrison sees the attack as primarily theological. He concludes, 'The writer neither desires nor expects that Christian charity or Christian morality of any kind will be preserved but believes that it will be enlarged and solidified into human charity and human morality.' G J Romanes' 'Agnostic Metaphysics' stresses the power of Nature, drawing man slowly towards greater power, a view which he takes as read, now that it has been revealed by the 'genius of Darwin'. Again the reviewer is quietly respectful. It is, perhaps, too ingenious to see the seeds of *Quality Street* and *The Admirable Crichton* as metaphysical comments anticipated, respectively, by these two papers. But Barrie clearly shares the problems addressed and has thought about them deeply, prior to a review which appeared on 15 September 1884.

Napoleon and the Superman: Barrie refers to Napoleon with obsessional frequency in his leaders. True, foreign policy was obviously part of his remit and the French problem could, logically, be related to the recent death and downfall of Prince Napoleon. But Barrie gives the Prince an undeserved centrality in order constantly to look back at his greatest ancestor. In a way Napoleon encapsulated the unresolved paradox of Christian virtues appearing to be a pattern for failure in the world of the Superman. There is no doubt that, as enemy to Britain, Barrie rejected the Emperor; but as small, lower-class, upwardly mobile hero he seemed at once to embody Darwinian principles and to be a type for Barrie himself. This accounts for the frequent attempts to rescue Napoleon in terms of a spirituality newly defined. In his first month with *The Nottingham Journal*, Barrie urged his readers to consider the greatness of Napoleon in rising above outside forces; in one of his last leaders (30 September 1884) he was still arguing on his behalf, albeit in guarded fashion, 'In his way, Napoleon was a religious man, though it was admittedly a way of his own.' Certainly, on the question of whether super-leader or the people made for better government, the youthful Scottish journalist had no doubts. 'The fondly foolish theory of the French Revolution,' he writes, 'may have been based on a benevolent philosophy but it was denied by the hierarchies of Nature, red in tooth and claw.' (*Journal*, 6 February 1883.) The Napoleonic Wars in *Quality Street*; Little Mary's Napoleonic hat; the Napoleonic tableau in *Peter Pan* — these are not quirks but essential symbols of metaphysical, literary and psychological conflict in Barrie's dramatic world. Nor have they suddenly appeared but have been refined as his thought developed from student days to journalism and the literary apprenticeship of his Victorian period.

Ireland, Doctors and Little Mary: Some readers may have found it unlikely that Barrie should have satirised English policy in Ireland with the subtlety presupposed by my analysis in Chapter Three. But, as leader writer for *The Nottingham Journal*, he had summed up the major political problem facing the English parliament, less than a month after his appointment. 'The real question as to the coming Session is "What will the Government in Parliament do about Ireland?"' (*Journal* 30 January 1883). Ireland remained the major topic for the leader writer throughout his twenty months of employment. Broadly he preferred to rely on an English solution. He even outlined a scheme of benevolently controlled emigration and found Parnell's position anathema. Yet, as he later enacted in *Little Mary*, the English seemed to assume that there was no difference between their affluent society and Ireland. In his leader of 1 March 1883, he reminded his readers that this was not the case. 'There are, however, in Ireland certain districts, the inhabitants of which trust for their sustenance entirely to the soil. When bad seasons come, such as those of the past years, the suffering of those poor creatures is terrible.' Such considerations lead him on to diet, doctors and vegetarianism, again as in *Little Mary*. The English now eat only what their doctors bid them (28 July 1884) and that is usually far too much. Vegetarianism is an alternative which he admires but does not dare (14 July 1884). There is, additionally, the problem of the two classes into which such persons divide, 'Those who believe in vegetables to a considerable extent only, and those who believe in nothing else. The latter are to be admired rather than imitated, the former to be imitated rather than admired.' Crucially, however, the English must cease believing that roast beef is 'the staff of life' and remind themselves that in the Bible and Ireland, simpler definitions remain, centred on bread and the potato respectively.

Plays and Players: Barrie seldom drops an idea; rather he refines and deepens early concepts and attitudes. It is, therefore, not surprising to find the germs of later dramatic plots in these early journalistic outpourings. Inevitably, also, he comments on actors and actresses, who will soon star in his plays. Toole's capacity for mime (as argued in Chapter Two) did impress him. 'After seeing Mr Toole, the audience go home and cannot make out why they laughed so much. But if they make a study of the subject, they will find that Mr Toole's facial expression was responsible for their merriment.' (4 August 1883). In the same piece he finds Ellen Terry delightfully 'arch' but given to 'attitudinising' — a dual judgement, which may account for his passing her over as first choice for any rôle until Alice Grey, the arch and attitudinising heroine of *Alice Sit-By-The-Fire* came along in 1905. Other chance remarks look forward — in a book review written on 26 November 1883, Barrie comments that many boys in Scotland model themselves on the Admirable Crichton as hero figure. Clearly, too, he read other columns, especially, 'A Lady's Column' for insight into the feminine mystery. One column in particular remained with him from *Quality Street* to *Dear Brutus*. Written on the 7 March 1883, it related hairstyles and headwear to the different ages of womanhood. Around seventeen, a girl's hair may still flow down but her ambition now is to have her 'hair knotted up behind', (*Dear Brutus*, Act 2). Later on, the lady wonders when to accept the bonnet of age — 'One of the secrets of a woman growing old gracefully is in knowing when to abandon hats and keep to judicious bonnets.' (*Quality Street*).

Notes

CHAPTER ONE: pages 3 - 24

1 W A Darlington, *J M Barrie* (London and Glasgow, 1938) p 150.
2 *Letters of Robert Louis Stevenson*, ed Sir Sidney Colvin, 5 vols (London, 1924) IV, 273.
3 James Agate, *The Selective Ego* (London, 1976) p 82.
4 William Archer, *The Old Drama and the New* (London, 1923) p 331.
5 J H Millar, *A Literary History of Scotland* (London, 1903) p 656.
6 Max Beerbohm, *Last Theatres* (London, 1970) p. 385. The article was written on the 9 September, 1908.
7 Henry Bett, *The London Quarterly Review*, October 1937, pp 477-81.
8 Hugh MacDiarmid, *Aesthetics in Scotland* (Edinburgh, 1984).
9 Hugh MacDiarmid, *Lucky Poet* (Edinburgh, 1972) p 396.
10 MacDiarmid, *Lucky Poet*, p 249.
11 David Daiches, 'The Sexless Sentimentalist', *The Listener*, 12 May, 1960, p 843.
12 Cynthia Asquith, *A Portrait of Barrie* (London, 1954) p 1. 'I at once felt Barrie's immensely strong personality, but could find no crack in what seemed an impenetrable shell of sadness and preoccupation.'
13 J M Barrie, *Sentimental Tommy* (London, 1896) Uniform Edition, p 63.
14 J M Barrie, *Margaret Ogilvy* (London, 1896).
15 Morris Fraser in *The Death of Narcissus* (London, 1976) continues this line.
16 I do have reservations about applying techniques used to study dreams for the interpretation of literature. See Francesco Orlando, *Toward a Freudian Theory of Literature* (Baltimore and London, 1934) pp 123-36.
17 Andrew Birkin, *J M Barrie and the Lost Boys* (London, 1979).
18 Barrie seems to have invaded the Quiller Couch family in a similar manner. See Birkin, pp 19-24, 32-4.
19 Denis Mackail, *The Story of J M B* (London, 1941).
20 Birkin, p 130.
21 Harry M. Geduld, *James Barrie* (New York, 1971) p 26.
22 Geduld, pp 112-13.
23 Geduld, p 119.
24 Geduld, p 64.
25 Daiches, p 841.
26 Daiches, p 841.
27 Daiches, p 843.
28 Barrie's letters are held by the Beinecke Library, New Haven, Connecticut. The one in question was written to Edward Spence and is dated 22 June, 1931.
29 Daiches, p 842. This contrast with Brown's novel is a leitmotiv in Scottish literary criticism.
30 Nico's comment (see Note 19) supports this viewpoint.

31 Quotations from the plays are taken from *The Definitive Edition of the Plays of J M Barrie* (London, 1942).
32 Wordsworth, *The Prelude*, Book V, Lines 548-57 (1805 Text).
33 John Allen, *A History of the Theatre in Europe* (London, 1983).
34 *Revels History of Drama in English*, General Editor, T W Craik; Vol VIII, *1880 to the Present Day* (London, 1978) pp 181-2.
35 W M Parker in *Modern Scottish Writers* (Edinburgh and Glasgow, 1917) warns that Barrie is difficult to pin down critically. 'Alas! quite a number of us have tried to catch hold of him, but he invariably slips away.' Nor are his antagonists the only guilty ones. Enthusiasm may also sweep away precision. Patrick Braybrooke, commenting on *The Little Minister*, finds it a work which 'just escapes being futile and the reason that it escapes such a fate, is to be found in the fact that its writer happened to be a genius.' Patrick Braybrooke, *J M Barrie: A Study in Fairies and Mortals* (London, 1924) p 123.
36 A S Collins, *English Literature of the Twentieth Century* (London, 1960) p 285.
37 *The Times*, 18 September 1902.
38 Cyril Maude, *The Haymarket Theatre* (London, 1903) p 212. In fairness other men of the theatre valued Shaw's opinions more highly. George Shelton, the actor, records, 'Shaw impressed me at once with his grasp of theatre values.' *It's Smee* (London, 1928) p 224.
39 Maude, p 215.
40 Cynthia Asquith, Barrie's secretary, records that she found ten different typescripts for his short play cum ballet, *The Truth about the Russian Dancers*. Asquith, *Portrait*, p 32.
41 George Rowell and Anthony Jackson, *The Repertory Movement* (Cambridge, 1984) pp 46-48.
42 A recent study of the thousand most popular plays on the British Stage accords Bridie only *The Anatomist*; Barrie has *Quality Street; The Admirable Crichton; Peter Pan; What Every Woman Knows* and *Dear Brutus. Harrap's Book of 1,000 Plays*, ed Steve Fletcher and Norman Jopling (London, 1989).
43 David Hutchison, 'Scottish drama 1900-1950' in *The History of Scottish Literature*, ed Cairns Craig, 4 vols. (Aberdeen, 1987-88) IV, 170.
44 Ian Campbell, *Kailyard: A New Assessment* (Edinburgh, 1981) pp 94-5.
45 George Blake, *Barrie and the Kailyard School* (London, 1951).
46 Blake, p 65.
47 Blake, p 8.
48 Beerbohm, p 386.
49 Blake, p 18. L Leclaire, *Le Roman Régionaliste dans les îles britanniques 1800-1950* (Clermont-Ferrand, 1954).
50 Blake, p 58.
51 Blake, p 15.
52 Hugh MacDiarmid, *Aesthetics in Scotland*, p 61.
53 Blake, p 13.
54 Thomas D Knowles, *Ideology, Art and Commerce: Aspects of Literary Sociology in the Late Victorian Scottish Kailyard* (Göteborg, 1983) p 89.
55 Cited by Knowles, p 82.
56 Leonee Ormond, *J M Barrie* (Edinburgh, 1987).
57 Jacqueline Rose, *The Case of Peter Pan* (London, 1984).
58 A D S Fowler, *A History of English Literature* (Oxford, 1987) p 358.
59 Fowler, p 359.

CHAPTER TWO: Pages 25 - 77

1   These Notebooks, like the vast majority of original Barrie material, are held
    by Yale University in the Beinecke Library, New Haven, Connecticut. They
    are part of the massive Walter J Beinecke Collection much of which is still
    uncatalogued. There are 48 Notebooks containing Barrie's jottings of ideas,
    titles, scraps of dialogue — a journalistic method which he maintained
    throughout his writing career.

2   A E Wilson in the *Definitive Edition* (p 1271) places the one-act pastiche of
    Vanity Fair, *Becky Sharp* in 1891. My evidence dates it for 1893 at Terry's
    Theatre. (Beinecke Collection, Barrie MSS B42). Like *Ibsen's Ghost*, this
    work reveals Barrie's skill in lighthearted satire. Both are, in fact, valuable
    pieces of literary criticism. Of his University writings, the major surviving
    example is the full-length play *Bohemia*. (Humanities Research Center,
    Austin, Texas). Its sole value lies in anticipating ideas later to be presented in a
    more sophisticated fashion (e.g. the Professor in love). Barrie rightly hoped it
    might be forgotten. (J M Barrie, *The Greenwood Hat* (London, 1937) pp
    181-2.

3   *The Times*, 17 April 1891.

4   *The Times*, 1 June 1891.

5   *The Times*, 7 January 1892.

6   Those who wish to argue that Barrie equated artistic value with a popularity
    measured in book sales or box-office receipts must somehow counter this
    strong contrary evidence.

7   See MacKail, *JMB*, p 19, pp 46-7.

8   By contrast, few of the later plays rely on national stereotypes.

9   Letter to M Albert Carré, Beinecke Library, Barrie Collection, A/3 (April
    1891).

10 Geduld, *Barrie*, p 105.

11 Allen Wright, *J M Barrie: The Glamour of Twilight* (Edinburgh, 1976) 53;
    Geduld, *Barrie*, p 101.

12 *The Daily Telegraph*, 26 February 1892. George Rowell in *The Victorian
    Theatre: 1792-1914* (Cambridge, 1975) sums up Robertson fairly. He is seen,
    stylistically, to be a good writer bringing some sort of respectability back to
    the comic stage. Rowell adds 'Robertson could not evolve a play of ideas
    because his own ideas were largely superficial.' (p 77).

13 *The Times*, 26 February 1892.

14 These notebooks are held in the Beinecke Library, Yale, Barrie MSS A/2.
    A/2.6; A/2.7.

15 Shelton, *It's Smee*, p 110.

16 Joseph Harker, *Studio and Stage* (London, 1924) p 239.

17 This poster is preserved in the Theatrical Museum, Tavistock Street, London;
    'Toole's Theatre, 1892'.

18 A fact revealed by H M Walbrook, *J M Barrie and the Theatre* (London,
    1922) p 35.

19 Irene Vanbrugh, *To Tell My Story* (London, 1949) p 29

20 Skelton, *Smee* p 110. Harker, *Studio* p 246 confirms this. 'Barrie', he notes,
    'was very quiet and undemonstrative . . . save in a few instances where his
    dictum was important. On these occasions he would assert himself with a
    sudden access of vigour, impressing on you his wishes in a way that quite
    plainly indicated that he knew exactly what he wanted and that he was capable
    of seeing that he got it.'

21   Patrick Chalmers, *The Barrie Inspiration* (London, 1938) p 185.

22   Recorded by Walbrook, *Barrie*, p 29.

23   This view is shared by some modern critics. See St John Ervine, *Oscar Wilde* (London, 1951) pp 188-220.

24   Consulted, Toole's Theatre 1891 (Theatre Museum).

25   *Illustrated London News*, March 1982.

26   *Bohemia*, if it proves anything, proves Barrie's knowledge of the classical tradition of the 'idée fixe' as a source for laughter. (See Henri Bergson, *Le Rire*, for a developed theory, based mainly on the practice of Molière).

27   *The Times*, 26 February 1892; *The Bookman* XXXIX (October 1910) p 13.

28   See n.14.

29   What becomes clear the more one immerses oneself in his attitudes to art is that though similar ideas are exhaustively and repetitively employed the literary context always differs. The re-definition is part of an aesthetic perspectivism, which will be discussed in Chapter Three.

30   Others include: Notebook 6—*Houseboat Granny*; Notebook 7—*Bluestocking*; Notebook 8—*That Houseboat*; Notebook 12—*Houseboat Blarney; The Mystery Man; The Lady Jane; The Floating Lily; The Water People; The Mermaid; The Cuckoo; The Mocking Bird; The Silent Pool.*

31   J M Barrie, *When A Man's Single* (London, 1888) p 196.

32   J M Barrie, *An Edinburgh Eleven* (London, 1889) p 101

33   *Ibid.* p 82. (In fact the pass rate in Medicine at that time was notoriously low.)

34   Darlington, *Barrie*, p 61.

35   'Definitive' simply means — as presented in the Definitive Edition. As will become clear, there can be no definitive (final; accepted) text of any Barrie play.

36   Barrie, *Man's Single*, p 174. See also Appendix A, *Plays and Players*.

37   Walbrook, *Barrie*, p 37.

38   To gain some sense of the 'norm', one should read, say, *The MacHaggis*. (See its unsurprisingly cold reception in *The Scotsman*, 26 February 1897.) Barrie's problem lay in writing at a time when justifiable national outrage at excessive parody co-existed with a heightened dramatic level of definition. In order to be comic one had to start from the latter norm in order to trigger any sense of incongruity from an audience whose knowledge of Scotland or Ireland was theatrical. Within that context he is clearly the most restrained of all practitioners in the area of nationally derived wit. He also counterpoints one national vision against another rather than following those who simply use London society as an ideal, against which the regions may 'hilariously' be contrasted.

39   This exchange is contained in the *Definitive Edition*, p 24.

40   J A Hammerton, *Barrie: The Story of a Genius* (London, 1929) p 186. He is, of course, describing the backcloth. This, like the one in *Walker, London*, was a work of art and became the source of much critical praise.

41   Chalmers, *Barrie*, p 186.

42   *The Times*, 26 June 1894.

43   Geduld, *Barrie*, p 101, perceptively concludes that 'Barrie could not make up his mind whether Professor Goodwillie was to be ridiculous or lovable, so he tried to make him both.'

44   Archer condemns this play more stridently than he does any other of Barrie's works. 'A calculated disloyalty to art, a patchwork of extravagant farce, mawkish sentiment, irrelevant anecdote.'

45   As considered in Chapter One.

46   *The Times*, 26 June 1894. The figure of the lover who is unaware of his state recurs also in Barrie's prose works but never so extravagantly as in the portrayal of Goodwillie.
47   Darlington, *Barrie*, p 5. In all other ways he had taken the theatre very seriously indeed.
48   Max Beerbohm, *More Theatres* (London, 1969) p 605.
49   *Ibid.* p 604.
50   In *A Kiss for Cinderella*, Cinderella has 'Scotch words sticking to her like bits of eggshell to a chicken' but one thinks of a fairytale type who happens to be Scottish not of a refugee from Thrums.
51   While accepting that major and minor cultures do not always obey the same canonical laws, I still see this situation as analogous to an English critic deciding that, say, *The Pickwick Papers*, is Dickens's only truly English novel. That bizarre premise accepted, it follows that he must be assessed only within the limitations of the picaresque and blamed for mocking his fellow countrymen!
52   Beinecke, Barrie Collection, A2/13.
53   *The Scotsman*, 26 June 1894. The idea of the male lover unaware of his state originates in the prose works. See *When A Man's Single*, where reference is made 'to the time it takes man to discover that he is in love.' (p 123).
54   See MacKail, *JMB*, pp 201-2; 218-19.
55   Walbrook, *Barrie*, pp 47-8.
56   Cited by Janet Dunbar, *J M Barrie: The Man Behind the Image* (London, 1970) p 97.
57   Chapter 8, 'The Courting of T'Nowhead's Bell'. Marriot's passion in Chapter 18 of *My Lady Nicotine* (London, 1890) resembles that of Goodwillie but the Notebooks argue for the dramatic character being separately conceived.
58   Henders discovers the all-important letter; Effie is Lucy White's confidante.
59   *The Ladies' Shakespeare* and *The Real Thing at Last*, Beinecke, Barrie Collection L33.2 and R.43.
60   William Archer, *The Theatrical World of 1894* (London, 1895) p 191. 'A mere patchwork of little mechanical devices, irrelevant anecdotes, "wheezes" and comic business.'
61   After carefully highlighting the contradictions implied by society's redefinition of truth and deceit, Jones escapes his own questions by sending his central character to Africa.
62   George Bernard Shaw, *Three Plays for Puritans* (London, 1947) p xxii. The Preface is dated 1900 but makes clear that Shaw's dissatisfactions came to a head in the mid-1890s.
63   It is noteworthy that, despite its failure, Barrie returns to many of the themes of *The Professor's Love Story*. In *The Admirable Crichton* he would satirise more thoroughly the useless lives of the upper classes, especially those who confuse play-acting with radicalism. The ideas that women are superior to men, that they value the power of their own love's purity above the object of it and that they may exaggerate slight duplicity into massive guilt will be returned to in *Quality Street*.
64   Cynthia Asquith, *Barrie* (London, 1954) p 21.
65   Though there were other reasons for his reaction, embarrassment was the main one.
66   *New York Sun*, 16 October 1931. The article looks back on the history of the *Empire Theatre*, following the news that it has been sold.
67   Cited by Walbrook, *Barrie*, p 54.

68 Cyril Maude, *Haymarket Theatre*, p 203.
69 *The Scotsman*, 8 November 1897.
70 Darlington, *Barrie*, p 79; P P Howe, *Dramatic Portraits* (London, 1913) p 117.
71 Walbrook, *Barrie*, p 50.
72 *The Scotsman, op. cit.* The phrase 'national drama' reveals an additional evaluative criterion. English critics might question the effectiveness of the humour as directed against the elders; Scottish critics also questioned its propriety.
73 Howe, *Portraits*, p 120.
74 Walbrook, *Barrie*, p 55.
75 Many critics, while accepting that the conclusion convulsed the audience, felt it also represented the last of too many sudden tonal changes. The sense that the play was, in this and other senses, an unhappy mélange was summed up by Archer's 'patchwork' metaphor.
76 *The Scotsman, op. cit.*
77 *The Times*, 8 November 1897. 'One almost loves them for their bigotry.'
78 I have used three early texts in particular. Beinecke, Barrie Collection, L54/2 and L54/4; British Library, Lord Chamberlain's MS. ADD 55635A. (This research also revealed that the 'national' humour was almost completely excised for the American productions.)
79 *The Times*, 14 September 1914.
80 Beerbohm, *Last Theatres*, p 208.
81 Beinecke, Barrie Collection, A2.9.
82 *Glasgow Herald*, 8 November 1897. This review also pays tribute to the music, based on old Scots folk tunes and composed by Sir Alexander Mackenzie.
83 Axel Olrik, 'Epic Laws of Folk Narrative' in Alan Dundas, *The Study of Folklore* (Englewood Cliffs, N.J., 1965) pp 129-41. In Ireland Yeats was exploring the possibilities of mythic drama in a different way. Darlington, *Barrie*, p 79, notes that Barrie has turned 'the little water-cress seller' of the novel 'into a princess in disguise' but does not pursue the idea.
84 Olrik, *op. cit.*, p 135
85 Olrik, *op. cit.*, p 132
86 In the novel, these associations were strong. When first we are introduced to Babbie, the narrator comments that, 'she came upon him (Dishart) like a witch.' (p 32). Later, she appears like 'a gypsy elf . . . She had an angel's loveliness . . . she was very human . . . Undoubtedly she was the devil.' (p 36).
87 Roland Barthes, *Mythologies* (London, 1984), p 143.
88 *The Scotsman, op. cit.*
89 MacKail, *JMB*, p 262
90 Dunbar, *Barrie*, p 109, argues that after Barrie had seen and been captivated by Maude Adams' performance in *Rosemary*, she urged him to write a dramatic version of *The Little Minister* for her.
91 Isaac F Marcosson and Daniel Frohman, *Charles Frohman* (London, 1916) p 161.
92 MacKail, *Barrie*, p 267.
93 This view of art as a substitute birth was mentioned in *The Professor's Love Story*. In Act 3 Goodwillie refuses to accept his sister's praise of his writings because he sees himself as inferior to a smith whose wife has just passed with her children. 'I saw his wife also, and a pair of such splendid children. I knew which of us two had been a success, Agnes.' (p 116)

94　*The Scotsman*, for example, sees Babbie as 'a capital acting part and no more.'

95　George Borrow, *The Romany Rye* (London, 1909) p 64. Borrow compares the gypsy to the cuckoo in this sense. Jasper (cuckoo) and Babbie (gypsy) do have much in common as free spirits in conventional communities.

96　For examples of the rowan having both significances see Thomas Davidson, *Rowan Tree and Red Thread* (Edinburgh, 1949).

97　Ronald Bryden, *The Unfinished Hero* (London, 1969) p 146.

98　Even the sympathetic MacKail sees this. 'Technically, in fact . . . this supreme effort at a big novel continually breaks down.' p 161.

99　Cited in *The Wind on the Heath: A Gypsy Anthology*, chosen by John Sampson (London, 1930) p 27.

100　Beinecke, Barrie Collection, A2.9; A2.10; A2.12.

101　See also Beinecke, Barrie Collection, L54.2. This text belonged to Frohman and was for the New York opening. Barrie has made revisions in Act I and IV in his hand. Other alterations appear to have been made by Maude Adams at rehearsal. It contains similar diatribes against the gypsies.

102　See the end of Act 2 Scene 2.

103　Beinecke, Barrie Collection, L54/4.

104　British Library, Lord Chamberlain's MS. ADD 53635A. In the novel, some passages present the same conflict. See, especially, Chapter XIX. The tighter dramatic form *of itself* transforms psychological variations into apparent contradiction. This may well have been the factor unforeseen by Barrie.

105　Both the translation of a major novel and the introduction of a variety of levels of interpretation make *The Little Minister* a more daring experiment than any of its dramatic predecessors.

106　Cited by Geduld, *Barrie*, p 106.

107　Geduld, *Barrie*, p 105.

108　Walbrook, *Barrie*, p 60.

109　In *Margaret Ogilvy* (London, 1896), the narrator confesses the problem openly. 'To-night I must make my hero say "Darling", and it needs both privacy and concentration.' (p 98). He finds amorous dialogue 'contrary to the Scotch nature' and composes it 'dourly with my teeth clenched.' (p 99). There is some self-parody, no doubt, but the problem was a real one.

110　Recalled by MacKail, *JMB*, p 300.

111　Beinecke, Barrie Collection, A2.16 (Entries 187, 191).

112　Walbrook, *Barrie*, p 66.

113　Ormond, *Barrie*, p 51

114　Beinecke, Barrie Collection, A3 (Pinero, 12/1/1913).

115　'All the conditions that she makes are that we live entirely out of England'. (Lord Augustus, Act 4 *Lady Windermere's Fan*). Earlier Lady Windermere had also thought of leaving the country with Darlington.

116　*The Profligate* was first produced in 1884. Pinero's *The Notorious Mrs Ebbsmith* (1895) is in the same tradition.

117　Einar Haugen, *Ibsen's Drama: Author to Audience* (Minneapolis, 1979).

118　Orley I Holtan, *Mythic Patterns in Ibsen's Last Plays* (Minneapolis, 1970) p 23.

119　Geduld, *Barrie*, pp 105-6.

120　His part was drastically reduced from the developed rôle set out in the original manuscript, Beinecke, Barrie Collection, W42. Characteristically, Barrie did not allow the lost material to go to waste, resurrecting the full character in *Mary Rose*. This intentional diminution of comedy deprived Barrie of his most important dramatic weapon — humour.

121   Strindberg in *The Father* (1887) had also dealt with the power given to woman through childbearing. His 'hero' sought solace in books as a subsidiary form of creation as well.

122   This aspect of Ibsen's drama is fully considered by John Nartham in *Ibsen's Dramatic Method* (London, 1952). 'Visual suggestions can add unspoken information where strict realism inhibits the statements of feeling and motive.' (p 12).

123   Speech given by Ibsen on 10 September 1874.

124   The problem of illegitimacy is considered in both.

125   Striking images, present in all the early dramas, are nonetheless most prevalent in *The Wedding Guest*. Mr Fairbairn, for example, describes himself as 'only a thing swaddled in comfortable phrases' while the image of Margaret as a 'stopped clock', powerful in itself, looks forward to *Peter Pan*, to Mrs Page in *Rosalind* and to *Mary Rose*.

126   The maturity of his critical ideas had been developed in the prose works, themselves a series of sub-genre experiments. I had forgotten that he was only a *theatrical* apprentice.

127   These articles were (in order of composition) — 'Barrie as Journeyman-Dramatist: A Study of *Walker, London*', *Studies in Scottish Literature*, XXII, 1985, pp 60-77; 'The Land of Myth and Faery: The Dramatic Version of Barrie's *The Little Minister*', *Scotia*, IX, 1985, pp 1-16.

128   Barrie's attempts to defeat this powerful convention seem slight to us but were regarded as daring in his own day. See especially Chapter Four.

129   Fay Compton, *Rosemary* (London, 1926) p 185.

130   J M Barrie, *The Greenwood Hat* (London, 1937) p 152.

131   An imitation, probably, of *The Wild Duck*. As it happens, the symbol of the duck, like Barrie's cuckoo, had not been part of the play as originally conceived. See Henrik Ibsen, *The Wild Duck*, ed D B Christiani (New York, 1968) p 149.

132   Beinecke, Barrie Collection, Ib.6.2.

133   Another Ibsen parody with serious critical relevance is Robert Buchanan's *The Gifted Lady*. It opened at *Toole's* in the same months as *Ibsen's Ghost*.

134   The Lord Chamberlain's text represents the next stage of revision after Ib.6.2.

135   J M Barrie, *An Edinburgh Eleven* (London, 1888).

136   In *Darwinism and The Study of Society*, ed Michael Banton (London, 1961) pp 17-35.

137   *Ibid.* p 29.

138   See Frederick Burkhardt, 'England and Scotland: The Learned Societies' pp 37-74 in Thomas F Glick, *The Comparative Reception of Darwinism* (Chicago, 1974).

139   J M Barrie, *Auld Licht Idylls* (London, 1888) p 5.

140   *Ibid.* p 49.

141   Charles Darwin, *The Descent of Man* (London, 1885) p 562.

142   The key word in Barrie's prose. It combines the sense of power with that of animal magnetism/personal charisma.

143   Darwin, *Descent* p 597.

144   J M Barrie, *Sentimental Tommy* (London, 1896) p 107.

145   The word referred to is his rival's surname after 'Jean'.

146   Darwin does accept that this superiority is due to biological and social factors. But the revolution which would be needed to offset this seems to him too radical and to involve so long a period of 'unnatural' behaviour as to be impractical.

147 Darwin, *The Origin of Species* (London, 1950) p 97.

148 Darwin, *Descent*, p 614. 'Sexual selection depends on the success of certain individuals over others of the same sex, in relation to the propagation of the same species; whilst natural selection depends on the success of both sexes, at all ages, in relation to the general conditions of life. The sexual struggle is of two kinds; in the one it is between individuals of the same sex, generally the males, in order to drive away or kill their rivals, the females remaining passive; whilst in the other, the struggle is likewise between the individuals of the same sex, in order to excite or charm those of the opposite sex, generally the females, which no longer remain passive, but select the more agreeable partners.'

CHAPTER THREE: Pages 78 - 154

1 Ormond, *Barrie*, p 84.

2 George Bernard Shaw, *Collected Letters*, ed D H Lawrence, 4 vols (London, 1972) II, 350. To Ada Rehan, 30.8.1904.

3 *The Times*, Thursday, 18 September 1902.

4 Wright, *Barrie*, p 55.

5 Roger Marivell, *Ellen Terry* (London, 1968) p 298. This judgement is based on four highlighted plays including *Quality Street* and *The Admirable Crichton*.

6 Lynette Hunter, 'J M Barrie: the Rejection of Fantasy', *Scottish Literary Journal*, V, 1978, 39-52 (p 39).

7 Shaw, *Plays for Puritans*, Preface pp vii-xxxvi. The Preface is dated 1900 but indicates that his dissatisfactions were formulated earlier.

8 The Uniform Edition (London, 1913-22) is used for the novels. The elder sister marries in the novel; the younger in the play.

9 Lord Chamberlain's Papers, British Library LCP 1902/27N.

10 *The Scotsman*, Thursday, 18 September 1902.

11 Max Beerbohm, *Around Theatres* (London, 1953), p 223.

12 Walbrook, *Barrie*, p 83. Hammerton gives strong support to this view. 'In my opinion the dramatist has never been better served in the interpretation of any of his creations than with the revival of *Quality Street* in August, 1921.' Barrie, *The Story of a Genius* (London, 1929), p 229.

13 Walbrook, p 81.

14 Beinecke Library, Yale, Barrie MSS A2/14.

15 Humanities Research Center, Austin, Texas, Barrie Hanley B, 'Phoebe's Garden'.

16 LCP 1902/27N, Act 3. In one instance this concern for garden imagery led him into an unconscious howler, later deleted. VALENTINE: Miss Lucy, I am at the garden gate. Do you think you will let me enter?

17 *The Times, op. cit.* See Chapter 1, n 33. Appendix A, *Plays and Players* suggests a source for the symbolism of the bonnet.

18 R D S Jack, 'From Novel to Drama: J M Barrie's *Quality Street*', *Scottish Literary Journal*, XIV, 2 1987, 48-61.

19 In LCP both Miss Henrietta and Patty are real foils to Phoebe, the former as a youthful but not so courageous rival, the latter as a lower-class parallel on the model of Effie in *The Professor's Love Story*.

20 Geduld, *Barrie*, p 111. (Livvy = Phoebe's 'niece').

21 Bruno Bettelheim, *The Uses of Enchantment* (Harmondsworth, 1976) p 245.

22   See Robert Scholes, *Structuralism in Literature* (New Haven, Conn., 1974) pp 44-6.

23   Beerbohm, *Around Theatres*, p 220.

24   Barrie's 'naturalistic' Acts are, of course, stylised. The distinction here is referential — we are encouraged to refer them to the laws of nature, not fantasy. There was, for example, a real blue and white room. See *Greenwood Hat*, Chapter XII.

25   In the earliest texts passersby include boys, girls, yokels, a clergyman, a maid and a postman. Later versions cut the lists down but (*Definitive Edition* p 275) the method is never abandoned. Sounds, too, such as the strains of the Military Band (*Definitive* pp 290, 293) provide variation within the same range of effect.

26   See Act 1, p 284.

27   Charles Darwin, *On the Origin of Species* (London, 1950) p 54. (Chapter Three).

28   'There is a satisfaction about living in *Quality Street* which even religion cannot give.' (Stage Directions, Act 1, p 275.) See also Appendix A, Darwin and Darwinism.

29   *Modern British Dramatists 1900-1945*, ed Stanley Weintraub, 2 vols (Detroit, 1982) I, 36.

30   The English translation of Weltanschauung loses the stronger philosophical associations intended.

31   *Fabian News*, VII, 8 July 1989, p 747.

32   This friendship/rivalry strengthened in later years when they both lived in Adelphi Terrace (1909-27). Shaw was also Barrie's seconder (1912) when the Scot was elected to the Academic Committee of the Royal Society of Literature, MacKail, *JMB*, p 435.

33   'My business is to fight for the Grand School — the people who are building up the intellectual consciousness of the race. My men are Wagner, Ibsen, Tolstoy, Schopenhauer, Nietzsche, who have, as you know, nobody to fight for them.' Shaw, *Letters*, II, 353 (27.8.1903).

34   Barrie, *Greenwood Hat*, p 6.

35   Patrick Bridgwater, *Nietzsche in Anglosaxony* (Leicester, 1972) p 13, citing Havelock Ellis's 'The Genius of Nietzsche'.

36   *Definitive Edition*. p 279. (She is listening through the floor. They all stoop or go on their knees to listen, and when they are in this position the RECRUITING SERGEANT enters unobserved.)

37   Nietzsche, *Beyond Good and Evil* (*Jenseits von Gut und Böse*), Section 259. I have used Nietzsche, *Werke*, ed G Colli und M Montinari (Berlin, 1967-78) as the text against which to check the English translations. If there seemed to me to be a problem I have included the German in the Note.

38   Cited by Alexander Nehemas, *Nietzsche: Life as Literature* (Cambridge, Mass., 1985) p 225. Nietzsche, *Untimely Meditations* (*Unzeitgemässe Betrachtungen*) II, 9.

39   Nietzsche, *Thus Spoke Zarathustra* (*Also Sprach Zarathustra*) I, 5.

40   Nietzsche, *Human All Too Human* (*Menschliches Allzumenschliches*) Section 111.

41   Nietzsche, *Beyond Good and Evil* (*Jenseits von Gut und Böse*) Section 270.

42   Peter Keating, *The Haunted Study* (London, 1989) p 133.

43   'For this reason it comes about that you think the passage, whose literal sense

you do not see, has to be understood spiritually only.' *Didascalicon*, VI, Chapter 10. (*Medieval Literary Theory and Criticism c1100-c1375*, ed A J Minnis and A B Scott (Oxford, 1989), p 85).

44 'And pass not in Thy mercy by them, / Nor hear their pray'r. / But for Thy people's sake destroy them, / An' dinna spare.'

45 Nietzsche, *Beyond Good and Evil* Section 270. 'Man', 'men' are translations of Menschen, which might in this context, more accurately, be rendered 'One'. Certainly Mensch includes women and so Phoebe!

46 See, for example, *Human All Too Human* Section 122, where the metaphor is put in the same scholastic context as in *Quality Street*. 'Blind pupils'.

47 Nietzsche, *Beyond Good and Evil* Section 21. Nietzsche prefers the French phrase.

48 This contrast between the travel-pilgrimage of, say, *The Canterbury Tales*, and enduring spiritual pilgrimage on the 'Field Full of Folk' (Langland, *Piers Plowman*) is a leitmotiv in Christian literature.

49 For the use of the Veil image in an early anticipation of Literature as Utility see Boccaccio, *Genealogia Deorum Gentilium* — Chapter XIV. Boccaccio and others used the image to translate the idea of levels of difficulty being conveyed in relation to the capacities of the audience. Barrie was doing the same thing.

50 Nietzsche, *Daybreak*, (*Morgenröte*) Section 113. Cited by R J Hollingdale, *Nietzsche* (London, 1973) p 85.

51 Nietzsche, *On the Genealogy of Morals* (*Zur Genealogie der Morale*) II, 16-19.

52 Nietzsche, *Thus Spoke Zarathustra*, I, 5.

52 Beinecke Library, Barrie Collection, A/3. (5/9/1935). For 'Anon' see *The Greenwood Hat*, Chapter 1; for McConnachie, J M Barrie *Courage* (London, 1922).

54 June Schlueter, *Metafictional Characters in Modern Drama* (New York, 1979) p 1. (Corp — lat. *corps* = earthbound).

55 Nietzsche, *The Will to Power* (*Wille zur Macht*), Section 520. (Cited, Hollingdale, p 131).

56 Nehamas, *Life as Literature*, p 47, Cf. Tzvetan Todorov, *Poétique* (Paris, 1968) p 17 'Mais dire, "toute est interprétation," ne signifie pas: toutes les interprétations se valent.' This is a more relativistic view than either Nietzsche or Barrie took.

57 Thomas Carlyle, *On Heroes and Hero-Worship*, ed Carl Niemeyer (Lincoln, Nebraska, 1966) p 55.

58 Nietzsche, *The Twilight of the Gods* (*Die Gotzendämmerung*), 'Die Wahre Welt übrig? die scheinbare vielleicht . . . Aber Nein! mit der wahren Welt haben wir auch die Scheinbare abgeschafft.'

59 Todorov, *Poetique*, p 36, 'Discourse' here translates Todorov's 'parole'. (Not entirely happily).

60 Arthur C Danto, *Nietzsche as Philosopher* (New York, 1965) p 109.

61 Nietzsche, *Beyond Good and Evil* Section 4.

62 The evidence suggests that Barrie may have known major Nietzschean ideas as early as the dramatic version of *The Little Minister*. Despite Sir James's originality of mind and natural propensity towards multi-definition personally, mutivalence linguistically, it is difficult to see either *Sentimental Tommy* or *Tommy and Grizel* existing in their precise form without some study of the German philosopher.

63 The rougher, more barbaric ages (though losing out in other ways) were more

favourable to the heroism of action. The 'case' of Crichton is presented by Barrie against these two backgrounds dramatically made possible by the creative powers of fantasy.

64   The audience contains the predecessors of Valentine and Susan.

65   Danto, *Nietzsche*, p 84.

66   Nietzsche, *The Genealogy of Morals* (*Zur Genealogie der Morale*) 'Deterring' translates 'Abschreckung'. (*Werke*, VI (2) p 333).

67   R L Green, *J M Barrie* (New York, 1961), p 32.

68   *Onward and Upward*, selected by James Drummond (Aberdeen, 1983). Barrie had earlier addressed the question of hypocritical forays by the aristocracy into the lives of the working class in Act Two of *The Professor's Love Story* with Sir George Gilding's hilarious combination of corn cutting and picknicking.

69   One of the Medieval versions of the world upside down associated with particular festivals. A boy took the rôle of the bishop for that day.

70   Beinecke Library, Barrie Collection, A2/18.

71   MacKail, *JMB*, p 288.

72   *Ibid*, p 312.

73   Beinecke Library, Barrie Collection, A2/15. The reference is in Act Three of what was then a three act play.

74   *Sir Thomas Urquhart: The Jewel*, ed R D S Jack and R J Lyall (Edinburgh, 1984) p 106. See also Appendix A, *Plays and Players*.

75   Irene Vanbrugh, *My Story*, p 67.

76   MacKail, *JMB*, p 33.

77   Roland Barthes, *Essais Critiques* (Paris, 1964). 'Le Théatre de Baudelaire': 'Il n'y a pas de grand théatre sans théatralité dévorante, chez Eschyle, chez Shakespeare, chez Brecht, le texte écrit est d'avance emporté par l'extériorité des corps, des objets, des situations; la parole fuse aussitôt en substances.' (p 42)

78   For a very brief history of Stage Lighting, see Tim Streader and John A Williams, *Create Your Own Stage Lighting* (London, 1985) pp 10-19. More detailed studies include Frederick Bentham, *The Art of Stage Lighting* (London, 1980).

79   W R McGraw, 'James M Barrie's Concept of Dramatic Action,' *Modern Drama*, 1964, p 136.

80   Case — as defined by Jolles.

81   *The Times Literary Supplement*, 14 November 1902, p 341. Max Beerbohm, *Around Theatres*, p 231, saw the play in terms of a revolution in theatre history. 'I think *The Admirable Crichton* is quite the best thing that has happened, in my time, to the British stage. New ground has been broken before. But the breakage has ever been made too furtively to attract other miners or too clumsily not to scare them to the old congested camp; nor, indeed, has the new ground been invariably worth breaking. That has remained the modern judgement; evaluatively *Crichton* has received a better press 'than any of the other Barrie plays considered in this book.' See Geduld, *Barrie*, p 29; Ormond, *Barrie*, p 98.

82   Thomas Moult, *Barrie* (London, 1928), p 149.

83   *The Times*, Friday, 5 November 1902. Many journalists did feel that Barrie's attack on the upper classes was too severe. Even Beerbohm, while applauding the general satire, was not quite at ease on this. 'The play left a somewhat bitter taste . . . the aristocrats, who began by being merely fools, are driven in the end into being consummate liars. *TLS* 1902, p 341.

84 Compare Wordsworth's use of the Platonic idea of a pre-existent state in *Ode on Intimations of Immortality*. Essentially the idea is justified by its utility in explaining Wordsworth's own experiences.

85 Ronald Grimsley, 'Jean-Jacques Rousseau, Philosopher of Nature,' pp 184-98, in *Philosophers of the Enlightenment*, ed S C Brown (Brighton, 1979) p 195.

86 The most primitive stage of society was not viewed idealistically by Rousseau. He saw the most stable state existing in the first social stage of development ('la première révolution'). Barrie recreates that stage but imports into it the products of an advanced civilisation.

87 J-J Rousseau, *Oeuvres Complètes*, ed B Gagnebin et M Raymond, 5 vols (Paris, 1959-66) I, 935.

88 Jean Terrasse, *Jean-Jacques Rousseau et la Quête de l'âge d'or* (Bruxelles, 1970) p 76.

89 J-J Rousseau, *The Political Writings*, ed C E Vaughan (Cambridge, 1915), i, 140. 'Je conçois dans l'espèce humaine deux sortes d'inégalité: l'une que j'appelle naturelle ou physique . . . l'autre, qu'on peut appeler l'inégalité morale ou politique.'

90 James Miller, *Rousseau: Dreamer of Democracy* (New Haven, 1984) p 109. See Appendix A, *Napoleon and the Superman* for an early anticipation of Barrie's opposition to democratic government.

91 Barrie, *Greenwood Hat*, p 37. Hippomenes (Barrie) in *The Nottingham Journal* often uses Carlyle's ideas as a starting point (e.g. 17.12.83).

92 They are, for Carlyle, interim heroes in an age of confusion and conditioned by that age. See John MacQueen, *The Rise of the Historical Novel* (Edinburgh, 1989) p 276.

93 B H Lehman, *Carlyle's Theory of the Hero* (Durham, North Carolina, 1928) p 59.

94 *Ibid*, p 79.

95 The audience dimension of an allegorical-utilitarian art (See n. 49) was, for Barrie and Nietzsche, honestly hierarchical. Some minds were more intelligent than others and capable of handling truths. But such art must be aware of the slower minds and not reveal even the simplest truths directly. This is, of course, a modern reinterpretation of the ideas expressed by Dionysius in *The Celestial Hierarchy*. The veils must at once conceal and reveal depending on the understanding and disposition of the reader. Geoffrey of Vinsauf sums up the situation economically in the *Poetria Nova* when he writes, 'Do not unveil the thing fully but suggest it by hints.' (*Amplificatio*, Section 2).

96 Ian Campbell, *Thomas Carlyle* (London, 1974) notes that Carlyle sees the Artist-Hero in these terms: 'altogether a product of these new ages.' (p 187).

97 Vanbrugh, *My Story*, p 68.

98 The assumption of power is very clearly stated even in the Definitive Text. Crichton himself notes it, 'I am Lord over all. They are but hewers of wood and drawers of water,' (p 398); his 'subjects' note it, Traherne, 'He is becoming a bit magnificent in his ideas,' (p 387) and Barrie as narrator/dramatist notes it, 'Never has he looked more regal, never perhaps felt so regal. We need not grudge him this one foible of his rule, for it is all coming to an end.' (p 401).

99 Nietzsche, *Genealogy of Morals*, II, 16-19. See Hollingdale, *Nietzsche*, pp 115-120.

100 Nietzsche, *Zarathustra*, Prologue 4.

101 My italics.

102 This had been stressed in *Quality Street*. The interrelationship of suffering as

one pole against exultation as another, to the additional polarity 'between barbarism and civilisation' in order to show that 'science as much as art is an instrument for the enhancement of life' is at once sound Nietzschean philosophy (Danto, *Nietzsche* p 60) and the more ambitious subject of *The Admirable Crichton*.

103 This is a complex topic, involving various perspectives. As Artist, Barrie saw himself confronting life to comfort others while testing them. See Danto, *Nietzsche*, pp 45-53.

104 Nietzsche, *Will to Power*, Section 108.

105 Nietzsche, *Will to Power*, Section 1018; Appendix A, *Napoleon and the Superman*.

106 Nietzsche, *Ecce Homo*. 'Wenn ich mein höchste Formel für Shakespeare suche, so finde ich immer nur die, dass er den Typus Cæsar concipirt hat.' (*Werke*, VI (3)) p 285.

107 As in *Hard Times*, where Gradgrind's philosophy summed up in the memorable phrase ('Facts, facts, facts') is set against Sleary's ('People must be amuthed') a formula which at once proclaims and evokes the comic alternative.

108 Compare Prospero in *The Tempest*. The structure of *The Admirable Crichton* recalls Shakespeare's Romances. This parallel once more sets the life and art of an adventurous but comparatively 'primitive' society against that of its refined Edwardian counterpart.

109 Howe, *Portraits*, p 126. 'The Hon Ernest Woolley has this particular importance in the comedy of J M Barrie, that he is the symbol of its reaction against the verbal decoration which, in its superficial aspect, was Wilde's.'

110 Johann Wyss, *The Swiss Family Robinson*, ed M J Godwin (London, 1814).

111 Captain Marryat, *Masterman Ready*, 3 vols (London, 1841-42), Chapter 27. Such stories, Barrie admits, were the staple reading of his childhood.

112 Barrie's aim is to address all intellectual levels with the greatest serviceable testing at all grades of ability.

113 Roget's importance will be fully discussed in Chapter Four.

114 *Treasure Island* first appeared under the pseudonym of Captain North in *Young Folks* (1 October 1881 to 28 June 1882).

115 R L Stevenson, *Treasure Island* (Edinburgh, 1895), *Works*, I, p 167 (Chapter 21).

116 See K J Fielding, *Charles Dickens* (London, 1966) p 104; pp 124-5; F D Fawcett, *Dickens the Dramatist* (London, 1952).

117 Charles Dickens, *David Copperfield* Chapter 17. 'Uriah, with his long hands slowly twining over one another, made a ghastly writhe from the waist upwards.' Heep's 'humility' translates itself into a variety of hand movements including pressing his palms together, 'shaving' his chin with his hands and taking his gloves on and off.

118 *The Admirable Crichton*, Berg Public Library, New York. This is an early typescript with holograph additions and corrections. A different ballad is to be found in Beinecke, Barrie Collection, A 55/1. It begins, 'In the shade of the old apple tree,/Love in your eyes I can see.'

119 J H Buckley, *William Ernest Henley* (Princeton, 1945) p 132.

120 *The Works of W E Henley*, 5 vols (London, 1921) IV, 86.

121 This might be linked with Nietzsche's theory of eternal recurrence. This argued that history revealed a limited number of states constantly recurring over the ages with minor modifications. In a sense, this parallels Barrie's

limited number of tale-types, embodying the major stories into which human life can, in essence, be categorised. Nietzsche advanced this theory as early as *The Gay Science* (*Die Fröhliche Wissenschaft*); see Section 341 in particular.

122   Urquhart, *The Jewel* p 73. Upon these roots 'all the rest are branched; for better understanding whereof with all its dependant boughs, sprigs and ramelets, I have before my lexicon set down the division thereof, making use of another allegory.' The 'allegory' or memorial device is that of the subdivisions of a city. This approach to language should be borne in mind when an undisputed influence — Roget — is considered (Chapter Four).

123   *Ibid.* p 63.

124   *Ibid.* Biographical Introduction, pp 1-11.

125   Barrie, *Edinburgh Eleven*, Chapter Two.

126   See George Elder Davie, *The Democratic Intellect* (Edinburgh, 1961).

127   Hugh Blair, a predecessor in the Regius Chair, was the major British authority on Rhetoric in the eighteenth century. (*Lectures on Rhetoric and Belles Lettres*, 2 vols 1783; *Essays on Rhetoric*, 1784). In Barrie's own day, the distinctive Scottish contribution had been assessed in A M Williams, *The Scottish School of Rhetoric* (London, 1897). James VI's much earlier contribution (1585) took the form of a handbook of poetics entitled 'The Reulis and Cautelis to be Observit and Eschewit in Scottis Poesie.' This is a clarion call for a distinctively Scottish Renaissance 'For albeit sindrie hes written of it in English, quhilk is lykest to our language, yit we differ from thame in sindrie reulis of poesie.' See David Reid, *The Party Coloured Mind* (Edinburgh, 1982) for a detailed assessment of Scottish rhetoric in the seventeenth century. A briefer discussion is contained in *Scottish Prose 1550-1770*, ed R D S Jack (London, 1972).

128   *The Letters of Robert Burns*, ed J Delancey Ferguson, 2 vols (Oxford, 1931) I, 108.

129   Without this consciousness, attempts to withstand the tendency of some English critics (notably Leavis in *The Great Tradition*) to underrate Scottish work through assuming it is *trying* to be English, degenerate into sociological rather than literary counterblasts.

130   Barrie, *Edinburgh Eleven*, p 17.

131   David Masson, *British Novelists and their Styles*, p 2. 'The Novel, at its highest, is a prose Epic, and the capabilities of the Novel as a form of literature, are the capabilities of Narrative Poetry universally, excepting in as far as the use of prose . . . may involve necessary differences.'

132   *Ibid.* p 299.

133   *Ibid.* p 291.

134   That is, in terms of Decorum, the interrelationship between theme and language. See E R Curtius, *European Literature and the Latin Middle Ages* (London, 1979).

135   Walbrook, *Barrie*, p 76.

136   Ormond, *Barrie*, p 96.

137   G A Lamacchia, 'Textual Variations for Act IV of *The Admirable Crichton*,' *Modern Drama*, 1970, p 417.

138   *Ibid.* p 408.

139   Star and Garter Performance, 1916.

140   1920 Revival, which ran at *The Royalty* for 134 performances.

141   John Berger, *G.* (1972, Chapter 3).

142   Flan O'Brien, *At Swim-Two-Birds* (1939, opening paragraph).

143   Christopher Norris, *Derrida* (London, 1987) p 225.

144   Shaw, *Heartbreak House* Act 3. (MRS HUSHABYE: Did you hear the explosions? And the sound in the sky; it's splendid: it's like an orchestra: it's like Beethoven. ELIE: By thunder, Hesione: it is Beethoven.) Shaw himself drew from the last Act of Chehov's *Three Sisters*.

145   *New York Times*, 10 March 1931.

146   Gillette's performances (1904-5: Lyceum, New York) were renowned for their brooding sense of menace. As such, they come closer to Barrie's original conception of the character in the *Notebooks*.

147   MacKail, *JMB*, p 534.

148   One of the lost opportunities of all time was the film industry's failure to harness the enthusiasms of Barrie, whose sympathies naturally lay with a mode which could transcend the Word and Time, visually. The situation with *Crichton* was lamentable; their handling of *Peter Pan*, tragically opaque.

149   *The Letters of J M Barrie*, ed V Meynell (London, 1942) p 61. All these variations and revisions, although they have behind them a consistent aesthetic view are also based in psychological necessity. 'I'm apparently so constituted that I can't possibly sit out a month's rehearsal without meddling and tinkering with the script.' Asquith, *Portrait*, p 37.

150   Theatre Museum, 'Wyndham's, 1903'. A cartoon by C Harrison shows two gentlemen in evening suits. Entitled 'Pages from my Album of Bores No. V', it shows one putting the other to sleep. 'The man who will tell you the plot of *Little Mary*.'

151   *The Times*, Friday, 25 September 1903.

152   *The Scotsman*, Friday, 25 September 1903.

153   Hammerton, *Barrie*, p 239.

154   William Archer, *Play-making: A Manual of Craftsmanship* (London, 1913) p 123.

155   *The Scotsman*, Friday, 25 September 1903.

156   Walbrook, *Barrie*, p 92. His loyalty is stretched to its limits by *Little Mary*. His real view is probably expressed by his consistently calling the heroine Moira Looney!

157   The Souvenir Edition of *The Stage* (No. 4), September 1903 was lavishly produced with mauve photographs. It includes one with the blurb — 'MOIRA: I must say it — Stomach.'

158   F J Harvey Darton, *J M Barrie* (London, 1929) p 58.

159   Hubert Carter's play opened fifteen days before *Little Mary*. Based on Diderot's *Le Neveu de Rameau*, it was concerned with many problems earlier addressed in *The Admirable Crichton*. In it Punchinello openly praises the virtues of the 'stomach': its voice, he argues is much louder than that of conscience.

160   J M Barrie, *Works*, Hanley B, *ABC*, Humanities Research Center, Austin, Texas, MS III/28. (Barrie concealed trick titles under the form *ABC* until the First Night.)

161   Geduld, *Barrie*, p 123.

162   Scholes, *Structuralism*, p 45.

163   Ormond, *Barrie*, p 239.

164   Moult, *Barrie*, p 151.

165   Scholes, *Structuralism*, p 45

166   In *The Cok and the Jasp*, the moral is written in terms of higher knowledge inapplicable to the cock-animal. It is criticised for being an enemy to knowledge when the tale suggested praise for valuing necessities above luxuries.

A clear tension or 'riddle' is presented to the reader. In *The Two Mice*, both fable and moral teach the value of unaspiring contentment. Only the odd phrase — 'Gild brother . . . and fre Burges' alerts the enquiring mind to a specifically historical reading, related to the recent rise of the Burgh in Scotland. For an analysis, which accentuates this 'testing', see John MacQueen, *Robert Henryson: The Major Narrative Poems* (Oxford, 1967).

167   By means of the booklet.

168   British Library, LCP 1902/20. (For Austin text, see n. 160.)

169   The fact that Barrie was split between a family famous primarily in the Renaissance period (Percy) and one currently in power (Cecil) has, itself, significance. (See the later section on Communication).

170   Dampier, *Voyages*, 4 vols (London, 1729) III, i, 97.

171   In the earliest notes for *Little Mary*, Beinecke, Barrie Collection, A2/23, there is a reference under October 1902: 'Shd be Quite in Christian Science Manner. Title — "The Chemist's Daughter." ' Lord Plumleigh refers to 'trance' (p 465) and Moira to death as passing 'upstairs' (p 481).

172   William Carleton, *The Black Prophet* (Shannon, 1972) p 221. The First Edition of this novel came out in 1847. The first major famine belonged to the earlier period which had attracted Barrie imaginatively in *Auld Licht Idylls* etc; the later famine involved him as a journalist.

173   The whole article is condescendingly paternalistic.

174   These utilitarian principles had been fully spelt out in Cecil's 1858 article. 'Theories of Parliamentary Reform'.

175   George Dangerfield, *The Damnable Question* (London, 1976) p 6. See also, Appendix A, *Ireland, Doctors and Little Mary*.

176   *Ibid.* p 12. 'After the Famine late marriages became and remained the rule.'

177   Max Beerbohm, *The Saturday Review*, 3 October 1903, p 423.

178   Scholes, *Structuralism*, p 45. The joke-story 'attacks inadequacies in language.'

179   Michael Meyer, *Henrik Ibsen: The Making of a Dramatist, (1818-1864)* (London, 1967), p 44. The Chapter is entitled 'The Apothecary's Apprentice'.

180   Many reasons occur for Herodotus' appearance as examplar of the classical tradition. His claim to be the father of fantasy rests on his use of myths and mythical figures (e.g. the wise adviser) into a vision of history which refused to accept simple answers. See K H Waters, *Herodotus the Historian* (London, 1985). Like Barrie, he strove to control this complexity through strict formal structures. See H R Immerwahr, *Form and Thought in Herodotus* (Cleveland, Ohio, 1966). Waters p 139 and pp 47-60 provides brief introductions to both topics.

181   Barrie, *The Greenwqood Hat*, Chapter XVI, p 180.

182   Thomas Carlyle, *Heroes*, p 45.

183   David, 'Napoleon Crossing the Alps'.

184   Armand Dayot, *Napoleon: Illustrations* (Paris, 1908) preserves the caricature. Napoleon is depicted about child's height and nicknamed 'Little Bouncing B'. This would make his appearance in *Peter Pan* (see Chapter Four) particularly appropriate. The idea of Addington as the Doctor is part of Gillray's private caricature-code. (See Draper Hill, *Gillray, the Caricaturist* (London, 1965) p 104.) Although Addington is the larger figure, he is wearing Pitt's boots and coat which dwarf him. The idea of two pygmies is thus created. Compare (for Addington) the 1802 sketch entitled 'Lilliputian Substitutes'. Napoleon's hat carries also the features of power. Little Mary, as a force for good, has only the rosette. (See n. 185.)

185   For the former, see especially 'The Plumb-pudding in danger; — or — State
       Epicures Taking un Petit Souper', Hill Illustration No. 96; for the latter 'The
       Corsican-Pest or Belzebub going to Supper', Hill Illustration No. 123. Hill
       notes also (p 128) the frequency with which caricaturists and engravers had
       'recourse to satirical black magic' as a means of accounting for Napoleon.
       Little Mary as a type of *white* magic would, therefore, have further ironic
       force for those aware of the caricaturist's art.

186   I have intentionally diverted much of the discussion on Gillray's influence to
       the Footnotes as it is not an essential part of my argument. Given, however,
       the publication of this massive work by Thomas Wright and R H Evans in
       1851, and the subsequent interest it evoked, ample evidence was available for
       Barrie. (It contained examples — graphic and/or descriptive — of almost all
       Gillray's work). The art of the caricaturist was bound to attract someone
       whose major loves were the visual and the exaggerated. There seem to be too
       many ironies and apposite images created and confirmed by a study of Gillray
       for his influence on the virtuosic *Little Mary* to be coincidental. The play must
       at least be related to the 'cartoon' tradition surrounding Napoleon and the
       images provided by that tradition for the enjoyment of the popular
       imagination. (See, Hill, *Gillray*, pp 128-9).

187   Barrie, *The Greenwood Hat*, Chapter XVI. This, the chapter on Genius,
       opens with an imagined dialogue between Barrie and Gilmour — 'Am I a
       genius? . . . I murmur it aloud, forgetting that my so-called friend Gilray (sic)
       is dining out to-night, so this is an admirable opportunity for communing
       pleasantly on the matter.' (p 175). The retrospective form of this book
       demands a later reaction on the early article. This takes the form of referring
       to Gilmour's sketch of Barrie, which faces the title-page. 'On re-examining the
       sketch one notes nevertheless that he has omitted the G as well as the Hat.'
       (p 181). It was this ability in sketching which appears to have suggested the
       Gilray *nom de plume* in the first place.

188   The Hat is important for Barrie both as a visual sign of his new respectability
       and, later, as the box for his old articles. The opening 'Apology' sums up all in
       Barrie's carefully modulated tone of ironic negation, which asserts as much as
       it denies both about himself and his friend. 'This is my favourite portrait of
       Anon (JMB), and it is sad to think that T L G (Gilmour), the master-hand, so
       far as I know never made another; he possibly there and then destroyed his
       tools in noble self-consciousness that with the first effort he had reached his
       pinnacle.' (*The Greenwood Hat*, p 4). See also Appendix A.

189   Compare the earlier portrait of a writer-peasant in *A Window in Thrums*, pp
       95-6. 'So he passed from youth to old age, and all his life seemed as a dream,
       except that part of it in which he was writing or printing, or stitching or
       binding *The Millenium*. At last the work was completed . . . You may care to
       know the last of Jimsy, though in one sense he was blotted out when the last
       copy was bound.' The ideas behind Reilly exist as early as 1889; Barrie's
       achievement lies in his varied presentation of them in relation to different
       personalities and developing philosophy.

190   See n. 184 and 'Little Bouncing B'; also Appendix A, *Napoleon and the
       Superman*.

191   Shaw, *Letters, 1898-1910*, p 383. If he did fully understand Barrie's complex
       message, the word 'pamphlet' — also used by Reilly — to describe three
       volumes indicates an awareness of how slight a part of the message the dietary
       plot represents. See Appendix A, *Ireland, Doctors and Little Mary*.

192   *Ibid.*
193   Bernard Shaw, *Plays Unpleasant* in *The Bodley Head Bernard Shaw* I, 26.
194   I am unaware how the Angels will intepret me but only too aware about the lack of awareness of the Angles. The Angels are comprehending me in a transcendant state of awareness (unaware as super-aware). The Angles are unaware of what I am trying to say to them (unaware as non-aware). Gregory I, as reported by Bede, was responsible for originating this form of Latin wit. 'Non Angli sed Angeli'. It is not, therefore, as abstruse as it might seem. At the same time, *Little Mary* is intended to comprehend the obvious *and* the abstruse.
195   Michael Holroyd, *Bernard Shaw: The Search for Love* (London, 1988) p 89.
196   *Ibid.* p 87.
197   LCP 1902/20 Act 1.
198   Nietzsche primarily in *The Birth of Tragedy* (*Die Geburt der Tragödie*) and *Human All Too Human*. Jakobson expands the idea of verbal multivalence on which Nietzsche and Barrie concentrated into the wider theory of dominance. See Roman Jakobson, *Selected Writings* (The Hague, 1981), 'The Dominant', III, 751-6.
199   Beerbohm, *Saturday Review*, p 423.
200   Bernard Shaw, 'Tolstoy: Tragedian or Comedian?' *Pen Portraits and Reviews* 263. For *The Quintessence*, see the edition and discussion presented by J L Wisenthal, *Shaw and Ibsen* (Toronto, 1979). The earlier edition of the text was the one available to Barrie when writing *Little Mary*.
210   Shaw, *Plays Unpleasant*, p 30.
202   William Archer, 'Ibsen and English Criticism', *Fortnightly Review*, New Series 46, 1 July 1889.
203   Nietzsche, *Human All Too Human*, Section 109.
204   Shaw, *Plays Unpleasant*, p 29.
205   Nietzsche, *Human All Too Human*, Section 287. 'A higher culture': Nietzsche writes 'einer höhen Cultur' but the context is comparative.
206   Nina Auerbach, *Ellen Terry: Player in her Time* (London, 1987) p 277.
207   The entry is for 15 March 1883.
208   *The Letters of Lewis Carroll*, ed Morton N Cohen, 2 vols (London, 1979) I, 489. The Dickens quotation is a variation on the last words of *Pickwick Papers*, Chapter xxxiv.
209   *Ellen Terry's Memoirs*, ed Edith Craig and Christopher St John (London, 1933) p 142; 'I think he wrote these letters for fun, as some people make puzzles, anagrams or Limericks!'
210   Misinterpretations: See Act 3 Scene 2 (especially lines 88-90); Act 3 Scene 3 (especially lines 118-33); Dogberry and the constables throughout. Multi-meaning: See especially Act 2 Scene 3 lines 16-17; 46-49 but also, throughout, the verbal badinage between Beatrice and Benedick. Hidden (riddling meaning): See especially Act 3 Scene 4 lines 40-60. References are to the *New Cambridge* text. This includes part of the Carroll letter as Appendix B, pp 157-8.
211   Anthony B Dawson, 'Much Ado about Signifying', *Studies in English Literature*, 22, 1982, pp 211-21.
212   Strictly, *Little Mary* in spite of its three Acts, is not a full-length play. It was preceded by a curtain-raiser, *Angelica's Lover*.
213   Austin, Hanley B III, 28.

214 *Ibid.* I, 18. These references have disappeared by the time the text goes to the Lord Chamberlain.

215 It seems almost certain that Barrie used them as an initial gauge of how much an audience might be expected to take. Ironically, their reaction very often resulted in the rejection of some of the clearer 'allegoric' signs, as these were also the oddest remarks on a naturalistic level. The intermediary text, which went to the Lord Chamberlain, provides a guide to what 'passed' this stage but was rejected by audiences during the run. LCP 1903/20 had Reilly adopting the *nom de plume* of 'Fullalove', an accurate allegoric translation of the spirit in which the play was written and the 'cure' offered. In Act 2, there are explicit references to Napoleon and the issue of national freedom. In Act 3, Moira had originally stated Reilly's opinion 'that Bacon never wrote Shakespeare, for no lawyer could have had such an organ.' In this manner, audiences were permitted by Barrie to choose their own literary medicine, though in the same sad spirit as Reilly permitted drugs.

216 EEG, *The Makers of Hellas* (London, 1903); see *Times Literary Supplement*, II, 1903, p 141. The ground is re-covered by Richard Onians, *The Origins of European Thought* (Cambridge, 1954) pp 13-15; 23-40.

217 The *TLS* reviewer criticises EEG for not stressing that paganism was a failed religious vision.

218 Barrie's low critical status makes this a regrettable rather than surprising situation.

CHAPTER FOUR: Pages 155-261

(a) *Peter Pan* = the play; Peter Pan = the character; *Pan* = the myth as treated in its various forms by Barrie; Pan = the pagan god.

(b) In view of the vast amount of material centring around *Pan*, I have had to control the organisation of this chapter with especial care. The Notes have become the resting place for many important ideas. They should, therefore, be consulted not only as confirmation for arguments within the text but as, in themselves, the source of further information/argument/opinion, excluded — with extreme regret — in the name of clarity.

1   Study of *Peter Pan*'s evolution involves at least an acquaintance with the following MSS and typescripts:

Notes:	Beinecke, Barrie Collection, P45/1903. Entitled 'Fairy', there are 466 of these, consecutively numbered. Andrew Birkin is preparing an edition of these crucial jottings.
Manuscripts:	Lilly Library, University of Indiana. Holograph: original manuscript and accepted as such by Barrie in correspondence.
Early Printed Texts. Three Act Format	Beinecke, Barrie Collection, P45/1904/05B. Full typescript of early Three Act form. Also has the introductory Notes by Barrie *On the Acting of a Fairy Play*. These give a clear indication of how he wished actors to interpret the work. Beinecke, Barrie Collection, P45/1904. Two typescripts with revision, of Act Three only.
Early Printed Texts. Five Act Format	Beinecke, Barrie Collection: For Act 1 P45/1905; For Acts 2, 3 and 4: P45/1905B; for Act 3: P45/1905CDE; for Act 5 (American version) P45/1905F
Epilogue:	Beinecke, Barrie Collection: P45/1908C

The Lord Chamberlain's Text has been stolen. Earlier scholars consulted it, so it did exist. On the other hand, there is something fitting about the disappearance of a play which Barrie, in the Dedication to the Collected Edition, claimed to have forgotten writing.

2   The Muse of drama.

3   Craig, *History of Scottish Literature*, IV, 170. It fares just as badly in other Histories. Maurice Lindsay (*A History of Scottish Literature*, London, 1977) can also dismiss it in a paragraph (p 373). In fairness, however, he seems disturbed at so doing and at the 'destructive dissection' to which the play has been subjected.

4   Roger Lancelyn Green, *Fifty Years of Peter Pan* (London, 1954), notes: 'Barrie is reported as saying, "it will not be a commercial success. But it is a dream-child of mine."' p 70. Green played Noodler in the 1943 tour with Alastair Sim as Hook and Ann Todd as Peter. His book is full of interesting insights and unique pieces of evidence.

5   'I am so anxious to see it on the stage that I have written another play (*Alice Sit-By-The-Fire*) which I will be glad to give you and which will compensate you for any loss on the one (*Peter Pan*) I am so eager to see produced.' Barrie cited by Green, *Fifty Years*, p 70.

6   Green, *Fifty Years*, p 70. Barrie probably approached Tree because his productions were renowned for an emphasis on spectacle.

7   Marcosson, *Frohman*, p 362.

8   Green, *Fifty Years*, p 84.

9   Asquith, *Portrait*, p 84.

10   Marcosson, *Frohman*, p 169

11   Eva Le Gallienne, *At 33* (London, 1934) p 213.

12   Gladys Cooper, *Gladys Cooper* (London, 1931) p 187.

13   Noel Coward, *Present Indicative* (London, 1937) p 47.

14   Harwood managed to combine darkness with grim humour. This was close to Barrie's intentions as revealed by the 'Fairy' Notes. Sim may be seen as carrying on the humorous line but he lost the ideas of the 'Dark and sinister man' (Note 347), 'awful to look on' (Note 355).

15   Angela du Maurier, *It's Only the Sister* (London, 1951) p 76.

16   Being an 'enchanted' house, it was not limited by the Unity of Place any more than Barrie. In his film scenario, Barrie makes even more use of its powers of flight. 'Little House lights up and then begins to move position.' (See Green, *Fifty Years*, p 218). On stage, the idea of movement was conveyed by its disappearance.

17   Mark Twain is cited in Phyllis Robbins, *Maude Adams: An Intimate Portrait* (New York, 1956) p 90. Kenneth Tynan, *Tynan on Theatre* (Harmondsworth, 1961) p 329.

18   Morton W Bloomfield, *Allegory, Myth and Symbol*, Harvard English Studies, Volume 9 (Boston, 1981) p 247.

19   The Notes for a 'Fairy' Play are written faintly and at speed. I am, therefore, grateful to Andrew Birkin for providing me with a full transcription.

20   The variety of Pan's origins was, especially, stressed by Francis Bacon in his treatment of the God in *The Wisdom of the Ancients*. The relevance of this will be studied later in the Chapter. Bacon's anticipation of the ideas, much later to be evolved by Darwin, resulted in many of his works being republished in the late 1880s. See Loren Eiseley, *Francis Bacon and the Modern Dilemma* (Lincoln, Nebraska, 1962) pp 39-46.

21 For Bacon's treatment of the Pan and Cupid myths, see Francis Bacon, *The Wisdom of the Ancients*, Sections VI and XVII. First composed in 1609, two new editions of this work appeared in 1878 and 1886.

22 Scholes, *Structuralism*, p 45.

23 Or, in another sense, from the alchemy of *Litte Mary*. Not only the fictive aristocrats had turned away from the 'phrenetic' quintessential panacea. It had been offered, on a different, 'phrenetic' level by Barrie to his own audience.

24 *The Stage*, December, 1904.

25 MacKail, *JMB*, p 350. October, 1903: '*Alice* was awaiting revision now, but the fairy play was taking most of his time. With more unimaginable thoroughness. There are nearly five hundred notes on it in one continuous series, and almost as many again, on separate sheets, as the work went on.'

26 Beinecke, Barrie Collection P45/1908C. More conveniently, the text is reprinted in a Special Edition of *John Bull*, 1957. Barrie appeared on stage at the end, dressed in black, holding his bowler hat, saying nothing.

27 Brian McHale, *Postmodernist Fiction* (New York, 1987) p 109.

28 Original Manuscript, Lilly Library, University of Indiana.

29 ARTIFICIAL: A myth which stresses rather than hides its nature as artifice.

30 Ormond, *Barrie*, p 108; Islay Donaldson, *Samuel Rutherford Crockett* (Aberdeen, 1989) p 196.

31 The idea of Imitation being the highest type of Art, if coupled with Invention, has its most powerful advocate in Quintilian. Few major authors, prior to the Romantic period, questioned this principle. Significantly, no negative literary usage of the word in English can be dated before the first decade of the eighteenth century.

32 Rose, *The Case of Peter Pan*. This is the literary study which is most in harmony with my own findings.

33 The 'Fairy' Notes include (No. 27) the idea of having 'Alphabetical biscuits'.

34 Stevenson: 'Silver called by Hook. (Speaks Silver's way — not imitation of actor).' Anderson: Note 186 'Cd Hans Anderson be a figure in play?' The ideas sustaining this through explicit echoing of his fairy tales (see 290) disappear but of course the fairytale remains. See Maureen Ann McGowan, *An Analysis of the Fantasy Plays of James M Barrie*. Unpublished PhD thesis, City University, New York, 1984, for a study of the play in terms of fairy-tale structures. She uses Propp's ground rules.

35 Charles Lamb, *'Dream Children' and 'The Child Angel'* (London, 1902).

36 Lamb, 'Dream Children' p 14.

37 The Punch and Judy motif (*Sentimental Tommy*, p 398) although it gives way to the harlequinade was also part of the planning in the Notes (e.g. Note 271 — 'Two fairies (dolls) in front of a glass quarrelling — worked a la Punch & Judy.' See *Punch* (1906) for a one-act continuation of this literary tradition.

38 Compare Note 277 'If smallest child became Pantaloon, it was thro' always imitating father'; Note 278 'Harlequin cd be tall youth,' etc.

39 Lilly MS Scene 6, pp 3-6. The conventions of the (Pan)tomime also suggested a harlequinade. A E Wilson, *Christmas Pantomime* (London, 1934) p 29. 'Between each act was introduced a comic fable on rigidly conventional lines about the courtship of Harlequin and Columbine in which Clown and Pantaloon figured.'

40 As explicated by Scholes, *Structuralism*, p 68. See Claude Lévi-Strauss, *Structural Anthropology* (Garden City, 1967).

41 Beinecke, Barrie Collection P35 (*Pantaloon*), Or54 (*Harlequin*). The full title of the latter should be noted.

42 See Green, *Fifty Years*, pp 122-3.

43 Angela Du Maurier, *Only the Sister*, p 78.

44 Anton Dolin, *Divertissement* (London, 1931). He had earlier appeared in Seymour Hicks' *Bluebell in Fairyland*, which Barrie and the Davies boys saw in December, 1901. Hicks called it 'A Musical Dream Play'.

45 This was William Nicholson. Although Nicholson was grateful to Barrie for giving him his 'first opportunity of coming to grips with the theatre', he lacked the Scot's ability to compromise in accordance with the teamwork element implied. That said, he was faced with some rather uncompromising actors whose vanity matched his own. Marguerite Steen, *William Nicholson* (London, 1943) records the battle between him and Du Maurier over 'a superb wig of purple chenille, arranged to look like snakes' and 'darker than the darkest thing imaginable' (p 98). Du Maurier, on his wife's advice, refused to wear this triumph of Nicholson's craft. She thought it made him look like a 'cross between Charles II and a fourteen-year-old schoolgirl.'

46 For someone who claimed to be shy of audiences, Barrie made a remarkable number of public speeches.

47 C S Lewis, 'On Three Ways of Writing for Children', in *Of Other Worlds*, ed Walter Hooper (London, 1966), p 47.

48 Beinecke, Barrie Collection, P.45/1904/05B. Note 5, p 2.

49 *The Scotsman*, 28 December 1904.

50 Eva Le Gallienne, *At 33*, p 216.

51 Geduld, *Barrie*, p 65. 'Unfortunately for Shaw, most children are not Shavians. They prefer *Peter Pan* to Shaw's *Androcles*.'

52 P54/1903.(259) The horror of growing up root idea of P; (171) If P a demon boy (villain of story) he is got round by mother at end; (202) P leaves children in wood dying; (268) P is flinging youngest out of window to take its place when girl wakes.

53 Daphne Du Maurier, *Gerald* (London, 1934) p 110.

54 J R R Tolkien, *The Monsters and the Critics* (London, 1983) p 144.

55 J C Trewin, 'The Creator of Peter Pan,' *Everybody's* 1 September 1951.

56 *Illustrated London News*, 7 January 1905.

57 A E Matthews, *Matty*, p 122. He confesses, 'It was quite a while before I had much idea of what it was all about.'

58 Gladys Cooper, *Cooper*, p 188.

59 Geduld, *Barrie*, p 55.

60 My earlier attempt at such criticism is in *Children's Literature*, 18, 1990, R D S Jack, 'The Manuscript of *Peter Pan*', pp 101-13.

61 *Ibid.* pp 107-9.

62 William Wordsworth, 'The Tables Turned', Stanza 6.

63 *The Bookman* (Supplement) Christmas, 1920, p 106.

64 Beinecke P45/1904/05B, Note 2. 'The scenic artist,' he adds, 'is another child in league with them'. (Actors and author).

65 Here 'dream' refers to the fantastic mode and the fantasy; 'real' and 'Reality' mark the Platonic distinction between shadow and form.

66 One could distinguish the fantastically real vision of the Nursery children from the fantastically Real (ideal) world of the Never Land and the imaginatively Real (artistic) realm of the harlequinade.

67 Lilly MS Scene 6, p 6. The relevance of this detail to the mother-artist opposition should also be noted.

68 This is the most explicit statement to be found in the earlier texts.

70 Beinecke P45 1904 Typescript 2, Scene 2, p 29. 'Mr Darling: [*a little bitter*] They will ask Michael to do the cricket and football now. Sic transit gloria mundi.'

71 R D S Jack, *Patterns of Divine Comedy* (Cambridge, 1989) p 96.

72 Birkin, *Lost Boys*, Chapter One. This covers the 1860-85 period.

73 Geduld, *Barrie* p 58.

74 *The Bookman*, 1905, p 110.

75 Eric Gould, *Mythical Intentions in Modern Literature* (Princeton, 1964) p 127.

76 *Roland Barthes: Selected Writings*, ed Susan Sontag (Oxford, 1982) p 99.

77 Rose, *Peter Pan*, p 35.

78 *Ibid*. p 76.

79 'Is' in the sense of being so identified in one of the photographs. Of course interchangeable rôles were the name of this game and so 'may be' is, strictly, more accurate. Hook's part — he was called the 'dark and sinister Captain Swarthy' in *The Boy Castaways* — was much coveted.

80 *American Imago*, 14, 1957, Skinner pp 111-41; Grotjahn pp 143-8. A rather more subtle psychiatric examination of Peter is to be found in *Psychoanalytic Review*, 43, 1955 (M Karpe, 'The Origins of Pan,' pp 104-10).

81 Frederick L Meisel, 'The Myth of Peter Pan', *The Psychoanalytic Study of the Child*, Vol 32 (New Haven, 1977) pp 545-64.

82 J M Barrie, *Peter and Wendy* (London, 1911) p 2.

83 Meisel, 'Myth of Pan', p 551.

84 He equates 'minimum narrative' with *Peter Pan*. Tzvetan Todorov, *The Fantastic* (Cleveland, 1973) p 163.

85 Meisel, 'Myth of Pan', p 558.

86 *Ibid*. p 561. The 'Fairy' Notes support Meisel's contentions. Note 259, cited earlier, does specifically define the root idea of *Peter Pan* to be 'The horror of growing up.' Many of the other Notes explore possible exchanges of gender and rôle, which never reach the play. They do indicate that the intention was an early one and bisexuality a necessary part of Barrie's plan.

87 Lamb, 'The Child Angel', p 20.

88 *The Bookman* (Supplement) Christmas, 1920, 'J M Barrie, The Tragedian', p 108.

89 Camillo Pellizzi, *English Drama* (London, 1935) p 166.

90 Laurence Irving, *The Precarious Crust* (London, 1971) p 84.

91 Chalmers, *Barrie Inspiration*, p 250.

92 Later to be defined as 'The Blot on Peter Pan' in the short story of 1927.

93 Burns, *Letters*, Second Edition (Roy), I, 123. 'I have bought a pocket Milton . . . the intrepid daring, and noble defiance of hardship, in that great Personage, Satan.' (Letter 114, to Mr William Nicol).

94 Humphrey Carpenter, *Secret Gardens* (London, 1985) p 185.

95 Cited, *Secret Gardens* p 186. Carpenter astutely counters, 'But Barrie himself is playing Herod to his own creation. At the heart of the sentimental dream is a cynical, mocking voice.'

96 Barthes, *Essais Critiques*, 'Introduction to the Structural Analysis of Narratives', p 259.

97 The Dedication to *Peter Pan* (and the literary theory sustaining that Dedication) encourages us to think of an author *primum inter pares* for the text as sequence of dramatic events. For that text as structure encompassing different levels of interpretation, the author's importance will vary depending

on which level is being highlighted (creatively or receptively). Compare McHale *Postmodernist Fiction*, p 202. 'The author flickers in and out of existence at different levels of the ontological structure.'

98 William Wordsworth, *Prelude*, Book V, lines 553-57.

99 Tolkien, *Monsters and Critics*, p 122. Tolkien also stresses the perfectionism necessary to meet the demands of sub-creation in all their minuteness. Barrie had shown such perfectionism from the revisions of *Walker, London* onwards.

100 Morton W Bloomfield, *Allegory, Myth and Symbol*, p 247. Scholes, *Structuralism*, p 68 also reminds us that 'myths take on a pleasing narrative form precisely in order to make palatable certain truths about the human situation which men have always found it difficult to contemplate.' Barrie's mode and professed critical aims thus complement one another.

101 Aquinas, *Exposition Perihermenias*, I, lect, 14. The translation is taken from the most convenient citation — St Thomas Aquinas, *Theological Texts*, translated by Thomas Gilby (London, 1955) p 98.

102 The question of authorship was wittily considered by Barrie over and over again. He wrote letters purporting to prove that Lady Bacon wrote Shakespeare's plays and, in *Shakespeare's Legacy*, concluded the Bard was Scottish. In fact, he never doubted at all and consistently rejected Bacon as 'too rational'. Barrie's conclusion is shared by many modern Shakespearean critics. Notably, John F Danby in Shakespeare's *Doctrine of Nature* (London, 1972) concludes from a study of Bacon on Pan: 'Bacon, in fact, might be charged with making his account of Nature's structure almost crudely rational.' p 23.

103 There is a convenient account of Bacon as a thinker anticipating Darwin and Frazer's *Golden Bough* in Eiseley, *Bacon and the Modern Dilemma*, pp 31-59.

104 Bacon's *New Atlantis* anticipates *The Admirable Crichton's* setting but also its philosophy of Nature. 'We cannot command nature except by obeying her.'

105 Francis Bacon, *The Wisdom of the Ancients and New Atlantis* (London, 1886) Pan, Section 6, p 36; Cupid Section 17, p 70. For choice of edition see Note 21.

106 *Ibid*, p 39.

107 Meisel, 'Myth of Pan', p 561. 'To get stuck in a narcissistic and bisexual solution is to end up like Captain Hook or the Captain in *The Little White Bird*. It is ultimately not satisfactory, and Barrie clearly shows where it leads. However, as a transitional position, it not only has its value, but it can be seen as a normal concomitant of a difficult developmental task.'

108 Cited Eiseley, *Bacon and the Modern Dilemma*, p 22. 'Every act of discovery advances the art of discovery.' In Bacon, Barrie would find support for his idea of the genius always being in advance of the perceptions of his audience.

109 Beinecke, Barrie Collection, P45 1904/05B, p 1. Barrie refers to the need to underplay farcical tendencies. The actors are reminded that the play works on the fiction of composition by a child, who is 'in deadly earnestness.' They must join this conspiracy by 'playing it in the same spirit.'

110 *Saint Augustine's Confessions*, edited and translated by William Watts, Loeb, 2 vols (London, 1912) pp 234-47.

111 Green, *Fifty Years*, p 122.

112 Dolin, *Divertissement*, p 26.

113 Pauline Chase, *Peter Pan's Postbag* (London, 1909), Introduction, p v.

114 Aquinas, *Exposition, Perihermenias*, i, lect, 14. (Gilby, *Theological Texts*,

p 99). For a fuller discussion of these distinctions and the drama of graded complexity for all levels of audience understanding, see Jack, *Divine Comedy*, pp 16-65.

115 Green, *Fifty Years*, p 72. She was also invited to go and get herself insured against accidents immediately!

116 Twenty-four members of the cast of fifty had speaking parts and so received such 'piecemeal' scripts. Barrie did not choose to 'rule' over a small dramatic world.

117 The italics are mine. Given that most of Barrie's hopes of conveying 'immortal longings' via his audience were doomed to failure, this area of success assumes great importance. A more specific focus for his triumph proved to be his actresses. Gladys Cooper writes of her sense of mystic continuity in her autobiography. As storyteller Barrie had captivated her in youth; subsequently she was to play out his stories but also to sit in the womb of his 'chimney corner,' listening to tales unborn: 'plays he has never written — and never will write.' *Cooper* p 189. She is particularly affected by the idea of continuous creation set against brief lives. Fay Compton was similarly troubled but uses Peter's immortality as a touchstone of the dilemma. 'Afterwards the little boy's father told me that the gentleman I had been talking to was Mr Barrie, and that at Christmas-time he would take me to see a lovely play that Mr Barrie had written about a boy who wouldn't grow up. It all happened just as he had said, and I told him how I would love to be Peter one day — and he thought maybe I would — and even that was to come true now! When I played Peter it was the fifteenth year he had refused to grow a day older.' *Rosemary*, p 188. Consistently, women have a more complex and accurate instinctive reaction to Barrie's feminine mind than men.

118 Matthews, *Matty*, p 155. Barrie had first explored the dramatic genre via *Ibsen's Ghost*, a parody cum act of literary criticism. With *Macbeth* he enters Film in the same witty, enquiring spirit. Beinecke, Barrie Collection R 43 'The Real thing at Last. Film: *Macbeth*.'

119 *Ibid*. The 'cinema' was itself a stage-set; the frontage of a picture house was built within a theatre. The title was written on a piece of cloth. Under it appeared the advice 'All snap — No Talky-Talky.'

120 MacKail, *JMB*, p 555. See Green, *Fifty Years*, 'Scenario for a Proposed Film of *Peter Pan*.' pp 171-218.

121 Green, *Fifty Years*, p 171. The same desire, earlier noted, to minimise dialogue had been expressed for *Pantaloon* and *The Origin of Harlequin*.

122 Ibid. p 178.

123 *Ibid*. p 194. This was a traditional mime in pantomime. The Policeman was 'elongated' behind a mangle, which produced a long cut-out figure. See Wilson, *Pantomime*, pp 29-48.

124 Barrie, *Letters*, p 201. 14 November 1924 to Cynthia Asquith. 'It is only repeating what is done on the stage and the only reason for a film should be that it does the things the stage can't do.' Yet again, Barrie defines genre via unique features. The opportunity of following the author's scenario still remains open for a film-maker despite Green's appeal for such an initiative in 1954.

125 Patricia Waugh, *Metafiction* (London, 1984) p 15.

126 J M Barrie, 'The Blot on Peter Pan', in *The Treasure Ship*, ed Cynthia Asquith (London, 1927).

127 Again this emphasis is more clearly revealed in the early texts. Lilly MS, V, 8. 'MR DARLING [*amazed*]: See here, Peter, this is my house, and I naturally

expect to be captain here.' (Peter in the rôle of Captain Peter — has just ordered cabs for all.)

128   Lilly MS, IV, 9; see Fig 6, p 192.

129   *Daily Telegraph*, 28 December 1904.

130   Beinecke, Barrie Collection P45/1903, No. 438. 'If Gerald [du Maurier] Pirate Capt — his imitations of actors [other villains he has killed].'

131   *Ibid.* No. 362, 'P. in black a stern figure of Fate — after success is drunk in himself à la Tommy [Sandys] — struts deck with others staring at him — like Napoleon on Bellerophon.'

132   In his argument that any species contained both male and female elements.

133   See P45/1903 No 296. 'P's worst agony of all that he will forget girl in a month.'

134   In this ending, Wendy's daughter Jane repeats the process of meeting and flying with Peter. In the final speech, Wendy foresees an unending continuity: 'I hope she will have a little daughter, who will fly away with him in turn — and in this way I may go on for ever and ever dear Nana, so long as children are young and innocent.'

135   *Peter Pan* (Definitive Text) pp 544-45. Barrie goes further in the Stage Directions reminding us that he is, also, weightless. This is a clear example of Peter suspending chosen elements in the Never Land, to allow himself a final spotlight and the heroic cry 'To die will be an awfully big adventure.'

136   *Tommy and Grizel*, p 168. 'He would have done it if he could. If we could love by trying, no one would ever have been more loved than Grizel.' Again p 380, when explaining his nature to Gemmell, he identifies the artist with self-consciousness. That, he claims, is the reason for the failure of his marriage. 'If I have greetin' eyes it was real grief that gave them to me, but when I heard what I was called it made me self-conscious.' His impotence was, I believe, directly related to an inability to abandon himself to natural passions. He felt, but at once, with the artist's instinctive analytic egoism, began to observe himself feeling; he could not love for watching himself in love.

137   See Note 52 to this Chapter. The Fairy Notes clearly show Pan to be at once hero and villain, capable in the latter aspect of leaving children in a wood gloatingly (202); flinging children out of windows (268) and of tipping them out of bed (276). The constant use of 'If' in these notes also reflects the knowledge that any chosen narrative is a simplification of possibility. 'If villain . . .' (378) = if I choose to emphasise the villainous aspects of Peter.

138   This parallel can only be apposite to a text working on at *least* three levels. First there is the appearance (the torturers think they are doing a good job of carpentry at the cross); then there is the reality (they are doing an evil job spiritually) and finally there is the Truth (they are being manipulated by God so that their actions proclaim God's benevolent purpose). Barrie, in *Peter Pan* evokes this complexity but obliterates the simplicity of Truth at the highest mimetic level. He substitutes for the comfort of revelation the challenge of perspectivism. See Jack, *Divine Comedy*, pp 101-3.

139   This trickery, within the Theology of Guile, was advanced by Christ (in hiding his divinity) as well as Satan in trying to establish the Saviour's true nature. Imagery of hook and fish is employed by Gregory of Nyssa. (See also n. 200).

140   Peter exists in the worlds of Bloomsbury, Never Land and Harlequinade. The Clown plays his rôle in the fourth world as represented in a form more clearly allied to the commedia dell' Arte and removed from *Peter Pan*.

141   Chaucer, *House of Fame*, Book 1, Line 1.

142   The Godfather of Moira Loney in *Little Mary*.

143   Charles Lamb, 'Dream Children,' p 14.

144   Gould, *Mythical Intentions*, p 136.

145   The device by which the Narrator in *The Little White Bird* claimed that his act of literary creation had pre-determined the birth of the child, so defeating the mother within linear time.

146   Beinecke, Barrie Collection, P45/1903 No. 51.

147   In *The Little White Bird,* nest, Wendy house and pram are all images associated with the womb and birth.

148   This idea also originated in the Notes and is carried through to both Lilly and Beinecke 1904/05B. It made very little dramatic sense and involved the hiring of a number of actresses for that scene alone.

149   First performed in April, 1917, this one-act play depended on the idea of one woman containing multiple personalities — witty, serious, coquette, mother, Very Woman, orator and murderess.

150   The song deals with the topic of love in old age for a faithful, married couple. As a controlled exercise in sentimental idealism it is a perfect embodiment of Wendy's hope for the future.

151   Recent anthropological discoveries had emphasised the magical powers conferred on the storyteller by primitive societies. In Beinecke, Barrie Collection P45/1903, Note 151, Barrie even toyed with the idea of making his monstrous Never Land animals long for stories.

152   MacGowan, *Fantasy Plays*, develops the idea of storytelling in *Peter Pan* very well; see especially pp 61-63.

153   *Peter Pan* (Definitive Text) p 571. Neither thought nor guilt has troubled the minds of Wendy or John particularly — 'no compunction for what they have done, not the tiniest fear that any just person may be awaiting them with a stick.' Wendy has made the choice to come out of childhood's egoistic eternal present; she has not yet issued from it.

154   Compare the rôle of the dramatist in *A Midsummer Night's Dream*.

155   This aspect of the myth was brilliantly translated into mime by Peta Lily in *Wendy, Darling*, performed at the Edinburgh Festival in 1988. The adult Wendy looked back on the idealisms and cruelties of her youth with just that mixture of regret and acceptance implied by the impossible myth.

156   I consulted a copy of this very rare book in the Beinecke Library. The full title is *The Boy Castaways of Black Lake Island*.

157   McHale, *Postmodernist Fiction*, p 113.

158   Roland Barthes, *Essais Critiques*, 'La Mort de l'auteur,' p 61. Translation taken from *Twentieth-Century Literary Theory*, ed K M Newton (London, 1988) p 155.

159   Barrie plays with the idea of only 'seeming' to understand the nature of the rôle he played in autobiographical spirit. He also fails to make clear whether the autobiography refers to his nature or to the type of *part* he liked to act when a boy in the Kirriemuir washhouse.

160   Barthes, *Selected Writings*, 'The Photographic Message', p 197. The editor of that collection, Susan Sontag, also considered the rôle of photography within structuralist theory. *On Photography* (Harmondsworth, 1977).

161   Barthes, 'The Photographic Message,' p 198.

162   The praise given, in holograph, on the manuscript of *Ibsen's Ghost* is repeated in Barrie's *Letters* and the Dedication to *Peter Pan*. 'The mightiest craftsman that ever wrote for our kind friends in front,' (p 491).

163 This went along with precisely the same mistrust of the exactitude of the word as in *Sentimental Tommy*. ('The language-maker was not modest enough to realise that he had only given designations to things . . . he believed that he had expressed through words the highest knowledge of things.' *Human All Too Human* No. 11).

164 A photograph of this scene is retained in the Theatre Museum; popular theatre necessarily tends to rely on stunning technical effects, as current West End London productions verify.

165 Words develop as part of the growth of society and 'the formation of a political society as the only way of escaping from perpetual strife.' (Brown, *Philosophers of the Enlightenment*, p 189). Like Shakespeare and Barrie, Rousseau groups the child, the primitive man and the savage in the earlier state. 'L'enfant, le paysan et le sauvage participent d'un même type d'humanité idéal.' Terrasse, *Rousseau*, p 230.

166 Beinecke, Barrie Collection, Or 54. Film techniques, in the form of a screen, were used to present these words. It does not appear that they were uttered. The text also indicates a link with Barrie's one attempt at Music Hall, *Rosy Rapture* (MS p 1 — 'Rosy appears in a new piece entitled *The Origin of Harlequin*.')

167 The parallels between these texts will be more fully explored in Section v of this Chapter.

168 On the highest level, as earlier argued, Peter may be manipulating the manipulator, in order to gain a final resounding victory. The theological parallel for this is the Doctrine of the Fortunate Fall.

169 A more overt sign of Hook's awareness of his own tragic definition is the 'Death' soliloquy, which opens Act 5.

170 Bergson in *Le Rire* identified risibility with the puppetlike reaction of the obsessed man or 'humour'. Deprived of the expected human fluidity, he was at once foreseeable and an emblem of comic incongruity.

171 But within a circular structure; Barrie uses dramatic structure again to counterpoint fictive order against flux. This, he does, in the spirit of Nietzsche. 'Fantastic edifices sprang forth insubstantial and unanchored from the forming imaginations of men.' (Danto, *Nietzsche*, p 128). The opposition between categorisation and flux also concerned Roget and lay behind his *Thesaurus*.

172 Compare Barrie's creature of air and music (Pan) with Shakespeare's creature of earth and music (Caliban).

173 Although Barrie probably had a higher opinion of the Edwardian audience's gullibility than he had of its intellect.

174 Tinker Bell, as earlier noted, received an Income Tax demand! Barrie's 'reality' of complete fictive insubstantiality gained the ultimate triumph of being transported in at least one person's imagination into the world of actuality outside the theatre.

175 Marcosson, *Frohman*, p 170.

176 It was a characteristic of Sentimental Tommy, that the more difficult he could make the artistic challenge, the more he liked it.

177 It was Cynthia Asquith to whom Barrie revealed the manipulative side of his complex personality. See Asquith, *Portrait* and Barrie *Letters*, pp 170-240.

178 He appeared, dressed all in black. In the Notes, he had toyed with giving this tragic, visual power to Peter. (Notes 294, 307).

179 Newspeak in Orwell's *1984*. Both Rousseau and Nietzsche had, of course, made the same connection and it is in their tradition that Barrie works.

180   Darwin, *The Descent of Man* (London, 1885) p 88.
181   *Ibid.* p 48.
182   *Ibid.* p 91. Darwin is quoting from Max Müller's article in *Nature*. 6 January 1870, p 257.
183   *Ibid.*
184   Barrie, *Peter Pan* (Definitive Edition) p 557 'The man is not wholly evil; he has a Thesaurus in his cabin, and is no mean performer on the flute.'
185   D L Emblem, *Peter Mark Roget* (London, 1970) p 101.
186   *Ibid.* p 255. Barrie did not share Roget's belief in 'the appearance of design in every part of every living thing,' though presumably he saw that as a possible interpretation of Nature's flux. He did share Roget's view that classification was a valid tool for enquiry, logical or imaginative.
187   Peter Mark Roget, *Thesaurus*, Facsimile of First Edition (Oxford, 1987) p viii.
188   *Ibid.* p xxiii.
189   Roget, *Thesaurus*, p x.
190   Emblem, *Roget*, p 137.
191   I am indebted to the pioneer work of Jacqueline Rose in this area.
192   As early as *Walker, London*, the first type of revision is illustrated when Baby O'Brien becomes Nanny O'Brien and Nanny Golightly changes to Bell. The more complex revision, based on different emphases on meaning at different levels of the text, is most clearly reflected in the Adam/Percy/Cecil variations in the MS of *Little Mary*.
193   Alan Gardiner, *The Theory of Proper Names* (London, 1957) p 7.
194   J G Frazer, *The Golden Bough* (London, 1900) 3 vols, I, 403.
195   Bertrand Russell, 'The Philosophy of Logical Atomism,' in *The Monist*, 1918, p 524.
196   See Notes (P45/1903) No. 300. 'Cecco' derives from a similar source. Note 437: 'Pirates called after boys, Cecco etc.' Cecco was the four year old son of Maurice Hewlett, whose play *Pan and the Young Shepherds* (London and New York, 1899), had influenced Barrie.
197   Peter is, also, the name of the type of the Christian Church. Barrie does not deny Christianity; he subsumes it into his world of doubt.
198   Virginia Woolf, *Mrs Dalloway* Grafton edition (London and Glasgow, 1989) p 79.
199   Frazer, *Golden Bough*, I, 412.
200   The tradition of the devil as a hungry fish unaware of the hook thrown to him by Christ is a strong one in Christian thought and led to the hook, like the fork and the bagpipes being iconographically associated with Satan. See Gregory of Nyssa, *Oratorio Catechetica*, 22-4, 26, 35. See also J A MacCulloch, *The Harrowing of Hell* (Edinburgh, 1930).
201   Frazer, *Golden Bough*, I, 403.
202   The history of taste in Shakeapearean criticism has recently been traced by Gary Taylor in *Reinventing Shakespeare* (London, 1990). The tradition of Dowden saw Shakespeare in the way Barrie saw himself, developing gradually from workshop to genius. The idea that *The Tempest* marked the crowning point of that achievement began with Coleridge but was fully formulated by the Victorian Biographical school. (See Taylor, pp 171-80).
203   Shakespeare, *The Tempest*, ed Frank Kermode, Arden Shakespeare (London and New York, 1985) p xlii.
204   *Three East European Plays*, ed Julius Hay *et al.* (Harmondsworth, 1970). In

The Memorandum the first government controls through an artificial language (Ptedype) based on the principle of redundancy; revolution brings in another power and another language (Chorukor) based on the opposite principle of similarity.

205 Literally 'the wondering' or 'the gazing' one.

206 I am grateful to my colleague Norman Macleod for pointing out this semantic property, as evidenced in phrases such as 'a thimble-full', 'from little acorns . . .', the 'kiss' as slight touch in billiards/snooker, 'I don't care a button'.

207 Mr Macleod also called my attention to the argot of confidence trickery.

208 Shakespeare, *As You Like It*. 2.vii.144.

209 Langdon Smith, 'Toast to a Lady'.

210 The necessary folly of vice derives from the implied opposition to God's beneficent plan — one of the premises being questioned in Pan. Such a man does not understand himself nor his relation to wider Nature. Herod was a major 'fool' figure in Medieval drama.

211 As 'King of the Kailyard' or 'Cabbage patch'.

212 Danto, *Nietzsche*, p 38. One of the attractions of Nietzsche's philosophy was his consistent attempt to parallel philosophical and linguistic conclusions. Nehemas, *Nietzsche: Life as Literature*, develops this premise.

213 This would seem self-evident but it is a factor tacitly ignored in much Barrie criticism. The anti-hero of Iris Murdoch's *The Sea, The Sea* spells out the facts, as they face a practising dramatist: 'In other arts we can blame the client; he is stupid, unsophisticated, inattentive, dull. But the theatre must, if need be, stoop — and stoop — until it attains that direct, that universal communication which other artists can afford to seek more deviously.' Barrie's answer — a multi-layered drama, working from sentiment to the hardest intellectual truths of all and addressing a triangle of audiences, narrowed by intellect and integrity at each higher level — is the purest Nietzschean drama of all. It reflects the German's key philosophical tenets that (i) there are no facts, only interpretations and (ii) the masters must face the cruellest visions but, in the name of utility, simplify them into solace for the slaves.

214 Fig 7, p 237.

215 Darwin, *The Descent of Man*. 'As far as concerns infants of from ten to eleven months old, it seems to me incredible that they should be able to connect certain sounds with certain general ideas as quickly as they do, unless such ideas were already formed in their minds.' (p 89). This is the linguistic equivalent of the Wordsworthian myth of the child possessing the highest mythic truth. It lies behind *Peter Pan* and is stated in 'The Blot'.

216 Darwin, *Origin of Species*, p 97. The closer one moved towards genius the more intense the struggle became. Interestingly, the key feature of 'perseverance', distinguished by Barrie in his own discussions of 'genius', is thought by Darwin (*Descent*, p 564) to determine victory between individuals otherwise identical.

217 In *Beyond Good and Evil*, Nietzsche singles out the belly as the 'reason man does not easily take himself for a god,' (Section 141). The frequency with which Barrie translates 'soothing myth' into loss of honesty in the face of food or the stomach may derive from this Nietzschean premise.

218 The Fairy Notes to *Peter Pan* show clearly that Barrie had first thought of setting his myth more clearly against a background of Fairytale convention as defined by the characters of Anderson and Grimm. (Woodcutters, hawkers,

tailors, seven dwarfs etc are propsed but omitted.) If the Harlequinade reached the first draft and then became *Pantaloon*, so this earlier potential matter found its form in the short story.

CHAPTER FIVE: Pages 242 - 261

1 Oh you of sane intellect, look closely at the doctrine which conceals itself under the veil of the strange verses.

2 William Donaldson, *Popular Literature in Victorian Scotland* (Aberdeen, 1986) pp 145-8; George Blake's arguments are recorded in Chapter 1, p 87.

3 In Barbour's *Bruce* for example, Robert the Bruce's early life is not consistent with the theme of liberty which, as Romance hero, he embodies. Barbour simply substitutes the early life of his grandfather. A similar technique here preserves Barrie's status as anti-hero by removing him from the working class.

4 The tendency rather is to preserve him as myth by simplifying the nature of his fantasies as an end in themselves. Cynthia Asquith supports the contrary view, as I have presented it. 'To my mind, the essential Barrie is not sentimental. The real sentimentalist refuses to face hard facts. Barrie does not. For all his reputed softness he is no escapist.' *Portrait*, p 218.

5 A representative curriculum will include for Scott, *Waverley, Redgauntlet* and *The Heart of Midlothian* but not *Ivanhoe, Kenilworth* or *Quentin Durward*. This is a thematic choice; literary excellence excludes in the sense that a truly second rate work such as *Peveril of the Peak* could not on any grounds be accepted. The first three are included because they are set in Scotland and reflect on Scottish History while the others noted reflect on English and/or French culture. Foreseeably, *The Prime of Miss Jean Brodie* is almost always the sole representative of the art of Muriel Spark.

6 R Cairns Craig, 'Peripheries', *Cencrastus*, 1982, No. 9, p 4.

7 One of the most valuable springboards for the development was Kurt Wittig's *The Scottish Tradition in Literature* (Edinburgh, 1958). It provided a simple overview working on precisely these principles.

8 It has Scots dialogue, heralds the coming of industrialism and makes its national, political and social comments in a direct, easily assimilable manner.

9 James VI's *Reulis and Cautelis* (1585) is the first of many attempts by this monarch to use literature as a method of political influence. He denies to poets the *divina furor*, preserving divinity to himself; he moves the sonnet towards panegyric — especially directed towards himself. Allan Ramsay's *Ever Green* (1724) provided an anthology including much earlier Scottish Poetry and proposed a national poetry movement to counterbalance not only excessive English but European influence.

10 James wrote of additional and specific strengths — stronger consonants in the context of alliteration. Ramsay thought of himself as inheriting not only the mantle of English neoclassicism but — again additionally — that of the Scottish makars.

11 Nietzsche, *The Gay Science*, Section 115.

12 J Caughie, 'Scottish Television: What would it look like?' in C MacArthur, *Scotch Reels: Scotland in Cinema and Television* (London, 1982) p 121.

13 R Cairns Craig, 'Visitors from the Stars', *Cencrastus*, 1983, No. 11, p 9.

14 So named because in Scotland at the time of their formation, 7% of the people owned 84% of the wealth. The company was committed to producing plays of

the Radical Left. Many of these, such as John McGrath's *The Cheviot, the Stag and the Black, Black Oil*, reached very high artistic standards.

15 See George Elder Davie, *The Democratic Intellect* (Edinburgh, 1961). The title covers a work concerned with the Scottish Universities during the Nineteenth Century.

16 Not only in *The Admirable Crichton* but in *The Professor's Love Story, Little Mary* and, later, in *What Every Woman Knows*.

17 The growth of Scottish Literary Journals for example is in itself a fine dvelopment, so long as they develop a broadly based readership or critics contribute also to journals with a wider literary base. The alternative to this is communication within an inner group about topics of interest to that group alone.

18 Peta Lily's performance drew much of its power from the idea of an older woman realising the largely unconscious and darker side to the attraction of Pan.

19 Nietzsche's doctrine is not, finally, a negative one. He himself saw it as a religion beyond religions and, in *Ecce Homo*, used the doctrine of eternal recurrence to argue that it was, indeed, the most advanced formula of affirmation yet devised by man. See Bernd Magnus, *Nietzsche's Existential Imperative* (Bloomington, 1978).

20 Ezra Pound, *ABC of Reading* (London, 1961) p 82.

21 *Gawain and the Green Knight*, Fitt II, lines 129-179.

22 Use of Vinsauf and Boccaccio along with Barthes and Derrida reveals many shared critical premisses.

23 *An Edinburgh Eleven*, p 67.

24 Spiritual levels of the text were more highly valued than moral or narrative.

25 Although the treatment of national and social divergences was farcical, it already centred on specific language features — 'Bang went saxpence'; 'caravan', 'Alhambra'. Thematic treatment was reserved for the Edwardian plays.

26 The conclusions centring on the domination of Babbie ('evil'; 'pagan'; 'chaotic') by Gavin ('good'; 'christian'; 'conventional') were completed but withdrawn. [See Chapter 2.]

27 'The Blot on Peter Pan', p 100.

28 This idea was promulgated by many Medieval thinkers and came to be generally accepted by Middle English and Middle Scots writers.

29 Fairy Note 222: 'wife & baby dancing (shadows on blind)'..

30 Flaubert recorded that he spent one afternoon's work replacing the comma he had removed in the morning.

31 Multivalence (in a more positive philosophical context) had been analysed by Aristotle (see *Physics* I, 2-3; *De Memoria* I, 450a-b.) A positive structural contrast to *Little Mary*'s deconstruction may be found in *Piers Plowman*. Truth may be defined as the pilgrim's goal in Passus I but 20 passus are needed to explore every meaning of Truth. For a fine exposition of this view, see James Simpson, *Piers Plowman: An Introduction to the B-text* (London, 1990) pp 26-38; 40-45.

32 Andrew Birkin records, 'As she was normally known as Sylvia, Barrie adopted "Jocelyn" as his own private pet-name for her.' (See *The Lost Boys*, Chapter 5).

33 Within the Never Land, animals, birds and fairies have different systems, all mastered by Peter; the games employ visual signs, sounds and music, all orchestrated by Peter. The characters have different 'literary' strengths, Pan's being dramatic, Wendy's narrative and Hook's poetic. To this must be added Barrie's own voice, unusually intrusive via text, stage-directions and Dedication.

Index

Abbreviations: *Walker, London* WL; *The Professor's Love Story* PLS; *The Little Minister* LMin; *The Wedding Guest* WG; *Quality Street* QS; *The Admirable Crichton* AC; *Little Mary* LMar; *Peter Pan* PP.

Aberdeen, Lord, 104
Adams, Maude, 48, 57, 70
Adelphi, The, 158
Admirable Crichton, The
(*See* Crichton, James)
Agate, James, 3
Allen, John, 14
Anderson, Hans Christian, 162, 289n34
Anon (Barrie's pseudonym) 96
(*See* Rôles)
Ansell, Mary, 10, 27, 30, 200
Archer, William, allusions to, 4, 6, 14, 62-3; and Shaw, 147; on individual plays, 42-3, 46, 131-2, 154
Aristotle, 230
Art, as Birth, 32, 67, 143-4, 162-3, 168-70, 188-9, 193-9, 205-7, 256; as deception, 12, 61-2, 202, 249-50; as Utility/Therapy, 103, 118-9, 127-8, 139-43, 147-54, 163-4, 239, 249-50; as Mimesis, 97-8, 177, 212, 241; as Power/Manipulation, 98-9, 114-5, 121-2, 126-7, 182, 185, 195-8, 200-2, 209-12; for Art's Sake, 100
Asche, Oscar, 151
Asquith, Cynthia, 47, 223, 238
Auerbach, Nina, 149

Bacon, Sir Francis, source for *Peter Pan*, 183-4, 193, 236, 255, 288n20; and Universal Language, 121, 183
(*See* Codes)
Barrie, David (brother) 7, 9
Barrie, David (father) 10

Barrie, Sir James Matthew, critical status: genius to joke, 3-5; in Scotland, 5-6, 17-23, 242-7; personality-based, 6-13; as dramatist 13-20; reaction 23-4; Barrie's literary theory 247-61;
APPRENTICE PLAYS: WL, reception, 27-8; visual power, 28-30; production, 30-1; evolution of text, 32-9; symbolism, 39-41; PLS, visual power, 41; comedy of stereotype, 42-4; evolution of text, 45-7; LMin, reception, 47-8; evolution of text, 48-56, 62; comedy of stereotype, 49-51; WG, and Ibsen, 62-3, 65-9; reception 63-4;
JOURNEYMAN PLAYS: QS, reception, 79-80; evolution of text, 81-5; mythic structure, 85-8; and Nietzsche, 89-95; and perspectivism, 95-101; and and language, 101-4; AC, evolution and performance, 104-8; and Will to Power, 108-30; LMar, as riddle, 131-2; as satire 132-4; as allegory, 134-8; on dramatic communication, 138-54;
PETER PAN: production, 155-9; play defined, 159-65; audience, 165-74; authorship, 174-8; as Fantasy, 181-5; author/God, 185-9; author/characters, 190-9; author/mother, 199-212; author/medium, 212-41;
OTHER PLAYS: *Alice Sit-By-The-Fire*,

48, 65, 156, 264; *Bandelero the Bandit*, 30; *Becky Sharp*, 268n2; *Bohemia*, 269n26; *Boy David, The*, 5, 18, 64, 250; *Dear Brutus*, 5, 13, 14, 44, 46, 85, 129, 250, 261, 264; *Ibsen's Ghost*, 25-6, 71-4, 188, 217, 258; *Kiss for Cinderella, A*, 58, 270n50; *Mary Rose*, 5, 13, 14, 17, 18, 19, 44, 85, 250, 261; *Origin of Harlequin, The* (ballet with words) 163, 165; *Pantaloon*, 163, 165, 172, 197-9, 218, 259; *Richard Savage* (with Marriott Watson) 25-6, 49; *Rosalind*, 13, 16; *Seven Women*, 60, 207; *Twelve Pound Look, The*, 76; *What Every Woman Knows*, 14, 19, 44, 48, 51, 65, 261; *Will, The*, 48; PROSE WORKS, *Auld Licht Idylls*, 20, 45-6, 75, 197, 244, 253, 260; *Better Dead*, 3; *Boy Castaways of Black Lake Island, The* (photographic narrative) 165, 176, 189, 197, 200; *Collected Speeches*, 165; *Edinburgh Eleven, An*, 34, 35, 74, 225, 253; *Farewell, Miss Julie Logan*, 59; *Greenwood Hat, The*, 111, 141; *Little Minister, The*, 9, 48-56, 74, 77, 197; *Little White Bird, The*, 21, 22, 165, 168-72, 188, 197, 199-207, 211, 255, 256; *Margaret Ogilvy*, 3, 7-11, 174; *My Lady Nicotine*, 34, 35; *Peter and Wendy*, 165, 197; *Peter Pan in Kensington Gardens*, 165; *Sentimental Tommy*, 7, 22, 26, 64, 69, 76, 79-80, 88-9, 96-7, 100-3, 114-5, 163, 196, 218, 244; *Tommy and Grizel*, 11, 89, 100-3, 163-4, 200, 205, 218; FILM SCENARIOS: *Macbeth or The Real Thing at Last*, 165, 189; *Peter Pan*, 165, 189-90, 193; NOTEBOOKS: allusions to, 8, 11, 25-6, 32, 36, 44, 46, 69, 80; *Notebook 6* (1885-8) 28, 34, 269n30; *Notebook 7* (1887-8) 28, 34, 269n30; *Notebook 8* (1888) 269n30; *Notebook 9* (1888) 60-1; *Notebook 10* (1889) 60-1; *Notebook 12* (1890) 60-1, 269n30; *Notebook 14* (1892) 82; *Notebook 16* (1894) 64, 66; *Notebook 18* (1899) 104, 105; *Fairy Notes*, 159, 162, 163, 167, 173, 184,

193, 196, 257, 287n1, 290n52, 294n137; *Notes on the Acting of a Fairy Play*, 166, 171, 287n1
Barrie, Mrs Margaret (mother) 7, 9-10
Barker, Harley Granville, 34
Barthes, Roland, 56, 106, 175, 180, 212-3, 215
Beerbohm, Max, critical precision, 5, 21, 43-4, 80; on national stereotypes, 51, 55, 138 (See Scottish stereotypes)
Bett, Henry, 5
Bettelheim, Bruno, 85
Birkin, Andrew, 8-9, 174
Blackie, Professor John Stuart, 262
Blair, Professor Hugh, 122, 281n127
Blake, George, as critic, 20-2, 75, 243, 246-7; *The Shipbuilders*, 20, 246
Bloomfield, Morton, 159, 182, 202n100
Boethius, *De Consolatione Philosophiae*, 183
Bookman, The, 178
Borrow, George, 58, 272n95
Boucicault, Dion, Jr. 64, 70, 106, 112, 156-7, 158
Bridie, James, 18, 266n42
Bright, Arthur, 51
British Weekly, The, 23, 243
Brown, George Douglas, *The House with the Green Shutters*, 12, 21, 245
Bryden, Ronald, 59
Burns, Robert, 4, 91, 122, 179, 208

Campbell, Ian, 19
Carleton, Royce, 45
Carleton, William, 136
Carlisle, Rosamund Countess of, 104
Carlyle, Thomas, 98; and heroism, 108-11, 140
Carpenter, Humphrey, 179
Carroll, Lewis, *Diaries*, 150
Carter, Hubert, *Punchinello*, 132, 282n159
Cartoons, of *Little Mary*, 131; of Napoleon, 141, 283n184
Case, The, defined, 86, 90 (See Story – types)
Cecil, Robert, Marquess of Salisbury, 137
Chalmers, Patrick, 41
Chase, Pauline, 187
Chaucer, Geoffrey, *House of Fame*,

199-200; *Nun's Priest's Tale*, 136, 179; *Pardoner's Tale*, 252
Chehov, Anton, 15
Chesterton, GK, 171
Chrystal, Professor George, 35
Christian Science, 136, 283n171
Cinderella, 58, 85, 211 (*See* Fairy-Tales)
Civic Repertory, The (New York) 158
Codes of Communication: drama, 145-54, 235-6; literary language, 233-5; mime, 29-30, 38, 39, 41-2, 106-7, 113, 116-7, 141, 216-8; music, 120-1, 123-4, 189, 220-1, 260; narration, 210-2, 231-3; poetry, 120-1, 123-4, 189, 220-1, 260; sound, 218-20 (*See* Bard; Universal Language)
Comedy, The, 45
Communication (*See* Codes of Communication)
Compton, Fay, 71, 81, 293n117
Conan Doyle, Sir Arthur, 104
Congreve, William, 19
Cooper, Gladys, 157, 164, 168, 293n117
Court Theatre, The, 14, 80
Coward, Noel, 158
Cowley, Abraham, 3
Craig, Gordon, 149
Craig, R Cairns, 244, 246
Crichton, James (The Admirable Crichton) 105
Crockett, S R, 22, 162

Daiches, David, 5, 11-3, 17, 43-4, 249
Daily Telegraph, The, WL 28, 29, PP 193
Dangerfield, George, 137
Dante, Alighieri, 93, 97, 111, 202, 248-9, 251, 253, 256
Danto, Arthur C, 99, 236
Darlington, WA, 3, 5, 8, 35, 48
Darton, FJ Harvey, 158
Darwin, Charles, as influence on Barrie, 73-5, 251-6, 262; as influence on Roget, 224-5, 260-1; metaphysical doubt, 144, 200, 235, 253; struggle for existence, 76-7, 87, 90, 113, 120, 139, 183, 197, 221-41, 250, 263 (*See* Roget, Peter Mark)
David, Jacques Louis, 141

Dekker, Thomas, 61
Democratic Intellect, The, 247
Derrida, Jacques, 127-8
Dickens, Charles, 41, 115, 119-20, 122, 280n107
Dionysius, Pseudo-, 111
Dodgson, Charles (*See* Carroll, Lewis)
Dolin, Anton, 164, 187
Donaldson, William, 243, 246-7
Duke of York's, The, 48, 105-6, 158
Du Maurier, Angela, 164
Du Maurier, Gerard, 158, 167
Dumbar, William, 245

Edinburgh University, 35, 74, 223-5, 253
EEG, *The Makers of Hellas* (*See* Jevons, Frank)
Ellis, Havelock, 88
Emery, Winifred, 48, 49
Empire, The (New York) 47, 158, 271n66
Endings, alternative, 39-41, 60-2, 84, 125-9, 161, 204-5
Eton College, 6, 165
Everyman, 92, 204, 208-9

Fairy-Tale, 12, 52-62, 79, 85, 86, 166, 239 (*See* Cinderella)
Fantasy, function of: 13-4, 95-6, 99, 101; and Herodotus, 140; and *Peter Pan*, 170-4; and Truth, 167; as Power, 182, 222; dishonest, 118-9; primacy of, 98-100 (*See* Herodotus)
Flaubert, Gustave, 259
Fowler, Alastair, 24
Fox, Edward, 14
Fraser, Campbell, 253
Frazer, Sir James, *The Golden Bough*, 226-9, 260 (*See* Names)
Freudian criticism, 7-11, 14, 176, 181, 265n16 (*See* Geduld, Harry M)
Frohman, Charles, 57, 106, 156-7, 222

Gaiety, The, 158
Garrick, The, 45, 64, 158
Gawain and the Green Knight, 161, 217, 252; pentangle, 252
Geduld, Harry M, 9-11, 13, 17, 62-3, 67, 74, 132-3, 168, 174 (*See* Freudian Criticism)
Genesis, I, v-ix, 225-6
Genius, 3-5, 115, 250-1, 284n187

Genre, defining characteristics, 12, 14-17, 26-7, 52-62, 129, 176, 189-90, 197-9, 203-6, 207, 213-50, 218, 238-41, 253
Gillette, William, Jr, 128
Gillette, William, Sr, 128
Gillray, Thomas, 141, 146, 283n184, 284n185-6
Gilmour, Thomas, 26, 141, 284n187-8
Gladstone, William, 137
Goldoni, Carlo, 19
Gould, Eric, 175, 202-3
Gower, John, 245
Grand, The, (Fulham) 132
Green, Roger Lancelyn, 104, 186, 288n4
Grotjahn, M, 177

Hammerton, J A, 41, 131
Hardy, Thomas, 4, 23
Harker, Joseph, 29, 70
Harrison, Frederic, 262
Harrison, Rex, 14
Harvey, Martin, 64
Hatton, Bessie, 45
Haugen, Einar, 66
Havel, Vaclev, 232, The Memorandum
Haymarket, The, 14, 16, 48
Henley, W E, 120, 137, 227
Henryson, Robert, 42, 134, 231
Hepburn, Katherine, 47
Herodotus, 140 (See Fantasy)
Homer, 120
Hope, Anthony, 179
Howe, P P, 49, 66
Hugh of St Victor, 91
Hunter, Lynette, 80
Hutchison, David, 18

Ibsen, Henrik: and Ibsen's Ghost, 71-4, 258; and symbolism, 82, 88, 209; and WG, 26-7, 62-9; Art as birth, 143-4; as apprentice, 138-9; Barrie's opinion of, 38, 70, 72, 116-7; early reception of, 4, 25-6; translations of, 73
WORKS CITED: Doll's House, The, 72; Ghosts, 72; Hedda Gabler, 67, 72; Little Eyolf, 67; Master Builder, The, 66-7; Rosmersholm, 66; Wild Duck, The, 66, 68, 72
Illustrated London News, The, 168

Images, (See Symbols and Images)
Imp, 72, 77, 247, 249 (See Meaning)
Ireland, 134-8, 263
Irving, H B, 54
Irving, Henry, 149, 151, 193, 234

James, VI and I, King of Great Britain, 122, 184, 245
James, Henry, 4
Jesperson, Otto, 147
Jevons, Frank, 152-4 (See E E G)
Jolles, André, 85-6, 225 (See Story, types of)
Jones, Henry Arthur, The Liars, 46-7
Joyce, James, Ulysses, 205

Kailyard School, 21-4, 73, 193, 243, 245, 253
Kaye-Smith, Sheila, 178, 249
Keating, Peter, 90
Knowles, Thomas, 23

Lady Audeley's Secret, 65
Lamacchia, G A, 126
Lamb, Charles, The Child's Angel, 162-3, 177; Dream Children, 162-3, 202, 212, 256
Langland, William, Piers Plowman, 252-3
Language (See Codes of Communication; Universal Language)
Leclaire, L, 21
Le Gallienne, Eva, 157, 167
Lévi-Strauss, Claude, 12
Lewis, C S, 166
Lighting (See Stage Lighting)
Lily, Peta, 249, 300n18
Lindsay, Sir David, Ane Satyre of the Thrie Estaits, 156
Listener, The, 6, 11
Llewelyn Davies Family, 8, 160, 167, 178, 213
Lloyds, 31
Lombard, Peter, 196
Lyceum, The (Edinburgh), 14
Lydgate, John, 245

McConnachie, 96 (Barrie's pseudonym) (See Rôles)
MacDiarmid, Hugh, 4, 5-6, 22, 164, 247
MacDonald, George, 162, 245

McHale, Brian, 161
MacKail, Denis, 8, 56, 57, 104-5, 129, 186
Mackenzie, Sir Alexander, 16
Maclaren, Ian, *Beside The Bonnie Brier Bush*, 22, 51, 243
MacQueen, John, 134, 282n166
Macrobius, 199
Marbury, Elizabeth, 57
Marcosson, Isaac F, 57, 222
Marryat, Captain Frederick, *Masterman Ready*, 119
Marx, Karl, 247
Masson, Professor David, 121-2, 247, 281n131
Matthews, A E, 168, 189
Maude, Cyril, 16, 48, 49
Maupassant, Guy de, 26
May, Ela Q: 'author of *Peter Pan*', 160
Meaning, levels of: allegory, 93, 110-11, 129, 149-54, 242, 257, 277n49 (*See* Veil); counterpointed, 40-1, 57-62, 66, 71-5, 77, 101, 247, 249 (*See* Imp); verbal multivalence, 33, 73, 102-3, 138
Meisel, Frederic L, 81, 184, 207-8, 291n86
Meredith, George, 4
Metafiction, 258-9
Millar, Hugh, 4-6, 21-2, 243
Miller, John, 74
Miracle Cycles, 220, 235, 252
Modes: multi-modes of *Pan*, 164; and perspectivism, 164-5, 258-61
Molière, 19
Monboddo, Lord, 74, 224
Moult, Thomas, 108, 134
Murdoch, Iris, *The Sea, the Sea*, 249, 297n213
Myth: artificial, 162; Christian, 94; creation, 160-1; defined, 12-7; function of, 15-7, 43, 82, 85; logic of, 52-62, 66-9, 103; Pan, 129, 141; perspectivist, 161-2, 175-8, 212, 241; Psyche, 174-6; Wordsworth, 170, 180 (*See* Story-types)

Names: titles, 34, 36, 82-4, 103, 105, 134; characters, 35-6, 102, 103, 105, 135-6, 143; power of, 117-8, 225-30, 239-40, 260 (*See* Frazer, Sir James)

Napoleon Buonaparte, 90-2, 111, 114, 140-1, 144, 229, 263; in Art, 191-3, 218, 254, 258, 263
Napoleonic Wars, 10, 75, 87-8, 253-63
Napoleon, Prince, 263
New Criticism, The, 7
New York Times, The, 128
Nicholson, William 164, 290n45
Nicodemus, Gospel of, 235
Nicoll, Robertson, 23, 243
Nietzsche, Friedrich: and fantasy, 98-100, 197; and guilt, 94-5, 112; heroic and lethargic eras, 113-4, 120, 148-50; influence, 183, 251-6; morality of whip, 90-4, 208, 250; perspectivism, 95-8, 99, 101, 129, 147-8, 236, 246, 250; reception in Britain, 88-9, 134; suffering, 91-2; verbal multivalence, 102, 154, 260-1; Will to Power, 105, 108-15, 120, 124, 126
Nineteenth Century, The, 262
Nordeau, Max, 88
Nottingham Journal, The, 75, 136, 183, 262-4
Noyes, Alfred, 174

Oedipus Complex, 8-11, 132-3, 141-3, 174-5, 181, 247 (*See* Barrie, Margaret)
Ogilvy, Margaret (*See* Barrie, Margaret)
Olrik, Axel, 52-8
Orchardson, Sir William, 192-3, 218, 258
Ormond, Leonee, 23, 65, 78, 125, 133
Orwell, George, 223

Palladium, The, 158
Pall Mall Gazette, LMin 48
Pantomime: conventions of in *Peter Pan*, 213, 289n30, 293n123
Paradise Lost, 179, 235
Paris, production of *Peter Pan*, 158
Parnell, Charles Stewart, 263
Pearl, The, 99
People's Journal, The, 75
Pinero, Sir Arthur Wing, 24, 27; *Profligate, The*, 66; *Second Mrs Tanqueray, The*, 65; *Sweet Lavender*, 79
Pirandello, Luigi, 97

Plato, 15, 44, 201-2
Pound, Ezra, 250-1
Prisoner of Zenda, The, 48

Queen's, The, 48
Quiller-Couch Family, 174
Quintilian, 122

Ramsay, Allan, 245
Reade, Winwood, 90
Riddle, The, 86, 132-4, 145-54, 239, 257 (See Story-types)
Robertson, Thomas, 28
Roget, Peter Mark: in Peter Pan, 102, 259; Thesaurus, 185, 223-5, 236, 251 (See Darwin, Charles)
Rôles: changing, 59-60, 95-8, 102-3, 207 (See Anon; McConnachie)
Romanes, G J, 262
Rose, Jacqueline, 23, 162, 175-6
Rousseau, Jean-Jacques, 108-10, 217-8
Russell, Bertrand, 227
Russian Doll, 173, 177, 212, 259

St Augustine, 71; De Civitate Dei, 183
St James's, The, 31, 64
Saint Thomas Aquinas, Exposition Perihermenias, 182-3, 292n114, 188
Saturday Review, The, 75
Savoy, The, 88
Schlueter, June, 97
Scholes, Robert, 86
Scotsman, The, PLS 44-5; LMin 48, 49, 51, 56, 62; WG 81, 82; LMar 131; PP 166-7, 168
Scott, Sir Walter, 21
Scottish, literary canon, 44, 244-7, 270n51
Scottish Playgoers Company, The, 18
Scottish: stereotypes, 17, 19-20, 26-7, 38, 42-4, 51 (See Beerbohm, Max)
Scottish, themes, 17-18
Shakespeare, William: and Barrie's parodies, 183, 189, 270n59; and Romance Structure, 85, 218, 230-3, 245; and theatre, 15
WORKS CITED: All's Well that Ends Well, 148; As You Like It, 46, 234; Hamlet, 234; King Lear, 85, 234; Macbeth, 18, 46, 125, 189, 234-5; Measure for Measure, 148; Midsummer Night's Dream, 235;

Much Ado About Nothing, 149-50, 258; Taming of the Shrew, 46; Tempest, 218, 230-3, 245; Troilus and Cressida, 148
Shaw, George Bernard: and Barrie, 13-17, 78, 154; and Darwin, 146; and Ibsen, 66, 68, 71, 148; and Nietzsche, 89; on women, 76; satirised by Barrie, 144, 258.
WORKS CITED: Androcles and the Lion, 167; Arms and the Man, 14; Devil's Disciple, 47; Doctor's Dilemma, 139; Heartbreak House, 128; John Bull's Other Island, 145, Man and Superman, 14; Widowers' Houses, 31, 47; You Never Can Tell, 16
Shelton, George, 29, 31
Shepperson, George, 74
Siddons, Sarah, 150-1
Sim, Alastair, 158, 167
Skinner, J, 177
Smith, Adam, 247
Sophocles, 153
Spark, Muriel, The Prime of Miss Jean Brodie, 245
Stage Lighting, 106, 120, 166, 182, 190
Star Theatre, The, (New York), 45
Stevenson, Robert Louis, 3, 119, 163
Story: types of, 256-7 (See Case; Myth; Riddle)
Strindberg, August, 143, 251, 273n121
Swiss Family Robinson, The, 118
Symbols and Images: baby/ring, 68-9, 84; cloak, 55, 58, 117; crocodile/crow, 209, 218-20, 255; cuckoo, 16, 39-41, 43, 84; garden, 82-4; gypsy, 52, 55-6, 58; hat/cap, 49-51, 84, 141, 254, 284n188; hook, 196-7, kennel/night-light, 206-7; kneeling, 91; locket, 68; moon, 59-60; pram/Wendy-house, 204; rice, 68-9, 84; ringlets, 84, 91; stage-set, 87-9; tower, 16, 66

Taylor, F H, 45
Tennyson, Alfred Lord, 4
Terriss, Ellaline, 81, 85
Terry, Ellen, 149-50
Theology of Guile, 196-7, 255
Thomas, Brandon, 64
Thomson, Joseph, 35

Time: divine, 181, 182, 185-90, 193-5,
202-5, 209-10, 254-6; human, 182,
196, 199-203, 204-5, 209-10, 220
Times, The: Barrie's qualities, 15;
Irish Land question, 137; *Ibsen's
Ghost*, 26; WL, 28, 30; PLS 41-2,
43; LMin 51, 52; QS, 79, 84-5; AC,
108; LMar 131
Times Literary Supplement, The, 108,
152, 278n81
Toole, J L, 33, 70, 72; and Barrie's
'shyness', 26, 31, 115; and mime, 30,
38, 216, 264; at Dumfries, 30
(*See* Codes of Communication)
Toole's Theatre, 27
Tree, Beerbohm, 156, 158
Trevelyan, Hilda, 187
Trewin, J C, 167
Twain, Mark, 158
Tynan, Kenneth, 158

Under the Red, Red Robe, 48
Unities, The, 187, 189-90
Universal Language, 121 (*See* Bacon,
Sir Francis; Codes of
Communication)
Urquhart, Sir Thomas, 105, 121, 224
(*See* Crichton, James; Universal
Language)

Vanbrugh, Irene, 27, 30, 32, 33, 106,
112
Vanbrugh, Violet, 63-4
Vaudeville, The, 79, 81
Vegetarianism, 145-6, 263-4
Veil, 93, 110-11, 129, 149-54, 242, 257,
277n49, 279n95 (*See* Meaning,
allegory)

Walbrook, H M, 39, 48-50, 63, 64,
66, 125, 131-2
Watson, Marriott, 25
Wellington, Duke of, 93
White Heather, The, 216
Wilberforce, Bishop, 260
Wilde, Oscar, 25, 27, 46, 107, 119,
258-9
WORKS CITED: *Lady Windermere's
Fan*, 31, 65-6; *The Importance
of Being Earnest*, 118
Women's Movement, The, 261
Woolf, Virginia, 77
Wordsworth, William, 13, 73, 108-9,
140, 170, 279n84

Yeats, W B, 89, 271n83